D1596180

THE FATHERS
OF THE CHURCH

A NEW TRANSLATION

VOLUME 135

THE FATHERS OF THE CHURCH

A NEW TRANSLATION

EUSEBIUS OF CAESAREA

AGAINST MARCELLUS
AND
ON ECCLESIASTICAL THEOLOGY

Translated with introduction and notes by

KELLEY MCCARTHY SPOERL

St. Anselm College, Manchester, New Hampshire

MARKUS VINZENT

King's College London

THE CATHOLIC UNIVERSITY OF AMERICA PRESS
Washington, D.C.

Cataloging-in-Publication Data is available
from the Library of Congress.
ISBN 978-0-8132-2991-1

Markus would like to dedicate this work to Martin Tetz (May 22, 1925–January 31, 2017), one of the twentieth century's most influential scholars of Eusebius of Caesarea's texts against Marcellus of Ancyra, Marcellus himself, and the historical environment of post-Nicaea. Tetz's death this year has taken away one of the keen readers and a great inspiration for young researchers. Markus still remembers his encouraging words when he started this project with an unpublished German translation (with Gerhard Feige), and his close critical readings by which he had followed the early steps of research on the relationship between Asterius, Marcellus, Apolinarius, and Eusebius. It is hoped that what has been achieved is following the trajectories that Martin Tetz had pursued throughout his entire life.

Kelley would like to dedicate her work on this long and arduous project to a seminal early influence in her life: her maternal grandmother, Mrs. Margaret Kelley Martin, who died in 1982. She was herself a fine linguist (as her father was, a small-town lawyer in a New England mill town filled with immigrants) and an avid reader, who encouraged and supported Kelley's love of books and study from a young age. More importantly, she was a woman of great faith and daily, fervent prayer, who endured by dint of them decades of agonizing suffering from arthritis in the years before hip replacements became common. She has given Kelley inspiration to carry on with this project over so many years despite obstacles and frustrations, and Kelley is sure and grateful that her beloved Gramma's prayers have brought her to its much-desired conclusion.

CONTENTS

AGAINST MARCELLUS

ON ECCLESIASTICAL THEOLOGY

INDICES

ACKNOWLEDGMENTS

The following is the fruit of well over twenty years of effort. Kelley Spoerl, working on Apolinarius's *Kata meros pistis* (itself dependent on Eusebius's earlier works) as part of her dissertation work at the University of Toronto, remembers long, tedious days of grinding through the Greek of Eusebius's anti-Marcellan works in the edition of Migne at the Toronto Public Library. Even so, the end of her research convinced her that these were seminal texts of the fourth century that had to be made more easily available to a general scholarly audience. Two reasons prompted her to start on a translation. A translation would make it easier for time-pressed scholars to locate critical passages in these texts for their own specialized research; it would also provide precious teaching materials for the middle of the fourth-century trinitarian debates, where translated texts for teaching in undergraduate as well as seminary and graduate programs are scarce on the ground. This situation gives students a skewed vision of the development of this key Christian doctrine because there are lots of materials for the beginning of the controversy and lots for the end, but not a whole lot for the middle. In an effort to help students of the Trinity understand how theologians got from A to C, Spoerl launched into this translation in the summer of 1992 or 1993; she can never remember which. Because of other professional commitments, the project proceeded very slowly over the course of the next nearly fifteen years.

The project received welcome new energy and impetus when Markus Vinzent asked if he could join in 2008, having himself worked for years on a German translation together with Gerhard Feige, now bishop of Magdeburg (Germany). He went through the translation, offering valuable corrections and adding most of the scholarly notes on the translation. He also constructed the indices. The introduction is a joint composition written mostly during Kelley's sabbatical from her work in the Theology Department of Saint Anselm College during the school year 2012–2013. This was the last of three sponsored leaves Kelley received from Saint Anselm College to work on this project (having had a Summer Research Grant in the summer of 1998 and a semester's sabbatical in the fall of 2003); she wishes to express her gratitude to the College for these opportunities. We are especially fortunate to have had a later version of the translation reviewed in detail by Dr. Mark DelCogliano of St. Thomas University and Dr. Aaron Johnson of Lee University. Dr. DelCogliano also offered useful comments on our introduction. We heartily thank both these generous scholars for sharing their expertise with us. We also thank our editor, Dr. Carole Monica Burnett of the Catholic University of America Press, for everything she did to help us improve this translation and for her skillful guidance through the final editing process. Of course, any remaining errors and infelicities remain our own.

ABBREVIATIONS AND SIGLA

Abbreviations

General

Gr.   Greek.

HE   *Historia ecclesiastica* (for several authors).

LXX   Septuagint.

RSV   Revised Standard Version.

Periodicals and Series

FOTC   Fathers of the Church. Washington, DC:
                The Catholic University of America Press, 1949—.

GCS   Die griechischen christlichen Schriftsteller (der
                ersten drei Jahrhunderte). Leipzig: J. C. Hinrichs,
                1897–1949; Berlin: Akademie-Verlag, 1953–2001;
                Berlin: De Gruyter, 2001—.

PG   Patrologia Cursus Completus: Series Graeca.
                Ed. J.-P. Migne. Paris, 1857–1886.

SC   Sources Chrétiennes. Paris: Cerf, 1941—.

Critical Editions and Translations

K./H.   *Eusebius Werke* IV: *Gegen Marcell, Über die kirchliche
                Theologie, Die Fragmente Marcells.* Edited by Erich
                Klostermann and Günther Christian Hansen. GCS.
                3d ed. Berlin: Akademie-Verlag, 1989.

Migliore   *Eusebio di Cesarea: Teologia ecclesiastica.* Translated
                by Franzo Migliore. Rome: Città Nuova Editrice, 1998.

Op.   Hans-Georg Opitz. *The Arian Debate up to the Year 328:
                Texts and Studies.* Unpublished manuscript.

Urk. Hans-Georg Opitz. *Urkunden zur Geschichte des arian-
      ischen Streites 318–328.* Berlin and Leipzig: De Gruyter,
      1934. Cited by document number.

V. or   Vinzent, Markus. *Markell von Ankyra: Die Fragmente
Vinzent und der Brief an Julius von Rom. VCSup* 39. Leiden:
        Brill, 1997; or Vinzent, Markus. *Asterius von Kappa-
        dokien: Die Theologischen Fragmente. VCSup* 20. Leiden:
        Brill, 1993.

Works of Eusebius of Caesarea

CM *Contra Marcellum.* The abbreviation *CM* is used in
    the notes for the Latin title of *Against Marcellus.*

ET *De ecclesiastica theologia.* The abbreviation *ET* is used
    in the notes for the Latin title of *On Ecclesiastical
    Theology.*

Sigla

< > words supplied by the editor of the Greek text

[ ] words supplied by the translators of this volume

SELECT BIBLIOGRAPHY

Primary Sources: Editions and Translations

Editions

Gaisford, Thomas. *Eusebii Pamphili contra Hieroclem et Marcellum libri.* Oxford: Typographeo Academico, 1852.

Eusebius Werke IV: *Gegen Marcell, Über die kirchliche Theologie, Die Fragmente Marcells.* Edited by Erich Klostermann and Günther Christian Hansen. GCS. 3d ed. Berlin: Akademie-Verlag, 1989.

Koetschau, Paul. "Anzeige und Rezension der Edition Klostermann." *ThLZ* 31 (1906): 597–600.

Montagu, Richard. *Eusebii Pamphilii Caesareae Palaestinae episcopi, de demonstratione evangelica libri decem, quibus accessere nondum hactenus editi nec visi contra Marcellum Ancyrae episcopum libri duo: de ecclesiastica theologia tres: omnia studio R.M. latine facta, notis illustrata: et indicibus loco suo necessariis locupletata.* Paris: Sonnius, Cramoisy and Morellus, 1628.

Rettberg, Georg. *Marcelliana, accedit Eunomii Ekthesis pisteos emendatior.* Göttingen: Vandenhoeck et Ruprecht, 1794.

Vinzent, Markus. *Markell von Ankyra: Die Fragmente und der Brief an Julius von Rom.* VCSup 39. Leiden: Brill, 1997.

Translations

Eusebio di Cesarea: Teologia ecclesiastica. Translated by Franzo Migliore. Rome: Città Nuova Editrice, 1998.

Select Secondary Bibliography on Marcellus of Anycra

Barnard, Leslie W. "Marcellus of Ancyra and the Eusebians." *GOTR* 25 (1980): 63–76.

———. "Pope Julius, Marcellus of Ancyra and the Council of Sardica: A Reconsideration." *RTAM* 38 (1971): 69–79.

Beskow, Per. *Rex gloriae: The Kingship of Christ in the Early Church.* Translated by Eric J. Sharpe. Stockholm: Almquist and Wiksell, 1962.

Dowling, M. J. "Marcellus of Ancyra: Problems of Christology and the Doctrine of the Trinity." Ph.D. diss., Belfast, 1987.

Feige, Gerhard. *Die Lehre Markells von Ankyra in der Darstellung seiner Gegner.* ETS 58. Leipzig: Benno Verlag, 1991.

———. "Markell von Ankyra und das Konzil von Nizäa (325)." Pages 67–136 in *Denkender Glaube in Geschichte und Gegenwart, Festschrift aus Anlass der Gründung der Universität Erfurt.* Edited by Wilhelm Ernst and Konrad Feieries. ETS 63. Leipzig: Benno Verlag, 1992.

Fondevila, José M. "Ideas cristológicas de Marcelo de Ancyra." *EE* 27 (1953): 21–64.

Foss, Clive. "Late Antique and Byzantine Ankara." *DOP* 31 (1977): 27–87.

Gericke, Wolfgang. *Marcell von Ancyra. Der Logos-Christologe und Biblizist. Sein Verhältnis zur antiochenischen Theologie und zum Neuen Testament.* TABG 10. Halle: Akademischer Verlag, 1940.

Green, H. Benedict. "Matthew 28:19, Eusebius, and the *lex orandi.*" Pages 124–41 in *The Making of Orthodoxy: Essays in Honour of Henry Chadwick.* Edited by Rowan Williams. Cambridge: Cambridge University Press, 1989.

Hanson, R. P. C. "The Source and Significance of the Fourth *Oratio Contra Arianos* Attributed to Athanasius." *VC* 42 (1988): 257–66.

Hockel, Alfred. *Christus der Erstgeborene: Zur Geschichte der Exegese von Kol 1:15.* Düsseldorf: Patmos-Verlag, 1965.

Hübner, Reinhard. "Gregor von Nyssa und Markell von Ankyra." Pages 199–229 in *Écriture et culture philosophique dans la pensée de Grégoire de Nysse.* Edited by Marguérite Harl. Leiden: Brill, 1971.

———. "Soteriologie, Trinität, Christologie. Von Markell von Ankyra zu Apollinaris von Laodicea." Pages 175–96 in *Im Gespräch mit dem dreieinen Gott. Elemente einer trinitarischen Theologie. Festschrift zum 65 Geburtstag von Wilhelm Breuning.* Edited by Michael Böhnke and Hanspeter Heinz. Düsseldorf: Patmos Verlag, 1985.

Kannengiesser, Charles. "Marcello di Ancira." Pages 2089–91 in vol. 2 of *DPAC.* Edited by Angelo de Berardino. 3 vols. Casale Monferrato: Marietti, 1983–1988.

Klose, Carl R. *Geschichte und Lehre des Marcellus und Photinus.* Hamburg: F. Perthes, 1837.

Le Bachelet, X. "Ancyre, conciles d'." Pages 1173–77 in vol. 1 of *DTC.* 15 vols. Edited by A. Vacant and E. Mangenot. Paris: Letouzey et Ané, 1908–1950.

Lienhard, Joseph T. "Acacius of Caesarea's *Contra Marcellum:* Its Place in Theology and Controversy." *StPatr* 48 (1987): 185–88.

———. "Basil of Caesarea, Marcellus of Ancyra, and 'Sabellius.'" *CH* 58 (1989): 157–67.

———. "*Contra Marcellum:* The Influence of Marcellus of Ancyra on Fourth-Century Greek Theology." 3 vols. Habilitätionsschrift, Albert-Ludwigs Universität zu Freiburg im Breisgau, 1986.

————. *Contra Marcellum. Marcellus of Ancyra and Fourth-Century Theology.*
Washington, DC: The Catholic University of America Press, 1999.

————. "Did Athanasius Reject Marcellus?" Pages 65–80 in *Arianism after Arius. Essays on the Development of the Fourth Century Trinitarian Conflicts.* Edited by Michel R. Barnes and Daniel H. Williams. Edinburgh: T&T Clark, 1993.

————. "The Exegesis of 1 Cor 15:24–28 from Marcellus of Ancyra to Theodoret of Cyrus." *VC* 37 (1983): 340–59.

————. "Marcellus of Ancyra in Modern Research." *TS* 43 (1982): 486–503.

————. "Two Friends of Athanasius: Marcellus of Ancyra and Apollinarius of Laodicea." *ZAC* 10 (2006): 56–66.

Logan, Alastair H. B. "Marcellus of Ancyra and Anti-Arian Polemic." *StPatr* 19 (1989): 189–97.

————. "Marcellus of Ancyra and the Councils of AD 325: Antioch, Ancyra, and Nicaea." *JTS* n.s. 43 (1992): 428–46.

————. "Marcellus of Ancyra, Defender of the Faith against Heretics—and Pagans." *StPatr* 37 (2001): 550–64.

————. "Marcellus of Ancyra on Origen and Arianism." Pages 159–63 in *Origeniana Septima.* Edited by W. A. Bienert and U. Küneweg. BEThL 137. Leuven: Leuven University Press, 1999.

————. "Marcellus of Ancyra (Pseudo-Anthimus), 'On the Holy Church': Text, Translation and Commentary." *JTS* n.s. 51 (2000): 81–112.

Loofs, Friedrich. "Marcellus von Ancyra." Pages 259–65 in vol. 12 of *RE.* Edited by J. J. Herzog. 24 vols. Leipzig: J. C. Hinrichs, 1896–1913.

————. "Die Trinitätslehre Marcells von Ancyra und ihr Verhältnis zur älteren Tradition." *SPAW* (1902): 764–81.

Macholz, Waldemar. "Der Dichter Prudentius in den Spüren Marcells von Ancyra." *ThStKr* 82 (1909): 577–92.

Molland, Einar, "'Des Reich kein Ende haben wird': Hintergrund und Bedeutung einer dogmatischen Aussage im nicäno-constantinopolitanischen Glaubensbekenntnis." Pages 234–53 in vol. 2 of Einar Molland, *Opuscula patristica.* Edited by Inger Marie Molland Stang. BTN 2. Universitet förlaget, 1970.

Möller, Wilhelm. "Marcellus, Bischof von Ancyra." Pages 22–25 in vol. 9 of *RE.* Edited by J. J. Herzog. Stuttgart/Hamburg, 1858. Pages 279–82 in vol. 9 of *RE.* Edited by J. J. Herzog and A. Hauck. Leipzig, 1881.

————. "Rezension von Theodor Zahn, *Marcellus von Ancyra* 1867." *ThStKr* 42 (1869): 147–76.

Montfaucon, Bernard de. "Diatriba de causa Marcelli Ancyrani." LI–LXVII in vol. 2 of Bernard de Montfaucon, *Collectio Nova patrum et scriptorum Graecorum, Eusebii Caesareensis, Athanasii, & Cosmai Aegyptii.* 2 vols. Paris: C. Rigaud, 1706.

Parvis, Sara. "The Canons of Ancyra and Caesarea (314): Lebon's The-
     sis Revisited." *JTS* n.s. 52 (2001): 625–36.
———. *Marcellus of Ancyra and the Lost Years of the Arian Controversy
     325–345*. Oxford Early Christian Studies. Oxford: Oxford University
     Press, 2006.
———. "Marcellus or Vitalis: Who Presided at Ancyra 314?" *StPatr* 34
     (2001): 197–203.
Pelland, Gilles. "La théologie et l'exégèse de Marcel d'Ancyre sur 1 Cor
     15:24–28: Un schème hellénistique en théologie trinitaire." *Greg* 71
     (1990): 679–95.
Pollard, T. E. "Marcellus of Ancyra: A Neglected Father." Pages 187–96
     in *Epektasis: Mélanges patristiques offerts au Cardinal Jean Daniélou*.
     Edited by Jacques Fontaine and Charles Kannengiesser. Paris:
     Beauchesne, 1972.
Pouderon, Bernard. "Muthodos, mustikos: L'hermeneutique de la
     Cohortatio ad Graecos restituée à Marcel d'Ancyre." *REAug* 49 (2003):
     267–83.
Pourchet, Maurice. "Marcel d'Ancyre et ses sources théologiques."
     Ph.D. diss., Rome, 1935.
Richard, Marcel. "Un opuscule méconnu de Marcel évêque d'Ancyre."
     MScRel 6 (1949): 5–24.
Riebe, Alexandra. "Marcellus of Ancyra in Modern Research." M.A.
     diss., Durham University, 1992.
Riedweg, Christoph. *Ps-Justin (Markell von Ankyra?): Ad Graecos de vera
     religione (bisher Cohortatio ad Graecos)*. SBA 24. Basel: Reinhardt, 1992.
Riggi, C. "La *dialogue* des Marcelliens dans le *Panarion* 72." *StPatr* 15
     (1984): 368–74.
Robertson, Jon M. *Christ as Mediator: A Study of the Theologies of Eusebius
     of Caesarea, Marcellus of Ancyra, and Athanasius of Alexandria*. OTM.
     Oxford: Oxford University Press, 2007.
Sansbury, Christopher. "Athanasius, Marcellus, and Eusebius of Cae-
     sarea: Some Thoughts on their Resemblances and Disagreements."
     Pages 281–86 in *Arianism: Historical and Theological Reassessments*.
     Edited by Robert C. Gregg. Philadelphia: Philadelphia Patristic
     Foundation, 1985.
Scheidweiler, Felix. "Marcellus von Ancyra." *ZNW* 46 (1955): 202–14.
Seeberg, Erich. *Die Synode von Antiochien im Jahre 324–325*. NSGTK 16.
     Aalen: Scientia, 1973.
Seibt, Klaus. "Ein Argumentum ad Constantinum in der Logos- und
     Gotteslehre Markells von Ankyra." *StPatr* 26 (1993): 415–20.
———. "Markell von Ancyra." Pages 83–89 in vol. 22 of *TRE*. Edited by
     Horst Robert Balz et al. 36 vols. New York: Walter de Gruyter, 1977–
———. "Markell von Ankyra (ca. 280–374 n. Chr.) und Asterius
     Sophista (ca. 270–ca. 350): Anmerkungen zu einer neuen Edition
     der Markell-Fragmente und der Epistula ad Iulium." *ZKG* 111
     (2000): 356–77.

———. *Die Theologie des Markell von Ankyra.* AKG 59. Berlin: Walter de Gruyter, 1994.

Simonetti, Manlio. "Ancora sulla paternità dello ps. Atanasiano "Sermo maior de fide." *VetChr* 11 (1974): 333–43.

———. "Su alcune opere attribuite di recente a Marcello d'Ancira." *RSLR* 9 (1973): 313–79.

———. "Sull'interpretazione patristica di Proverbi 8:22." Pages 9–87 in Manlio Simonetti, *Studi sull'Arianesimo.* VSen n.s. 5. Rome: Editrice Studium, 1965.

Spoerl, Kelley McCarthy. "Athanasius and the Anti-Marcellan Controversy." *ZAC* 10 (2006): 34–55.

———. "Two Early Nicenes: Eustathius of Antioch and Marcellus of Ancyra." Pages 121–48 in *In the Shadow of the Incarnation: Essays on Jesus Christ in the Early Church in Honor of Brian E. Daley, S.J.* Edited by Peter W. Martens. Notre Dame, IN: University of Notre Dame Press, 2008.

Stead, Christopher. "'Eusebius' and the Council of Nicaea." *JTS* n.s. 24 (1973): 85–100.

Tetz, Martin. "*Ante omnia de sancta fide et de integritate veritatis:* Glaubensfragen auf der Synode von Serdika (342)." *ZNW* 76 (1985): 243–69.

———. "Die Kirchweihsynode von Antiochien (341) und Marcellus von Ancyra: Zu der Glaubenserklärung des Theophronius von Tyana und ihren Folgen." Pages 199–218 in *Oecumenica et Patristica: Festschrift für Wilhelm Schneemelcher zum 75. Geburtstag.* Edited by Damaskinos Papandreou, Wolfgang A. Bienert, and Knut Schäferdiek. Stuttgart: Kohlhammer, 1989.

———. "Markellianer und Athanasios von Alexandrien. Die markellianische *Expositio fidei ad Athanasium* des Diakons Eugenius von Ankyra." *ZNW* 64 (1973): 75–121.

———. "Zum altrömischen Bekenntnis. Ein Beitrag des Marcellus von Ancyra." *ZNW* 75 (1985): 107–27.

———. "Zur strittigen Frage arianischer Glaubenserklärungen auf dem Konzil von Nicaea (325)." Pages 220–38 in Hanns Ch. Brennecke et al., eds., *Logos. Festschrift Luise Abramowski*, Beihefte zur Zeitschrift für Neutestamentliche Wissenschaft 67. Berlin and New York: De Gruyter, 1993.

———. "Zur Theologie des Markell von Ankyra I. Eine Markellische Schrift 'De incarnatione et contra Arianos.'" *ZKG* 75 (1964): 217–70.

———. "Zur Theologie des Markell von Ankyra II. Markells Lehre von der Adamssohnschaft Christi und eine pseudoklementinische Tradition über die wahren Lehrer und Propheten." *ZKG* 79 (1968): 3–42.

———. "Zur Theologie des Markell von Ankyra III. Die pseudoathanasianische *Epistula ad Liberium*, ein markellisches Bekenntnis." *ZKG* 83 (1972): 145–95.

Toom, Tarmo. "Marcellus of Ancyra and Priscillian of Avila: Their Theologies and Creeds." *VC* 68 (2014): 60–81.

Vinzent, Markus. *Asterius von Kappadokien: Die theologischen Fragmente, Einleitung, kritischer Text, Übersetzung und Kommentar. VCSup* 20. Leiden: Brill, 1993.

———. "Die Entstehung des 'Römischen Glaubensbekenntnisses.'" Pages 185–409 in *Tauffragen und Bekenntnis. Studien zur sogenannten 'Traditio Apostolica', zu den 'Interrogationes de fide' und zum 'Römischen Glaubensbekenntnis.'* Edited by Wolfram Kinzig, Christoph Markschies, and Markus Vinzent. AKG 74. Berlin: Walter de Gruyter, 1999.

———. "Die Gegner im Schreiben Markells von Ankyra an Julius von Rom." *ZKG* 105 (1994): 285–328.

———. "Gottes Wesen, Logos, Weisheit und Kraft bei Asterius von Kappadokien und Markell von Ankyra." *VC* 47 (1993): 170–91.

———. *Pseudo-Athanasius, Contra Arianos IV. Eine Schrift gegen Asterius von Kappadokien, Eusebius von Cäserea, Markell von Ancyra und Photin von Sirmium. VCSup* 39. Leiden: Brill, 1996.

Willenborg, Franz August. *Über die Orthodoxie des Marcellus von Ancyra.* Münster, 1859.

Zahn, Theodor. *Marcellus von Ancyra. Ein Beitrag zur Geschichte der Theologie.* Gotha: F. A. Perthes, 1867.

Select Secondary Bibliography on Eusebius of Caesarea

Abramowksi, Luise. "Der Geist als 'Band' zwischen Vater und Sohn— ein Theologoumenon der Eusebianer?" *ZNW* 87 (1996): 126–32.

Armstrong, Jonathan J. *The Role of the Rule of Faith in the Formation of the New Testament Canon According to Eusebius.* Lewiston, New York: The Edwin Mellen Press, 2014.

Bardy, G. "La théologie d'Eusèbe de Césarée d'après *L'Histoire Ecclésiastique.*" *RHE* 40 (1955): 5–20.

Barnes, Timothy D. *Constantine and Eusebius.* Cambridge, MA: Harvard University Press, 1981.

Beeley, Christopher. "Eusebius' *Contra Marcellum*, Anti-Modalist Doctrine and Orthodox Christology." *ZAC* 12 (2009): 433–52.

Berkhof, H. *Die Theologie des Eusebius von Caesarea.* Amsterdam: Uitgeversmaatschappij Holland, 1939.

Bigelmair, A. "Zur Theologie des Eusebius von Caesarea." Pages 65–85 in *Festschrift für Georg von Hertling.* Edited by Görres-Gesellschaft zur Pflege der Wissenschaft im Kath. Deutschland. Kempten: Kösel'sche Buchhandlung, 1913.

Campenhausen, Hans von. "Das Bekenntnis Eusebs von Caesarea (Nicaea 325)." *ZNW* 67 (1976): 123–39.

DelCogliano, Mark. "The Eusebian Alliance: The Case of Theodotus of Laodicea." *ZAC* 12 (2008): 250–66.

———. "Eusebian Theologies of the Son as the Image of God before 341." *JECS* 14 (2006): 459–84.

Eusebius, Christianity and Judaism. Edited by Harold W. Attridge and Gohel Hata. Detroit, MI: Wayne State University Press, 1992.

Foakes-Jackson, F. J. *Eusebius Pamphili, Bishop of Caesarea and First Christian Historian: A Study in the Man and His Writings.* Cambridge: W. Heffer and Sons, Ltd., 1933.

Gero, Stephen. "The True Image of Christ: Eusebius' Letter to Constantia Reconsidered." *JTS* n.s. 32 (1981): 460–70.

Gressmann, Hugo. *Studien zu Eusebs Theophanie.* TU 23.3. Leipzig: J. C. Hinrichs, 1903.

Gwynn, David M. *The Eusebians: The Polemic of Athanasius of Alexandria and the Construction of the 'Arian Controversy.'* OTM. Oxford: Oxford University Press, 2007.

Heil, Ute. "Athanasius und Eusebius. Zum Rückgriff des Athanasius auf Euseb von Caesarea." Pages 189–214 in *Drei griechische Apologeten: Origenes, Eusebius, und Athanasius.* Edited by A. C. Jacobsen and J. Ulrich. Frankfurt am Main: Peter Lang, 2007.

Holland, D. L. "Die Synode von Antiochien (324/325) and ihre Bedeutung für Eusebius von Caesarea und das Konzil von Nizäa." *ZKG* 81 (1970): 163–81.

Hollerich, Michael J. *Eusebius of Caesarea's Commentary on Isaiah: Christian Exegesis in the Age of Constantine.* Oxford Early Christian Studies. Oxford: Clarendon Press, 1999.

Inowlocki, Sabrina, and Claudio Zamagni, eds. *Reconsidering Eusebius: Collected Papers on Literary, Historical, and Theological Issues.* Leiden: Brill, 2011.

Johnson, Aaron P. *Eusebius.* London: I. B. Taurus, 2014.

———. *Eusebius of Caesarea: Tradition and Innovation.* Edited by Aaron P. Johnson and Jeremy Schott. Washington, DC: Center for Hellenic Studies, 2013.

Kannengiesser, Charles. "Eusebius of Caesarea, Origenist." Pages 435–66 in *Eusebius, Christianity, and Judaism.* Edited by Harold W. Attridge and Gohel Hata. StPB 42. Leiden: Brill, 1992.

Lee, S. *Eusebius of Caesarea, On the Theophania or Divine Manifestation of Our Lord and Saviour Jesus Christ.* Cambridge, UK: Duncan and Malcolm, 1843.

Luibhéld, Colm. *Eusebius of Caesarea and the Arian Crisis.* Dublin: Irish Academic Press, 1981.

———. "Eusebius of Caesarea and the Nicene Creed." *ITQ* 39 (1972): 299–305.

Lyman, J. Rebecca. *Christology and Cosmology: Models of Divine Activity in Origen, Eusebius, and Athanasius.* OTM. Oxford: Clarendon Press, 1993.

————. "Substance Language in Origen and Eusebius." Pages 257–66 in *Arianism: Historical and Theological Reassessments*. Edited by Robert C. Gregg. Philadelphia: Philadelphia Patristics Foundation, 1985.

Mackett, John K. "Eusebius of Caesarea's Theology of the Holy Spirit." Ph.D. diss., Marquette University, 1992.

Moreau, J. "Eusèbe de Césarée de Palestine." 1437–60 in DHGE 15. Edited by R. Aubert and E. Van Cauwenbergh. 31 vols. Paris: Letouzey et Ané, 1963.

————. "Eusebius von Caesarea." Pages 1052–88 in *RAC*, vol. 6. Edited by Franz Joseph Dölger et al. 24 vols. Stuttgart: Hiersemann, 1950–.

Mühl, M. "Der λόγος ἐνδιάθετος und προφορικός von der älteren Stoa bis zur Synode von Sirmium 351." *ABG* 7 (1962): 239–68.

Munos Pacios, R. "La mediación del Logos, preexistente a la encarnación, en Eusebio de Cesárea. *EE* 43 (1968): 381–414.

Nielsen, Sylvia. *Euseb von Cäsarea und das Neue Testament.* Theorie und Forschung 786. Theologie 43. Regensburg: Roderer, 2003.

Opitz, H.-G. "Euseb von Caesarea als Theologe." *ZNW* 34 (1935): 51–59.

Pollard, T. E. "Eusebius of Caesarea and the Synod of Antioch (324–325)." Pages 459–65 in *Überlieferungsgeschichtliche Untersuchungen*. Edited by Franz Paschke. TU 125. Berlin: Akademie Verlag, 1981.

Prestige, G. L. "Ἀγέν[ν]ητος and γεν[ν]ητός and Kindred Words in Eusebius and the Early Arians." *JTS* 4 (1923): 486–96.

Ricken, F. "Die Logoslehre des Eusebios von Caesarea und der Mittelplatonismus." *TP* 42 (1967): 341–58.

————. "Zur Rezeption der platonischen Ontologie bei Eusebius von Kaisareia, Areios und Athanasius." Pages 114–17, 326, 331, in *Metaphysik und Theologie*. Edited by K. Kremeer. Leiden: Brill, 1980.

Robertson, Jon M. *Christ as Mediator: A Study of the Theologies of Eusebius of Caesarea, Marcellus of Ancyra, and Athanasius of Alexandria*. OTM. Oxford: Oxford University Press, 2007.

Rousseau, Philip. "Eusebius of Caesarea." Pages 141–44 in vol. 3 of *The Oxford Encyclopedia of Ancient Greece and Rome*. 7 vols. Edited by Michael Gagarin and Elaine Fantham. New York: Oxford University Press, 2010.

Ruther, R. R. "The Knowledge of God in Eusebius and Athanasius." Pages 229–42 in *The Knowledge of God in the Graeco-Roman World*. Edited by J. Mansfield, R. van den Broek, and T. Baarda. Leiden: Brill, 1988.

Schwartz, E. "Eusebios" in *Real-Encyclopädie der classischen Altertumswissenschaft*. Edited by A. Pauly, G. Wissowa. 3d ed. (1907): 1370–1439.

Simonetti, Manlio. "Eusebio e Origene. Per una storia dell' origenismo." *Aug* 26 (1986): 323–34.

Spoerl, Kelley McCarthy. "Anti-Arian Polemic in Eusebius of Caesarea's *Ecclesiastical Theology*." *StPat* 32 (1997): 33–38.

Stead, Christopher. "'Eusebius' and the Council of Nicaea." *JTS* n.s. 24, 1 (1973): 85–100.

Stevenson, J. *Studies in Eusebius*. Cambridge: Cambridge University Press, 1929.

Strutwolf, Holger. *Die Trinitätstheologie und Christologie des Euseb von Caesarea: Eine dogmengeschichtliche Untersuchung seiner Platonismusrezeption und Wirkungsgeschichte*. FKDG 72. Göttingen: Vandenhoeck und Ruprecht, 1999.

Thielman, F. S. "Another Look at the Eschatology of Eusebius of Caesarea." *VC* 4 (1987): 226–37.

Three Greek Apologists: Origen, Eusebius, and Athanasius. Edited by Anders-Christian Jacobsen and Jörg Ulrich. Frankfurt am Main: Peter Lang, 2007.

Trisoglio, F. "Eusebio di Cesarea e l'escatologia." *Aug* 18 (1978): 173–82.

Vinzent, Markus. *Pseudo-Athanasius, Contra Arianos IV: Eine Schrift gegen Asterius von Kappadokien, Eusebius von Cäsarea, Markell von Ankyra, und Photin von Sirmium*. VCSup 36. Leiden: Brill, 1996.

Wallace-Hadrill, David S. *Eusebius of Caesarea*. Westminster, MD: Canterbury Press, 1961.

———. "Eusebius of Caesarea." Pages 537–43 in vol. 10 of *TRE*. Edited by Horst Robert Balz et al. 36 vols. New York: Walter de Gruyter, 1977–.

Warmington, B. H. "Eusebius of Caesarea and some Early Opponents of Athanasius." *StPatr* 32 (1997): 59–64.

Weber, Anton. *Arche: Ein Beitrag zur Christologie des Eusebius von Cäsarea*. Munich: Verlag Neue Stadt, 1965.

Weis, Matthias. *Die Stellung des Eusebius von Cäsarea im arianischen Streit*. Trier: Paulinus-Druckerei, 1919.

Willing, Meike. *Eusebius von Cäsarea als Häreseograph*. PTS 63. Berlin: Walter de Gruyter, 2008.

Young, Robin Darling. "*Theologia* in the Early Church." *Comm* 24 (1997): 681–90.

INTRODUCTION

INTRODUCTION

I. Justification for the Translation

There has been tremendous interest in the evolution of fourth-century trinitarian thought over the past fifty years. Several major overviews of the period have been published,[1] in addition to specialized studies devoted to those theologians who would later be characterized as orthodox proponents of trinitarian doctrine such as Athanasius,[2] the Cappadocians,[3]

1. For example, Manlio Simonetti, *La crisi ariana nel IV secolo,* SEAug 11 (Rome: Institutum Patristicum Augustinianum, 1975); Frances Young, *From Nicaea to Chalcedon: A Guide to the Literature and its Background,* 2d ed. with Andrew Teal (Grand Rapids, MI: Baker Academic, 2010); R. P. C. Hanson, *The Search for the Christian Doctrine of God: The Arian Controversy 318–381* (Edinburgh: T & T Clark, 1988); John Behr, *The Nicene Faith* (Crestwood, NY: St. Vladimir's Seminary Press, 2004); Lewis Ayres, *Nicaea and its Legacy: An Approach to Fourth-Century Trinitarian Theology* (New York: Oxford University Press, 2004); Khaled Anatolios, *Retrieving Nicaea: The Development and Meaning of Trinitarian Doctrine* (Grand Rapids, MI: Baker Academic, 2011).

2. For example, Annik Martin, *Athanase d'Alexandrie et l'église d'Egypte au IVe siècle (328–373)* (Rome: École française de Rome, 1996); Khaled Anatolios, *Athanasius: The Coherence of his Thought* (London: Routledge, 1998); Xavier Morales, *La théologie trinitaire d'Athanase d'Alexandrie* (Paris: Institut d'études augustiniennes, 2006).

3. Another sampling: Volker Henning Drecoll, *Die Entwicklung des Trinitätslehre des Basilius von Cäsarea* (Göttingen: Vandenhoeck & Ruprecht, 1996); Bernard Sesboüé, *Saint Basile et la trinité: un acte théologique au IVe siècle: le rôle de Basile de Césarée dans l'élaboration de la doctrine et du langage trinitaires* (Paris: Desclée, 1998); Stephen M. Hildebrand, *The Trinitarian Theology of Basil of Caesarea: A Synthesis of Greek Thought and Biblical Truth* (Washington, DC: The Catholic University of America Press, 2007); Mark DelCogliano, *Basil of Caesarea's Anti-Eunomian Theory of Names: Christian Theology and Late-Antique Philosophy in the Fourth-Century Trinitarian Controversy* (Leiden: Brill, 2010); Christopher Beeley, *Gregory of Nazianzus on the Trinity and the Knowledge of God: In Your Light We Shall See Light* (New York: Oxford University Press, 2008); Michel R. Barnes, *The Power of God: Duna-*

3

and Augustine.[4] Since the 1980s, however, many patristic studies have focused more attention on those thinkers deemed in
the fourth century and subsequently as "Arian" or "Neo-Arian"
heretics. Premier among such figures are Arius of Alexandria[5]
and Asterius of Cappadocia,[6] but important studies, too, have
been published on other thinkers, more neutrally described
as "non-Nicene": first of all on Eusebius of Caesarea[7] and others in the developing Homoian,[8] Homoiousian,[9] and Heter-

---

mis in Gregory of Nyssa's Trinitarian Theology (Washington, DC: The Catholic University of America Press, 2001); Andrew Radde-Gallwitz, *Gregory of Nyssa and the
Transformation of Divine Simplicity* (New York: Oxford University Press, 2009).

   4. Lewis Ayres, *Augustine and the Trinity* (New York: Cambridge University
Press, 2010).

   5. Rudolph Lorenz, *Arius Judaizans?* (Göttingen: Vandenhoeck & Ruprecht,
1979); Robert C. Gregg and Dennis E. Groh, eds., *Early Arianism: A View of
Salvation* (Philadelphia: Fortress Press, 1981); Robert C. Gregg, ed., *Arianism:
Historical and Theological Reassessments* (Cambridge, MA: Philadelphia Patristic
Foundation, 1985); Michel René Barnes and Daniel H. Williams, eds., *Arianism
After Arius* (London: Continuum International Publishing Group–T & T Clark,
1993); Rowan Williams, *Arius: Heresy and Tradition* (London: Darton, Longman
and Todd Ltd., 1987; repr., Grand Rapids, MI: Wm. B. Eerdmans Publishing
Co., 2002); Thomas Böhm, *Die Christologie des Arius* (St. Ottilien: EOS Verlag,
1991); Charles Kannengiesser, *Arius and Athanasius: Two Alexandrian Theologians*
(Variorum Reprints; Brookfield, VT: Gower Publishing Company, 1991).

   6. Wolfram Kinzig, *In Search of Asterius. Studies on the Authorship of the Homilies on the Psalms*, FKDG 47 (Göttingen: Vandenhoeck & Ruprecht, 1990);
Markus Vinzent, ed., *Asterius von Kappadokien. Die theologischen Fragmente*, VCSup
20 (Leiden: Brill, 1993).

   7. Timothy D. Barnes, *Constantine and Eusebius* (Cambridge, MA: Harvard
University Press, 1981); Jörg Ulrich, *Euseb von Caesarea und die Juden*, PTS 49
(Berlin: Walter de Gruyter, 1999); Aryeh Kofsky, *Eusebius of Caesarea against
Paganism* (Leiden: Brill, 2000); H. A. Drake, *Constantine and the Bishops; The Pol-
icy of Intolerance* (Baltimore: John Hopkins Press, 2002); Holger Strutwolf, *Die
Trinitätstheologie und Christologie des Euseb von Caesarea*, FKDG 72 (Göttingen:
Vandenhoeck & Ruprecht, 1999); Aaron P. Johnson, *Eusebius* (London: I. B.
Taurus, 2014).

   8. Hanns Christof Brennecke, *Studien zur Geschichte der Homöer: Der Osten
bis zum Ende der homöischen Reichskirche* (Tübingen: Mohr/Paul Siebeck, 1988);
Winrich Alfried Löhr, *Die Entstehung der homöischen und homöusianischen Kirchen-
parteien: Studien zur Synodalgeschichte d. 4. Jh.*, Bonner Beiträge zur Kirchen- und
Theologiegeschichte 2 (Witterschlick: Wehle, 1986); Jörg Ulrich, *Die Anfänge der
abendländischen Rezeption des Nizänums* (Berlin: Walter de Gruyter, 1994).

   9. J. N. Steenson, "Basil of Ancyra and the Course of Nicene Orthodoxy"

oousian[10] movements, all united to one degree or another by opposition to the Nicene assertion that the pre-existent Son of God incarnate in Christ is ὁμοούσιος or consubstantial with his Father. But in recent years there has been an impressive accumulation of scholarship in both English and German devoted to a one-time ally of Athanasius in the pro-Nicene camp: namely, Marcellus of Ancyra, who was condemned and deposed at Constantinople in 336 for denying the hypostatic existence of the Son.[11] Michel Barnes[12] has argued persuasively that the theological reaction to Marcellus in the decades following his condemnation, especially in the Greek East, was as determinative for the shape of orthodox trinitarian doctrine as the reaction to Arius's teaching. To appreciate his claim, it is imperative to familiarize oneself with the literature composed in the period to counter what were seen as the errors of Marcellus. Studies have looked at both texts expressly composed *contra Marcellum* (or *Sabellium,* one of the fourth century's favorite code names for the bishop of Ancyra) and ones that combine an anti-Marcellan perspective with an anti-"Arian"[13] one, as well as the numerous

---

(Ph.D. diss., Oxford University, 1983); Hanns Christof Brennecke, *Hilarius von Poitiers und die Bischofsopposition gegen Konstantius II. Untersuchungen zur dritten Phase des arianischen Streites (337–361),* PTS 26 (Berlin: Walter de Gruyter, 1984); Mark Weedman, *The Trinitarian Theology of Hilary of Poitiers* (Leiden: Brill, 2007).

10. Thomas A. Kopacek, *A History of Neo-Arianism,* 2 vols. (Cambridge, MA: Philadelphia Patristic Foundation, 1979); Richard P. Vaggione, *Eunomius of Cyzicus and the Nicene Revolution,* Oxford Early Christian Studies (New York: Oxford University Press, 2000).

11. Gerhard Feige, *Die Lehre Markells von Ankyra in der Darstellung seiner Gegner* (Leipzig: Benno Verlag, 1990); Klaus Seibt, *Die Theologie des Markell von Ankyra* (Berlin: Walter de Gruyter, 1994); Markus Vinzent, ed., *Markell von Ankyra: Die Fragmente; Der Brief an Julius von Rom,* VCSup 39 (Leiden: Brill, 1997); Joseph T. Lienhard, SJ, *Contra Marcellum: Marcellus of Ancyra and Fourth-Century Theology* (Washington, DC: The Catholic University of America Press, 1999); Sara Parvis, *Marcellus of Ancyra and the Lost Years of the Arian Controversy, 325–345,* OTM (New York: Oxford University Press, 2006).

12. Michel R. Barnes, "The Fourth Century as Trinitarian Canon," in *Christian Origins: Theology, Rhetoric and Community,* ed. Lewis Ayres and Gareth Jones (London: Routledge, 1998), 47–67.

13. Recognizing that many of the claims that Athanasius attributes to Arius in, for example, his *Orationes contra Arianos,* really come from Asterius.

conciliar pronouncements, especially from the 340s and 350s, that incorporate standard slogans and scriptural exegeses typical of anti-Marcellan polemic.[14] All of these literary expressions of the anti-Marcellan perspective, however, trace their inspiration and often a good deal of their argumentation to the first anti-Marcellan texts, which were composed in the 330s by Eusebius of Caesarea: 1) the *Against Marcellus* (Κατὰ Μάρκελλον), primarily a pastiche of quotations from Marcellus's work *Against Asterius,* which, according to our reading, Eusebius wrote to justify the ultimate decision of the Constantinopolitan council that deposed Marcellus in 336; and 2) the *On Ecclesiastical Theology* (Ἡ Ἐκκλησιαστικὴ Θεολογία), composed after the *Against Marcellus* in the years leading up to Eusebius's death in 339, which contains not only more valuable source material from Marcellus, but, critically, Eusebius's considered theological response to Marcellus, one that is repeated and reworked to great constructive effect in subsequent fourth-century Greek theology. Hence to understand the development of the latter under the influence of the anti-Marcellan tradition that Eusebius initiated, scholars and students of the period must have access to these critical early texts. To date, however, this access has been limited because of the lack of translations of these works in modern languages.[15] The translation in the present

14. The works of Feige and Lienhard (both his monograph and numerous articles) are useful in this regard. One should also note the work of Reinhard M. Hübner, *Die Schrift des Apolinarius von Laodicea gegen Photin (Pseudo-Athanasius, Contra Sabellianos) und Basilius von Caesarea,* PTS 30 (Berlin: Walter de Gruyter, 1989); Markus Vinzent, *Pseudo-Athanasius, Contra Arianos IV: Eine Schrift gegen Asterius von Kappadokien, Eusebius von Cäsarea, Markell von Ankyra, und Photin von Sirmium,* VCSup 36 (Leiden: Brill, 1996); Franz Xaver Risch, ed., *Pseudo-Basilius Adversus Eunomium IV–V: Einleitung, Übersetzung und Kommentar,* VCSup 16 (Leiden: Brill, 1992). Spoerl's doctoral dissertation ("A Study of the *Kata Meros Pistis* of Apolinarius of Laodicea"; University of Toronto, 1991), 212–318, examined the anti-"Arian" and anti-Marcellan elements of the trinitarian theology of Apolinarius of Laodicea.

15. An Italian translation of the *On Ecclesiastical Theology* was published in the late 1990s, which the author, Franzo Migliore, correctly identified as the "absolutely" first translation ever of one of these works into a modern language: *Eusebio di Cesarea: Teologia ecclesiastica,* trans. Franzo Migliore (Rome: Città Nuova Editrice, 1998). The titles of the two works in the present volume

volume has been made in hopes of rectifying this omission and facilitating further study of this important period in doctrinal history. We include here both Eusebian texts, the *Against Marcellus* and the *On Ecclesiastical Theology,* the better to appreciate the evolution of Eusebius's trinitarian thought over the course of the 330s.

In our opinion, the study of these texts taken together has many advantages. Eusebius's anti-Marcellan works, the last treatises in the long and illustrious career of a scholar-bishop important to early Christianity as a church historian and apologist, will expand scholars' comprehensive understanding of the thought of this significant figure, shedding new light upon earlier works that have been fortunate enough to receive the benefit of translation and the increased study that translation generates. In addition, these texts are among the few complete texts available from the immediate post-Nicene period, and thus are invaluable in illuminating the initial theological response to the first ecumenical council, even if the creed of the council itself is not discussed in any explicit way in these works. For both scholars and students, these texts will render more comprehensible the abundant scholarship already published about Marcellus and the anti-Marcellan tradition in recent decades, and, it is hoped, will inspire and facilitate the production of more scholarship on the subject. Yet because of the pre-history of the relations of Eusebius and Marcellus before the council (to be recounted below), to which these texts allude at various points, their study can also provide new insight into the theological debates that preceded Nicaea in 325, and the ecclesial and theological dynamics at work at the council itself.[16] These texts, moreover, are important not only for their trinitarian content, but also for Christological

will be abbreviated in accordance with their Latin titles: *CM* (*Contra Marcellum*) for *Against Marcellus,* and *ET* (*De ecclesiastica theologia*) for *On Ecclesiastical Theology.*

16. This was already recognized in the early twentieth century by the great scholar of the period Hans-Georg Opitz. In his yet unpublished studies of the collection of documents pertaining to the origin of the Arian debate, Opitz pointed out that one of the major sources for the description of the ante-Nicene events and for the years after the first ecumenical council of the year 325 was Eusebius's long-neglected works against Marcellus. Hans-Georg

statements, which we have argued in print were influential on the doctrine of Apolinarius of Laodicea.[17] A translation of *On Ecclesiastical Theology* in particular will enable scholars more easily to consider the impact the anti-Marcellan debate had on the development of orthodox teaching on the person of Christ, as well as the Trinity.

Aside from the significance these texts have for doctrinal development, they have much intrinsic interest. Reading them, we are thrown into a philosophical, exegetical, and dogmatic discourse that reveals the theological viewpoints of several discussants, all of whom claim orthodoxy for their own positions. This further confirms the conclusion of much recent scholarship that the council of Nicaea was far from settling the question of the relation between God the Father and his Son, Jesus Christ, let alone addressing how the Holy Spirit relates to both. At the same time, the argument between Eusebius and Marcellus that is developed in these texts is a debate about references and traditions. For the first time, we learn, Origen is invoked as foundational for Christian thinking; we see that Eusebius begins to use the concept of "Church Fathers";[18] we also discover the relevance of theological schools and their genealogies of teachers and students. For both Marcellus and Eusebius, it is important to consider who was trained by whom and to what extent theology was influenced by pagan wisdom or Scripture. Perhaps ironically, while the debate between Eusebius and Marcellus would give rise over time to more stereotyped "heresies"

Opitz, "The Arian Debate up to the Year 328: Texts and Studies" (unpublished manuscript).

17. Markus Vinzent, "Direct or Discrete—On Inter-textuality and Counter-textuality in Athanasius, *Orations against the Arians I–III*," StPat 52 (2012): 113–27; idem, *Pseudo-Athanasius, Contra Arianos IV*; Kelley McCarthy Spoerl, "Apolinarian Christology and the Anti-Marcellan Tradition," *JTS* n.s. 45 (1994): 545–68. More recently, see Christopher A. Beeley, "Eusebius' *Contra Marcellum*. Anti-Modalist Doctrine and Orthodox Christology," *ZAC* 12 (2009): 433–52.

18. See Markus Vinzent, "Origenes als *Postscriptum*. Paulinus von Tyrus und die origenistische Diadoche," in *Origeniana Septima. Origenes in den Auseinandersetzungen des 4. Jahrhunderts*, ed. W. A. Bienert and U. Kühneweg, BETL 137 (Leuven: University Press, 1999), 149–57; Thomas Graumann, *Die Kirche der Väter*, BHT 118 (Tübingen: Mohr Siebeck, 2002).

(namely, "Semi-Arianism" and "Neosabellianism"), they often critique one another in terms of heretical categories that had been in existence for centuries. Although the canon itself is undisputed, the interpretation of Scripture is far from standardized, and what we see throughout Eusebius's anti-Marcellan works are the traces of a passionate debate about the exact meaning of numerous controverted texts. The core theological ideas of creation, the generation of the Son, salvation, the economy, and the eschatological future are controversial issues, and none of them are settled at the time Eusebius composed these books. The books read like a lively, vital debate that seeks to discover what "Ecclesiastical Theology" (a new term that Eusebius invents), or, to put it into our own language, what Christianity is about.

II. The Genesis of Eusebius of Caesarea's Anti-Marcellan Works

The dispute between Eusebius of Caesarea and Marcellus of Ancyra that led to the composition of the texts translated here likely had its roots in the pre-Nicene period. Biographical information about both figures is scanty, but it is clear that by the time their paths crossed in the 320s, both men were bishops: Eusebius in Palestinian Caesarea since approximately 313,[19] Marcellus of Ancyra certainly before 314, the year he presided at a council in his Galatian city.[20] The occasion for their closer

19. For more specific information about Eusebius's education and activities prior to the outbreak of the controversy regarding Arius of Alexandria's teaching, one may consult D. S. Wallace-Hadrill, *Eusebius of Caesarea* (Westminster, MD: The Canterbury Press, 1961), 11–38; Barnes, *Constantine and Eusebius*, 94; Johnson, *Eusebius*, 1–24.

20. What little is known about Marcellus prior to his appearance as bishop at the Council of Ancyra in 314 is discussed in Parvis, *Marcellus of Ancyra*, 8–10; a history of scholarship on Marcellus is given by Seibt, *Die Theologie des Markell von Ankyra*, 15–202; on works of Marcellus other than the one excerpted and discussed by Eusebius, see Martin Tetz, "Zur Theologie des Markell von Ankyra I. Eine Markellische Schrift 'De incarnatione et contra Arianos,'" *ZKG* 75 (1964): 217–70; Christoph Riedweg, *Ps.-Justin (Markell von Ankyra?), Ad Graecos de vera religione (bisher "Cohortatio ad Graecos"). Einleitung und Kommentar*, SBA 25/1.2 (Ba-

interaction was the debate generated by the preaching of the presbyter Arius in Alexandria, Egypt. While the exact chronology of when concern about Arius emerged in his diocese and steps were taken to discipline him for views regarded as heretical is unclear, we know that at some point in either the late teens or early 320s,[21] after being condemned and expelled for heresy in Alexandria,[22] Arius traveled about the eastern Mediterranean seeking support for his views in hopes of eventual rehabilitation. One of his letters mentions that Eusebius of Caesarea lent his name to the cause;[23] another document indicates that Eusebius wrote to Euphrantion of Balaneae to explain the legitimacy of Arius's views.[24] Sometime in the period Eusebius of Nicomedia convened a council in Bithynia in Asia Minor to overturn Arius's condemnation in Alexandria.[25] Afterwards Eusebius of Caesarea wrote to bishop Alexander of Alexandria to persuade him to readmit Arius to communion in the diocese,[26] an effort that was unsuccessful, as in the wake of it, Alexander sent out two letters to bishops outside of Egypt reiterating Arius's heresy and the impossibility of his readmission to communion without a full recantation of his views.[27] Sozomen reports that Eusebius of Caesarea reacted by convening a council of bishops in Palestine to press again for intervention in favor of

---

sel, 1994); Alastair H. B. Logan, "Marcellus of Ancyra (Pseudo-Anthimus), 'On the Holy Church': Text, Translation and Commentary," *JTS* 51 (2000): 81–112.

21. A good overview of the problems surrounding this topic appears in Williams, *Arius: Heresy and Tradition*, 48–61, and in Parvis, *Marcellus of Ancyra*, 68–75.

22. See Arius's letter to Eusebius of Nicomedia, Urk. 1.2 in Hans-Georg Opitz, *Athanasius Werke: Urkunden zur Geschichte des Arianischen Streites 318–328*, Bd. 3.1 (Berlin: Walter de Gruyter, 1934), 1.

23. Urk. 1.3 (Op., 2), in Arius's letter to Eusebius of Nicomedia. A translation may be found in *A New Eusebius: Documents Illustrative of the History of the Church to A.D. 337* (London: S.P.C.K., 1980), 344–45.

24. Urk. 3 (Op., 4–6).

25. Urk. 5 (Op., 12), from Sozomen, *HE* 1.15.

26. Urk. 7 (Op., 14–15).

27. Urk. 14–15 (Op., 19–31). A translation of Alexander of Alexandria's letter to Alexander of Thessalonika can be found in William G. Rusch, ed., *The Trinitarian Controversy* (Philadelphia: Fortress Press, 1980), 33–44.

Arius,[28] suggesting that the conflict was developing into a stale-
mate in the east between the bishops who supported Arius and
those who condemned him, and this at a time when Constantine's victory over Licinius gave him the opportunity to pro-
mote the unity and welfare of the Church east and west that he
was convinced was the key to his political success. Accordingly,
sometime in 324, Ossius of Cordoba was sent to Alexandria in
an attempt to resolve the controversy;[29] this effort too failed,
and it was announced at the time that a larger synod of bishops from the eastern and western parts of the empire would
be held the next year.[30] The location originally announced was
Marcellus's home see of Ancyra, though in the event the council was moved to the city of Nicaea. The initial choice to hold
the council in Ancyra, however, might suggest that Marcellus
and his diocese had by this time somehow become known to
Constantine, and that the Emperor may have thought of Marcellus as a particularly reliable supporter for his policy of bringing unity back to the Church; if that was the case, Constantine
must have changed his mind prior to the decision to move
the venue to Nicaea. Theognis was bishop of Nicaea; he, too,
was a supporter of Arius and ally of Eusebius of Caesarea, although apparently early on not as outspoken as he. (Together
with Eusebius of Nicomedia, Theognis was condemned only by
the council of Nicaea itself.)[31] In the end, Constantine's stated reasons for changing the location of the council were that
Nicaea was a more convenient location for the bishops of Italy
and the rest of Europe, had a more accommodating climate,

28. Urk. 10 (Op., 18, from Sozomen, *HE* 1.15).

29. Eusebius of Caesarea, *v.C* 2.63, in *Eusebius Werke,* Bd. 1.1, *Über das Leben des Kaisers Konstantin,* ed. Friedhelm Winkelmann, GCS 61 (Berlin: Akademie Verlag, 1975), 73; Socrates, *HE* 1.7.1, in *Sokrates, Kirchengeschichte,* Günther Christian Hansen and Manja Kirinjan, eds., GCS n.f. Bd. 1 (Berlin: Akademie Verlag, 1995), 13; Sozomen, *HE* 1.16.5, in *Sozomenus, Kirchengeschichte,* 2d ed., Joseph Bidez and Günther Christian Hansen, eds., GCS n.f. Bd. 4 (Berlin: Akademie Verlag, 1995), 36.

30. Urk. 18.14–15 (Op., 40). A partial translation of this text (preserved in Syriac) is available in *A New Eusebius,* 354–57.

31. Urk. 28 (Op., 63). See also their interpretation of events in their letter from exile, Urk. 31 (Op., 65–66).

and allowed him to be present himself at the council.[32] Perhaps
Theognis, not already condemned and branded as pro-Arian
before the council, had a supporting voice in Constantia, since
two years after the Council Rufinus reports that on her death-
bed, she had asked for Arius's recall from exile—thus showing
that Arius and his allies had powerful supporters close to the
emperor.[33]

But even before the Ancyran/Nicaean council was held, one
last attempt to resolve the conflict over Arius's teaching took
place in December of 324. A council was held in the city of Antioch after the bishop, Philogonius, had died, and Eustathius
was elected as his replacement.[34] Theological issues were discussed, and this time the leaders of the council came out in favor of Alexander, not Arius. They produced a creed, which they
required all present to sign. Eusebius of Caesarea along with
Theodotus of Laodicea and Narcissus of Neronias refused and
received a provisional punishment of excommunication for
their "Arian" views, leaving open the possibility of their rehabilitation at the larger synod to be held in the summer of 325.[35]
The change of location of the planned ecumenical council
and the theological and political struggles in the aftermath of
the council of Antioch can still be traced in Eusebius's *Against
Marcellus*. The debate that is discussed in *Against Marcellus* relates to the most difficult time in Eusebius of Caesarea's life, his

32. Urk. 20 (Op., 41–42). Translation in *A New Eusebius*, 358.

33. See Rufinus, *HE* 1.11 (PL 21: 482–83) or 10.12 (*Eusebius Werke* Bd. 2:
Die Kirchengeschichte, T. 2, (Buch VI–X), ed. Eduard Schwartz und Theodor
Mommsen, GCS n.f. Bd. 6 (Berlin; Akademie Verlag, 1999), 976–78; Socrates,
HE 1.25 (Hansen, 72–73), 1.39 (ibid., 90–91), 2.2 (ibid., 93–94); Sozomen,
HE 2.27 (Bidez/Hansen, 88–91); 2.34 (ibid., 99–100); Theodoret, *HE* 2.2, in
Theodoret, Kirchengeschichte, 3d ed., Leon Parmentier and Günther Christian
Hansen, eds., GCS n.f. Bd. 5 (Berlin: Akademie Verlag, 1998), 94–96; Phi-
lostorgius, *HE* 1.9, in *Philostorgius, Kirchengeschichte*, 2d ed., Joseph Bidez and
Friedhelm Winkelmann, eds., GCS 21 (Berlin: Akademie Verlag, 1972), 9–11.
On the life of Constantia, see Hans A. Pohlsander, "Constantia," *Ancient Society*
24 (1993): 151–67.

34. John Chrysostom, *Philogon* (PG 48: 747–56). See also Theodoret, *HE*
1.7.10 (Parmentier/Hansen, 32).

35. Urk. 18–19 (Op., 36–41).

condemnation by Antioch (in 324/325), and what happened to him at and after Nicaea.

As Marcellus had access to and quotes from a body of pre-Nicene correspondence between the primary bishops involved, he himself must have been part of, or at least must have been well informed about, the debate generated by Arius's teaching prior to Nicaea. Whether, as Sara Parvis contends, Marcellus had already come out in favor of the anti-Arian, Alexander-supporting wing of the eastern episcopate,[36] is less clear. In any case, the first time Marcellus is unambiguously attested as opposing Arius's teaching—and thus by extension, that of his supporters, including Eusebius of Caesarea—was at the council of Nicaea.[37] This may have been the first time Eusebius and Marcellus had encountered one another in person—Eusebius having been seated after he tendered his personal creed to the council and had its orthodoxy recognized. He eventually signed off on the Nicene creed, though he gave a nuanced interpretation of it in a letter to his diocese.[38] Interestingly, despite the fact that in his letter to Julius, Marcellus claims that he had already refuted at Nicaea those bishops who had written to the bishop of Rome,[39] his name does not appear on the earliest lists of signatories to the Nicene creed, though Parvis argues he may have been influential in drawing up the canons of the council.[40]

We have no information about the dealings of Eusebius and Marcellus with one another for the two years following Nicaea; instead, historians report the outbreak of a pamphlet war between Eustathius of Antioch (who, it must be remembered, was bishop of Antioch at the council at which Eusebius and his allies received provisional excommunication for heresy before Nicaea) and Eusebius of Caesarea, wherein the two bishops accused one another of heresy—Eustathius accusing Eusebius for

36. Parvis, *Marcellus of Ancyra*, 50.

37. Marcellus says as much in his letter to Julius, bishop of Rome. See Vinzent, *Markell von Ankyra*, 124, 2–3; on this letter see Martin Tetz, "Zum altrömischen Bekenntnis. Ein Beitrag des Marcellus von Ancyra," *ZNW* 75 (1984): 107–27.

38. Urk. 22 (Op., 42–47). Translation in *A New Eusebius*, 364–68.

39. Marcellus, *ep. ad Iul.* (Vinzent, 124,3).

40. Parvis, *Marcellus of Ancyra*, 91–94.

his support of Arius, Eusebius accusing Eustathius of Sabellian-ism for his interpretation of the Nicene ὁμοούσιος.⁴¹ At the au-tumn synod of the diocese of Coele-Syria in the fall of 327, Eu-stathius was deposed as bishop of Antioch and sent into exile.⁴² Within less than a year, a second replacement for Eustathius had died, and Eusebius of Caesarea himself was proposed for the Antiochene see; he refused the appointment out of consid-eration for the Nicene canon that prohibited the translation of bishops from one see to another, and Euphronius was appoint-ed instead. He survived a year in the position, to be replaced by Flacillus, the dedicatee of *On Ecclesiastical Theology*.⁴³ From the harsh remarks about Eusebius and Paulinus of Tyre⁴⁴ that ap-pear in his text *Against Asterius,* Parvis contends that Marcellus was incensed at what happened to Eustathius, and held Euse-bius (who by one report presided at the council that deposed Eustathius)⁴⁵ responsible for the downfall of one whom he re-garded as a paragon of orthodoxy.⁴⁶

It was not long after Eustathius's deposition that the imme-diate catalyst emerged for the composition of the work that Eusebius quotes extensively in both *Against Marcellus* and *On Ecclesiastical Theology*. Sometime before the fall of 328, Asterius of Cappadocia had composed a tract in defense of Eusebius of Nicomedia, one of Arius's defenders from the earliest stages of the controversy. (He had convened the pre-Nicene council in Bithynia to overturn Arius's condemnation, after which Euse-bius of Caesarea had written to Alexander of Alexandria.) Nev-

41. Socrates, *HE* 1.23.6 (Hansen, 69–70).

42. The date and circumstances of Eustathius's deposition, the subject of some controversy in the literature, is discussed in Parvis, *Marcellus of Ancyra,* 101–7. The date offered here reflects Parvis's reconstruction of events.

43. Eusebius of Caesarea, *v.C.* 3.59–62 in Winkelmann, 111–17.

44. Paulinus had been a rival to Eustathius during the latter's tenure in the Antiochene episcopate and held the see alone for six months after Eustathi-us's deposition; on Paulinus see Vinzent, "Origenes als *Postscriptum*. Paulinus von Tyrus und die origenistische Diadoche."

45. Theodoret, *HE* 1.20.4 (Parmentier, 70). See Timothy D. Barnes, *Atha-nasius and Constantius: Theology and Politics in the Constantinian Empire* (Cam-bridge, MA: Harvard University Press, 1993), 17.

46. Parvis, *Marcellus of Ancyra,* 101–7, 117.

er ordained because he had sacrificed during the Great Per-
secution, Asterius was a philosopher from Cappadocia whom
Athanasius attests to have been an early defender of[47] and even
the source for the theology of Arius and his allies.[48] Epiphanius and Philostorgius identify him as a pupil of Lucian of Antioch.[49] Marcellus does not mention Lucian, but twice claims
Paulinus of Tyre to have been the "father" of Asterius.[50] Paulinus had also written a letter in support of Eusebius of Nicomedia, presumably addressed to Alexander of Alexandria.[51] Asterius wrote his tract in defense of Eusebius of Nicomedia, who,
apparently in a private letter that was only addressed to Paulinus,[52] had voiced views that must have nevertheless become
public. In support of Eusebius, Asterius traveled around Syria
in the spring and summer of 329 giving readings from his *Syn-
tagmation*.[53] Several major scholars now believe that Marcellus
wrote his book in response to Asterius's activities, and hence
the tract often goes by the name *Against Asterius*.[54] In the fol-

47. Athanasius, *syn.* 20.1 (Opitz, 247); *Ar.* 1.30.7, in *Athanasius Werke*, Bd.
1.1, ed. Martin Tetz (Berlin: Walter de Gruyter, 1996), 140, 23–141, 3, and 32
(Tetz, 141–42); 3.2.1 (Tetz, 307, 38); and 60.4 (Tetz, 373, 18–19).

48. Athanasius, *decr.* 8.1 (Op., 7) ("Arius transcribes" what "Asterius has
written"); 20.2 (Op., 16–17) (Asterius learned from the Eusebian bishops, and
"Arius learned from him [Asterius]"); see also *syn.* 18.2 (Op., 245).

49. Epiphanius, *haer.* 76.3, in *Epiphanius III: Panarion haer. 65–80, De fide*,
2d ed., Karl Holl and Jürgen Dummer, eds., GCS 37 (Berlin: Akademie Verlag, 1985), 343–44; Philostorgius, *HE* 2.14 (Bidez/Winkelmann, 25). See also
Urk. 1.5 (Op., 3), wherein Arius addresses Eusebius of Nicomedia as a "fellow
Lucianist."

50. See Marcellus, *fr.* 18; 122 (K./H., 87; 84; Vinzent, 18; 114). (Here and
later we give the numberings of Marcellus's fragments according to the edition of Vinzent [here fragments 18 and 122], followed by the numberings in
brackets of the older edition of Klostermann/Hansen [here fragments 87 and
84], followed by the page numbers in the edition of Vinzent [here p. 18 and
p. 114].)

51. So Hans-Georg Opitz, "The Arian Debate up to the Year 328: Texts and
Studies" (unpublished manuscript).

52. Marcellus, *fr.* 18 (K./H., 87; Vinzent, 18).

53. See Parvis, *Marcellus of Ancyra*, 100–101, 112–16. The report of Asterius's travels in support of his treatise appears in Socrates, *HE* 1.36.3 (Hansen,
86), a fuller account of what Athanasius describes in *syn.* 18.3 (Op., 245).

54. It should be noted that because of his interpretation of the relation-

lowing five or six years, the book received sufficient circulation that Eusebius was able to compose his *Against Marcellus* incorporating extensive quotations from it.[55]

With Eustathius off the scene in the east since the fall of 327, it seems that the supporters of Arius began efforts to remove from the eastern episcopacy another one of his opponents, Athanasius of Alexandria, who had been deacon to bishop Alexander of Alexandria and present with him at the Council of Nicaea, and from the year 328, his successor in the see of Alexandria. Without arguing explicitly against Athanasius's theological views, the supporters of Arius accused Athanasius of using violence in his diocese against any and all either with whom he disagreed or who did not recognize his authority as bishop—for example, Meletian schismatics.[56] Significantly, there is evidence that Constantine ordered a council of bishops to meet in Caesarea circa 334 to investigate the charges against Athanasius, at which Eusebius would have presided.[57] The council carried out an investigation of his behavior and condemned Athanasius, but Constantine chose not to put the decision into effect.[58] Another attempt to dislodge Athanasius from his see was made at a council in Tyre in 335, and this time Marcellus was present, as well as Eusebius of Caesarea. Eusebius's ally Flacillus of Antioch presided at the council, which was interrupted by a mandatory side trip to Jerusalem to join Constantine in celebrating the dedication of the Church of the Holy Sepulchre in Jerusalem. Marcellus and Eusebius came into open conflict at this council: to begin with, Marcellus refused to communicate with Arius at the dedication ceremonies in Jerusalem and objected to the deposition of Athanasius when it

---

ship between Marcellus and Constantine, Seibt proposes a different title for the work, the *Opus ad Constantinum Imperatorem.* For more on this, see Seibt, *Die Theologie des Markell von Ankyra,* 460–89.

55. See Parvis, *Marcellus of Ancyra,* 118–23.

56. On this, see Barnes, *Constantine and Eusebius,* 206–7, 224–44; *Athanasius and Constantius,* 10–33.

57. Sozomen, *HE* 2.25.1 (Bidez/Hansen, 84); Theodoret, *HE* 1.28.2 (Parmentier/Hansen, 163).

58. Athanasius, *apol. sec.* 65.4 (Op., 144). For more details on the council, see Barnes, *Constantine and Eusebius,* 234–35.

was finally voted upon.[59] Having foiled the emperor's cherished attempts to restore harmony after more than ten years of conflict in the eastern episcopate, Marcellus felt obliged to write to Constantine himself to defend himself from the charge of willful recalcitrance. Without mentioning Arius himself, but targeting Asterius, the "defender" of the Eusebians,[60] Marcellus accused his opponents of outright polytheism, accusing Eusebius of Nicomedia explicitly (along with Paulinus of Tyre and Narcissus of Neronias) of believing in multiple gods and likening their ideas to those of earlier Christian heretics and pagan philosophers.[61] The effort did not help his cause: he was called to a council in Constantinople in July 336, wherein his theological views were scrutinized and deemed wanting,[62] after which Marcellus was deposed and sent into exile, possibly in Illyricum.[63] Basil was appointed in his stead. Eusebius of Caesarea was present at this council, and we learn from the *Against Marcellus* that the decision of the council fathers to depose Marcellus from his see was not unanimous.[64] Apparently because of a strong resistance to the condemnation of Marcellus, the bishops who were in favor of the deposition urged Eusebius to defend their vote; hence Eusebius composed the *Against Marcellus* after the synod to comply with their wishes.[65] In fact, the two books of the work address the two chief charges against Marcellus: first, in Book 1, of divisive, un-collegial behavior in laying such bald charges of heterodoxy against respected bishops, and second, in Book 2, of overt theological errors, laid out through a series of longer or shorter quotations from Marcellus's tract *Against Asterius*.

As Eusebius himself admits,[66] the *Against Marcellus* was not

59. See ibid., 234–44; Barnes, *Athanasius and Constantius,* 22–25; Parvis, *Marcellus of Ancyra,* 123–27.

60. See Marcellus, *fr.* 9; 18 (K./H., 35; 87; Vinzent, 12,1–3; 18,4).

61. See Marcellus, *fr.* 115–118 (K./H., 98; 81; 82; 85; Vinzent, 108–110).

62. Parvis, *Marcellus of Ancyra,* 127–32.

63. Ibid., 135–36.

64. Eusebius at *CM* 2.4.30 (K./H., 58) admits that some bishops who attended the synod believed that Marcellus "was treated unjustly," the reason, as he states, that made it "especially necessary" for him to write *Against Marcellus.*

65. Vinzent, *Markell von Ankyra,* xix.

66. See the preface to the *ET* (K./H., 62).

intended as a systematic refutation of the errors embedded in
Marcellus's theology. It is instead a work composed for a specific polemical purpose—to present Marcellus's behavior and
teaching in such a negative light as to justify his deposition from
episcopal office and the removal of his voice from contempo-
rary theological discussion. Another attempt to refute Marcellus, and, significantly, to offer his own responses and corrections to Marcellus's errors, presented itself after Constantine's
death in May of 337; in its aftermath, his successor in the east,
Constantius, declared an amnesty allowing exiled bishops to return home to their native sees.[67] Many scholars place the composition of *On Ecclesiastical Theology* between the declaration of
this amnesty and Eusebius's own death in May of 339, as part of
an effort to prevent Marcellus from resuming his see. Parvis has
suggested that, like the *Against Marcellus*, it may have been composed for an Antiochene council held in the winter of 338/339,
at which Flacillus of Antioch presided, that decreed a second
deposition for Marcellus.[68] In the event, whether at this council
or not, Marcellus was deposed again by the spring of 339 and
sent into exile, first probably to Illyricum and then certainly to
Rome by the winter of 339, where he met up with Athanasius of
Alexandria, who had also been deposed a second time in the
wake of the amnesty of 337. By this time, Eusebius was dead.
Marcellus seems to have remained in exile until about the year
361, when he returned to Ancyra. He lived there until approximately 374.[69]

III. Theological Analysis

1. Asterius's Controversial Theology as Seen by Marcellus

In order to understand the theology of Eusebius in his anti-
Marcellan works, we have to know something of the theology
of Marcellus. And to understand that, we need to know something about Marcellus's conflict with Asterius, which prompted

67. Barnes, *Athanasius and Constantius,* 34; Parvis, *Marcellus of Ancyra,* 136–46.
68. Parvis, *Marcellus of Ancyra,* 156.
69. Ibid., 245–52.

the composition of the treatise against which Eusebius reacted. Asterius's relation to the original catalyst for the trinitarian
controversies, Arius, remains unclear. According to Athanasius,
the latter learned from the former, while post-Nicaea, Asterius
was seen as the defender of the supporters of Arius.[70] Whatever
the nature of the relation between the two was, their theologies
show demonstrable similarities, but also significant differences.
They differ in their main theological concerns, and they are influenced by different philosophical backgrounds. From the surviving fragments, especially those that Athanasius provides, we
can see that Asterius is influenced by Middle-Platonism and that
his thought bears some affinities to Philo of Alexandria, but also
to a Porphyrian reading of Plotinus, while Arius is closer to Plotinus himself. These differences are evident in their descriptions
of God's nature. Asterius differentiates primarily between those
essential characteristics of God that define who he is and those
essential characteristics that are proper to him, but which he can
share with whom and what he generates and creates.[71] So the
prime distinction is not between God and creation or between
Father and Son, but between the utterly transcendent divine being[72] and everything else. The divine being itself is characterized

70. See Athanasius, *decr.* 8.1 (Op., 7); 20.2 (Op., 16–17); see also *syn.*, 18.2
(Op., 245); Marcellus, *fr.* 9; 18 (K./H., 35; 87; Vinzent, 12,3; 18,4).

71. See Vinzent, *Asterius von Kappadokien*, 41–48.

72. On the translation of οὐσία: one of the challenging features of this translation project was determining how we would render in English the trinitarian
terms οὐσία and ὑπόστασις. The differentiation of these terms, seemingly syn-
onymous in the pre-Nicene period as well as in the anathemas appended to the
creed of the council of Nicaea, was critical in the development of the trinitarian orthodoxy confirmed at the Council of Constantinople in 381. Granted, it
is likely, as some scholars have noted, that fourth-century theologians may not
have seen the assignment of fixed meanings to these terms as essential to the
formulation of orthodoxy as modern theologians do. Even so, the assignment of
precise definitions to these controverted terms *was* an important part of helping
Christian thinkers identify what was one and what was three in the Christian
godhead. Hence it is understandable that as modern scholars of the trinitarian
debates, we would be interested in Eusebius's usage of these terms, and we expect other scholars to be so too. To translate them, however, in the sense of later usage—"substance" for οὐσία, "person" or "subsistence" for ὑπόστασις—runs
the risk of attributing a clarity and precision to Eusebius's trinitarian theology

5

by only two incommunicable essential characteristics, namely,
the state of being "ingenerate" and "eternal," a Middle-Platonic
pair of concepts that we can already find in Philo of Alexandria.[73] That God is also without beginning and invisible, that he
creates out of himself, that he is source, God, generator, Father,
power, Logos, Wisdom, Lord, King, teacher, being, savior, light,
and so forth, and that he is one, the one alone, perfect, and true,
are all implications of his ingenerate and eternal being. All those
implications, however, are not exclusive to him, contrary to his
designation as "ingenerate" and "eternal." Except for these two
characteristics, all the others can be communicated. Oneness,
therefore, as mentioned, counts among those qualities that God
is able to share even with his creatures. Or, as Asterius says: "See,
there is even only one single Sun, and one Earth."[74] Yet, "ingenerate" and "eternal" denote God alone.

Like Asterius, Arius takes "ingenerate" and "eternal" as
characteristics of God's being, but Arius not only adds that
God is "ineffable"; in contrast to Asterius he takes God's "oneness" as an exclusive characteristic of God. Moreover, most
probably under the influence of Plotinus, Arius asserted that
oneness is even a more distinctive characteristic of God than
all others, in fact, the main characteristic of the transcendent.
In the preserved fragment of his *Thalia*, oneness even precedes
God's characteristic of being "ingenerate." He is μόνος οὗτος.[75]

---

that may not have been there when he was writing his anti-Marcellan works in
the 330s. We think there is evidence in these works for some erosion of the syn-
onymity of these terms that had been the case in the pre-Nicene period. Others,
however, may disagree. Hence in the interest of avoiding the overdetermination
of what Eusebius (and others in the debate with him) meant by these terms and
allowing those who read this translation to draw their own conclusions, we have
taken the following course of action on this vexing issue. We have chosen to
transliterate ὑπόστασις as "hypostasis," which is simply the most obvious, direct
way to alert the reader to the occurrence of this key term. To translate οὐσία,
then, we have used the word "being" but have consistently throughout the text
tagged the occurrence of this term with a footnote, indicating that the word
here translates οὐσία.

73. Philo, *Opif.*, 171.
74. Asterius, *fr.* 24 (Vinzent, 94).
75. Arius, *Thalia*, in Athanasius, *syn.* 15 (Op., 242,10).

Central to this text is the idea of God being one or God being Oneness (μονάς), something Marcellus shares with Arius and which differentiates both Arius and Marcellus from Asterius and Eusebius. How the latter defends Asterius on this point against Marcellus can be seen in his criticism in *On Ecclesiastical Theology* 2.5, where Eusebius writes about Marcellus:

> ... Having asserted that the monad is indivisible, and that there is one hypostasis of God and of the Word within him, according to him one would have to think that the one who was incarnated was none other than the God who is over all.[76] But if the monad is indivisible, God and the Word within him are one and the same thing, and who, then, would someone say is the Father and who is the Son, since the underlying reality[77] is one? And so in this way, Marcellus, introducing him who is one and the same, a Son-Father, renewed [the error of] Sabellius.[78]

To Eusebius (as for Asterius, but in contrast not only to Marcellus, but also to Arius), the designation of "oneness" (μόνος / μονάς) cannot be the distinct conceptualization of God's being. Already in his *Against Marcellus* 2.4 Eusebius called Marcellus's understanding of God's "Oneness" a fall into the "depth of irrationality."[79] Eusebius had grasped that the concept of salvific mediation was at stake, as we will see further below.

The differences between Asterius's and Arius's identification of the essential characteristics and their different transcendentals of the divine led to alternative interpretations of the generation of Son (and Spirit). For Arius, the Son was unlike God, the Father, "the one," who is ingenerate, invisible, and incomprehensible. The Son was seen as the beginning of the many that did not share in any of God's essential characteristics. In contrast, Asterius credits the Son (as he does all creatures) with all the divine characteristics that he takes as transcendentals, except for being "ingenerate" and "eternal." Unlike in Arius's thought, where God was not always Father, but only God when

76. Rom 9.5; Eph 4.6.
77. τοῦ ὑποκειμένου.
78. *ET* 2.5 (K./H., 103.2–8).
79. *CM* 2.4.13 (K./H., 55).

the Son and the creation did not exist,[80] in Asterius, God was always Father like a doctor who has the power of healing even prior to actively healing.[81] While Arius posits a more rigid transcendence of God, Asterius emphasizes his transcendental nature and the likeness of God to his creation and the similarity of Father and Son, "the one [who begot] one; the perfect a perfect, the King a King, the Lord a Lord, the God a God, unchanged[82] image of [his] being[83] and will and glory and power."[84] As a result, Asterius and Arius developed very different views of mediation.

According to Asterius (as in Philo),[85] since God could not be encountered by his creatures, but had to be mediated, the Son exerted his mediatory role by being a creature essentially like those creatures to whom he mediated God's gifts, even if he was the first of them and their mediator. As God had chosen a man, Moses, to pass on his law to his fellow people, so the

---

80. This is evident in Arius's *Letter to Alexander of Alexandria* 4 (= Urk. 6, Op., 13, 8–13): "And God, being the cause of all things, is unbegun (ἄναρχος) and altogether sole, but the Son, being begotten apart from time by the Father, and being created and found before ages, was not before his generation; but, being begotten apart from time before all things, alone was made to subsist by the Father. For he is not eternal (ἀΐδιος) or co-eternal (συναΐδιος) or co-unbegotten (συναγέννητος) with the Father, nor has he his being together with the Father, as some speak of relations, introducing two unbegotten (ἀγεννήτους) beginnings (ἀρχάς), but God is before all things as being Monad and Beginning (ἀρχή) of all." Translation adapted from *A New Eusebius,* 346.

81. See Asterius, *fr.* 14 (Vinzent, 88).

82. Mark DelCogliano argues that the Greek term ἀπαράλλακτος should be translated as "indistinguishable," because while Asterius uses Christ's identity as "image of God" to assert the distinction between Father and Son on the level of hypostasis, at the same time he is asserting that the Son is an "indistinguishable image" of the Father which conveys an "epistemic" unity between them that guarantees that the Son can "accurately and truthfully represent [the Father] in every way and thus transmit knowledge of him." See Mark DelCogliano, "Eusebian Theologies of the Son as the Image of God before 341," *JECS* 14 (2006): 459–84, esp. 465–71.

83. οὐσίας.

84. Asterius, *fr.* 10 (Vinzent, 86).

85. See Philo, *Mut.* 27–29 (God creates through the medium of his power); *Spec.* 1.60 (God creates without a touch by himself). See also further references and commentary by H. A. Wolfson, *Religious Philosophy* (Cambridge, 1961), 133–35.

Son, the first creature, passed on God's salvation to the other creatures, in order that "through the similar the similar beings would be able to become" what he is.[86] Arius, in turn, believed in the sole revelatory power of God, the Father; he asserted that the Son neither knows the Father, nor sees him, nor can recognize his own being.[87] Only God "himself is the teacher of Wisdom."[88] Mediation happens "each according to one's own measure by that power by which God is able to see";[89] hence God's intellect and will determine how the Son and any other creature can bear to see the Father.[90] Although Arius calls the Son a "more powerful God,"[91] he is far from being "the" God, a differentiation between the Son and the highest transcendent divinity, known already from Origen, to which Eusebius will refer numerous times in his anti-Marcellan works.[92]

Interestingly, Marcellus in his book neither mentions nor discusses Arius and his theology, but he must have known about them from his participation at Nicaea, if not from the debate that preceded the council, as we have discussed above. Taking note, however, of the differences between the respective theologies of Arius and Asterius is important in order to understand the remote background to the debate between Eusebius and Marcellus, as Eusebius himself maintains a third position that is neither fully that of Arius nor that of Asterius. Moreover, although Marcellus is also critical of others who defended Arius, the opponent with whose work he is most familiar and eager to dispute is Asterius:

> For if Asterius has believed that "God is Maker of all things,"[93]
> it is clear that even he himself will confess along with us that

86. Asterius, *fr.* 47 (Vinzent, 112).

87. Athanasius, *syn.* 15.3 (Op., 243, 14–15).

88. Ibid. (Op., 242, 18).

89. Ibid. (Op., 242, 22–23).

90. See ibid. (Op., 242, 19–20).

91. Ibid. (Op., 243, 13).

92. Origen, *Jo.* 2.12–18, in *Origène, Commentaire sur S. Jean,* ed. Cécile Blanc, SC 120 (Paris: Éditions du Cerf, 1966), 214–18. See Eusebius, *CM* 1.1.30 (K./H., 7); 1.4.46 (K./H., 27); *ET* 2.14 (K./H., 114–18).

93. Asterius, *fr.* 21 (Vinzent, 92).

the one [God] has always existed and never received a beginning of his existence, while the other things have both come
to be by him and have come to be out of nothing. For I do not
think to someone who says that there also are certain things
that are ingenerate [he would say that he also believed this,
but] that he is firmly convinced that the sky and earth and everything in the sky and upon the earth came to be from God.
Well now, if he were to believe this,[94] it would be necessary for
him also to confess that there was nothing other than God.
Thus the Word possessed his own glory, since he was in the
Father.[95]

With this statement, Marcellus reveals that he shares certain
ideas with Asterius, but also wishes to modify them considerably.

a. Marcellus and Asterius on Word and "Words"

To begin with, both Asterius and Marcellus believe that God
is the Creator of all things, and that God has always existed
while the creation has been created out of nothing; hence it did
not exist before it was created. And although Asterius was later accused by Athanasius of teaching two Words and Wisdoms
of God, a coeternal Wisdom of God through which the Son as
Wisdom has been created,[96] Marcellus himself believes this to
be an incorrect interpretation of Asterius. Ironically, Eusebius
will accuse Marcellus of teaching the same thing: that he assumes an inner Logos or Wisdom of God that then became an
external Logos or Wisdom.[97] Perhaps Eusebius was not too far
from the truth, as Marcellus admitted that he believed (like Asterius) that the Word was "in the Father." Moreover, the Word's
generation, in Marcellus's reading of Asterius, was a deliberate
act of the will of God, a topic Marcellus thought was better left
unexplored.[98]

---

94. See Asterius, *fr.* 21; 27; 29 (Vinzent, 92, 96).
95. Marcellus, *fr.* 76 (K./H., 103; Vinzent, 68,1–10).
96. See, for example, Athanasius, *syn.* 18 (Op., 245–46).
97. See Eusebius, *CM* 1.1–2 (K./H., 1–2).
98. See Asterius, *fr.* 5–6 (Vinzent, 84); Eusebius, *CM* 1.4.10–11 (K./H., 19).

b. The Word's status as image of God and his glory

Marcellus and Asterius both speculated about the Son's status as the "image of the invisible God" (Col 1.15).[99] Marcellus shares with Asterius the view that images show the things of which they are images, even if the represented things or people are absent.[100] Yet Marcellus's own exposition of the Pauline doctrine led him to deny the existence of a pre-incarnate visible Word: "If it is the case that while God is invisible the Word also is invisible, how can the Word be in and of himself 'image of the invisible God,'[101] seeing as he, too, is invisible?"[102] To Marcellus, the Word only became visible once it had assumed human flesh in the Incarnation. By contrast, Asterius believed that the pre-incarnate Word (who as pre-incarnate was obviously invisible) was the image of God, as he makes clear in his *fr.* 10, where he asserts that God had generated "the only-begotten Word and firstborn of all creation, the one [who begot] one; the perfect a perfect, the King a King, the Lord a Lord, the God a God, unchanged image of [his] being and will and glory and power ..."[103] These differing views of the Word's status as image, then, generate differing evaluations of the Word's glory. Given Asterius's conviction that the Word is the image of God the Father even prior to the Incarnation, he speaks of the power that was given to the Word (Mt 28.18; Jn 17.2; 5.21–22) as a "pre-cosmic glory."[104] For Marcellus, for whom the Word becomes image of God only in the Incarnation, the attribution of glory to the Word can only be a "cosmic" or economic one—that is, one revealed only after creation has come into existence. A further difference between the two thinkers on this point is that Marcellus sees the Word possess-

99. See Asterius, *fr.* 10–13 (Vinzent, 86–88); Eusebius, *CM* 1.4.30–31 (K./H., 24); 2.3.23–27 (K./H., 48–49), and *ET* 1.20.14 (K./H., 93) and 2.23 (K./H., 133–34).

100. See Asterius, *fr.* 13 (Vinzent, 88); Eusebius, *ET* 2.23 (K./H., 133–34).

101. See also Asterius, *fr.* 11 (Vinzent, 88).

102. Marcellus, *fr.* 54 (K./H., 93; Vinzent, 48,4–10).

103. Asterius, *fr.* 10 (Vinzent, 86); Eusebius, *CM* 1.4.33–34 (K./H., 24–25); Marcellus, *fr.* 113 (K./H., 96; Vinzent, 106,6–9).

104. Asterius, *fr.* 36 (Vinzent, 100).

ing his "own glory,"[105] while Asterius admitted that both the
eternal glory and that of the incarnate Word was not that of the
Word itself, but always was and remained God the Father's.[106]

*c. The unity of Father and Son and Marcellus's rejection of
two hypostases*

Marcellus and Asterius also differed in how they conceived
of the unity of the Father and Son. According to Asterius, the
relation between the Word and the Father was one of harmony
of words and deeds,[107] a relation of two different beings or hypostases (or of three, if one added the Spirit), not one of identity, although he believed (as Philo did)[108] that God was eternal
intellect and had in himself a Logos and a Wisdom that were
ingenerate, were always together with God, and were identical
with him.[109] Building on the latter, Marcellus maintained that
such an intimate relationship was so much the reality of God's
inner being that one had to call it a "μονάς," "oneness," whereas
only within the temporal economy of the Incarnation (and not,
as Asterius put it, prior to the creation), was that oneness extended into a threefoldedness, a τριάς.[110] "For it is impossible that the
three, being hypostases, could be united in a monad, unless the
Trinity were previously to take its beginning from the monad.
For the holy Paul said that those things are gathered up[111] in
[the] monad, which in no way belong to the oneness of God; for
only the Word and the Spirit belong to the oneness of God."[112]

105. Marcellus, *fr.* 76 (K./H., 105; Vinzent, 68,9–10); *fr.* 77 (K./H., 104;
Vinzent, 68,11–13).
106. See Asterius, *fr.* 36 and 38 (Vinzent, 100; 102); Eusebius, *CM* 2.2.26–
29 (K./H., 39–40); Marcellus, *fr.* 54 and 74 (K./H., 93 and 73; Vinzent, 48,7–
10; 62,5–64,14).
107. See Asterius, *fr.* 39–40 (Vinzent, 102); Eusebius, *CM* 2.2.15–25 (K./H.,
37–39); Marcellus, *fr.* 73 and 74 (K./H., 71/73; Vinzent, 62–64).
108. See Philo, *Opif.* 8–9; 100; *Mut.* 259–64.
109. See Asterius, *fr.* 64–73 (Vinzent, 124–34).
110. See Asterius, *fr.* 39–40 (Vinzent, 102); Eusebius, *CM* 1.4 (K./H., 29,8–
12); 2.2 (K./H., 37,29–31); Marcellus, *fr.* 74–75 and 125 (K./H., 73–74, 72;
Vinzent, 62,5–66,27).
111. Eph 1.10.
112. Marcellus, *fr.* 47 (K./H., 66; Vinzent, 42,1–4); see also Marcellus, *fr.* 48
(K./H., 67; Vinzent, 42,5–44,8).

Consequently, Marcellus strongly criticized Asterius's assertion of two or three hypostases in the Christian godhead.[113]

d. The emergence of the Son

One of the significant ways in which Asterius and Marcellus differed in their theologies was in the diverse similes they utilized to explain the "coming forth" of the Son. Asterius used the Porphyrian example of a human father and son and explained that even before the father actually becomes a father, he always had the potential to become a father, but once the father had generated a son, this son was a different being or hypostasis from his father.[114] Marcellus counters this example with two similes of his own, one that applies to the Logos in God, and the other to the generated and incarnated Logos. For the Logos in God, Marcellus refers to our human intellect (using the term "word") and states, "For it is not possible to separate the word from a man in power and hypostasis. For the word is one and the same with the man, and is separated [from him] in no other way than by the activity alone of the deed."[115] And with regard to both, the Logos in God, with whom God creates and generates this world, and the incarnate Logos, he introduces the example (similar to that of the architect, which Philo uses)[116] of the sculptor who conceives a statue first in his mind before he carries out the actual design:

> But if, using a small human example from our experience,
> one were to explain the divine activity as through an image,
> it would be as if some man knowledgeable in making statues,

---

113. Marcellus, *fr.* 47; 75 (K./H., 66; 74; Vinzent, 42,1; 64,25).

114. See Asterius, *fr.* 52 (Vinzent, 116), and also Asterius, *fr.* 14; 15; 22; 54; 75 (Vinzent, 88; 90; 92; 118; 140); Eusebius, *ET* 2.19.21 (K./H., 126); Marcellus, *fr.* 85 (K./H., 63; Vinzent, 74,1–5); on Porphyry and his background, see Aristotle, *Metaph.* 1033b32 and 1032a24; Philo, *Ebr.* 30; 184; Porphyry, *Sent.* 32. Asterius, in keeping with this metaphor, uses the language of begetting and generation, maybe even privileges it over the language of creating, different from Arius, who mixes them all together. This will be important for Eusebius, who at *ET* 1.10 (K./H., 68,18) dismisses any idea that creation can be an acceptable way to describe the Son's emergence.

115. Marcellus, *fr.* 87 (K./H., 61; Vinzent, 76,5–10).

116. See Philo, *Opif.* 20.

wishing to form a statue, first considers within himself its type and character and then figures out how much width and height would be suitable for it. He scrutinizes the proportion of the whole in each part, and after having prepared the right amount of bronze[117] and outlined beforehand in his mind the future statue with a clear mental picture of it, being conscious of the cooperation of his reason, with which he makes his calculations and with which he is accustomed to do everything (for nothing beautiful comes to be without reason).[118] When he begins this perceptible work, he exhorts himself as he would another, saying, "Come now, let us make, let us form a statue." Just so does God, the Lord of the universe, in making a living statue from earth, exhort himself with nothing but His own Word, saying, "Let us make man ..."[119]

The names in Marcellus for the sculptor's inner faculty are different from those in Asterius. Marcellus calls it philosophically Word (λόγος), inner perception (διάνοια), and intellect (ἐπιστήμη), while Asterius keeps closer to Pauline terminology and calls it Word (λόγος), wisdom (σοφία), and power (δύναμις) (1 Cor 1.24).[120] To Marcellus the simile serves as "a small human example from our experience," but it highlights that, unlike in Asterius, for Marcellus the Word is always the inner capacity of God, even when God is acting as creator and savior in this world. When Scripture presents him speaking to himself (Gn 1.28), we might get the impression that God has a plural nature, but in truth, God is one single being, not divided into two. The same happens during the generation and Incarnation of the Word. Even here, God remains the single Monad, as the Trinity is nothing but an enlargement with regard to God's salvific action and only for the time of this action, and, as a result, God's active power is more properly called "Word," instead of "Son," especially if, as in Asterius, the notion of "Son" is used against the background of Asterius's anthropological-genetic example of a dyohypostatic father-son relationship.

117. See Prv 8.27.
118. Again, in the sense of rationality.
119. Gn 1.26; Marcellus, *fr.* 98 (K./H., 58; Vinzent, 88,18–90,7).
120. Asterius, *fr.* 64 (Vinzent, 124).

e. The kingship of Christ

Another area in which Marcellus and Asterius shared an important theological claim but explained it in starkly different ways concerned the "kingship" of Christ. In a lengthy discussion, Marcellus develops his view of "kingship" (or one might even say "emperorship" since Marcellus wrote his treatise with the intention that Constantine the emperor would read it)[121] of human beings and their restoration through the King or Emperor Christ.[122] Based on his theology of image, Asterius had confessed, as we have seen before, that "the" God had generated "the only-begotten Word and firstborn of all creation, the one [who begot] one; the perfect a perfect, the King a King, the Lord a Lord, the God a God, unchanged image of [his] being and will and glory and power…"[123] While Asterius, therefore, believed that the Lord was king (or emperor) like God the king (or emperor), Marcellus expresses anxiety that if the Lord was not himself "the" king (or emperor), but only an envoy or servant of him, he would not be trustworthy and could not guarantee the salvation of fallen humanity. Contrary to Asterius, therefore, Marcellus develops his own theology of kingship in the broader context of his eschatology, based on his explanation of 1 Cor 15.28, probably the most contentious part of his work that he himself had to modify, at least partially, as one can see from his letter to Julius of Rome of the year 340/341.[124] In his discussion with Asterius, he states that the incarnated Logos had to become "king over the Church":[125]

> … clearly so that the man who had previously been deprived of the kingdom of heaven might be able to obtain the kingdom through the Word. For this reason, God devised this economy, since he wished that this man, who had previously been de-

121. See Eusebius, *CM* 2.4.30–31 (K./H., 58,16–24).

122. Marcellus, *fr.* 99–114 (K./H., 111; 112; 113; 114; 115; 116; 106/108; 105/117; 119; 120; 121; 60; 41; 122; 96; 97; Vinzent, 90,9–108,5).

123. Asterius, *fr.* 10 (Vinzent, 86); Eusebius, *CM* 1.4.33–34 (K./H., 24–25); Marcellus, *fr.* 113 (K./H., 96; Vinzent, 106,6–9).

124. Marcellus, *ep. ad Iul.* (Vinzent, 126,11–13).

125. See Ps 2.6.

prived of the kingdom because of disobedience, might become Lord and God. Therefore, the most holy prophet David says prophetically, "The Lord reigns; let the earth rejoice."[126]

And Marcellus adds that this beginning of Christ's kingdom was the Lord taking on human flesh.[127] Being king, and not only "image of the king," was vital for the salvation of humanity, who had fallen away from God's kingdom and instead had been deceived by the powers of the devil, as Marcellus read in 1 Cor 15.24. And, as Marcellus continued to read in Paul, he came to another conclusion (which surprised himself, as he notes), which Eusebius and later orthodoxy would reject, saying: "For he must reign until he has made his enemies his footstool."[128] That is, Marcellus, almost naïvely, draws the literal conclusion: "Thus the holy Apostle says that this [is] the end of the kingdom of our Lord Christ, namely, when he puts all things under his feet."[129] Paul's verse perfectly fitted Marcellus's theology, according to which the trinitarian activity of the divine power was the rescue action for this world within a strictly monotheistic framework. Therefore, the idea that this trinitarian activity had a beginning in the Incarnation met with the corresponding concept of an end of this action in the eschaton when finally the devil with his powers would be defeated and the Word's flesh would be left behind. This particular claim of Marcellus's will provoke almost vitriolic opposition from Eusebius in the conclusions of both the *Against Marcellus* and the *On Ecclesiastical Theology*.[130]

f. The role of the Holy Spirit

Although the Father-Son relation was certainly the focus of the debate between Asterius and Marcellus, the role of the Spirit is discussed between them, even if this element of the debate is later neglected by, for example, Athanasius.[131] In the debate

126. Ps 96.1 (RSV 97.1). Marcellus, *fr.* 99 (K./H., 111; Vinzent, 10–15).

127. Marcellus, *fr.* 100 and 101 (K./H., 112; 113; Vinzent, 92,1–10).

128. Ibid.; 1 Cor 15.25.

129. Marcellus, *fr.* 101 (K./H., 113; Vinzent, 92,8–10).

130. Eusebius, *CM* 2.4.19–28 (K./H., 56–58); *ET* 3.8–12 (K./H., 165–69).

131. All fragments by Asterius concerning the Spirit derive solely from Marcellus and Eusebius.

about the inner Word of God (which was assumed, as we have
seen, by both Asterius and Marcellus) Marcellus reports that
his opponent admitted that "the Holy Spirit" "proceeds from
the Father."[132] In contrast to Marcellus's own view, according
to which such procession underlined the undividedness of the
one godhead even during its "broadening" into a Trinity for
the time of the economy, Asterius derived from it the necessity
of asserting the three hypostases of God,[133] namely, that "it is
necessary to think that the Father is truly Father and that the
Son is truly Son and likewise [regarding] the Holy Spirit."[134]
The "likewise" indicates that Asterius did not understand the
procession in the same anthropological way as he saw the generation of the Son by the Father, although he saw the Spirit—
like the Son—as derived and generated by the Father and not
by the Son, in the same way as he saw the entire creation derived and generated by the Father through the Son.[135] The Spirit, therefore, is not the Son, but a third hypostasis that has only
come into being in a manner similar to the Son's coming from
the Father. The point of similarity is that both Son and Spirit
derive from the Father, yet the Son without mediation and the
Spirit mediated through the Son, as the Son is mediator of the
Father. According to Asterius, therefore, the Son will be the one
through whom the procession of the Spirit takes place. As in
any Platonic mediation scheme, mediation, however, means a
reduction in being. Hence, the Son is less than the Father and
the Spirit lesser still than the Son or the Father. Asterius must
have read this Platonic reductionist scheme in Luke 1.35, where
it is said that the Spirit "overshadowed" Mary,[136] and, therefore,

132. Marcellus, *fr.* 48 (K./H., 67; Vinzent, 42,6–7); see also Jn 15.26; Asterius, *fr.* 59 (Vinzent, 120); Eusebius, *ET* 3.4 (K./H., 158,3–4).

133. See Asterius, *fr.* 61 (Vinzent, 120); Marcellus, *fr.* 50 (K./H., 69; Vinzent, 44,13–14).

134. Asterius, *fr.* 60 (Vinzent, 120); see Eusebius of Nicomedia, *ep. Paulin.*
(= Urk. 8 in Op., 15–17). Marcellus, *fr.* 1 (K./H., 65; Vinzent, 4,8–9).

135. That Asterius understood derivation as "generation" has been shown in
Vinzent, *Asterius von Kappadokien*, 277; see also Ps.-Athanasius, *dial. III de Trin.*
4 (PG 28: 1208 D–1209A); Ps.-Athanasius, *dial. c. Macedon.* 14 (PG 28: 1313B).

136. See Marcellus, *fr.* 61 (K./H., 54; Vinzent, 54,1–5); Eusebius, *CM* 2.2.4
(K./H., 35,21–25); *ET* 2.1.1 (K./H., 99,17–21).

could not be equated with the divine light of the Father. This "reductionist" scheme of creation and salvation—or, in Asterius's eyes, protective shielding of creatures from the overpowering and potentially deadly pure hand of God—is made explicit with regard to the Son. According to Asterius, the Son was light and shone above all things in the noetic world, himself being one of the noetic beings (like the sun that is shining on everything by being one of those created elements that receive its sunshine).[137] Thus the Son made the divine light of the Father bearable by the creation, as "the God of the universe, when he decided to make the created nature, recognized that it could not stand the all-powerful hand of God."[138] As the Son was both less divine than the Father and at the same time protected creation from the overpowering pure nature of God, so likewise the Spirit further reduced the threat that divine power presented to creation. Mary was not touched by the direct, full divine light of the Father, but the Son was engendered in her by the shadow of the Spirit, whose divinity was proportionate to her capacity to receive. On this understanding of the Incarnation, one can see the need for Asterius's clear distinction between the hypostases of the Father, Son, and Spirit. Contrary to Asterius, however, Marcellus insisted that the Spirit was never a cause of shadow or darkness and that the Savior himself in Jn 4.24 spoke of the Spirit as "God" and "light,"[139] both of which claims counter Asterius's reductionist view. Marcellus may have had in view the reference to the "Power of the Most High," mentioned in Luke 1.35, even if it is not present in his quoted text as we have it. Eusebius, who informs us of this debate about the Spirit, sides with Asterius and rejects Marcellus's criticism of Asterius.

g. Summary

Marcellus, as we have seen, builds in many ways on Asterius's ideas: for example, of the intrinsic existence of a Logos and

137. See Asterius, *fr.* 23 (Vinzent, 94).
138. Asterius, *fr.* 26 (Vinzent, 94).
139. See Marcellus, *fr.* 64 (K./H., 57; Vinzent, 54,10–12).

Wisdom of God and also of the hypostatically differentiated[140] but harmonious existence of Logos and Power in the economy. In both cases, compared to Asterius's understanding of the relation between Logos and God or Father, Marcellus even loosens this relation by stating that after the Incarnation the Logos had not only his own glory, but also his own will—different from, separated from, and even contrasting with that of the Father. This is evident in Marcellus's exegesis of Christ's agony in Gethsemane.[141] And yet Marcellus altered Asterius's concept by denying a pre-cosmic existence of this separation between Father and Logos and restricting it to the fleshly economy of the Incarnation of the Word, which he understood as an extension of the eternal oneness, a temporal extension that went hand in hand, not with the creation of time and cosmos, but with the salvific Incarnation. Hence, Marcellus interpreted the contentious scriptural verses like Prv 8.22–31, which played such an important role in the pre-Nicene debate together with others like Ps 109.3, as applying to the generation of the Logos in the Incarnation, not his generation or creation at the beginning of time and cosmos.[142] Without doubt, both Asterius and Marcellus wanted to maintain the belief in monotheism, but also to explain the salvific and mediatory role of Christ, the Lord and Son.[143]

2. Marcellus's Errors in the Eyes of Eusebius

Eusebius has numerous objections to the theology of Marcellus, and traces them to two fundamental deficiencies in Marcellus's character and education. To begin with, as we see from the opening chapters of the *Against Marcellus*, Eusebius accuses

---

140. See, for example, Asterius, *fr.* 52 (Vinzent, 116); Eusebius, *ET* 2.19 (K./H., 123,7–12); Marcellus, *fr.* 85 (K./H., 63; Vinzent, 74,1–5).

141. See Marcellus, *fr.* 74 (K./H., 73; Vinzent, 62,5–64,14).

142. See Asterius, *fr.* 48–49 (Vinzent, 114); Eusebius, *CM* 1.2.4 (K./H., 12); Marcellus, *fr.* 26–46; 57 and 60 (K./H., 6; 12; 10; 11; 13; 14; 15; 16; 126; 17; 18; 19; 20; 21; 28; 29; Vinzent, 50,7–12; 52,13–15).

143. See Asterius, *fr.* 51 (Vinzent, 116), and Marcellus, *fr.* 92 (K./H., 78; Vinzent, 80,13–82,12).

Marcellus of envy and jealousy[144] of his episcopal colleagues, of a lamentable lack of respect in disparaging their orthodoxy, all but accusing them of outright polytheism.[145] He goes on elsewhere in both works to suggest that Marcellus's outlandish ideas arise from a similar arrogant disrespect for other forms of authority—whether that of Scripture,[146] the Church's tradition[147] (which would include its practice of liturgy, in baptism[148] an unassailable witness to a robust doctrine of the Trinity that, in Eusebius's view, Marcellus conspicuously lacks), and foregoing Church "fathers,"[149] among whom Eusebius numbers Origen of Alexandria,[150] of whom his own teacher, Pamphilus, was a disciple. Most serious of all these charges, however, is Marcellus's inability to read Scripture correctly (and refusing to be guided by others more learned than himself); hence a good deal of both works is devoted to extensive discussion of texts such as John 1.1[151] ("In the beginning was the Word ..."), Prv 8.22[152] ("The Lord created me as the beginning of his ways"); 1 Cor 15.28[153] ("When all things are subject to him, then the Son himself will also be subjected to him who put all things under him ..."); Col 1.15[154] ("He is the image of the invisible God ..."); and 1 Cor 8.6[155] ("For us one God the Father, from whom are all things, and one Lord Jesus Christ, through whom are all things," which will become an important text for the entire anti-Marcellan tradition). Marcellus's inability to read Scrip-

144. *CM* 1.1.1 (K./H., 1).

145. *CM* 1.4.39 (K./H., 26), citing Marcellus, *fr.* 116 (K./H., 81; Vinzent 108,11–15).

146. Refutation of Marcellus's erroneous interpretation of Scripture is implied in the *CM*, but systematically conducted throughout the *ET*. See the preface to the latter in K./H., 62, section 2.

147. *CM* 1.1.36 (K./H., 8).

148. *CM* 1.1.9 (K./H., 3); *ET* 3.5.22 (K./H., 163).

149. *CM* 1.4.3 (K./H., 18); 1.4.16 (K./H., 20); *ET* 1.14.2 (K./H., 74).

150. *CM* 1.4.3 (K./H., 18).

151. For example, *ET* 2.10.4–8 (K./H., 111–12).

152. *ET* 3.1–3 (K./H., 137–57).

153. *ET* 3.14–16 (K./H., 170–75).

154. *ET* 1.20.14, sections 72–74 (K./H., 93).

155. For example, see *ET* 1.6.1 (K./H., 64–65); 1.20.8, sections 55–56 (K./H., 90); 1.20.12, section 67 (K./H., 92); *ET* 2.2.1 (K./H., 100).

ture properly, aside from leading to obvious errors in laying out the sequence and history of biblical events,[156] leads to serious problems in both his trinitarian and Christological doctrines.

Summarizing an exposition that unfolds across nearly two hundred pages of Greek text, Eusebius's core objection to Marcellus's teaching centers on both his misunderstanding of the second person's identity as "Word of God" and his overprivileging of this term in Christological discourse.[157] As Marcellus himself admits, and Eusebius notes over and over again in his refutation, Marcellus sees Christ's identity as "Word of God" as his fundamental identity,[158] the identity he has from eternity long before creation and the beginning of salvation history and the identity to which he will return when salvation history is complete. The Word is eternally in the Father, as one *prosopon* (πρόσωπον),[159] one being (οὐσία),[160] and one hypostasis (ὑπόστασις)[161] with him. Hence in Eusebius's eyes, Marcellus teaches that Father and Son are the same, thus repeating the errors of the third-century heretic Sabellius.[162] The Word "comes forth"[163] for the purposes of creation and salvation history, and at a specific moment in time ("not four hundred whole years ago,"[164] as Mar-

---

156. This is the focus of *CM* 1.2 (K./H., 9–13).

157. See especially *ET* 2.9.12 (K./H., 110).

158. For example, Marcellus, *fr.* 94 (K./H., 46; Vinzent, 84,2), where he insists that the Word is "chiefly and truly" Word (κυρίως τε καὶ ἀληθῶς ὑπάρχων λόγος).

159. Marcellus, *fr.* 92 (K./H., 78; Vinzent, 80,18); *fr.* 97 (K./H., 76; Vinzent, 86,3).

160. This is clear from Marcellus's criticism of the idea of multiple οὐσίαι in the godhead in *fr.* 116 (K./H., 81; Vinzent, 108,11–15), 117 (K./H., 82; Vinzent, 110,1–7), and 120 (K./H., 83; Vinzent, 112,16–23), and also in Eusebius's criticism of the idea that the unity of Father and Son is based on a "coalescence of one being" (*ET* 3.18.3–4; see especially lines 29–30, K./H., 179).

161. Eusebius accuses Marcellus of teaching this at *ET* 2.5 (K./H., 103); 3.17.6 (K./H., 177); 3.19.3 (K./H., 180). It is clearly implied by Marcellus's disapproval of the notion of multiple hypostases in the godhead in, for example, *fr.* 85 (K./H., 63; Vinzent, 74,1–5); 47 (K./H., 66; Vinzent, 42,1–4); 50 (K./H., 69; Vinzent, 44,13–14).

162. *ET* 2.5 (K./H., 103).

163. Marcellus, *fr.* 109 (K./H., 121; Vinzent, 102,1–21); 110 (K./H., 60; Vinzent, 104,1–11).

164. Marcellus, *fr.* 103 (K./H., 115; Vinzent, 94,8,6); 104 (K./H., 116; Vinzent, 94,17–18).

cellus specifiés, writing circa 330) acquires a second hypostasis in the humanity of Jesus of Nazareth.[165] Once, however, salvation history is complete, the Word will return into the Father, leaving the humanity that was previously assumed to a fate unknown.[166]

Eusebius sees numerous deficiencies in Marcellus's explication of the Savior's status as Word. He will be sharply critical of the analogies Marcellus uses to illustrate the latter, notably the sculptor planning the design of a statue,[167] suggesting that such an analogy indicates that the Word is merely the rational faculty of God the Father, thus a component of the divine being or an accident[168] that exists within its being, which renders the latter synthetic or composite.[169] Without its own hypostasis, the Word in Marcellus's defective understanding is a "mere" word,[170] ephemeral and insubstantial,[171] used to communicate God's will[172] or to express his commands,[173] with affinities to the Stoic λόγος ἐνδιάθετος / λόγος προφορικός (the interior men-

165. This is suggested in Marcellus, *fr.* 97 (K./H., 76; Vinzent, 86,8–11) and 85 (K./H., 63; Vinzent, 74,1–3): that Asterius claims (in Marcellus's view, erroneously) that the Word constitutes a separate hypostasis from that of the Father on the basis of the flesh that it assumed in the Incarnation.

166. See the discussions in Marcellus, *fr.* 106 (K./H., 117; Vinzent, 96,4–100,3) and especially 109 (K./H., 121; Vinzent, 102,1–21).

167. Marcellus, *fr.* 98 (K./H., 58; Vinzent, 88,18–90,8).

168. The specific discussion of the Son/Word as an "accident" (συμβεβη-κός) appears at *ET* 2.14.4 (K./H., 115) and 3.2.1 (K./H., 138–139).

169. Eusebius, *ET* 1.5.1 (K./H., 64); 2.14.4 (K./H., 115); 3.3.63 (K./H., 156–157).

170. Eusebius, *CM* 1.1.15 (K./H., 4); 1.1.32 (K./H., 7–8); 2.2.8 (K./H., 36); 2.2.43 (K./H., 43); 2.4.21 (K./H., 56); *ET* 1.18.4 (K./H., 80); 1.20.9, section 64 (K./H., 91).

171. ἀνυπόστατος: *CM* 1.1.32 (K./H., 7); 2.2.32 (K./H., 40); 2.4.21 (K./H., 56); *ET* 1.20.4, section 15 (K./H., 83); 1.20.5, section 30 (K./H., 86); 1.20.9, section 64 (K./H., 91); ἀνούσιος: *CM* 2.4.21 (K./H., 56); *ET* 1.20.4, section 15 (K./H., 83); 1.20.5, section 30 (K./H., 86).

172. The λόγος σημαντικός: *ET* 1.17.2 (K./H., 77); 1.17.4 (K./H., 78); 1.17.7 (K./H., 78); 1.20.4, section 11 (K./H., 82); 1.20.5, section 25 (K./H., 85); 1.20.6, section 36 (K./H., 87); 1.20.6, section 39 (K./H., 87); 1.20.6, section 46 (K./H., 88); 1.20.29, section 91 (K./H., 97); 2.8.1 (K./H., 106); 2.11.1 (K./H., 112); 2.24.3 (K./H., 135).

173. The λόγος προστακτικός: *CM* 2.2.8 (K./H., 36); 2.2.11 (K./H., 36); *ET* 2.8.1 (K./H., 106).

tal word and the exterior expressed word).[174] The notion that the Word "comes forth" or expands out of the divine Monad and then contracts or returns into it at the end of time suggests that the transcendent, immaterial Christian godhead is corporeal.[175] Yet contrary to the interpretation that Marcellus's Word is ephemeral, essentially passing in its nature, Eusebius also criticizes Marcellus's assertion of the eternity of the Word. Though the Cappadocians will later contest this, Eusebius automatically concludes that if the Word is eternal as his Father is, he must also be "ingenerate" (ἀγένητος) or "unbegotten" (ἀγέννητος) as the Father is. In Eusebius's estimation, such is to assert two first principles and thus (mis)lead Christians into polytheism.[176] Thus, Marcellus's defective interpretation of the Savior's status as Word leads to a theology that fails to find its proper place between two extremes: a Jewish monotheism that was commendable for its time, but which does not acknowledge the revelation of God's Son in Jesus Christ, and the pagan worship of multiple gods that Eusebius saw being gradually vanquished in his lifetime with the advent of Constantine.[177]

While raising legitimate concerns about Marcellus's insufficiently trinitarian doctrine of God, Eusebius also draws out some of the negative Christological implications of Marcellus's theology. Again, many of them derive from Marcellus's overemphasis on the Savior's identity as Word. Here the extremes between which Eusebius thinks a correct Christology should find its place are the Christologies of Paul of Samosata and Sabellius. To take the latter error first, Eusebius will argue that because Marcellus's "Word" does not possess his own hypostasis

174. λόγος ἐνδιάθετος: *ET* 1.17.7 (K./H., 78); 2.11.1 (K./H., 112); 2.14.20 (K./H., 117); 2.15.2 (K./H., 118); 2.15.3 (K./H., 119); 2.15.4 (K./H., 119); λόγος προφορικός: *ET* 1.17.7 (K./H., 78); 2.14.20 (K./H., 117); 2.15.2 (K./H., 118); 2.15.4 (K./H., 119); 2.17.6 (K./H., 121). Eusebius expresses this distinction alternatively as the λόγος κατὰ διάνοιαν/λόγος κατὰ προφοράν at *ET* 2.15.1 (K./H., 118).

175. *ET* 2.6.2–3 (K./H., 103); 3.3.64 (K./H., 157).

176. *CM* 2.2.1 (K./H., 35); *ET* 2.3.3 (K./H., 102), but especially *ET* 2.12.2–3 (K./H., 113–114).

177. For example, *CM* 1.1.11–14 (K./H., 3–4); *ET* 1.2 (K./H., 63); 1.8.1 (K./H., 66); 1.20.29, section 89 (K./H., 96).

in his pre-incarnate state, he and the Father are "the same."[178]
Consequently, since they are so, one can fairly conclude that
it is the Father who takes flesh in the Incarnation, and suffers
the saving death on the cross for the sins of humanity.[179] This
is the classic third-century Christological heresy denounced by
Tertullian as "patripassianism."[180] As for the other error, Eusebius will claim that because, again, the Word has no hypostatic distinctiveness, but can be seen as a "communicating word"
or "word of command," such as came to the prophets of the
Old Testament, the Word's presence to the human Jesus can
legitimately be seen in terms of the prophetic call of a human
being[181]—not the advent of an incarnate God. Such would render the Savior a mere man (the charge of psilanthropism);[182]
yet if one went on to say that that man was eventually honored
and exalted as anointed king for his service and virtue,[183] such
would be the heresy of adoptionism,[184] all these ideas associated in Eusebius's mind with the teaching of Paul of Samosata,[185]
who was deposed as bishop of Antioch in 268 for claiming, in
Eusebius's words, that Jesus of Nazareth was the Christ of God
but not the pre-existent Son of God himself.[186]

Eusebius sees Marcellus's overprivileging of the Christological title "Word" also evident in his claim that all other scrip-

178. For example: *CM* 1.1.17 (K./H., 4); *ET* 1.1.3 (K./H., 63); 1.5.2 (K./H., 64).

179. *CM* 2.2.5 (K./H., 35); *ET* 1.1.4 (K./H., 64); 2.5 (K./H., 103), but especially 2.1.1 (K./H., 99); 2.4.2 (K./H., 102); 2.12.3 (K./H., 114) (for the idea
that the Father suffered the Passion).

180. Tertullian, *Adv. Prax.* 1–2.

181. *CM* 2.4.27–28 (K./H., 57–58).

182. *CM* 1.4.59 (K./H., 29); 1.4.64 (K./H., 30); *ET* 1.3.1 (K./H., 63); 1.7.1
(K./H., 65); 1.20.6, section 43 (K./H., 88); 1.20.6, section 45 (K./H., 88). It is
important to note that Eusebius emphasizes this aspect of Marcellus's Christology partly because he reports more than once that Marcellus accused *him*
of the same error at *CM* 1.4.46 (K./H., 27), 1.4.59 (K./H., 29), and 1.4.64
(K./H., 30).

183. As suggested by the Christological hymn of Phil 2.

184. Explicitly referred to at *CM* 2.1.9 (K./H., 33).

185. References to Paul appear at *ET* 1.14.2 (K./H., 74); 1.20.6, section 43
(K./H., 88); 3.6.4 (K./H., 164).

186. Eusebius discusses the case of Paul of Samosata in his *HE* 7.27–31.

tural titles ascribed to the Savior apply to him either in his incarnate state[187] or, if they occur in the Old Testament, prophetically.[188] Such titles include important ones like "Son" or "King," but also include "Image of God." As we saw above, Marcellus thought the latter term could only apply to the incarnate Word because only material things can be images of invisible ones;[189] as Eusebius will argue at length in *ET* 1.20, such titles do apply to the pre-incarnate second person; he will particularly insist that the pre-incarnate Word and Son is image of God, and this will be an important plank in his defense of the second person's divinity.[190] Eusebius sees more troubling aspects of Marcellus's restriction of the title "King" to the Word's incarnate career. Given that the Incarnation is motivated by the economic soteriological concern to re-establish divine sovereignty over the human race, lost through sin, Marcellus reasons that it is inappropriate to call the Word "King" before he assumes the humanity through which he will re-establish that sovereignty. Hence he will say that Christ's kingdom has a beginning—when the Word became incarnate.[191] But Marcellus also claims that Christ's kingdom will have an end—specifically, when divine sovereignty has been re-established over creation and Christ hands over the kingdom to his Father.[192] At this point, Marcellus asserts that the Incarnation itself will have an end; the Word will be separated from the flesh he assumed and return into the undifferentiated divine Monad from which it came forth at creation.[193] Marcellus declines to speculate

---

187. *CM* 2.1.1–3 (K./H., 31–32); 2.3.2 (K./H., 44), with especial reference to Marcellus, *fr.* 8 (K./H., 49; Vinzent, 10,18–12, 2).

188. *ET* 1.19.2 (K./H., 80), with regard to Marcellus, *fr.* 7 (K./H., 42; Vinzent, 10,7–17).

189. Marcellus discusses the title "image of God" in dialogue with Asterius, who attributed it to the pre-existent Son in *fr.* 51–56 (K./H., 90–95; Vinzent, 46–50).

190. *ET* 1.20.14, sections 72–74 (K./H., 93): 2.23 (K./H., 133–34).

191. Marcellus, *fr.* 100 (K./H., 112; Vinzent, 92,1–3), 103 (K./H., 115; Vinzent, 92,14–94,9).

192. Marcellus, *fr.* 102 (K./H., 114; Vinzent, 92,11–13), 107 (K./H., 119; Vinzent, 100,4–7).

193. This is discussed in Marcellus, *fr.* 105–109 (K./H., 118, 117, 119, 120, 121; Vinzent, 96–102).

about the fate of the discarded humanity.[194] Probably no other claim of Marcellus's scandalizes Eusebius as much as this one. He sees in it a complete rejection of the Church's soteriological and eschatological teaching, arguing that it makes no sense to offer to believers as Christian hope an eternal life in a glorified body modeled on that of the Savior—if the Savior himself will have no body in the kingdom of heaven.[195] The passion and eloquence with which he articulates his own vision of the afterlife at the end of the *On Ecclesiastical Theology*[196] are a touching testimony to the hope of salvation that animated the bishop of Caesarea as he finished what would be his final work.

3. Eusebius's Response to Marcellus's Theology

a. Trinity

The positive trinitarian theology that Eusebius constructs in the treatises translated here seeks to situate itself between three poles, all of which represent errors that misrepresent the nature of the God revealed in the Old and New Testaments. Obviously, polytheism is erroneous, and it was the grace of the Old Testament to reveal the one God to the Israelites. But it was the grace of the New Testament to reveal that that one God possessed a Son who pre-existed creation and was revealed in Jesus of Nazareth.[197] But the revelation of God's Son in Christ must be understood in the correct way; if one does not distinguish properly between the Father and the Son revealed in Jesus Christ (saying they are "the same," which Eusebius will repeatedly attribute to the third-century heretic Sabellius),[198] one will not advance beyond a strict Jewish monotheism.[199] At the same time, one can go wrong in over-distinguishing the Father and Son in one

194. Marcellus, *fr.* 109 (K./H., 121; Vinzent, 102).

195. *CM* 2.1.10–11 (K./H., 33).

196. *ET* 3.14–18 (K./H., 170–179), though the subject is also discussed at the end of the *CM* 2.3.36–2.4.1–28 (K./H., 51–58).

197. *CM* 1.1.10–11 (K./H., 3).

198. *CM* 1.1.17 (K./H., 4); *ET* 1.1.4 (K./H., 63); 1.5.2 (K./H., 64).

199. *ET* 1.20.8, section 55 (K./H., 90); 2.2.1 (K./H., 100); 2.2.5 (K./H., 101); 2.14.19–20 (K./H., 117); 2.22.5 (K./H., 133).

of two ways, both of which misrepresent the revelation of the Christian God in Christ. If one says that the Son is a creature of the Father (the error associated with Arius and Asterius), one compromises the real divinity that the Son has by virtue of his begetting by the Father.[200] At the same time, if one asserts (as Marcellus did) that the Word is eternal as the Father is, one will inadvertently assert two ingenerate or unbegotten beings in a way that will endanger Christian monotheism.[201] Indeed, it is a tricky obstacle course through which Eusebius must travel to formulate a trinitarian doctrine that is faithful to revelation and to avoid the numerous pitfalls over which he considers theologians in his immediate past to have stumbled.

The basic shape of Eusebius's trinitarian doctrine starts, as Asterius's did, with his assertion of the Father as the ingenerate or unbegotten eternal source (ἀρχή) of divinity.[202] Before the creation of the cosmos, and hence before "all the ages,"[203] the Son comes into existence through the Father's begetting. While Eusebius (similar to Arius, according to whom God is "unbegotten," "without source," "eternal")[204] will ultimately say that the manner of the Son's begetting is unknowable,[205] he will insist that it occurs in an immaterial way, free of any kind of passion associated with animal or human generation.[206] This insistence may be made in view of Arius's suggestion that begetting wrongly understood conveys either incorrect materialistic notions of deity or Gnostic ideas of "emanation,"[207] but

200. *ET* 1.9–10 (K./H., 67–69). On this passage, see Kelley McCarthy Spoerl, "Anti-Arian Polemic in Eusebius of Caesarea's *Ecclesiastical Theology*," *StPat* 32 (1997): 33–38.

201. *ET* 2.12.2 (K./H., 113–114).

202. For example, *ET* 1.2 (K./H., 63); 2.6.1–2 (K./H., 103); 2.7.1 (K./H., 104); Asterius, *fr.* 1–4, though he speaks of the single αἴτιος or cause instead of the single ἀρχή, source (Vinzent, 82).

203. *CM* 1.4.23 (K./H., 22); *ET* 1.2 (K./H., 63); 1.8.2–3 (K./H., 66); 1.17.9 (K./H., 78).

204. Arius, *Thalia*, in Athanasius, *syn.* 15 (Op., 242,11–13); *Letter to Alexander of Alexandria* 2 (Op., 12,4).

205. *ET* 1.2 (K./H., 63), but especially 1.12 (K./H., 70–72).

206. *ET* 1.12.8–10 (K./H., 72).

207. Arius's *ep. Eus.* (= Urk. 1.4 in Op., 2, 7–8), and his statement of faith in Urk. 6.3 (Op., 12), and 5 (ibid., 13).

also to avoid Marcellus's (mis-)reading of Asterius's anthropo-
logical/genetic simile for the generation of the Son. Again, as
noted above, Eusebius's "positioning" of his trinitarian theology places it in dialogue not only with opponents like Marcellus,
but with one-time allies. Although Eusebius will on occasion
use other similes for the Son's origin from the Father (already
used by Tertullian)—the ray from the sun,[208] the stream from
the fountain[209]—Asterius's genetic simile of human reproduc-
tion will be retained by Eusebius as his favorite to counter two
aspects of Marcellus's thought that he thinks are problematic:
Marcellus's overprivileging of the Christological title "Word"
and his vague assertion of the Word's origin in his "coming
forth" from the Father. Eusebius will highlight two advantages from stressing the genetic rather than the linguistic simile.
First, the genetic simile enables him to assert the Son's divinity,
which had been challenged by Arius's and Asterius's claim that
the Son was created.[210] Yet at the same time, the genetic simile
allows Eusebius (as it did for Asterius) to assert against Sabelli-
us/Marcellus (who according to Eusebius claimed that Father
and Son were "the same") that Father and Son instead were
distinct personal entities, just as human sons are distinct from
their fathers. This assertion, in turn, enables the Christian to
make much better sense of the witness of the New Testament,
for example, those Johannine passages in which Christ speaks
of being "sent" by his Father on his salvific mission[211] or the
Pauline passages that speak of Christ as a mediator between
God and men or God and the angels.[212]

It should be noted that in some passages where Eusebius tries
to argue that the trinitarian assertion that Father and Son constitute distinct personal entities makes for more coherent scriptural exegesis, he uses the word πρόσωπον when, as was typical

208. *ET* 1.8.3 (K./H., 66); 1.12.9 (K./H., 72); see, for example, Tertullian,
Adv. Prax. 8.

209. *ET* 1.2 (K./H., 63); 1.8.3 (K./H., 66); see, for example, Tertullian,
Adv. Prax. 8.

210. *ET* 1.9–10 (K./H., 67–69).

211. *ET* 1.20.5, section 19 (K./H., 84); 1.20.6, section 39 (K./H., 87); 2.7.6
(K./H., 104); 3.5.8–9 (K./H., 161).

212. *CM* 1.1.32–33 (K./H., 7–8).

for the period, he identifies different speakers (whether Father
or Son) in such passages.[213] Hence it is not unreasonable to assume that Eusebius would be comfortable identifying Father
and Son as distinct *prosopa,* and such language persists in subsequent Greek texts under the influence of the anti-Marcellan
tradition initiated by Eusebius.[214] More frequently, however, he
prefers to say that Father and Son constitute different and dual
hypostases.[215] This is an assertion made prior to Eusebius by
both Arius[216] and Asterius,[217] and more remotely by Origen;[218] it
will receive the stamp of orthodoxy at the Council of Constantinople in 381. A critical development in the process was the
distinction between οὐσία and ὑπόστασις, οὐσία referring to the
divine being in itself, ὑπόστασις referring to the distinct persons of the Trinity who share that single divine being. In *fr.* 116
and 117,[219] Marcellus accuses Eusebius of having asserted that

213. We see the use of the term πρόσωπον with regard to the exegesis of
Christ's mediatorship at *ET* 2.21.4 (K./H., 130). It is also used at *ET* 1.20.9,
section 63 (K./H., 91), to explain how the language of Christ's obedience in
Phil 2 requires the assumption of different πρόσωπα. Πρόσωπον is used repeatedly in *ET* 3 in scriptural exegesis; see, for example, 3.1.1 (K./H., 138);
3.2.1 (K./H., 138); 3.2.31 (K./H., 144); 3.2.32 (K./H., 145); 3.3.39 (K./H.,
152). On the "prosopographical" exegesis of Scripture and its implication in
the fourth-century trinitarian debates, see Michael Slusser, "The Exegetical
Roots of Trinitarian Theology," *TS* 49 (1988): 461–76.
214. For example, in the "Long-lined Creed" of 344, anathema 4, in
A. Hahn, ed., *Bibliothek der Symbole und Glaubensregeln der alten Kirche* (Breslau,
1897; repr., Hildesheim: Georg Olms, 1962), #159, 193; the creed of the Council of Sirmium in 351 that condemned Marcellus's disciple Photinus, anathema 19, condemning the assertion of one πρόσωπον in the Christian godhead
(Hahn, #160, 198); the Homoiousian letter of George of Laodicea from 358
(Epiphanius, *haer.* 73.12–22, especially 16); and Apolinarius's *Kata meros pistis*
1.167.19; 13.171.21; 14.172.3; 15.172.14; 19.173.23–24; 24.175.21–22; 25.176.3.
All Apolinarian references are to the edition of Hans Lietzmann, *Apollinaris
von Laodicea und seine Schule* (Tübingen: J. C. B. Mohr, 1904; repr., Hildesheim:
Georg Olms Verlag, 1970), citing by chapter, page, and line number.
215. For example: *ET* 1.20.6, section 40 (K./H., 87); 2.7.1–2 (K./H., 104).
216. See, for example, his statement of faith in Urk. 6.4 (Op., 13, 7).
217. As Marcellus claims in *fr.* 50 (K./H., 69; Vinzent, 44,13–14), and 85
(K./H., 63; Vinzent, 74,1–5). See also *fr.* 61–62 in Vinzent's edition of the Asterian fragments (Vinzent, 120–122).
218. For example, Origen, *Jo.* 2.75 in SC 120, 254.
219. Marcellus, *fr.*116–117 (K./H., 81–82; Vinzent, 108,11–110,7).

Father and Son constituted two οὐσίαι in the pre-Nicene period and one may well ask whether Eusebius retained the functional equivalence of these terms, which even the anathemas attached to the Nicene creed endorsed, thus rendering the terms inter-changeable for multiple divine "things." Three observations are relevant here. First, nowhere in the anti-Marcellan works does Eusebius employ the Nicene watchword ὁμοούσιον. At the same time, secondly, nowhere in the anti-Marcellan works do you find as bald a statement of the existence of multiple οὐσί-αι in the Christian godhead as Marcellus accuses Eusebius of making in the pre-Nicene period. Yet, thirdly, there is at least one obscure passage in the *ET* in which Eusebius may allude indirectly to the existence of multiple, though unequal, οὐσίαι in the Christian godhead.[220] Nevertheless, it is our impression at present that the fact that Eusebius repeatedly uses the term *hypostasis* when discussing the personal distinctions between Father and Son indicated by Scripture and arising from their different ontological relations as source and offspring does suggest that he, whether consciously or not, promotes a seman-tic shift in the connotation of the term that will ultimately be fruitful for the final formulation of trinitarian doctrine. It will be the task of the renewed study of Eusebius's anti-Marcellan works that this translation hopes to encourage to determine whether this impression is well-founded or not.

While the assertion that the pre-existent Son constitutes a distinct second hypostasis is central to Eusebius's anti-Marcellan rhetoric, the bishop of Caesarea, especially in the *On Ecclesias-tical Theology*, expresses anxiety about its potential compromise of Christian monotheism: how can there really be one Christian God if the Father is divine and the Son is divine too?[221] Euse-bius's solution of this dilemma is as follows. There is one God because the Father is one eternal source or ἀρχή of divinity.[222] As

220. *ET* 2.23.1–2 (K./H., 133, lines 12–26): "For it does not introduce two unbegottens or two things without source, as has been said many times by us, *nor does it introduce two beings parallel to one another because of their equal glory*, and for this reason not two gods, but it teaches one source and God and that the same is Father of the only-begotten and beloved Son ..." (emphasis added).

221. *ET* 2.7.1–3 (K./H., 104).

222. *ET* 1.11.3 (K./H., 69–70); 2.6.1 (K./H., 103); 2.7.1 (K./H., 104); 2.23.1

Asterius did previously, Eusebius therefore asserts that he is the "only true God."[223] The Son is God as Son of the Father who is the only true God. Hence, the Father is "the" God, while the Son is God,[224] which we have traced back to Origen.[225] Another way Eusebius has of expressing this insight will be to specify that the divinity the Son has by virtue of his begetting is the "paternal" divinity, a divinity that comes from and belongs primordially to the Father.[226] The same logic would seem to underlie Eusebius's assertion at *ET* 1.10 that the Son has a "natural relationship" to the Father, by virtue of the Father's begetting, phrasing that suggests Eusebius would be comfortable asserting that Father and Son share a single divine nature, which the Son derives from his Father, though he says nothing explicit on this point in the anti-Marcellan works.[227] In general, however, if we would seek the expression that Eusebius would prefer using to express the unity of the Father and Son other than the ὁμοούσιος he found unsatisfactory, it might well be in the assertion of the single source (ἀρχή) of divinity that Father and Son share.

Two features of Eusebius's theology that will be problematic from the perspective of later orthodoxy arise in tandem with this assertion of the Son's derived divinity that Eusebius thinks preserves Christian monotheism. To begin with, because the Son is God, but not "the" God, and has a divinity that belongs primordially to the Father, Eusebius will make many statements that handbooks of patristic theology would characterize as "subordinationist."[228] He will assert, among other statements, that

(K./H., 133). For more on this aspect of Eusebius's thought, see Anton Weber, *Arche: Ein Beitrag zur Christologie des Eusebius von Cäesarea* (Munich: Verlag Neue Stadt, 1965).

223. Citing Jn 17.3: *ET* 1.11.4 (K./H., 70); 2.22.1–2 (K./H., 132); 2.23.2 (K./H., 133).

224. We see this distinction made in Eusebius's exegesis of the Prologue of John's gospel in *ET* 2.14 (K./H., 114–18).

225. See above, n. 92.

226. *ET* 1.2 (K./H., 63); 3.6.1 (K./H., 164); 3.15.5 (K./H., 172); 3.18.4 (K./H., 179); 3.20.2 (K./H., 181).

227. *ET* 1.10.3 (K./H., 69).

228. The best example of this feature of Eusebius's thought is in *ET* 1.11.3–6 (K./H., 69–70).

the Son has a lesser glory than the Father's,[229] another point of agreement with Arius and Asterius,[230] and that he is, as in Asterius,[231] obedient[232] to the Father, and prays to the Father[233] as his God. He is consistently presented as the subordinate agent of his God and Father, as in Asterius, helping[234] the Father in the work of creation,[235] bringing the law to the Israelites, and appearing in Old Testament theophanies,[236] and through his government establishing the Father's dominion over the universe.[237] While recent scholarship is correct to suggest that this aspect of Eusebius's thought has been unfairly overemphasized at the expense of his genuine attempts to assert the Son's real divinity,[238] especially in opposition to defects he saw in his one-time ally Arius of Alexandria, it is a marked aspect of Eusebius's theology of the Son that should not be discounted.

The second claim that arises from the assertion of the Son's derived divinity is Eusebius's ambiguous denial of eternity to the Word. We say "ambiguous" because there are real contradictions in Eusebius's thought on the issue in the anti-Marcellan works, though recent scholarship has supported the idea that Eusebius in fact retained this Origenist doctrine from his studies with his teacher Pamphilus.[239] There is evidence to support such a contention. As we have noted before, Eusebius will say

229. *ET* 2.7.8 (K./H., 105).

230. As suggested in his *Thalia*, quoted by Athanasius in *syn.* 15 (Op., 242–243) and *Ar.* 1.6.5 (Tetz, 115, 16–18); Asterius, *fr.* 10; 35–36; 46 (Vinzent, 86; 100; 112).

231. Asterius, *fr.* 40 (Vinzent, 102).

232. *ET* 1.11.4 (K./H., 70); 1.20.9, section 63 (K./H., 91); 2.7.5–6 (K./H., 104).

233. *ET* 1.11.4 (K./H., 70); 1.20.6, section 46 (K./H., 88); Asterius, *fr.* 38–40 (Vinzent, 102).

234. See Asterius, *fr.* 34 (Vinzent, 100); *ET* 1.20.3, section 5 (K./H., 81) and 2.14.9 (K./H., 116).

235. *ET* 1.8.3–4 (K./H., 66–67); 3.3.53–58 (K./H., 155–156).

236. *ET* 2.21.1–4 (K./H., 130).

237. *ET* 1.13.2 (K./H., 73); 1.20.5, section 30 (K./H., 86); 2.17.7 (K./H., 121); 3.2.17 (K./H., 142); 3.3.5 (K./H., 146).

238. Christopher A. Beeley, *The Unity of Christ: Continuity and Conflict in Patristic Tradition* (New Haven: Yale University Press, 2012), 88.

239. Ibid., 92–93.

numerous times throughout these texts that the Father begets the Son "before all ages"[240]—that is, before the creation of the universe and the time that measures its change. Significantly, Eusebius attributes this expression to Origen in *CM* 1.4.[241] Likewise, in the anti-Marcellan works there are a number of assertions that the pre-existent Son is always with the eternal Father or always coexists with him.[242] Lastly on this point, suggestions that the Son is eternal appear in Eusebius's considerations regarding the Son's status as image of God.[243] Again, Marcellus had insisted that all images must be visible; hence the Word only becomes "image of God" with the Incarnation of the latter in a physical, perceptible body. Eusebius is at pains in both the *CM* and the *ET* to attack this claim, asserting that the Son has this status before his coming in the flesh.[244] The assertion is important for Eusebius to support his claims for the Son's divinity,[245] and he will insist, much like Asterius[246] (and contrary to Arius), that the Son as image is "most like"[247] the Father, or represents the Father's divinity "in the closest way possible" and "to the most accurate degree."[248] Such statements are evidently important sources for the Homoiousians' approach to trinitarian doctrine in the late 350s. We see more evidence relevant to the theme of the Son's eternity at *ET* 1.20.6,[249] wherein Eusebius says the Son is the image of the Father, even in having an *immortal* life.

240. See above, n.203.
241. *CM* 1.4.23 (K./H., 22).
242. *ET* 1.8.2 (K./H., 66); 2.14.14: "Thus the Word, that is to say, the only-begotten Son, was with God, his own Father; he coexisted with him and was always and everywhere present with him …" (K./H., 116,34–117,1); 3.3.56 (K./H., 155); 3.4.6 where he speaks of the Son "always coexisting" with the Father (K./H., 159, 9–10).
243. Some examples: *CM* 1.4.35 (K./H., 25); *ET* 1.2 (K./H., 63); 1.20.14 (K./H., 93); 2.7.16–17 (K./H., 106); 2.14.7 (K./H., 115); 2.17.3 (K./H., 120); 2.20.15 (K./H., 129–130); 2.23.1 (K./H., 133); 3.21.1 (K./H., 181).
244. Very explicitly stated at *ET* 1.20.14, sections 72–74 (K./H., 93).
245. *ET* 1.2 (K./H., 63).
246. Asterius, *fr.* 10 (Vinzent, 86).
247. *CM* 1.4.35 (K./H., 25); *ET* 2.14.7 (K./H., 115).
248. *ET* 2.17.3 (K./H., 120); 3.21.1 (K./H., 181).
249. *ET* 1.20.6, section 33 (K./H., 86).

Hence the suggestion that Eusebius embraced or was at least favorable to the notion of the Son's eternity is not without textual support in the anti-Marcellan works. It seems fair, however, to assert that statements supporting the Son's eternity exist in tension in these texts with passages that otherwise seem clearly to deny eternity to the second person of the Trinity. It does seem axiomatic for Eusebius to say that eternity and the status of being ingenerate imply one another; if you attribute one of these qualities to a divine person, you must attribute the other to that person too.[250] He thinks Marcellus is seriously in error to assert that the Word/Son is eternal, because such would suggest that the Son, too, is ingenerate; that leads directly to the idea that there are two ἀρχαί, two first principles in the godhead, and hence polytheism instead of monotheism.[251] Consequently, Eusebius does not directly say that the Son is eternal or eternally begotten, as, for example, Alexander of Alexandria did in the immediate period before Nicaea.[252] Hence it is fair to say that there is a lack of clarity in Eusebius's teaching on this point, created by Eusebius's explicit denial of the Son's eternity alongside his assertion of his coexistence with the eternal Father and status as living image of the immortal Father. This ambiguity will have to be resolved in subsequent Greek theology with the retrieval of the Origenist doctrine of the Son's eternal generation, which in particular will contest Eusebius's assumption that only the ingenerate can be eternal.

Significant for the authentically trinitarian aspects of Eusebius's theology in the anti-Marcellan works is his doctrine of the Holy Spirit. For the most part, Eusebius's anti-Marcellan works are predominantly binitarian, focused on the relationship between the first and second members of the Trinity. Yet there are important pneumatological statements in both works. For example, in *ET* 3.4–6, Eusebius deploys that same kind of exegetical argument around the Spirit's sending that he used to defend the personal distinctness of the Son. Eusebius criticizes Marcel-

250. *CM* 2.2.2 (K./H., 35); *ET* 2.3.3 (K./H., 102).
251. *ET* 2.12.2 (K./H., 113).
252. Based on Heb 1.3. See the letter of Alexander of Alexandria to Alexander of Thessalonika 52 (Op., 28,2).

lus's way of understanding how the Spirit comes forth from the
Father, since it is said even of Satan in Job (1.12; 2.7) that he
"went forth from the Lord." In the case of the Spirit, sending is
equivalent to going forth and requires that what is sent be distinct from the sender, and that permanently. One has to think
of the Spirit what is said by Daniel of the "thousands of thousands" (Dn 7.10): that when they stood "by the throne of God,"
they were neither God nor the throne, but distinct from both
while being close to them. In addition, such scriptural statements implying the "being with" and "going forth" of the Spirit
indicate that he must be hypostatically distinct from Father and
Son. Hence it is not unreasonable to suppose that Eusebius, if
put to the point, would assert that the Spirit, too, constitutes another hypostasis or πρόσωπον alongside those of the Father and
Son. The "being with" of the Spirit close to the throne of God in
turn leads to language that suggests the coexistence of the Spirit with Father and Son and thus the same ambiguity on the question of the Spirit's eternity that we see in Eusebius's doctrine of
the Son. The Spirit, too, at *ET* 3.4 is said to be "likewise" "always
together" with the Father and Son.[253] On the Spirit's divinity, we
note that while Eusebius will speak in two places of the "divine
Spirit" in discussions of prophetic inspiration and the inspiration of Scripture,[254] in *ET* 3 he explicitly claims that the Spirit
is created by the Son,[255] and as such is subordinate to him,[256]
although "outstanding in honor and glory and privileges, greater and higher than any [other] intellectual and rational being
(for which reason he has also been received into the holy and
thrice-blessed Trinity)."[257] The Spirit's role as "Counselor" is, for
Eusebius, another unmistakable proof that he is inferior to the
Father and Son as a mediator of God's power to human beings.
The Father had to create human nature first, and the Son had to
prepare it, before the Spirit was received by it.[258] The assertion

253. *ET* 3.4.9 (K./H., 159,26–29).
254. *ET* 1.20.29, section 87 (K./H., 96); 2.20.5 (K./H., 128).
255. *ET* 3.6.1 (K./H., 163–64).
256. *ET* 3.5.18 (K./H., 162).
257. *ET* 3.5.17–18 (K./H., 162,28–31).
258. *ET* 3.5 (K./H., 159–63).

of the Spirit's created status is another legacy from Origen,[259] but Eusebius's reiteration of the teaching does not seem to have elicited much negative comment at the time the anti-Marcellan works were composed. Nevertheless, it would remain an element of Eusebian theology that would have to be addressed in the subsequent anti-Marcellan tradition,[260] perhaps in acknowledgment of Eusebius's own statement that the Church's teaching on the Holy Spirit needed "greater amplification and clarification."[261]

b. Christology

The Christology of Eusebius's anti-Marcellan works is among the most intriguing elements of these often overlooked texts. As we have already indicated, Eusebius was quick to discern the Christological difficulties that arose from Marcellus's failure to account for the ontological distinctiveness of the pre-existent second person of the Trinity, to attack them, and to craft an alternative Christology that attempts to address the deficiencies of Marcellus's model. The following is a brief sketch of the main features of Eusebius's Christology.

Eusebius is emphatic that the subject of the Incarnation is the pre-existent Son of God, the second person, a hypostasis distinct from that of the Father. Again, failure to distinguish adequately between the first and second persons of the Trinity prior to the Incarnation leads to the error of patripassianism, the notion that it was the Father who became incarnate.[262] Eusebius has a number of ways of describing the manner of the Incarnation: most often he speaks of the Son assuming or taking the flesh[263] or assuming the body;[264] in one instance he

259. Origen, *Jo.* 2.73–76 (SC 120, 252–56).
260. See Kelley McCarthy Spoerl, "Apollinarius on the Holy Spirit," *StPat* 37 (2001): 571–92.
261. *ET* 3.5.15 (K./H., 162,12–13).
262. See above, n. 179.
263. For example, "took" or "assumed" flesh, *CM* 1.1.22 (K./H., 6); 1.1.23 (K./H., 6); 2.1.2 (K./H., 32); *ET* 1.2 (K./H., 63); 1.16.2 (K./H., 76); 2.18.2 (K./H., 122).
264. *ET* 1.6.2 (K./H., 65); 1.7.3 (K./H., 65); 1.20.3, section 2 (K./H., 81); 2.23.4 (K./H., 134).

will speak of assuming man.[265] In another illustration of the way that the desire to avoid earlier heresies shapes Eusebius's Christology, Eusebius will stress that the flesh that the Word assumed is real, not illusory, thus avoiding the error of Docetism, a charge that had already been implicated in post-Nicene Christological debate in the writings of Eusebius's adversary Eustathius of Antioch, who accused "Arian" opponents [Eusebius?] of denying that Christ had a human soul, and thus compromising the reality of the Incarnation.[266] The latter is particularly interesting in view of the fact that it is clear from statements in both the *Against Marcellus* and the *On Ecclesiastical Theology* that Eusebius eliminates a human soul from the incarnate Son. Interestingly, Eusebius makes statements to this effect in both his anti-Marcellan works,[267] suggesting that it was one of his immediate and foundational responses to the Christology he discerned in Marcellus's book against Asterius, though Spoerl has suggested that Eusebius may also have come to this conclusion in the course of his post-Nicene debate with Eustathius of Antioch.[268] Indeed, it is likely that Eustathius's Christology is in the background here, since the bishop of Antioch did explicitly assert the presence of a human soul in Christ. Marcellus did not do the same, though it is not unreasonable to suggest he could, too, have endorsed this idea because of his assertion

265. *ET* 1.3.1 (K./H., 63), in describing some variety of Docetism.

266. *ET* 1.7.1 (K./H., 65). For more discussion of this, with the relevant references, see Kelley McCarthy Spoerl, "Two Early Nicenes: Eustathius of Antioch and Marcellus of Ancyra," in *In the Shadow of the Incarnation: Essays on Jesus Christ in the Early Church in Honor of Brian E. Daley, S.J.*, ed. Peter W. Martens (Notre Dame, IN: University of Notre Dame Press, 2008), 121–48.

267. The idea of the Word/Son existing in the assumed flesh in place of a [human] soul (ψυχῆς δίκην) appears at *CM* 2.4.24 (K./H., 57) and *ET* 1.20.6, section 40 (K./H., 87), both in contexts in which Eusebius criticizes Marcellus's conceptualization of the second person of the Trinity as Word, charging that it denies the Son/Word his own living and subsisting hypostasis, and leads directly to the notion that it is the Father who is incarnate.

268. Kelley McCarthy Spoerl, "Apollinarius and the First Nicene Generation," in *Tradition and the Rule of Faith in the Early Church: Essays in Honor of Joseph T. Lienhard, S.J.*, ed. Ronnie J. Rombs and Alexander Y. Hwang (Washington, DC: The Catholic University of America Press, 2010), 109–27, especially 119.

that Christ has a will distinct from the Father's and realistic human emotions when anticipating his Passion.[269]

Since the issue of Christ's human soul is a significant aspect of Eusebius's theology, it is worth laying it out in some detail. The first occurrence of this idea appears at *CM* 2.4.24, in the context of discussion of the Marcellan claim that Eusebius seems to find most offensive, that the body assumed by the Word in the Incarnation would be abandoned after the conclusion of salvation history:

> Therefore, will the body stand alone without [the] Word in immortal and incorruptible irrationality and inactivity? And how will the Word itself return into God and be united again with him after its separation from the flesh? Consequently, was he [the Word] not in God when he coexisted with the flesh, although he was in him in every respect, being both co-eternal with him [and] one and the same with God? How, then, did he come to be in the body? If indeed he dwelt in it in place of a soul, he will consequently be in a hypostasis distinct from the Father, both living and subsisting in the flesh that he assumed. What, therefore, hindered [Marcellus from] confessing that he was the living Son of God even before the constitution of the world?[270]

Clearly what Eusebius thinks is erroneous here is the idea that the assumed body would continue to exist after the Word's return into God. It would exist, moreover, "irrational" and "immobile" because the Word, which presumably animates it, would not be present to it. This is already a clue to Eusebius's working Christological model. Eusebius then goes on to indicate that Marcellus's Christological model makes the conception of the Incarnation even before the end of time difficult: if the Word must "return" into God at the end of time, does this mean that he was not "in God" while the Incarnation was taking place? To suggest such would contradict Marcellus's own teaching that the Word is "in God," "coeternal," and "one and the same" with him. The phrasing here indicates that all three

269. For example, Marcellus, *fr.* 74 (K./H., 73; Vinzent, 62–64).
270. *CM* 2.4.24 (K./H., 57, 3–12).

of the previous claims are ones made by Marcellus—not Eusebius. We would argue, then, that the next line in this passage represents Eusebius's position: "If he dwelt in it in place of a soul, he will consequently be in a hypostasis distinct from the Father, both living and subsistent in the flesh that he assumed. What, therefore, hindered [Marcellus from] confessing that he was the living Son of God even before the constitution of the world?" This is clearly Eusebius's Christological model: Christ is the pre-existent, living, and subsisting Son, who has his own hypostasis distinct from that of the Father, which is the subject of the Incarnation and which operates in the assumed flesh in place of a soul.

The second passage wherein we see Eusebius's implicit denial of a human soul in Christ appears at *ET* 1.20.6, and it occurs in a similar context to the statement above, which is exploring the Christological implications of the notion (suggested by John's prologue) that the Word was "in God." Eusebius says:

> If the Word, while dwelling in the flesh when he was teaching upon the earth, was outside the Father, living, subsisting, and moving the flesh in place of a soul, he was clearly another besides the Father, and again he and the Father existed as two hypostases, and so every effort of Marcellus has been proven to be in vain ...[271]

Again, Eusebius intends this statement to counter Marcellus's denial of a distinct hypostasis of the Son, which he thinks creates great difficulty in conceptualizing the Incarnation. Without the assertion of the Son's distinct hypostasis, a literal interpretation of the Johannine prologue suggests that the Word somehow comes "out of" God at the Incarnation, leaving "the" God without his own Word and thus irrational. One must in contrast assert the Son's hypostasis as the subject of the Incarnation and, moreover, as that which "moves" the flesh (as suggested in the *CM* passage above) and (one presumes) provides its rationality. Eusebius goes on to assert:

271. *ET* 1.20.6, section 40 (K./H., 87,24–28).

> For if the Word who dwelt in the body existed outside of God,
> but was united and joined to God so as to be one and the same
> with him, he [Marcellus] must of necessity admit that either
> it is the Father himself in the flesh, or the Son who subsists in
> himself and acts in the body, or the soul of a man, or, if none
> of these, that the flesh moves itself spontaneously, being with-
> out soul and without rationality.[272]

Eusebius posits four Christological options here, only one of
which seems reasonable: 1) the patripassian assumption (Father incarnate in the flesh); 2) the subsisting Son acting in the
body; 3) the soul of a man animating the body; or 4) that the
flesh moves by itself, without any rationality. Given his preference for identifying the incarnate Word as the pre-existing Son
who subsists in himself by virtue of having his own hypostasis,
it is clear that Eusebius sees option 2 as the only viable manner
of interpreting the Incarnation. This is reinforced a bit later in
the passage, where Eusebius explicitly says:

> And if Marcellus denies that this [Son] subsists, the cause
> must be that he supposes him to be a mere man, composed of
> body and soul, in no way different from the common nature of
> human beings. But this teaching too has been cast out of the
> Church. Indeed, long ago the Ebionites and lately the Samo-
> satene and those called Paulinians after him, because they
> thought this, paid the penalty for their blasphemy.[273]

Thus a close analysis of these two texts indicates that Eusebius denied that the incarnate Son had a human soul along
with the body he assumed. The reason why Eusebius makes this
assumption would seem to be, particularly from the evidence
just cited from *ET* 1.20.6, section 43, his anxiety that if the Son
assumes a humanity that includes a human soul, Christ will be
a mere man, thus driving those who would assert this into the
psilanthropism and adoptionism associated with the teaching
of Paul of Samosata. Yet as we see above, Eusebius thinks it
equally wrong to suppose that the body that the Son assumed
was without intelligence altogether, which would make its ac-

272. *ET* 1.20.6, section 41 (K./H., 87,29–35).
273. *ET* 1.20.6, section 43 (K./H., 88,4–9).

tions irrational.[274] Hence some provision must be made for a rational presence moving the body of Christ, but it would seem that for Eusebius that presence is provided by the supremely rational Son and Word who acts in place of a human soul in the assumed body. Such a reading of Eusebius's Christological statements may be supported by statements in which Eusebius speaks of the "instrument" of the body,[275] the body as a tool deployed by the indwelling Son, the language of "dwelling" or "indwelling" the flesh also appearing a number of times in both anti-Marcellan works.[276] This is the Apolinarian model of Christology before the fact, and its articulation within an anti-Marcellan context illuminates the appearance of the same Christology in Apolinarius's treatise *Kata meros pistis*, which is saturated with commonplaces from anti-Marcellan rhetoric.[277]

In addition to this noteworthy aspect of Eusebius's Christology, his anti-Marcellan works contain a number of intriguing remarks about the relationship of divinity and humanity in Christ that point forward to debates that will reach greater intensity in the later fourth and early fifth centuries. To begin with, there is some evidence in these texts that Eusebius was aware of how some might interpret Marcellus's suggestion that the humanity assumed by the Son in the Incarnation was a hypostasis separate from that of the Son himself. Indeed, Marcellus's suggestion that this was the case,[278] combined with his robust portrayal of the psychological reality of the Savior's humanity (evident in his exegesis of the Gethsemane episode of the gospels),[279] could well give rise to the notion of what patristic handbooks call a "dyoprosopic" Christology, the idea that

274. 1.20.6, sections 41–42 (K./H., 87–88).

275. *ET* 1.13.5 (K./H., 73).

276. *CM* 2.4.24 (K./H., 57); *ET* 1.6.1 (K./H., 65); 1.20.6. sections 40, 44 (K./H., 87, 88).

277. On this, see Spoerl, "Apollinarian Christology and the Anti-Marcellan Tradition."

278. See *fr.* 85 (K./H., 63; Vinzent, 74,1–5): "Well, then, who does Asterius think it is who says, 'I am who am,' the Son or the Father? For he said that 'there are two hypostases of the Father and of the Son,' looking at the human flesh that the Word of God assumed and because of it imagining that this is so …"

279. Marcellus, *fr.* 74 (K./H., 73; Vinzent, 62,5–64,14).

Christ incorporates two distinct personal realities, the divine Son of God and the human Son of Man. This Christological model emerges more clearly later in the fourth and fifth centuries with theologians like Diodore of Tarsus and Theodore of Mopsuestia, but some (possibly Eusebius and very likely Apolinarius) may have seen an early adumbration of this model in Marcellus's Christology. A couple of statements in the anti-Marcellan works suggest that Eusebius is eager to quash any such notion, asserting in various ways instead that the incarnate Son/Word is a "single subject of existence,"[280] or "one agent in two lives."[281] The latter idea is particularly evident when Eusebius says that the Son of God became the Son of Man at his human birth—thus showing that the primary identity of Christ is pre-existent Son of God, who then himself becomes Son of Man when he assumes the human body.[282] Very significant for Eusebius's idea that the incarnate Savior is the same person as the pre-existent Son is a statement he makes in an early chapter of the *On Ecclesiastical Theology:* "[The Church] confesses that *the same* (τὸν αὐτόν) became Savior and Son of Man, being Son of God before he also became Son of Man, and that he became this, which he was not, because of the ineffable abundance of the Father's love for humankind."[283] Obviously, the language of "the same" becomes an important vehicle for expressing this insight into the singularity of Christ's person, right up to the Chalcedonian Definition of 451.

At the same time as Eusebius seems to want to avoid any notion that the humanity that the Son of God assumes in the Incarnation has hypostatic independence, he also seems concerned in a few places to uphold the ontological distinction between the divinity of the assuming Son and the created humanity (or at least body) that he assumes, another issue that will become important in Christological debate later in the century. We see evidence of this debate in the Apolinarian

280. Beeley, "Contra Marcellum," 445.

281. J. Rebecca Lyman, *Christology and Cosmology, Models of Divine Action in Origen, Eusebius, and Athanasius* (Oxford: Oxford University Press, 1993), 116.

282. *CM* 1.1.27 (K./H., 7).

283. *ET* 1.3 (K./H., 64,5–8).

fragments: if divinity and human body constitute one person in the Savior, does this change the humanity in some way? Does it somehow become less human—for example, uncreated—because of its union with the Son of God? The question, moreover, becomes more acute when the attribution of consubstantiality to the Son gains greater acceptance in the Greek East as the century progresses. The question then becomes: does the flesh share in the assuming Son's divine consubstantiality with the Father?[284] Eusebius, obviously, never addresses this issue because of his disuse of the Nicene watchword ὁμοούσιος in the anti-Marcellan works. He does, however, seem to want to maintain the integrity of the flesh as created and not divine. He makes it clear that while the Son of God is the same as the Son of Man, the Son of God is not the same as the body he assumed.[285] He goes on in the same treatise to state that God is separated *by nature* from the earthly flesh.[286] This could be read as suggesting that Eusebius would endorse the idea of two natures in Christ. Would Eusebius have also endorsed the idea that in taking on flesh, the Son of God assumes a body that is not only of another nature from that of himself, but of another being or οὐσία? A provocative statement appears in *CM* 1.4, wherein Eusebius criticizes Marcellus's idea that the Incarnation only involves an extension of the godhead in activity, not an actual Incarnation of the godhead, or rather, of one of the hypostases of the godhead, itself.

284. We see evidence of this discussion in Apolinarius, *fr.* 41.213.31–33, 112.233.32–33, 146.242.19–22 (denials that Christ's body is ὁμοούσιος with God), *fr.* 148.246.30–247.4 (the flesh does not become uncreated because of the Incarnation), and *fr.* 121.237.11–12 (Christ is not changed into the flesh he assumed). Spoerl explored some of the origins of this discussion in "Apollinarius and the Homoiousians" (paper presented at the Boston College Colloquium in Historical Theology, Boston, Massachusetts, 30 July 2010).

285. *ET* 1.7.3 (K./H., 65,31–33): "For it is necessary to search for the Son of God who is truly living and subsisting, and who is neither the same as the body that he assumed nor the same as the God and Father."

286. *ET* 1.12.8 (K./H., 72,12–15): "By as much, however, as God who transcends the universe was differentiated and separated by nature from earthly flesh, by so much is it necessary to think that the manner in which the Father begot the Son is differentiated from the generation of fleshly things."

But he [Marcellus] would say that he has come to be in the
body likewise by activity alone and not by the hypostasis of
being (οὐχὶ δὲ οὐσίας ὑποστάσει). For he says that coexisting
with the body by active energy alone (by moving it and doing
all the things related in the gospels), he was united by virtue of
being (οὐσίᾳ) to God, existing as a Word inseparable and indistinguishable from him. If, then, he should say these things, let
him answer us who have asked whether the activity of the Word
has come to this flesh alone, but not also to the other holy men
of God?[287]

This is a difficult passage to interpret, but a few things are
clear. Eusebius thinks the notion of God extending himself
solely in activity in the Incarnation makes the latter event too
similar to the call of the Old Testament prophets, thus compromising the unique pre-existent divinity of Christ and the reality
of a divine incarnation. With the deployment of the language
of οὐσία, and by implicitly criticizing the idea that throughout
the Incarnation the Son remained "united by virtue of being
(οὐσίᾳ) to God" (which would follow from Marcellus's insistence that Father and Son share one οὐσία, not two or more),
Eusebius seems to suggest that the Incarnation involves the
Son of God taking on a being different from the one he had
in his pre-incarnate life. As we saw earlier with his trinitarian
terminology, it is hard to decide whether Eusebius makes any
clear distinction between the two terms of οὐσία and hypostasis, such that one could argue he is using οὐσία more in the
sense of *nature*, the ontological constitution of the humanity
the Son of God assumes, or in the sense of hypostasis as person. Yet it seems clear that Eusebius wants to say that the Incarnation involves the assumption of an entity that is fundamentally different from the entity that does the assuming—without
this involving the assumption of another person wholesale
(which seems to be the point of his rhetoric that the same Son
of God becomes the Son of Man with his birth from the Virgin
Mary). Hence again, we may see here another early indication
of a concern to distinguish clearly between humanity and di-

287. *CM* 2.4.25–26 (K./H., 57,12–18).

vinity in Christ while maintaining his unity of person that will be more systematically addressed later in the century.

One aspect of Eusebius's Christology that is absolutely clear is his conviction that once the Son of God assumes the human flesh, that flesh will remain inseparable from the Son of God. As we have noted above, Eusebius sees Marcellus's assertion that the body would be cast off after the conclusion of salvation history as unforgivably discordant with the Church's eschatological and soteriological teaching. His insistence that Christ will remain an incarnate king over redeemed humanity would be affirmed in various credal statements following the publication of the anti-Marcellan works.[288] In addition, Eusebius's assertion that the incarnate Son would always remain incarnate is another idea that is affirmed at Chalcedon.

To summarize briefly, the positive contributions Eusebius makes in his anti-Marcellan works to later Christological orthodoxy would be driven by his articulation of a concern to assert the single personal identity of the pre-existent Son of God and the incarnate Christ. We might like to describe this concern as one for the "unity of person" in Christ, though as we have suggested throughout this introduction, Eusebius still represents a preliminary stage in the Church's reflection about the differences between the categories of nature, person, and substance, and does not express this concern as explicitly and systematically as later theologians will do. While stressing this concern, Eusebius is aware that one must account for the difference between divinity and humanity in Christ, and he makes at least one attempt to explain such with his reference to the distinction in being that pertains between the Son of God and the body he assumed. Lastly, Eusebius insists upon the permanence of the Incarnation once it is undertaken; Christ remains for him the model of the resurrected life for Christians. The most negative aspect of Eusebius's Christology would be his equally emphatic denial of a human soul in Christ. Given Apo-

---

288. Clauses countering this Marcellan claim about the end of Christ's kingdom begin to appear in creeds associated with the Antiochene Dedication Council of 341. On this, see J. N. D. Kelly, *Early Christian Creeds*, 3d ed. (Essex, UK: Longman, 1972), 263–74.

linarius's own explicitly anti-Marcellan stance in the *Kata meros pistis*, the Christology of Eusebius's anti-Marcellan works is surely a factor (among others) in shaping the model that would ultimately result in the condemnation of the bishop of Laodicea in 377. While articulated out of the legitimate anxiety that Marcellus's Christology generated, this dimension of Eusebius's thought would prove a wrong, though influential, turn in the Christological speculation of the fourth century.

IV. The Influence of Eusebius's
Anti-Marcellan Works

Despite the lack of modern-language translations, there has been some work over the past twenty-five or thirty years on Eusebius's anti-Marcellan works and the enduring influence they had on Greek theology in the fourth century. American scholars, such as Joseph T. Lienhard, and German scholars building upon the work of Hans-Georg Opitz, such as Martin Tetz, Reinhard M. Hübner, Markus Vinzent, Luise Abramowski, Klaus Seibt, and Gerhard Feige, have contributed greatly to the appreciation of the importance of Eusebius's last works for subsequent formulations of trinitarian theology in the Greek East as the fourth century progressed.[289] The following is an attempt to provide an overview of recent scholarship on this influence.

---

289. See, for example, Martin Tetz, "Zur Theologie des Markell von Ankyra II. Markells Lehre von der Adamssohnschaft Christi und eine pseudoklementinische Tradition über die wahren Lehrer und Propheten," *ZKG* 79 (1968): 3–42; idem, "Zur Theologie des Markell von Ankyra III. Die pseudoathanasianische *Epistula fidei ad Liberium*, ein markellisches Bekenntnis," *ZKG* 83 (1972): 145–94; idem, "Markellianer und Athanasios von Alexandrien. Die markellianische *Expositio fidei ad Athanasium* des Diakons Eugenios von Ankyra," *ZNW* 64 (1973): 75–121; idem, "Die Kirchweihsynode von Antiochien (341) und Marcellus von Ancyra," in *Oecumenica et Patristica, Festschrift Wilhelm Schneemelcher* (Chambésy and Geneva, 1989): 199–217; idem, "Zur strittigen Frage arianischer Glaubenserklärungen auf dem Konzil von Nicaea (325)," in Hanns Ch. Brennecke et al., eds., *Logos. Festschrift Luise Abramowski*, Beihefte zur Zeitschrift für Neutestamentliche Wissenschaft 67 (Berlin and New York: De Gruyter, 1993): 220–38; Luise Abramowski, "Die Synode von Antiochien 324/25 und ihr Symbol," *ZKG* 86 (1975): 356–66. For the works of the other scholars mentioned, see the bibliography.

1. Credal Formulas

The study of Eusebius's anti-Marcellan works reveals the frequent appearance of standard, even stereotyped, characterizations of Marcellus's erroneous theology and positive trinitarian statements that Eusebius articulates in opposition to them. Eusebius himself at various points in the *Against Marcellus* and the *On Ecclesiastical Theology* seeks to express his interpretation of the Church's theology in credal-style statements without, however, adopting any single one by preference. At the same time, there is evidence that Marcellus and his supporters responded to criticism with credal formulations of their own. As has been shown elsewhere,[290] such credal form production, wherein one formula is a counter-form of an adversary's, led to an explosion of creeds in both East and West in the period following the composition of Eusebius's anti-Marcellan works. Some examples of this are the four creeds of the Dedication Council of Antioch from 341, the second of which is the most explicitly and aggressively anti-Marcellan while drawing on the creed of Marcellus's main opponent Asterius.[291] In contrast, the letter to the eastern bishops around Eusebius of Nicomedia that Julius of Rome composed after the Roman synod of the year 340 explicitly declared Marcellus's statement and belief to be orthodox. Nevertheless, Marcellus and some of his views were condemned in both the synodical letter and the creed issued by the eastern bishops who left the council at Serdica (the date of which is disputed but was likely held in 343) to meet in Philippopolis, whereas Marcellus with a number of supporters formulated the so-called Western Serdicense, a creed that found its way into many Western churches that endorsed the council fathers' support for Marcellus.[292] Anti-Marcellan

290. See Markus Vinzent, "Die Entstehung des römischen Glaubensbekenntnisses," in *Tauffragen und Bekenntnis. Studien zur sogenannten* Traditio Apostolica, *zu den* Interrogationes de fide *und zum* Römischen Glaubensbekenntnis, ed. Christoph Markschies, Markus Vinzent, and Wolfram Kinzig, Arbeiten zur Kirchengeschichte 74 (Berlin: Walter de Gruyter, 1999), 185–410.

291. Ibid., 167–72.

292. Ibid., 172–76; see Markus Vinzent, *Der Ursprung des Apostolikums im Urteil der kritischen Forschung*, FKDG 89 (Göttingen: Vandenhoeck & Ruprecht,

arguments, combined with clear criticism of Asterius, Eusebius, and Marcellus's disciple Photinus of Sirmium, appear in the *Ekthesis Makrostichos* or the "Long-Lined Creed," which was brought to Italy by four eastern bishops after an Antiochene council of 344 in an attempt at reconciliation between eastern and western bishops—whose disagreement about the condemnation and depositions of Athanasius and Marcellus had been significant factors in their estrangement in the years since the latter's depositions in the mid-330s.[293] The continued influence of Eusebius's characterization of and response to Marcellus can still be detected in the creed that the Council of Sirmium in 351 produced, where the debate, however, has moved on and is now focused on criticism of the theology of Marcellus's disciple Photinus of Sirmium.[294] That this series of creeds should share a similar anti-Marcellan stance is further explained by the fact that the creeds of Philippopolis, the *Ekthesis*, and Sirmium 351 elaborate by means of additional anathemas and explanatory material on the fourth creed of the Dedication Council of 341, and follow what Markus Vinzent called a kind of "building block" hermeneutics of credal development.[295]

2. Explicitly Anti-Marcellan Tracts

The influence of Eusebius's anti-Marcellan works was evident in the period after the bishop of Caesarea's death not only in credal statements, but also in prose works. In many respects, these works continue the complicated debates between multiple theologians (Arius, Asterius, and Marcellus) that preceded and influenced the composition of Eusebius's anti-Marcellan works. For example, Eusebius's immediate successor in the see of Caesarea, Acacius of Caesarea (in office from approximately

2006); Luise Abramowski, "Die dritte Arianerrede des Athanasius. Eusebianer und Arianer und das westliche Serdicense," *ZKG* 102 (1991): 389–413; Martin Tetz, "'Ante omnia de sancta fide et de integritate veritatis.' Glaubensfragen auf der Synode von Serdika," *ZNW* 76 (1985): 243–70.

293. Vinzent, "Die Entstehung," 176–78.

294. Ibid., 178–81.

295. See Wolfram Kinzig and Markus Vinzent, "Recent Research on the Origin of the Creed," *JTS* n.s. 50 (1999): 535–59.

340 to 356), composed a treatise *Against Marcellus*, apparently to defend Asterius the Sophist (who was present at the council) against Marcellus's criticisms at the Dedication Council in Antioch in 341, but embarks on topics that were also central and partially common to both Asterius and Marcellus.[296] Likewise, anti-Marcellan arguments, combined with clear criticism of Asterius, Eusebius, and Marcellus's pupil Photinus of Sirmium, appear in another document possibly from the early 340s, the Pseudo-Athanasian *Fourth Oration against the Arians,* which Markus Vinzent has proposed was the first theological treatise that Apolinarius of Laodicea composed.[297] And again, the Pseudo-Athanasian *Against the Sabellians,* for which Reinhard M. Hübner has also posited Apolinarian authorship circa 360, continues and extends Eusebius's anti-Marcellan argumentation.[298] Other examples of anti-Marcellan prose works include the short piece by Apolinarius, *Quod unus sit Christus,*[299] and the sermons entitled *De fide* and *Adversus Sabellium* (now preserved only in Latin) by Eusebius of Emesa.[300] Though the latter work condemns the theology of "Sabellius," Marcellus is mentioned under the title of "Galatian,"[301] and otherwise theses associated with Marcellus as well as ideas derived from Eusebius's anti-Marcellan polemics are evident in these texts. This should not

296. The text may be found in Epiphanius, *haer.* 72.6–10 (Holl and Dummer, 260–65). See also Lienhard, *Contra Marcellum,* 182–86.

297. Vinzent, *Pseudo-Athanasius, Contra Arianos IV,* 58–88, and now Markus Vinzent, "Pseudo-Athanasius, *Oratio contra Arianos IV*—Apolinarius' earliest extant work," in Silke-Petra Bergjan, Benjamin Gleede, and Martin Heimgartner, eds., *Apolinarius und seine Folgen* (Tübingen: Mohr Siebeck, 2015), 59–70. Vinzent used the edition from A. Stegmann, "Die pseudoathanasianische 'IVte Rede gegen die Arianer' als *Kata Areianon logos* ein Apollinarisgut" (Ph.D. diss., Würzburg, Tübingen, 1917), 43–47.

298. The text may be found at PG 28: 96–121. See Hübner, *Die Schrift des Apolinarius von Laodicea gegen Photin (Pseudo-Athanasius, Contra Sabellianos) und Basilius von Caesarea.*

299. For this see Lietzmann, *Apollinaris von Laodicea und seine Schule,* 159–60, 209, 296.

300. For the editions, see *Eusèbe d'Emèse, Discours conservés en latin,* ed. E. M. Buytaert, 2 vols. (Leuven: Peeters, 1953, 1957), 79–127.

301. See Eusebius of Emesa, *De fide* 24, vol. I, 93 (Buytaert); see also Lienhard, *Contra Marcellum,* 194–95.

surprise scholars, as Eusebius of Emesa, though originally from Mesopotamia, came to Palestine in the post-Nicene period to study Scripture with Eusebius of Caesarea. Significantly, after his death (no later than the spring of 359), George, bishop of Laodicea, wrote an encomium of Eusebius of Emesa, suggesting a strong theological affinity between Eusebius of Emesa and the Homoiousian trinitarian thinkers, which included George, as well as Marcellus's successor in the see of Ancyra, Basil.[302] One can discover the influence of Eusebius of Caesarea and the anti-Marcellan tradition in *Catechesis* 15 of Cyril of Jerusalem, specifically on the issue of the final fate of the incarnate Word, attacking the idea that Christ's kingdom would come to an end after the reintegration of the Word into the primal divine Monad.[303] The similarity of outlook shared by Eusebius of Emesa and Cyril of Jerusalem with Eusebius of Caesarea was the subject of an important study by the French scholar Ignace Bertin in the late 1960s, though he still uses the now-outmoded title "semi-Arian" to characterize the theologies of all three.[304] He does not extend that characterization to the members of the Homoiousian party that emerged after the Council of Ancyra in 358, but it is clear that the Homoiousians, known from the two documents preserved in Epiphanius, also continue the Eusebian anti-Marcellan tradition, and in fact represent the final form of the Eusebian theology that developed in response to Marcellus.[305]

3. Tracts Against Sabellius and Arius

The two texts mentioned above as possible works by Apolinarius of Laodicea, the Pseudo-Athanasian *Contra Arianos IV* and the *Contra Sabellianos*, it should be noted, combine anti-Marcellan rhetoric with criticism, much as one sees in *ET* 1.10, of the Arian or Asterian idea that the second person of the Trinity is cre-

---

302. Lienhard, *Contra Marcellum,* 186–97.

303. Ibid., 197–99.

304. Ignace Bertin, "Cyrille de Jérusalem, Eusèbe d'Emèse et la théologie semi-arienne," *RScPhTh* 52 (1968): 38–75.

305. Lienhard, *Contra Marcellum,* 187, 211–12.

ated. Again, this is evidence of the multi-faceted nature of early anti-Marcellan debate, wherein Eusebius seeks to place his own theology between the extremes of Marcellus's modalism and the excessive differentiation of Father and Son that would compromise the Son's divinity that Eusebius sees in Arius and Asterius's theology. Traces of what a patristic heresiologist might call "anti-Arianism" appear in these two pseudo-Athanasian works, but are much more obviously pursued in a text that has been unambiguously attributed to Apolinarius of Laodicea, the short trinitarian text the *Kata Meros Pistis* or *The Detailed Confession of the Faith*.[306] Produced probably between 357 and 362 or 363, this text (if it is not a compound of texts) exhibits two features: attacks against Marcellan theses under the term "Sabellius," as well as criticism of the Asterian/Arian error of worshiping a created, not divine, Word. As in Pseudo-Athanasius's *Contra Arianos IV*, there is positive reference to the Nicene ὁμοούσιον[307] in the text, as well as a reference to the eternal generation of the Son.[308] The text is otherwise distinguished by its clear engagement with the Pneumatomachian debate that began to emerge in the late 350s and statements that are expressive of Apolinarius's distinctive Christology. This Apolinarian text closely follows the earlier hybrid text of Pseudo-Athanasius's *Contra Arianos IV* and draws upon the Eusebian anti-Marcellan tradition while moving toward a more explicitly pro-Nicene account of divine unity. In this genre we include Basil of Caesarea's *Contra Sabellianos et Arium et Anomoeos*[309] and the short homily entitled *Adversus Arium et Sabellium* attributed to Gregory of Nyssa[310] though pseudonymously.[311] Both of these texts likely come from the 370s or even later.

306. Spoerl, "A Study of the *Kata Meros Pistis* by Apollinarius of Laodicea."
307. Apolinarius of Laodicea, *KMP* 27.176.21. Markus Vinzent notes that if such texts as the *Contra Arianos IV* are by the young Apolinarius writing in the early 340s, he would have the priority over Athanasius of Alexandria in the reappropriation of the Nicene ὁμοούσιος for a theological account of divine unity; see Vinzent, *Pseudo-Athanasius, Contra Arianos IV*, 376–77 with note 912.
308. Apolinarius of Laodicea, *KMP* 26.176.15–16.26.
309. Edition in PG 31: 600B–617B.
310. Edition in PG 45: 1281–1301.
311. Karl Holl, "Über die Gregor von Nyssa zugeschriebene Schrift 'Ad-

Both the assertion of the Nicene ὁμοούσιον and the doctrine of eternal generation cause these hybrid anti-Marcellan texts to mark a new stage in the reception of Eusebius, one that significantly promoted the reconciliation and synthesis of foregoing approaches to the Christian doctrine of God: the approach that wanted to stress the unity of the divinity shared by Father, Son, and Spirit, and the approach that was concerned to preserve the distinction of the persons revealed in Scripture. Yet while acknowledging the presence within these texts of new elements that represent important developments in trinitarian thought beyond the contributions of Eusebius, it should be remembered that Eusebius himself in his anti-Marcellan works wished to correct some of the errors associated with the teaching of Arius, and that this impulse had been evident in Greek theology at the Council of Nicaea, as we see from the anathemas appended to the creed formulated there.[312] Hence it should not surprise that, just as it seems that some anti-Marcellan writers beginning with Eusebius incorporate some anti-"Arian" rhetoric into their theologies, so some pro-Nicene writers incorporate anti-Marcellan rhetoric into their theologies. For example, Spoerl has demonstrated that Athanasius of Alexandria, despite having been allied with Marcellus from the early 340s while both were in exile in Rome,[313] also incorporates characteristic elements of anti-Marcellan rhetoric in his anti-Arian works of the 340s and 350s.[314]

---

versus Arium et Sabellium,'" *ZKG* 25 (1904): 380–98; Reinhard M. Hübner, "Gregor von Nyssa und Markell von Ankyra," in *Écriture et culture*, ed. M. Harl (Leiden: Brill, 1971): 199–229, at 211–12; Elias D. Moutsoulas, Γρηγόριος Νύσσης (Athens: Eptálophos, 1997), 327–29.

312. This was an observation Rowan Williams made in response to Spoerl's presentation at the 1995 Oxford Patristic Conference, "Anti-Arian Polemic in Eusebius of Caesarea's *Ecclesiastical Theology*."

313. On this, see Parvis, *Marcellus of Ancyra*, 179–85.

314. Kelley McCarthy Spoerl, "Athanasius and the Anti-Marcellan Controversy," *ZAC* 10 (2006): 34–55. If *Contra Arianos IV* has Apolinarian authorship, Vinzent theorizes that the source of this rhetoric in Athanasius could have been Apolinarius; see Markus Vinzent, "Pseudo-Athanasius, *Oratio contra Arianos IV*—Apolinarius' earliest extant work," in *Apolinarius und seine Folgen*, 59–70.

V. Overview of the Major Contributions
of Eusebius's Anti-Marcellan Works to
Fourth-Century Theology

Examining the texts that develop the portrayal of Marcellus's theology and the response to it initially presented in Eusebius's anti-Marcellan works enables us to see through time the major contributions Eusebius and his followers in the anti-Marcellan tradition made to the overall shape of orthodox trinitarian theology. Although the presentation of Marcellus's theology becomes increasingly stereotyped as anti-Marcellan literature continues to be produced over the course of the fourth century, certain ideas that Eusebius initially introduces in response to Marcellus also become progressively more refined and compelling to the theologians, both self-identified "pro-Nicenes" and those who would not choose to identify themselves as such. Some of the most important of these ideas include:

1) The assertion that the incarnate Word is Son before the Incarnation because of his begetting from the Father. Marcellus was clear on this point; for him the generation of the Son was the Word's taking flesh from Mary. This is the reason why he preferred the title "Word" as the most accurate title for the pre-existent Christ and why he rejected the Father-Son simile for the Word's generation. Although Marcellus had himself strengthened the distinction between the incarnate Son and the Father, by asserting they had two different wills, he denied the idea that God and Logos were "two hypostases" even during the Incarnation.[315] The other hypostasis (or person?) that Marcellus sees in Christ does not belong to the Word, but to the man Jesus, whom the Word assumed. Eusebius and those after him insist on the appropriateness of the title "Son" for the pre-existent offspring of the Father, in the process reinforcing the ontological process of begetting as the means by which a second being or hypostasis arises, whom, in response to Marcellus, Eusebius already called a hypostasis and πρόσωπον distinct from that of the Father.[316] This stress has two advantages,

315. See Marcellus, *fr.* 48 (K./H., 67; Vinzent, 44,2–8).
316. See *ET* 1.20.9 (K./H., 90–91).

which Eusebius and his successors will exploit theologically: in promoting a genetic simile for the Son's origin, anti-Marcellan theologians will be better equipped to argue for the Son's similarity to the Father in the order of divinity, the better to quash the "Arian" notion of his artificial creation. Indeed, Eusebius, building on Asterius's theology, will use the language of begetting to stress the "likeness" of the Son to the Father in a way that points directly toward the Homoiousian stance of the late 350s. At the same time, stressing the pre-incarnate offspring's status as a begotten Son, and thus other as hypostasis and πρόσωπον than the Father, enables Eusebius and his successors to articulate the difference between Father and Son in a meaningful way as two persons over against Marcellus's stress on the oneness and identity between the Father and his Logos.

2) It is the anti-Marcellan tradition that will assert over against Marcellus that the Son's status as image pertains to him even in his pre-existent state, not only in his incarnate one, as Marcellus thought. This assertion will also reinforce the anti-Arian idea of the Son's ontological likeness to the Father that supports claims to his equal divinity.

3) Clearly one of the main contributions of the anti-Marcellan tradition to the later shape of trinitarian orthodoxy is the mainstreaming of the use of the term *hypostasis* for what will become the personal distinction between Father, Son, and Spirit in the Christian godhead. This development arguably takes longer to crystallize than may seem to be the case at first glance. We may see the tentative beginnings of a consensus at the Council of Alexandria in 362, but that consensus does not become truly widespread until the early to mid-370s, culminating in the definition offered at the Council of Constantinople in 381. Nevertheless, the fact that Eusebius consistently uses this term in the context of arguing for a meaningful ontological distinction between the persons of the Trinity, while still arguing for their shared divinity, does start to erode the terminological equivalence between οὐσία and hypostasis that we see in the Nicene anathemas in a way that will ultimately lead to the Cappadocian differentiation of these terms. While this distinction has probably received a level of attention among scholars that is disproportionate to the

interest paid to it by the theologians themselves of the fourth century (and this would include Eusebius), it is nevertheless clear that the assertion of the formula "three hypostases" and the differentiations of persons for the distinctions between Father, Son, and Spirit are traceable back to Asterius and Eusebius and their successors in the anti-Marcellan tradition.

4) Eusebius's objections to some of the troubling implications of Marcellus's eschatological teaching obviously have become part of the confessional traditions of many Christian denominations up to the present day, in that the Nicene-Constantinopolitan creed includes the statement aimed directly at Marcellus that Christ's kingdom will have no end. Yet it should be noted that the inclusion of this clause in the Nicene-Constantinopolitan creed represents not only a correction of Marcellus's eschatological teaching; it is part and parcel of a critical response to Marcellus's Christological teaching. It is hoped that the publication of this translation will enable students and scholars of fourth-century Greek theology to appreciate more fully the interaction between trinitarian theology, Christology, and eschatology in the debates generated by the emergence of Arius in the early fourth century. As Eusebius's criticisms of Marcellus make clear, statements about Christ's pre-existent status are inextricably intertwined with and mutually dependent on statements about his incarnate and his eschatological existence. Eusebius clearly wants to assert over against Marcellus that Jesus Christ had a pre-existent life as Son of his divine Father, begotten from him, and that he will have as a result his own life in his glorified body in the ages to come. But Eusebius also wants to assert that the one we know as Jesus Christ is identical in the order of hypostasis (and person?) with that pre-existent Son. The humanity assumed by the Word is not a distinct hypostasis or person, as Marcellus suggested. Some of Eusebius's Christological arguments are heresiologically phrased and stereotype Marcellus's concerns, simplifying these and framing them along earlier stereotypes from the third century, such as the adoptionist teaching credited to Paul of Samosata, or from the second century, such as the monarchianism credited to Sabellius. This is why in some instances he and some of his successors in the anti-Marcellan tradition (particularly af-

ter the emergence of Photinus of Sirmium) uncritically assimi-
late Marcellus's teaching to that of Paul of Samosata or Sabellius.
Eusebius is adamant that the subject of the healing, teaching,
and suffering Messiah is the divine Logos, and in that sense we
can describe his Christology as unitive in orientation. When
brought into dialogue with reflection on Marcellus's idiosyncratic eschatology, it is clear that Eusebius also asserts the insight—to
be reiterated in the teaching of the Council of Chalcedon over
a hundred years later—that once the Son assumes humanity in
the Incarnation, that Incarnation will persist into the new age.

At the same time, however, while there is no question that Eusebius's reflections in this domain become part of the Church's
orthodox teaching, another dimension of his unitive Christology is his explicit rejection of a human soul in Christ, which
he thinks implies a heretical adoptionist Christology. The desire
to avoid adoptionism was conditioned by Eusebius's response to
Marcellus's idea of two different wills in the incarnate Christ,
which Eusebius heresiologically equated with what was believed
to be the teaching of Paul of Samosata in the mid-third century, but represents a significant departure from the teaching of
Origen, whom Eusebius and his teacher Pamphilus revered. Giv-
en the influence of the Marcellan and anti-Marcellan traditions
on the theology of Apolinarius of Laodicea[317]—and likely of his
predecessors in the Syrian see, including Eusebius's close friend
and ally Theodotus[318]—it has been suggested that some of the
roots of Apolinarius's idiosyncratic theology are in part traceable back to Marcellus, Asterius, and Eusebius.[319] Nevertheless,
despite this problematic aspect of his portrait of the incarnate
Word, the positive contributions of the entire debate, presented
here by Eusebius in his two works, to Christological orthodoxy
in the Christian tradition should be neither overlooked nor un-
derestimated.

317. Spoerl, "Apollinarian Christology and the Anti-Marcellan Tradition."
318. On their relationship, see Mark DelCogliano, "The Eusebian Alliance:
The Case of Theodotus of Laodicea," *ZAC* 12 (2008): 250–66.
319. See Vinzent, *Pseudo-Athanasius, Contra Arianos IV, passim.*

VI. Some Notes about the Translation

To render Eusebius into a modern language is no easy task. Although across his career he wrote extensive historical, exegetical, dogmatic, and apologetic works, studies that often include substantial quotations from other authors, it is noticeable how his own, often long-winded and verbose, if not wearisome, prose contrasts with the more concise style of other authors. Even if Marcellus himself does not write as Plotinus or Porphyry does, but develops a pre-Byzantine, sometimes atticizing court-style, Eusebius, especially in the opening chapters of his treatises, tries to overtake Marcellus in his effort to overshadow his opponent, whom he calls an inexperienced "novice author."[320] Long, sometimes very long, clauses make the comprehension of the main argument often difficult; hence, in order to make the text easier to grasp, the translation either shortens those clauses and breaks them up into shorter sentences, or makes the line of arguments clearer. Yet despite the often embroidered and sometimes periphrastic or repetitious style, Eusebius's works against Marcellus still show the mature strength of consistent theological thinking, a reflection that gets to the point of the debate, develops serious arguments, and from beginning to end seems tireless in adding fragment to fragment of his opponent while counter-arguing detail after detail of them. The final product of our efforts is neither an easy translation nor an easy read, yet, given the importance of these texts outlined above, we took heart in what Jerome said as he translated works of Origen of Alexandria: namely, that the task was necessary, and he "had found" himself "forced to translate" him,[321] but we also have to add that we also quite enjoyed it.

320. *ET* 1.20.6, section 45 (K./H., 88).
321. Jerome, *ep.* 85.3 (Eng. trans., Nicene and Post-Nicene Fathers, Second Series, 6, p. 182).

AGAINST MARCELLUS

BOOK ONE

HE UNDERLYING reason for his [Marcellus's] writing was hatred of his fellow men, but the root of this was jealousy and envy, which indeed also cast countless others into the most extreme evil. Yes, from the beginning, jealousy and envy brought about fratricide.[1] Driven on by these impulses, he wrote this one and only treatise (though it was of no use); right from the start this man[2] was determined to make war upon the holy ministers of God, instead of speaking and writing against the great and numerous body of heretics who were bringing his territory into ruin.[3] If only the saving Word had had any effect on him, this would indeed have been his primary task, like a good shepherd driving out the enemies of the Church of God of the (2) Galatian people as if they were wolves and wild beasts. But this man, who disregards his territory as if it were some dry land full of creeping things spewing out darts of venom, having boiled over needlessly and in vain, discharged his rage against the ministers of God. And not against just anybody, but against those conspicuous among all for their life in the grace of God, and their philosophical con-

1. See Gn 4.1–16.

2. By setting up this contrast between "this man," Marcellus, and the "holy ministers of God," Eusebius suggests Marcellus is an inexperienced writer, perhaps even a layman. He, of course, was not, but already one of the inspirations behind the Nicene condemnation of Arius. In any case, Eusebius's phrasing here is consistent with the insinuation that Marcellus not only grievously neglected his pastoral duties in his own diocese, but out of ignorance polemicized against his theological opponents.

3. It is unclear whom Eusebius has in mind here—the wolves and beasts may recall Justin's and Irenaeus's heretics, the Valentinians and the Pontic wolf, Marcion (Justin, 1 *Apol.* 58; Irenaeus, *haer.* 1.27.4; 3.12.12), or the Montanists or others.

duct; and <not those living> alone, but even those who have fallen asleep in Christ, and those of these whose fame is sung, as it were, throughout the whole inhabited world especially because of the excellence of [their] service of God and [their] study of holy words. But he spoke of these men in a disparaging way not one time, but many times and in different ways, having mercilessly leveled false accusations (3) and calumnies against them. Then he even used curses against them, such as women use in battle, railing and uttering curses at those who have done no wrong to him.[4] For this reason the treatise ran on even beyond what was necessary to a great (for him) and immeasurable length, since, all told, it came (4) near, I estimate, to ten thousand lines to complete the one tract.[5] Therefore, as one might expect, having sharpened an abusive tongue against the holy ministers of God and having exercised beforehand [his] irreverence and disrespect against these [ministers], going further he next advanced to the most important thing of all, subjecting the only begotten and beloved Son of God to these sorts of godless blasphemies, such as it will be better to hear him, but not me, saying a little later.

(5) Having then, however, made use of his words up to this point, I shall hold back, without adding many words to contradict and refute them, as the men who are blasphemed by him are certainly neither unknown nor obscure, but are known among all, (6) even when they are not mentioned, nor is [his] blasphemy against the Christ of God something contested and difficult to discover—hence there is no need for some great and more verbose zeal to refute it. Thus to all who have received the Church's grace,[6] great and small alike, the empty babbling of this foreign theologian has been made manifest, even by its mere quotation. For this reason I will make use of only brief

4. Eusebius indicates that Marcellus not only attacked Asterius (who was secretary of Dianius of Caesarea in Cappadocia), but also bishops who had not been involved in the debate; see *Lib. syn. ad synod. Antioch. anno 341*, ed. J. D. Mansi, *Sacrorum conciliorum nova et amplissima collectio* (Florence: Expensis Antonii Zatta, 1759–1798) II, col. 1350.

5. If this were correct, the book cannot have been much longer than what we now have as fragments, as our word count is already around 16,000 words.

6. Eusebius refers here to baptismal grace.

notes, organizing the treatise with method and orderliness, only hinting at (7) the sheer absurdity of the views that will be introduced. But before progressing to his words I would necessarily advise those reading the man's treatise, especially if indeed there are any men from Galatia,[7] not to be unmindful of the holy statement of Paul the Apostle, who, writing to those very Galatians, exhorted [them] not to turn away from "the one who called" them "in [the] grace of Christ to another gospel," for "there is no other," as he himself said, "even if there are certain men who trouble" them (8) "and wish to distort the gospel of Christ."[8] And it is necessary to turn one's mind to that [remark] which, addressing even himself, the great Apostle made for the shaming of those who were attempting to turn the men away [from the right faith], when he said, "but even if we or an angel from heaven shall proclaim to you a gospel other than the one we have proclaimed to you, let him be anathema."[9] (9) Indeed, having taken up this [theme], he repeats it a second time, saying, "As I have proclaimed and I now say again: if someone proclaims to you a gospel other than that which you received, let him be anathema."[10]

But what in the world was this gospel instead of which there was no other one,[11] if not, I suppose, that very gospel that indeed it is recorded that the Savior publicly proclaimed when he was handing it over to his disciples, saying, "Go, make disciples of all nations, baptizing them in the name of the Father and (10) of the Son and of the Holy Spirit"?[12] For he alone through the mystical regeneration has given to us this grace of the knowledge of the holy Trinity, since neither Moses nor any prophet provided this to the people of old. For it was fitting for the Son of God alone to proclaim to all human beings the paternal grace, since

7. It is not clear here to whom Eusebius refers.
8. Gal 1.6–7. "I am astonished that you are so quickly deserting him who called you in the grace of Christ and turning to a different gospel—not that there is another gospel, but there are some who trouble you and want to pervert the gospel of Christ." (RSV)
9. Gal 1.8.
10. Gal 1.9.
11. The correction of Klostermann is unnecessary.
12. Mt 28.19.

indeed, "The law was given through Moses," but only through "Jesus Christ," as through (11) an "only-begotten Son," did "grace and truth" come.[13] For this reason rightly did the one [Moses], in the manner of a tutor, hand over to the people of old in their infancy "elements of the beginning of the ways of God,"[14] on the one hand prohibiting [the] error of polytheism, while on the other, announcing the knowledge of one God. But the saving grace, which provides to us a certain transcendent and angelic knowledge, unveiled for all to see the ancient mystery that had been hidden in silence from the people of old, announcing that the very God who is beyond the universe[15] [and] who was known to the men of old is at the same time God and Father of the only-begotten Son, supplying as well the power of the Holy Spirit through the Son to those (12) deemed worthy. Thus the Church of God received and preserves the holy, blessed, and mystical Trinity of Father, Son, and Holy Spirit as its saving hope through the regeneration in Christ. And this was the gospel that the great Apostle testifies it is not lawful to change "for another gospel [though] there is no other"[16] still up to the present through the letter to them, crying out to [the] Galatians, "Even if we or an angel from heaven proclaims to you a gospel other than you received, let him be anathema,"[17] commanding [them] long ago, as is right, not to heed either bishops or rulers or teachers if one of them should distort the true statement of the faith. (13) But who was this [man][18] who teaches [us] to know God as Father and hands over [to us] the knowledge of a Son of God and the zeal to participate in a Holy Spirit? Indeed, these things would be the distinguishing features of Christians alone, this being the way in which, I think, the (14) holy Church of God distinguishes itself from the Jewish way [of life]. For as that way [of life] rejected the polytheistic and Greek error by [the] confession of one God, so also the exceptional knowledge concerning the Son that belongs to

13. Jn 1.17–18.
14. Heb 5.12.
15. Rom 9.5.
16. Gal 1.6–7.
17. Gal 1.8.
18. Klostermann's emendation <ἦ> is unnecessary.

the Church introduced something greater and more complete, teaching [human beings] to know the same God as Father of an only-begotten Son, a Son who is truly existing and living and subsisting. In saying, "For as the Father has life in himself, so also he has given to the Son to have life in himself,"[19] the only-begotten of God himself taught [this], (15) so that the Father is truly Father (not being called so only in name, nor having acquired the title falsely, but [being] in truth and deed Father of an only-begotten Son) and also the Son is truly Son. But he who supposes that the Son is a mere word and testifies that he is only Word and many times says this very thing, that he is nothing other than Word, remaining within the Father while he is resting but being active in the crafting of the creation, just like our word that rests when we are silent but is active when we are speaking, would clearly agree with a certain Jewish and human conception [of the Word], but deny the true Son of God.

(16) Indeed, if someone were to ask one of the Jews if God had a word, to be sure, he would say, "I suppose so"—since every Jew would confess that he has both not only a word, but many words. But that he also has a Son, he would no longer (17) confess [this] when asked. But if not a Jew but one of [the] bishops were to introduce this belief, granting that he is only a word united to God and [that] this is eternal and unbegotten and both one and the same with God, on the one hand being called by different names of Father and Son, while on the other, existing as one in being and hypostasis[20] [with the Father], how could it not be clear that he is clothing himself in the mantle of Sabellius, and has made himself a stranger to both the knowledge and the grace in Christ? For the law of the Church commands us neither to question, nor to dispute, nor to ask whether or not the only-begotten Son of God existed or pre-existed; but it teaches by means of a confessed and unambiguous faith with great courage and boldness to confess that God is a Father of a Son, the Only-begotten, and to name neither the Son Father nor the Father Son, but to worship on the one hand the Father

19. Jn 5.26.
20. οὐσίᾳ δὲ καὶ ὑποστάσει.

who is ingenerate, and eternal and without source and first and only, but on the other to believe that [the Son] has been begotten by the Father and subsists and is alone only-begotten Son, (18) and also to acknowledge him as God as being truly Son of God.

Therefore, if someone were to appear to contradict these [truths], and defined this Word of God as being like the one in men, <how would he avoid being refuted> since he neither understands nor realizes that nothing mortal or human must be attributed to the God who is beyond the universe, nor altogether any of the things that occur to our understanding, even if the divine Scriptures, teaching those who read them as if they were certain very young children, speak about him in a more human way, applying to him hands and feet and eyes and voice and words and a mouth and a face and countless other things of this sort? These things, indeed, must be transferred to ideas befitting God, so that they might not imagine there is anything mortal or human in God; for the Savior himself taught [that] "God is spirit, and those who worship him must worship in spirit and truth."[21] (19) But if [God is] spirit, it is clear that [he is] divine, greater than any perceptible and composite body, so as to have neither a perceptible word, coming from a tongue and listened to by mortal ears through speech, nor a tongue nor a voice nor a face nor any other thing that is comparable to a mortal and (20) human conception. For if the holy Apostle taught that there is something else "which eye has not seen nor ear heard nor has occurred to the heart of man" of the sort "which God has prepared for those who love him,"[22] the giver of these things would himself be more ineffable than all these ineffable things, so that it would be more true by far to say in the theology concerning him that neither has eye seen nor ear heard nor has (21) the knowledge of the comprehension of him come "into the heart of man." But the same saying would also apply about the generation of the Son. So the Savior himself would become a worthy interpreter of these sacred mysteries for us, claiming in this way somewhere, "All things have been given to

21. Jn 4.24.
22. 1 Cor 2.9.

me by my Father, and no one knows the Son except the Father, nor does (22) anyone know the Father except the Son."[23]

Therefore then, if anyone were to contradict these [words] and dare to say

that even the Son, to whom the Father has given all things, did not subsist, but were to define him as word as only like [the word] in human beings, at one time resting in God like the one that is silent among us, but at another time being active like [the word] that is uttered in speaking among us;

then to say that this very [word] at a certain time not four hundred whole years ago took flesh (I know not how) and through it has fulfilled the human economy and at that time became Son of God and as Jesus Christ both was called King and is addressed as image "of the invisible God," and "firstborn of all creation,"[24] never having received these titles ever before;

then in addition to this sort of madness, he neither granted unending life and eternal kingdom to Christ, whatever time frame he has in mind, but would introduce an end to him that is neither auspicious nor such as the Savior himself promised to those who would be made worthy through him of the gospels, having promised eternal life and immortal resurrection and [the] kingdom of heaven to those who love him;

(23) but would claim that at that time, in accordance with the expected hope of these, the things of the everlasting kingdom would endure for all the others, but that a complete deprivation of all these things would be the lot of Christ himself alone, his kingdom having come to an end, while the flesh that he assumed would be left behind abandoned, while the Word himself, who pre-existed in God, being separated from the body (even if this were to be undying and immortal), would be united to God, so as to become one and the same again with God just as he also was previously;

(24) then what extravagance of impiety could be left to him [who makes such claims]?

For this reason, then, the witness of the apostolic command is needed, which said to these [Galatians]: "Even if an angel

23. Mt 11.27.
24. Col 1.15.

from heaven shall announce a gospel different from the one you received, let him be anathema."[25] But I was wonder-struck when I was reflecting upon the Apostle's thinking. For just as if he were prophesying the future to the Galatians themselves, he explained more precisely the theology of the Savior, in that passage in the beginning of the letter to them, in which he wrote in a more surprising way than usual[26] as follows: "Paul an apostle, not by men (25) nor through a man but through Jesus Christ."[27] At any rate, one would not find him writing in this way to others—because, as we know, there were no others to whom he wrote in this way concerning the faith. For just as he brought correction to those who supposed that Christ was a mere man, teaching that he was not a man at the beginning of the letter, so proceeding further he said to the same [readers], "My gospel, which was proclaimed to you, is not according to man, nor did I receive it from a man, nor was I taught it, but through a revelation of Jesus Christ,"[28] (26) through which he again shows that Jesus Christ was not a man. And he again clarified further on what he was, if not a man, saying, "when God took pleasure in choosing me from my mother's womb to reveal his Son in me."[29] You see that he addressed the Savior clearly as

---

25. Gal 1.8–9.

26. Eusebius finds Paul surprising in the opening of Galatians as the Apostle specifies mediation between God and man through Christ, who is divine as well as human. Eusebius is at pains to stress his anti-Marcellan position, but, as one can see here, also deviates from Asterius (therefore the note on the "surprise"). Marcellus saw the divine Logos as the mediator; Asterius believed Christ mediated God's grace through his humanity, whereas Eusebius (with Paul in Galatians) sees that Paul stated that he had become Apostle "not by men nor through a man but through Jesus Christ." See Asterius, *fr.* 47 (112 V.): "See, then, also through Moses he [God] guided the people out of Egypt and has given the Law, although he [Moses] too was only a human being; hence, it is possible that through the same [the Son as a human being] the same can happen [mediatorship of God's grace, salvation, law-giving]." Eusebius tries to communicate a middle position between Asterius and Marcellus, and introduces the idea that Christ is both God and man; hence he reflects neither Marcellus's view (that Christ is mediator only as God) nor Asterius's position (that Christ is mediator only as human).

27. Gal 1.1.

28. Gal 1.11–12.

29. Gal 1.15–16.

Son of God (27) and because of this as God. And that he knew that he was Son of God even before [his] coming in the flesh he shows in the clearest way possible, adding in the same letter to Galatians: "But when the fullness of time came, God sent his Son, born of a woman."[30] Therefore not now, but before he was born of a woman, the Father sent a Son who exists and pre-exists, so that he who was of old Son of God might also become Son (28) of man, having been born "of a woman." But he teaches that he also became a mediator of the law of Moses,[31] defining the purpose of the mediation, by saying, "What then? The law was given because of transgressions until the seed came to whom it had been promised, ordained through angels by [the] hand of a mediator. Now a mediator implies more than one; but God is one."[32] You hear that in these [words] the Apostle taught [those] same Galatians to know from (29) [that passage] that God is one, and that the mediator between God and angels is one. Indeed, he also showed this in other [remarks], saying, "For there is one God, and one mediator between God and men, [the] man Jesus Christ."[33] But when, on the one hand, he named him mediator between "God and men," quite rightly he called him "man" because of the Incarnation. But when, on the other hand, he introduced the same as mediator not between God and men but between God and angels, he no longer named him "man," but he says only that he is "mediator," having said that the law was ordained (30) "through angels by [the] hand of a mediator,"[34] and clarifying the name of the mediator necessarily by a distinction in saying, "Now a mediator implies more than one; but God is one."[35] Consequently neither would "the" God be the mediator (for of whom could he also become a mediator?) nor would the mediator himself be "the" God, (31) for "a mediator implies more than one."[36] But rather

30. Gal 4.4.
31. See Asterius, *fr.* 47 (112 V.).
32. Gal 3.19–20.
33. 1 Tm 2.5.
34. Gal 3.19.
35. Gal 3.20.
36. In this passage Eusebius relies upon the Origenist distinction between the Father as "the" God and the Son as God. See introduction, pp. 23, 45.

he stood between these two. Who these were between whom
[he stood] [Paul] makes clear by naming angels and "the" God.
He says that the Son of "the" God, being between them ["the"
God and angels], has received the law with his own hand from
the Father, but that it was ordained for the first people [the
Jews] through angels. Thus on that basis the Son was mediator
between God and angels, before (32) he became "mediator between God and men."

And he was not, as a mere word of God, non-subsistent,[37] existing as one and the same with God (for he would not then be
a mediator); but he existed and pre-existed as "only-begotten
Son full of grace and truth."[38] And he acted as a mediator for
the Father when he provided the law to men "through angels."
And indeed, when teaching on this basis the ignorant and unlearned regarding the theology of the Son of God, the Apostle
confirmed this, saying, "a mediator implies more than one."[39]
For it is not natural (33) for a mediator to be defined in relation to one thing. For this reason, this mediator does not imply
one party, but necessarily operates between two parties, being
neither of those between whom he is, so that he is thought to
be neither "the" God who is over all[40] nor one of the angels,
but in between and a mediator between these, when he medi-
ates between the Father and angels. As once again, when he became "mediator between God and men,"[41] being between each
rank, he belongs to neither one of those ranks between which
he is mediator. Neither is he himself the one and only God, nor
is he (34) a man like the rest of men. What then, if neither of
these, [is he] if not an only-begotten Son of God, now having
become a mediator between men and God, but very long ago
in the time of Moses existing as mediator between God and
angels? And writing these things to them, passing them down,
I suppose, in this way the great Apostle says, "The law having
been ordained (35) through angels by [the] hand of a media-

37. ἀνυπόστατος.
38. Jn 1.14.
39. Gal 3.20.
40. Rom 9.5; Eph 4.6. The phrase "over all" appears frequently.
41. 1 Tm 2.5.

tor. Now a mediator implies more than one; but God is one."[42] Therefore, "there is one God" and "one mediator of God" for all creatures, the saving mediation beginning not now, but even before his divine appearance among men, as (36) the statement thus showed. Given that these things have been laid out in brief to the same Galatians from the only letter addressed to them, and that the saving faith provides the mystical regeneration "in the name of the Father and of the Son and of the Holy Spirit,"[43] and that in addition to the divine writings the universal Church of God from one end of the earth to the other confirms the testimonies from the divine Scriptures by its unwritten tradition, now it remains also to examine in detail the statements of Marcellus and to undertake the demonstrations that were promised by us, lest anyone think that the man is unjustly disparaged by us. (37) My present goal being to discuss briefly what has been said, I will not recount all the statements of the man, but I will make use of only those that are most significant; through them I will make my argument, having gone over the most, as it were, egregious ones. But before I lay out what he has said, I think it is necessary in the first place to show to my readers that he did not understand correctly the most obvious statements of the divine Scriptures, so that it might be known to those who were still ignorant of him[44] what sort of man was driven to dare [to say] such things.

Chapter 2

(1) Therefore, to begin with, the prophet Zechariah arose at the time of the return from Babylon and mentioned the great priest Jesus,[45] that is, the son of Josedek, who together with Zerubbabel led those who had returned from Babylon. This fine fellow and wondrous author [Marcellus], being ignorant of

42. Gal 3.19–20.
43. Mt 28.19.
44. This shows that Marcellus's book, and perhaps he himself, was not known by all the people whom Eusebius intended to address.
45. Zec 3.1–2. The Hebrew name "Joshua" is in fact a form of the Greek name "Jesus."

these things, cites the statement of Zechariah in which he mentions Jesus, but having gotten the historical referent completely wrong, (2) he supposed he spoke about Jesus, [the] successor to Moses. And again, where the Apostle wrote in the letter to the Galatians in this way, "the Jerusalem that is above is free, which is our Mother,"[46] he either forgot or did not know or even deliberately distorts the statement, writing, however:

> "Our Jerusalem is above. For she is in bondage with her children."[47]

(3) And again, where our Savior said to Peter, "Get behind me, Satan; you are a stumbling block to me, because you do not think of the things of God but of the things of man,"[48] not having understood in what sense the statement was made to the Apostle and for what sort of reason, he says that these things were said to the Devil. But he proposes such tremendous errors at the same time under a single section [of his treatise], writing with these very words in this way:

> That there is no name that is greater than "Jesus" among those who are named on earth, the gospel testifies in that passage where the angel said to Mary: "Do not be afraid, Mary, for you have found favor with God. And behold, you will conceive in your womb and bear a son, and you will call his name (4) Jesus. He will be great, and will be called Son of the Most High."[49] This is also clear from the prophecy of Zechariah, which had prophesied long ago concerning this name. For it says, "The Lord showed to me the great priest Jesus standing before the angel of the Lord, and the Devil standing at his right hand to accuse him. And the Lord said to the Devil: 'The Lord, who has chosen (5) Jerusalem, rebuke you.'"[50] For when did he rebuke him? When he joined the man beloved by him to his own Word. He says, "He who has chosen Jerusalem," [mean-

46. Gal 4.26.
47. Small middle section of Marcellus, *fr.* 4 (1 K./H.) (8,5–6 V.), taken from Gal 4.25–26.
48. Mt 16.23.
49. Lk 1.30–32.
50. Zec 3.1–2.

ing] quite clearly, this one belonging to us, about which the Apostle says, "Our Jerusalem is above. (6) For she is in bondage with her children."[51] For at the time when he was in that great Jerusalem, that is, in our Church, he rebuked the Devil in accordance with the prophecy, having said, "Get behind me, Satan, because you are a stumbling block to me."[52] Therefore, this [Jesus] is the great priest (7) of whom Jesus in the past preserved the type. For it was not possible for that man [Jesus] to be called a great priest, even though he was honorable in every way, because not even Moses was called great (for Moses was great in this respect, that he was even called "servant of God" and was named God of the Pharaoh by God himself).[53] (8) But if because of this someone were to think that Jesus was said to be great because he was deemed worthy to lead the people into the Holy Land and did many other wonders, let him also know through this, that the attribution of greatness to Jesus referred not so much to the action of the type, but to his [Jesus's] leading of his people a little later into this great city of Jerusalem that was to come.[54]

You see how great his ignorance was, having completely lost track of the historical referent, and not having been able to identify (9) the Jesus who was indicated by the prophet Zechariah. For the one was son of Josedek of [the] tribe of Levites, having received the high priesthood from the family of Aaron, on account of which he was also deemed "great priest," just as the prophet teaches, saying, "and [the] Lord showed to me Jesus the great priest."[55] (10) But the successor of Moses, who led the people into the Promised Land and who also did many other miracles, was a son of Nun, of the tribe of Ephraim, which had nothing to do with the priesthood. Well now, having deviated to so great an extent from the most obvious sense of the [biblical] statement and having been ignorant of the straight-

51. Gal 4.25–26.
52. Mt 16.23.
53. Ex 14.31; Ex 7.1.
54. Marcellus, *fr.* 4 (1 K./H.) (6,12–8,18 V.).
55. Zec 3.1.

forward facts of the narrative, how could this fellow [Marcellus] be worthy to teach the highest theology?

And with regard to Peter, likewise (11) it is necessary to know in what sense it was said to him "Get behind me" and what the [proper] interpretation of the name of Satan is and why he also said he [Peter] was a "stumbling block," and how at almost nearly one and the same time it was said to him both "Blessed are you, Simon bar Jonah"[56] and (12) "Get behind me, Satan,"[57] and what the meaning of the expression "to follow behind" the Savior is. Right afterward, he himself explains [this], adding next, "If anyone wishes to follow me, let him deny himself and take up his cross and follow me,"[58] which Peter himself in fact did (13) a little later, having been perfected by martyrdom. But it is also necessary to inquire why he blessed him and why he rebuked him. But he [Marcellus], having taken none of these things into consideration, declared that these things were said (14) to the Devil, contrary to Scripture. And was this the only thing about which he was ignorant? No, but proceeding on again, having mentioned the resurrection of our Savior [and] having then wished to show that even before him in prophetic times someone was raised from the dead, he again makes mistakes here too, saying that first Elisha the prophet raised [a child] from the dead;[59] not knowing that even before Elisha, Elijah the great resurrected the son of the widow when he had died, as (15) one can learn from the third book of Kings.[60] But he also seems to have been ignorant of these things in what he wrote as follows:

> Therefore, the Apostle says that he is not only "firstborn of the new creation,"[61] but also "firstborn of the dead"[62] for no other reason, it seems to me, but so that through the expression "firstborn of the dead" one might grasp how the expression

56. Mt 16.17.
57. Mt 16.23.
58. Mt 16.24.
59. LXX 4 Kgs 4.35 (RSV 2 Kgs 4.35).
60. LXX 3 Kgs 17.22 (RSV 1 Kgs 17.22).
61. Col 1.15; 2 Cor 5.17; Gal 6.15.
62. Col 1.18.

"firstborn of all creation" is to be understood. For our Lord Jesus Christ was not the first to rise from the dead, but the man who was raised by Elisha the prophet rose before [him],[63] and Lazarus rose before his resurrection,[64] and at the time of the Passion "many bodies of those who had fallen asleep"[65] rose.[66]

(16) But Marcellus seems to me to have taken even this without carefully considering it; I mean the statement that "many bodies of the saints who had fallen asleep" were raised before him [Christ]. For he did not take into consideration the whole text of the gospel when it teaches that "after (17) *his* <raising>"[67] the bodies of the saints were raised.

But you would find him running into error even in his presentation of the apostolic statement. For, on the one hand, the divine Apostle, writing these sorts of things to the Romans, says, "having been chosen for [the] gospel of God, which had been promised beforehand through his prophets in [the] holy writings concerning his Son, who came from [the] seed of David according to [the] flesh, (18) having been ordained Son of God in power according to the spirit of holiness."[68] But, on the other hand, [this fellow], with I do not know what intention, even here distorts the apostolic statement, when he writes "having been *fore*ordained," instead of "having been ordained," so that he [Christ] might be like those (19) who were foreordained "according to [his] foreknowledge."[69] Thus he says in this way with these very words:

> Therefore, just as God the Almighty long ago foreordained the Church, so also [did he foreordain] the fleshly economy of Christ, through whom he foreordained to call the race of the God-fearing "into adoption,"[70] having laid the foundation [for him] beforehand in his mind. Because of this, the Apostle

63. LXX 4 Kgs 4.35 (RSV 2 Kgs 4.35).
64. Jn 11.44.
65. Mt 27.52.
66. Marcellus, *fr.* 12 (2 K./H.) (14,6–13 V.).
67. Mt 27.52, 53.
68. Rom 1.1–4.
69. Eph 1.11.
70. Eph 1.5.

expressly proclaimed him who "in the Holy Spirit" is "foreordained Son of God."[71]

And again he says in other [words]:

This is he about whom Paul said, "The foreordained Son of God."[72]

(20) But even here he not only distorts the apostolic statement, but even the very sense through the addition of the preposition [be]*fore*. But pursuing the same line of argument, when the Psalm includes [the statement], "From the womb before the morning star I begot you,"[73] the fellow has used even in this case a preposition that is absent [from the biblical text] in order to reprimand (21) the one [Asterius] who does not make claims similar to the ones he does. Therefore, listen to how he writes, saying:

Well then, because of this, it seems good to me (22) to consider in detail now what I have not yet considered previously. For most of what was written by him [Asterius] has become clear to us from what has already been said. For [Scripture] says, "From the womb before the morning star I brought you forth."[74] For he [Asterius] somehow altogether believed that suppression of the preposition *from* would concur with his heretical opinion. For this reason he took away the central idea expressed by this word because he wanted to show [the Son's] initial birth from above.[75]

And since he exerted himself powerfully in these [remarks] on behalf of his own error, while having accused the man [Asterius] who wrote correctly, having himself said nothing, he hands over to those who come upon it the same testimony of the reading. (23) And proceeding on again, the same man introduces the Savior saying, "I am the day," claiming somewhere in this way:

71. Rom 1.4; Marcellus, *fr.* 37 (19 K./H.) (36,1–5 V.).
72. Rom 1.4; Marcellus, *fr.* 112 (122 K./H.) (106,1 V.).
73. Ps 109.3 (RSV 110.3).
74. Ibid.
75. Marcellus, *fr.* 57 (28 K./H.) (50,7–12 V.).

For since it was dark previously because of the ignorance of the fear of God, and since the day was going to appear (for [Christ] says, "I am the day"), [Scripture] most fittingly called the star [the] "morning star."[76]

(24) And in another place he says,

For since after the assumption of the flesh he is proclaimed both "Christ" and "Jesus," as well as "life"[77] and "way"[78] and "day."[79]

And again proceeding on, he presents the statement of the Apostle:

"Our Jerusalem is above."[80]

(25) And why should I continue on at length, since it is possible for him who wishes on the basis of what has been said to read the same sorts of things throughout the whole treatise and to consider the carelessness of the man? Listen to him, because of his carelessness, calling many times Solomon a prophet and invoking the "prophecies" of Proverbs. (26) Therefore, just as he says in these [remarks]:

For this reason, the most holy prophet Solomon said, "Receive instructions in wise dealing,"[81] and again, "words of the wise and their riddles,"[82]

he calls the proverb a prophecy, and again:

For this reason, this most wise prophet seems to me also to have uttered the first words of the prophecy in the form of a proverb.[83]

---

76. Marcellus, *fr.* 58 (30 K./H.) (52,1–3 V.).

77. Jn 11.25; 14.6; 1 Jn 1.1–2; 5.20.

78. Jn 14.6.

79. Jn 9.4; this passage comes from a small middle section of Marcellus, *fr.* 3 (43 K./H.) (6,1–3 V.).

80. Small middle section of Marcellus, *fr.* 4 (1 K./H.) (8,5–6 V.), taken from Gal 4.25–26.

81. Prv 1.3.

82. Prv 1.6; Marcellus, *fr.* 24 (123 K./H.) (28,17–18 V.).

83. Marcellus, *fr.* 25 (124 K./H.) (28,19–20 V.).

(27) And a second and third time and many times, as I said, he does this, being ignorant that "there are varieties of gifts"[84] but still "the same Spirit" and to one "is given the utterance of wisdom" according to the Apostle, "to another utterance of knowledge according to the same Spirit, to another faith by the same Spirit, to another prophecy."[85] (28) For this reason Solomon has been attested to have received gifts of wisdom, "for [the] Lord gave to Solomon wisdom," as Scripture says, "and he was made wise beyond all men."[86] But neither having acquired the prophetic life nor the distinctive mark of prophecy, which is known from [the statement] "Thus says the Lord" and similar [statements], (29) he makes his declarations through his own words. But [that] fellow [Marcellus], having paid no attention to any of these things, granting, as it were, some gift to the man, calls him [Solomon] a prophet, not having understood that the prophets "went around in skins of sheep and goats, in want, afflicted, mistreated."[87] And he says that the proverbs are his prophecy [even if] the divine Scripture nowhere teaches [this], although he [Solomon], the very wisest man, together with [the] Holy Spirit, gave to this book [the] name Proverbs, to another Ecclesiastes, and to the third Song (30) of Songs, applying these titles not on the basis of a godless or human calculation.

But he also tries to interpret the very divinely inspired Scripture of him [Solomon] by means of Greek models, having paid no heed to Paul the Apostle when he said, "we did not receive the spirit of the world but the Spirit that comes from God, so that we might see the things that were given by God to us; and we do not speak these things in learned words taught of human wisdom, but in learned [words] taught of [the] Holy Spirit, teaching spiritual things to the spiritual. But the psychic man does not receive the things of the Spirit of God. For [they] are folly to him, and he cannot know that they are judged spiritual-

84. 1 Cor 12.4.
85. 1 Cor 12.8–10.
86. LXX 3 Kgs 5.9–10 (RSV 1 Kgs 4.29–30).
87. Heb 11.37.

ly."[88] But having been ignorant even of these things, the noble man tries to place before us the meaning of the holy Proverbs on the basis of Greek writings, writing in this way in these very words:

Chapter 3

(1) For it is not out of place, I think, at this time to remind you in the present discussion of a few of the non-Christian proverbs. "Either he is dead or he is teaching letters." One would suppose on the basis of its wording that this proverb was said against those who teach letters, since another one of them also said, "You taught letters; I went to school." But those who wrote the commentaries alleged that this was not the case. Rather, they say, when the Sicilians conquered the Athenians in battle, they spared only those who claimed to be educated, leading them as teachers to [their] children, but killed all the rest. And when some of those who had fled and returned home were asked by the Athenians about some of their relatives, they allege that they said, "Either he is dead or he is teaching letters."

(2) But what about [the proverb] "A goat to the knife"? Someone might suppose—if I may put down what has been said about it before—that the proverb was said because of the fact that the goat that is about to be sacrificed looks up at the knife. But the ancients, you can be sure, did not say this. For the expression would not have been a proverb if indeed this were so (for it was logical to think this if you take the saying literally). But they allege that this was said with regard to those who bring evil on themselves. For [they say] Medea, in Corinth, after she had killed her children, hid the knife on the spot. But when the Corinthians, in obedience to an oracle that had been given to them, were sacrificing a black goat and did not have a knife, the goat, digging with its hoof, uncovered Medea's knife and was sacrificed with it.

(3) But "What does [the saying] 'Enough of the oak!' mean?" someone says. For it is impossible to understand the proverb at first glance. The ancients, as they said, ate acorns

88. 1 Cor 2.12–14.

before the cultivation of grain, [but] when, as they thought, this type of nourishment was later discovered, taking note of it and rejoicing in the change, they said, "Enough of the oak!" And this, they said, was [the meaning of] the proverb.[89]

(4) Again, another proverb was articulated by most of the wise men among them in many and various books. It is necessary to mention at present what those who have chosen to interpret proverbs have written about it, but[90] so that we might refute Asterius, who also knows from his non-Christian studies exactly what the point of the proverb is, though at present he pretends to be ignorant so that he might seem to lend persuasiveness to his own viewpoint through the use of a proverbial statement. [The proverb] is "the skill of a Glaukos." The non-Christian wise men who mentioned this proverb (5) explained it variously. For a certain one of them said that Glaukos was a man who had become knowledgeable in a certain skill, which was the most wondrous of many, but which perished at sea along with that man, since no one has heard of it since. But another, having testified that Glaukos had an excellent knowledge of music, says that four bronze disks, which were made by him, achieved a concordance of sounds as a result of a certain harmony in the striking. And so on this basis the proverb was articulated. (6) Yet another one says that of [the] votive offerings of Alyattes, a mixing bowl with a wondrous stand was offered, something made by Glaukos of Chios. And another [says that] Glaukos himself dedicated at Delphi a bronze tripod, which he crafted from its materials in such a way that when struck forcefully, the feet on which it rested and the upper casing and the garland on the basin and the rods extended through the middle resonated with the sound of a lyre. And again another says that the proverb was articulated with regard to a certain Glaukos who believed that he had made something even greater.

89. Cf. Theophrastus, *On Piety, apud* Porphyry, *Abst.,* 2.5.6.

90. The editor Wendland and following him Klostermann/Hansen have thought there was a lacuna in the text. As one can see from the manuscript corrections of V^c and V^*, there must, indeed, have been a corruption. Yet the text makes sense without assuming a lacuna: Marcellus indicates that he, as Asterius has done before him, is using an interpreter, not to support Asterius's interpretation, however, but to refute him.

(7) You see how the difficulty of the proverb is also demonstrated through this, through [the fact that] those who wished to explain this proverb do not agree on the same interpretation. Thus the point of the proverb seems to be something difficult to find even among the non-Christians. For this reason also a certain one of the wise men among them, having collected the proverbs spoken by many men and in different ways, has written six books on them, two (8) in meter, four in prose. Non-Christians called these "proverbs" for no other reason, it seems to me, than because when they read the proverbs of the most wise Solomon and came to know through them that there is nothing to learn clearly at first glance from their wording, they, too, desiring to emulate the prophetic writing, wrote in the same way as he [Solomon]. Then, since they could think of no other name more suitable than that, they also named these proverbs.[91]

(9) Through these sorts of comparisons, Marcellus attempts to teach the Church of God [how] to understand the divinely inspired Scriptures. But I presented this whole long and verbose digression because I wanted to show the folly of the massive and importunate ambition with which the man has operated, having made a show of the writings of the Greeks, while (10) ignoring the holy [Scriptures]. For he would never have fallen into such great folly if he had remembered the apostolic commands, through which he [the Apostle] exhorts [us] to use "the gifts given by God to us," to speak "not in words taught by human wisdom, but taught by [the] Spirit, (11) teaching spiritual things to the spiritual,"[92] [and] had not failed to understand in what sense [this statement] was made: "the psychic man does not receive the things of the Spirit of God. For [they] are folly to him, and he cannot know that they are judged spiritually."[93] But having been ignorant of these things, he supposed that the wise men of Greece acquired knowledge of the wisdom granted by God to Solomon, and having this knowledge, emulated (12) the prophetic writing, as he himself says. And how were

91. Marcellus, *fr.* 23 (125 K./H.) (24,1–28,16 V.).
92. 1 Cor 2.12–14.
93. Ibid.

the psychic men able to know and emulate divine things and
yet did not know that "spiritual things" are judged "by the spiritual," given that the holy Apostle declared that a psychic man
cannot receive "the things of the Spirit of God"? But although
the same man said that the psychic man cannot know spiritual
things "because they are judged spiritually," the noble fellow
[Marcellus], contradicting the Apostle, claims that the (13) authors of Greek proverbs had written in the same way as Solomon [wrote]. And, indeed, he says this, using these very words:

> When they read the proverbs of the most wise Solomon and
> came to know through them that there is nothing to learn
> clearly at first glance from their wording, they, too, desiring
> to emulate the prophetic writing, wrote in the same way as he
> [Solomon].[94]

And see again in another way from the[se] very comparisons
how greatly he deviated from the truth, having said that the
Greeks have written in the same way as Solomon. (14) For on
the one hand, Solomon, impelled by God-given wisdom, dedicated all of his writing to the benefit and salvation of souls by
means of the word of godly piety; but for the sake of the exercise of the reader's understanding, he made use of obscure
metaphors, turns of phrase, and expressions conveyed through
riddles. And there is testimony of this in the beginning of the
book, [where it says], "Having listened to these, a wise man
will be wiser, and the thoughtful man will acquire guidance,
and he will reflect on a parable (15) of dark words, both the
words and riddles of wise men," and again, "to receive turns of
phrase."[95] And that this is also the case, it is easy to learn from
the things contained in the book, which otherwise cannot be
known, unless we pass from the surface meaning to the deeper
meaning underneath it. Such is the statement "By the leech,
three daughters were loved with love, and the same three did
not plaster it up. And the (16) fourth was not content to say
what was sufficient,"[96] and "Wisdom built her house, and set up

94. Marcellus, *fr.* 23 (125 K./H.) (28,11–14 V.).
95. Prv 1.5–6; 1.3.
96. Prv 30.15.

seven pillars; she has slaughtered her beasts and has mixed her wine in a mixing bowl,"[97] and all the other statements similar to these, which are impossible to understand in another way, either at first reading or from some story, but solely according to the metaphorical and analogical sense of the wording.

The proverbs that were exhibited among the Greeks, however, (17) received their beginnings from certain stories. For the proverb "Either he is dead or he is teaching letters" was said, he says, because of this story; and because of yet another deed of this sort that happened, the statement "A goat to the sword" was said. And the proverb "Enough of the oak!" likewise [was said], because of the time when acorn-eaters ceased [consuming] this sort of food. But even if a certain Glaukos, having become knowledgeable in some skill, was described in different ways by those afterward who disagreed about these things in [their] writing about him, what does this have to do with the divinely inspired Proverbs? Unlike the Greek proverbs, these [proverbs] do not admit solution on the basis of a certain story. Consequently, not only in ignorance and without understanding of the divine Scriptures, but also in opposition to the Apostle, Marcellus declared that the wise men of Greece, reading the Proverbs of Solomon, learned [from them] and imitated the prophetic writing and (18) wrote in the same way he did. Since I have said these things for the purpose of demonstrating the fact that the man had not read the divine Scriptures in the appropriate way, the time now also calls for a consideration of his unsound belief about the faith, since he imagines things that are contrary to the Church's teaching and has rejected both it and those who preside over it.

Chapter 4

(1) I will present first the statements through which he attempts to contradict what was written correctly and in accordance with Church teaching, rejecting those who wrote it, and having waged all but total war upon all. First he compos-

97. Prv 9.1–2.

es the refutation against Asterius, then against Eusebius the
(2) great,[98] and then he turns to the man of God, the so truly
thrice-blessed Paulinus, on the one hand a man honored with
the highest office of the Church of Antioch who on the other
served the Church of Tyre in a most distinguished way, and he
shone so brightly in the episcopacy [there] as (3) to claim the
good of the Antiochene church as his own.[99] But this wondrous
author mocks even this man, who had lived blessedly, and died
blessedly, and fell asleep a long time ago and who now sleeps
in peace, and whom nothing troubles any longer. And having
turned from this fellow, he makes war on Origen, whose life
also ended long ago. Next he battles against Narcissus, and per-
secutes the other Eusebius[100] and rejects all of the ecclesiastical
fathers together, content with none whatsoever except (4) himself alone.[101] Therefore he writes, making hostile mention of all
of them by name in this way:

> Well then, I will begin to refute each of those things that were
> written incorrectly from the letter that was written by him [As-
> terius]. He has written that "he believes in the Father, God Al-
> mighty, and in his Son the only-begotten God, our Lord Jesus
> Christ, and in the Holy Spirit."[102] And he says that he "learned
> this way of piety from the divine Scriptures."[103] (5) And when
> he says this, I approve these statements wholeheartedly, for this
> way of piety—namely, to believe in Father, Son, and Holy Spir-
> it—is common to us all. But when, failing to grasp the divine
> meaning, he tells us in a more human sense through a certain
> contrived theory that the Father is Father and the Son (6)
> Son, it is no longer without danger to praise this theory. For
> the consequence of this sort of theory is that the heresy lately

98. Of Nicomedia.

99. As one can see from further below where the same term μεταποιέω appears (19,10 K./H.), Paulinus must have demanded the see of Antioch as his
own—and apparently was criticized for this by Marcellus.

100. Of Caesarea.

101. This gives us an insight into the structure of Marcellus's one book, the
restoration of which has been attempted by Klaus Seibt, followed (with slight
alteration) by Markus Vinzent in his critical edition of Marcellus's fragments.

102. Asterius, *fr.* 9 (86,1–3 V.).

103. Asterius, *fr.* 9 (86,4–5 V.).

invented by these men is aggravated, which clearly is easy to show, I think, from his remarks. For he said that "it is necessary to think that the Father is truly Father and that the Son is truly Son and likewise [regarding] the Holy Spirit."[104]

(7) Marcellus said these things against Asterius, not content with the claim that "it is necessary" to confess "that the Father is truly Father and the Son is truly Son and likewise [regarding] the Holy Spirit." For this reason, he immediately attempts to refute the statement concerning these [points] through more extensive remarks. For he wishes to confess that the Christ is a mere [word] resembling even the human word, but not a truly living and subsisting Son. (8) And though he said that this heresy [was] invented very recently, it must be shown as he continues that he has in mind Origen, who lived long ago, as one who believes the same things as those who are now being slandered by him. But I have also read a great many ecclesiastical treatises of men more ancient than Origen, and various letters of both bishops and synods written long ago, through which one and the same (9) outline of the faith is revealed. Therefore, not rightly has he [Marcellus] rejected it, saying that this heresy has been invented just recently by those who are being slandered. A little after these things, he goes on and addresses in hostile fashion not only Asterius, but also the great Eusebius, for the episcopacy of whom many illustrious provinces and cities have contended, in this way:

I will remind you of the things that [Asterius] himself wrote when he recommended the evil writings of Eusebius, so that you might know that he clearly departs from the (10) former profession. For he has written as follows in these very words: "For it is the chief aim of the letter to refer the generation of the Son to the will of the Father and not to represent begetting as involving suffering on the part of 'the' God. This very idea the wisest of the Fathers revealed in their own treatises, guarding against the impiety of the heretics, who falsely claimed that 'the' God's generation [of the Son] was in some way corporeal

104. Asterius, *fr.* 60 (120 V.); see Eusebius of Nicomedia, *ep. ad Paulin. Tyr.* (= Urk. 8; III 15–17 Op.); Marcellus, *fr.* 1 (65 K./H.) (2,3–4,9 V.).

and subject to suffering, which they declared were the emana-tions."[105]

(11) And in addition to these statements, he next composes an expanded refutation, after which he begins again, saying:

Therefore Asterius, wishing to defend Eusebius (who wrote so badly), himself became his own accuser, having made mention of both "the nature of the Father and the nature of the Begot-ten."[106] For it would have been much better to have left lying unexamined "the depth of the thought of Eusebius that lay in a short statement,"[107] as he himself wrote, than, having subjected it to a lengthy examination, to have brought the wickedness of the letter into the light.[108]

(12) After other remarks, he adds:

But now let us examine one statement from the writings of Asterius. For this man said, "The one is the Father who begot from himself the only-begotten Word[109] and the firstborn of all creation …"[110] Having linked the two [titles], he wrote "only-begotten" and "firstborn," although there is a great difference between these names, (13) as is easy to understand even by those who are very uneducated. For it is clear that the only-begotten, if he were really only-begotten, can no longer be firstborn, and if the firstborn were [really] firstborn, he cannot be only-begotten.[111]

And in these remarks, he censures Asterius in vain, for the statements come not from him but from the divine Scripture that [speaks of] the Son of God as at one time an only-begotten Son and at another as firstborn of all creation. (14) And again he adds to these remarks, saying:

---

105. Asterius, *fr.* 5 (84 V.); Marcellus, *fr.* 2 (34 K./H.) (4,10–17 V.).
106. Asterius, *fr.* 8 (86 V.).
107. Asterius, *fr.* 6 (84 V.).
108. Marcellus, *fr.* 9 (35 K./H.) (12,3–8 V.).
109. Jn 1.18.
110. Col 1.15; first part of Asterius, *fr.* 10 (86,1–2 V.); see also Marcellus, *fr.* 113 (96 K./H.) (106,2–14 V.).
111. Marcellus, *fr.* 10 (3 K./H.) (12,9–16 V.).

But having departed from the true knowledge, he revealed
to us even now his contrived theory. For not having the will
to construct it for himself "out of the divine Scriptures,"[112]
he goes back to those whom he considers to be "the wisest
fathers," alleging [that] "this very idea the wisest of Fathers
(15) revealed in their own treatises."[113] Asterius says that these
fathers of his have expressed their opinion and have written
their dogma concerning God on the basis of their own conviction. For the (16) word "dogma" implies human will and
judgment. And that this is so, the dogmatic skill of doctors
gives sufficient testimony to us, as well as the so-called dogmas
of the philosophers. And that the decisions of the Senate are
still even now called the dogmas of the Senate, no one, I think,
is ignorant.[114]

But Marcellus was also compelled to say these things, having
forgotten the apostolic statement about the Savior: "he abol-
ished the law with its commandments and ordinances [*lit.*, dog-
mas]."[115] But he also finds fault with the necessity of following
the fathers, although the divine Scripture says, "Ask your father, (17) and he will inform you; your elders, and they will tell
you,"[116] and, "Do not remove the ancient landmark that your an-
cestors set up."[117] Still angry because he [Asterius] called Paulinus blessed, mentioning him together with Eusebius again with
hostility, he writes in this way:

> For [Asterius], having wished to defend Eusebius, who wrote
> such a bad letter, said that "first he [Eusebius] composed the
> letter, not expounding the dogma in the manner of a teacher,
> for it was written neither to the Church nor to the unlearned
> but to the blessed Paulinus."[118] He said the latter was blessed

112. Excerpt from Asterius, *fr.* 9 (86,4–5 V.); see also Marcellus, *fr.* 1 (65
K./H.) (2,6–7 V.).

113. Excerpt from Asterius, *fr.* 5 (84,2–3 V.); see also Marcellus, *fr.* 2 (34
K./H.) (4,14–15 V.) and 18 (87 K./H.) (18,9 V.); Origen, *de princ. I praef.*

114. Marcellus, *fr.* 17 (86 K./H.) (16,10–18,3 V.).

115. Eph 2.15.

116. Dt 32.7.

117. Prv 22.28.

118. Asterius, *fr.* 7 (84 V.).

for this reason—that he held the same opinion as Asterius. Therefore, seeing that we have learned who the "wisest fathers"[119] of Asterius were, I think it follows that we say who also became the teacher of Paulinus and others. (18) For it should be entirely clear to us from the letter of Paulinus who his teacher was.[120]

And after offering some intervening remarks, he again repeats the same slander [against Paulinus], that he misinterpreted Origen, saying in this way:

Not remembering the evangelical teaching, Paulinus wrote these things, confessing that "some are moved in this way by themselves, while others (19) were led in this way by the interpretations of the aforementioned men."[121] Then finally, adding it as if it were the crowning flourish of the demonstration, he appended to his own letter [a passage] from the sayings of Origen, as if he [Origen] could be more convincing than the evangelists and the apostles. And the words are these: "It is time now to take up again the subject of the Father, the Son, and the Holy Spirit, and to explain a few of the matters that were previously put to the side. Regarding the Father, since he is inseparable and indivisible, he becomes (20) Father of a Son, not having cast him forth, as some men think. For if the Son is something cast forth by the Father and an offspring from him, such as the offspring of living beings are, it is necessary that he who cast forth and he who has been cast forth be a body."[122]

(21) Then immediately after the presentation of the sayings of Origen, he continues, saying:

Origen wrote these things because he did not want to learn from the holy prophets and apostles about the eternity of the

119. Excerpt from Asterius, *fr.* 5 (84,3 V.); see also Marcellus, *fr.* 2 (34 K./H.) (4,14–15 V.) and 18 (87 K./H.) (18,9 V.); Origen, *de princ. I praef.*

120. Marcellus, *fr.* 18 (87 K./H.) (18,4–12 V.).

121. Paulinus of Tyre, *ep.* (= Urk. 9; III 17–18 Op.).

122. Origen, *de princ.* 4.1.28. See on this fragment M. Vinzent, "Origenes als *Postscriptum.* Paulinus von Tyrus und die origenistische *Diadoche*," in *Origeniana Septima. Origenes in den Auseinandersetzungen des 4. Jahrhunderts,* ed. W. A. Bienert and U. Kühneweg, BETL 137 (Leuven: University Press, 1999), 149–57; Marcellus, *fr.* 19 (37 K./H.) (18,13–20,4 V.).

Word. But having made more of his own efforts, he dared to describe in vain a second hypostasis of the Word.[123]

But he [Marcellus] contradicts even these things that were said correctly by Origen concerning the fact that one must not suppose that the begetting of the divinity of the Son is corporeal and subject to suffering, especially because he [Origen] has granted a hypostasis to the Son. And he carries on, speaking ill of Origen again and contradicting in these remarks what was written correctly by him:

> It is clear that Origen relied upon his own opinions when he wrote these sorts of things, from the fact that he frequently even contradicts his own views. Therefore, in another passage, he says certain things regarding God, which it is fitting to recall. (22) He writes as follows: "For God did not begin to be a Father, as if he were prevented [before], as men who have become fathers were [prevented] by not being able to be fathers before. For if God is always perfect, and he always has the power to be a Father, and if it is good for him to be Father of such a Son, why does he delay and deprive himself of the good, and, so to speak, of that [power] by which he is able to be a father? And indeed the same thing must also be said about the Holy Spirit."[124] (23) Therefore, if Origen also wrote this, how did the blessed (according to him [Asterius]) Paulinus think it was dangerous to conceal this passage, but that he should use contradictory passages for the support of his own opinions, for which we might say Origen himself could not take responsibility?[125]

In these remarks, Marcellus lied when he said that Origen said contradictory things, not having been able to understand that through the previous statement he showed the incorporeality and impassivity of the Father, while through the second statement he showed that the Son has been begotten not in time but before all ages. (24) But again after other remarks about Origen the same fellow writes these things:

123. Marcellus, *fr.* 20 (38 K./H.) (20,5–8 V.).

124. Origen, *comm. in Gen.* 1.1, in Pamphilus, *apol.* 3 (PG 12: 46C; 17: 561A).

125. Marcellus, *fr.* 21 (39 K./H.) (20,9–22,6 V.).

And yet, if it is necessary to speak the truth concerning Origen, it is fitting to say this, that having just abandoned the teachings of philosophy, and having decided to occupy himself with the divine words before [he had gained] an accurate comprehension of the Scriptures, because of a great ambition resulting from his non-Christian education, he began to write sooner than was appropriate. He was led astray by the arguments of philosophy, and composed certain things incorrectly because of them. And this is clear: for it was while still under the influence of the dogmas of Plato (25) and the distinction between the first principles in his thought, that he wrote the book *On First Principles* and gave this title to the treatise. But [this is] the strongest proof that he drew the beginning of his remarks and the title of the book from no other source than from the statements made by Plato. For in the beginning he wrote as follows: (26) "Those who have believed and who have been convinced";[126] you will find this remark was made in this way in the *Gorgias* of Plato.[127]

Not even if he had quoted [Plato], would it have brought disgrace to Origen because when he says "those who have believed and who have been convinced," he also adds immediately afterward: "'grace and truth have come through Jesus Christ'[128] and Christ is the truth according to what was said by him, 'I am the truth.'"[129] For what sort of commonality could there ever be between these things (27) and Plato? No book of Plato *On First Principles* is remembered, nor did Origen think in the same way about first principles as Plato did, since he [Origen] knew that the first principle alone is ingenerate and without source and beyond the universe, and that this is Father of one only-begotten Son, through whom all things came into existence. And the fellow who lied about Origen even in these remarks (28) adds [more] after other statements, saying:

For although Asterius said, "the Word was generated before the ages,"[130] the passage itself proves that he is lying; so that

126. Origen, *de princ. I praef.*
127. See Plato, *Gorg.* 454d–e; Marcellus, *fr.* 22 (88 K./H.) (22,7–19 V.).
128. Jn 1.17.
129. Jn 14.6.
130. Asterius, *fr.* 17 (90 V.).

he is not only in error regarding the fact[s], but also regarding the letter. For if Proverbs says, "Before the age, he founded me,"[131] how did he [Asterius] say, "he was generated before the ages"?[132] For it is one thing for him [Christ] to have been founded before the age, and another "to have been generated before the ages."[133]

(29) Having said these things and added other remarks for the purpose of overthrowing the claim that the Son was generated before the ages, he adds in these very words:

I ask those who read the holy [Scriptures],[134] who have truly received, as it were, seeds and principles of this interpretation, to add more complete demonstrations to those that have been said, so as to refute still more the convictions of those who are distorting the faith. For in truth they have "left behind" the God who begot them, and "dug for themselves broken cisterns."[135]

(30) Having launched these sorts of calumnies, he also through them immediately afterward tries to show that the Son is not the image of God, saying in this way:

It follows, I think, to speak briefly also about the image. For [Asterius] has written: "The one who was begotten from him is another, 'who is the image of the invisible God.'"[136] Asterius calls to mind "the image of the invisible God"[137] for this reason, so that he might teach that "God is as different from the Word as even a man seems to differ from his own image."[138]

(31) And after some intervening discussion, he continues:

Therefore, it is absolutely clear that before the assumption of our body the Word in and of himself was not "image of the

---

131. Prv 8.23.

132. See Asterius, *fr.* 17 (90 V.).

133. Asterius, *fr.* 17 (90 V.); Marcellus, *fr.* 36 (18 K./H.) (34,11–16 V.).

134. See Irenaeus, *haer. I praef.* (SC 264, 26).

135. Jer 2.13; Marcellus, *fr.* 46 (89 K./H.) (40,9–14 V.).

136. Col 1.15; Asterius, *fr.* 11 (88 V.); see also *fr.* 13 (88 V.).

137. Excerpt from Asterius, *fr.* 11 and 13 (88 V.).

138. See Asterius, *fr.* 52–55; 75 (116–118,14 V.); Marcellus, *fr.* 51 (90 K./H.) (46,1–5 V.).

invisible God."[139] For it is natural for the image to be seen, so that through the image that which has hitherto been invisible might be seen.[140]

And he adds:

How then has Asterius written that the Word of God is an "image of the invisible God"?[141] For images reveal those things of which they are the images even when they are absent, so that even he who is absent (32) seems to appear through them. If it is the case that while God is invisible the Word also is invisible, how can the Word be in and of himself an "image of the invisible God,"[142] seeing as he, too, is invisible?[143]

And proceeding on, he again casts aspersions, saying in this way:

How do those men "full of deceit and villainy,"[144] to speak as the Apostle does, refer the passage to what they think is [Christ's] first creation,[145] even though David clearly said these things about his generation according to the flesh?[146]

(33) And having offered a [more] extensive statement in the intervening material, he carries on:

Therefore, what will [Asterius] say in response to these points? For I do not think that he has anything to say about this, nor do I think he would confess clearly and undisguisedly even

139. See Col 1.15; Asterius, *fr.* 11 (88 V.); see also *fr.* 13 (88 V.).
140. Asterius, *fr.* 13 (89 V.); Marcellus insists that only the incarnate Word can be the image of God, because he is visible, and that this is the point of images, to make the invisible visible. His attack on Asterius presupposes, however, that Asterius himself had taught that images make the invisible visible, and yet that he applied this making of the Word visible to the pre-incarnate generation of the Word. Marcellus, *fr.* 53 (92 K./H.) (46,10–48,3 V.).
141. Excerpt from Asterius, *fr.* 11 and 13 (88 V.).
142. Ibid.
143. Marcellus, *fr.* 54 (93 K./H.) (48,4–9 V.), while the last phrase is missing; see Eusebius of Caesarea, *CM* 2.3 (48,33–49,5 V.), where the full fragment is given.
144. Acts 13.10.
145. See Asterius, *fr.* 13–14; 23; 25; 30; 35 (90; 94; 96; 100 V.).
146. Marcellus, *fr.* 60 (29 K./H.) (52,13–15 V.).

to others what he himself hides in his own mind, as one can clearly learn from what he has written. For he says that "the one is the Father who begot from himself the only-begotten Word and firstborn of all creation, the one [who begot] one; the perfect a perfect, the King a King, the Lord a Lord, the God a God, an unchanged[147] image of [his] being[148] and will and glory and power …"[149] These statements clearly prove his (34) defective belief about the divinity. For how can "the Lord, who is begotten, and God,"[150] as he said before, be an image of God? For an image of God is one thing, and God another. And so if he is an image, he is not Lord and God, but an image of [the] Lord and God. But if he is really Lord and God, the Lord and God can no longer be an image of [the] Lord and God.[151]

(35) And he said these things in complete ignorance, not having understood that even the Son can at one time be said [to be] living image of his own Father, since he is like the Father as much as possible. Indeed, the Scripture also teaches this, which says, "Adam lived two hundred and thirty years, and he begot according to his likeness and according to his image, (36) and he gave him the name Seth."[152] And concerning the divinity of the Son, the Apostle teaches, saying, "who, though he was in the form of God, did not regard equality with God as something to be grasped at, but emptied himself,"[153] and again, "who is the radiance of [God's] glory and [the] exact imprint of [his] hypostasis."[154] And in other passages, it has been said, "[He is] [the] radiance of eternal light, [the] spotless mirror of the activity of God, and [the] image (37) of his goodness."[155] Again, the Apostle in saying, "seeing that you have stripped off

147. See introduction, p. 22 n. 82.

148. οὐσίας.

149. Asterius, *fr.* 10 (86 V.); already quoted in Marcellus, *fr.* 10 (3 K./H.) (12,10–12 V.).

150. See Asterius, *fr.* 11 (88 V.) and Marcellus, *fr.* 51–52 (90–91 K./H.) (46,1–9 V.).

151. Marcellus, *fr.* 113 (96 K./H.) (106,2–14 V.).

152. Gn 5.3.

153. Phil 2.6–7.

154. Heb 1.3.

155. Wis 7.26.

the old self with its practices, and have clothed yourselves with the new self, which is being renewed in knowledge according to the image of its creator,"[156] clearly (38) does not teach that the image of God is said to be the flesh. But having passed on [from that topic], again Marcellus writes against the bishops as follows:

> For, you see, Asterius's doctrine does not cause us so much pain,[157] if he was compelled to write such things, but the fact that even some of those who seem to hold positions of leadership in the Church, having forgotten the apostolic tradition, and having preferred non-Christian [doctrines] to those divine, dared to teach and write things of this nature, which are no less erroneous than those mentioned before.[158]

(39) And after other remarks, he adds:

> For having read the letter of Narcissus, who presides at Neronias, which he has written to a certain Chrestos, Euphronius, and Eusebius, as to how "Ossius the bishop asked him if he would also say in this way, as Eusebius of Palestine does, that there are two beings,"[159] I learned from his writings that he answered that "he believed that there were three beings."[160]

Having said these things, he passes from Narcissus to Eusebius [of Caesarea], reproaching him (40) because he confesses the Word of "the" God to be God.[161] So he writes these things also about him:

> One may clearly and easily learn from those very remarks that were written by him [Eusebius of Caesarea] into what great

156. Col 3.9–10.

157. See Asterius, *fr.* 10–11 (86–88 V.).

158. Marcellus, *fr.* 115 (98 K./H.) (108,6–10 V.).

159. οὐσίας; first part of the fragment of the epistle by Narcissus of Neronias to Chrestus, Euphronius, and Eusebius (= Urk. 19; III 41 Op.).

160. οὐσίας; Marcellus, *fr.* 116 (81 K./H.) (108,11–15 V.). Second part of the fragment of the epistle by Narcissus of Neronias to Chrestus, Euphronius, and Eusebius (= Urk. 19; III 41 Op.).

161. Although this is not a fragment of Marcellus, it still is a report about Marcellus's text that goes beyond the quotation (indicated by the "also" in the next sentence).

blasphemy he fell, having dared to separate the Word from
"the" God and to call the Word another God, who is separated
from the Father in being[162] and power. (41) For he has written
as follows in these very words: "Of course, the image[163] and the
one of whom he is the image are not to be thought of as one
and the same thing, but as two beings,[164] two things,[165] and two
powers, corresponding to the number of their names."[166]

And he adds these remarks in evil slander, saying:

Well then, how have these men, following the same evil path
of those who are not Christian, not chosen both to teach and
write the same things [as they did], since Eusebius has spoken
like both Valentinus and Hermes, and Narcissus like both
Marcion and Plato?[167]

(42) Then, immediately afterward, he strings together a long
and rambling disquisition, alleging that "... he had learned by
hearsay that Eusebius preached something one time when he
was in Laodicea."[168] About such things, of which he had no
knowledge, having learned them from hearsay, he writes in addition, saying:

On the contrary, it was necessary to cry with tears and mourn-
ing to the Lord: "We have sinned, we have been impious, we
have broken the law,"[169] and we have done what is evil in your
sight, and now repenting, (43) we ask to obtain your lovingkindness. It was fitting and appropriate to say these things to
him because of the "immeasurable goodness and loving-

162. οὐσίᾳ.
163. See, for example, Eusebius of Caesarea, *dem. ev.* 4.2.2. and 5.2.21.
164. οὐσίαι.
165. See Origen, *c. Cels.* 8.12.
166. Marcellus, *fr.* 117 (82 K./H.) (110,1–7 V.). See the fourth part of Eusebius of Caesarea, *ep. ad Euphr. Bal.* (= Urk. 3,4; III 5,11–6,2 Opitz), first reported, then quoted.
167. See (Marcellus?), *de sancta eccl.* 9. The Marcellan authorship is uncer-
tain; see Klaus Seibt, "Marcell von Ancyra," *Theologische Realenzyklopädie* 22
(1992): 83–89, 85; Marcellus, *fr.* 118 (85 K./H.) (110,8–11 V.).
168. First part of Marcellus, *fr.* 119 (99 K./H.) (110,12–13 V.). This first part
had not been recognized as Marcellus's fragment (see V. *ad loc.*).
169. Dn 9.15.

kindness of God."[170] And yet it followed that the God who governs with lovingkindness and justice responded by saying: "If an enemy taunted me, I would bear it; if he who hates me dealt insolently with me, I would hide from him. But you, my equal, my guide, my familiar friend, we used to hold secret converse together; (44) within God's house we walked in fellowship."[171] For that he attends to us who are his servants we know from his statement, for he said, "Behold, I will be with you all the days of your life, even to the end of the age."[172] Thus it would be entirely appropriate, I think, to add also to the foregoing the following words: "Let death come upon them, let them go down to Hades alive, because wickedness is in their hearts."[173] For Scripture says that those who are dead in the ignorance of impiety are swallowed up by Hades. For they are really dead, even though they seem to live.[174]

(45) And again, immediately following these remarks, he censures Eusebius "... for having preached in the church one time when he was passing through Ancyra, the very thing," he says, "he has learned through hearsay."[175] Angry at this, he writes such things:

> But the Apostle writes these sorts of things concerning the faith of the Galatians. But Eusebius, confounding the apostolic intention (on account of which the Apostle said this for the aforementioned reason, "My children, with whom I am in tra-

170. Ti 3.4.
171. Ps 54.12–15 (RSV 55.12–14).
172. Mt 28.20.
173. Ps 54.16 (RSV 55.16).
174. Second part of Marcellus, *fr.* 119 (99 K./H.) (110,13–112,15 V.).
175. Although this is not a literal quotation, it needs to be read together with the previously quoted fragment of Marcellus that mentions Eusebius in Laodicea. If Hans-Georg Opitz is correct, the fragments belong to the time immediately preceding Nicaea. In his unpublished introduction to the *Urkunden zum Arianischen Streit* I, Opitz writes, "The aggressive narration of Marcellus and the hardly restrained anger of Eusebius leave the historical events in the dark. But perhaps one can interpret the sayings of the two by concluding that Eusebius stuck to his position that he held in Antioch and even made it public in a homily at the see of the third person who had been condemned there, Theodotus of Laodicea" (trans. Vinzent).

vail until Christ be formed in you!"),[176] attacked the Galatians for "not having the right belief about God." (46) For he was truly in travail with a certain sharp and bitter labor, because he knew that the Galatians did not think about piety as he did, nor did they speak of "two beings,[177] things, powers, and Gods."[178]

Pay heed to these remarks, how he rails bitterly at him who said no more, as he himself writes, than the apostolic word. And now he confesses that Eusebius "speaks of two gods," on the grounds that he calls the Son of "the" God "God" together with the Father. Proceeding on in the remarks immediately following, as if he had forgotten those ideas he had just criticized, he attempts to slander the same [Eusebius] for having said that Christ is a mere man. (47) Next he adds to the previous remarks a certain great and voluminous load of nonsense, stringing together for himself both truths and falsehoods,[179] all but just like those who say, "Our lips are our own; who is Lord of us?"[180] (48) through which he shows, just as I said at the beginning of this treatise, that he attacked the writing out of overwhelming enmity and hatred of his brothers.[181]

And having turned from these matters, he once again represents Asterius as the protagonist in a tragedy, spinning out a long-winded statement about him, too, how he went about traveling, and where and when and to whom he went. But having dropped him, he again turns to the man of God Paulinus, writing these things in these very words:

176. Gal 4.19.

177. οὐσίαι.

178. Marcellus, *fr.* 120 (83 K./H.) (112,16–23 V.). See notes to Marcellus, *fr.* 119; above, note 168; see Asterius, *fr.* 54–55 (118 V.), Paulin. in Marcellus, *fr.* 121 and 122; Paulin., *ep.* (= Urk. 9,2–4; III 18,4–8 Op.).

179. Literally, "things that are and things that are not."

180. Ps 11.5 (RSV 12.4).

181. This reveals that from the beginning, Eusebius wrote this book not only because fellow bishops had asked him to write it, but also because he saw himself being attacked by Marcellus, one of his "brotherly" co-bishops.

(49) Convinced by these remarks, even Paulinus, the father
of this man [Asterius], does not hesitate to speak and to write
these things, saying at one time that "Christ is a second God"
and that "he [this one] has become a more human God," and
at another time asserting that "he is a creature." That this is
so, [I cite as evidence the fact that] he even once said in front
of us, when he was passing through Ancyra, that "Christ is a
creature."[182]

(50) And again, making the whole story up, he [Marcellus]
says that he refuted Paulinus. Then he slanders the blessed
man for having said that "there are many gods," and having left
Paulinus behind, he again rattles on about Eusebius, claiming:

> Eusebius of Caesarea has also written in this vein and himself
> holds the same opinion about gods as Paulinus and those who
> are not Christian. (51) For he has written not that there is
> one only God, but that "the only true God is one."[183] Having
> learned this, then, from this source, Paulinus, too, father of
> Asterius, thought "there are newer gods."[184]

And in these remarks, he blames those men as if they were
introducing belief in [multiple] gods, while he himself denies
the divinity of the Son. And having presented the statement of
Eusebius, he does not understand that the statement teaching
that the Father is [the] only (52) true God was not his, but our
Savior's, who said, "so that they may know you, the only true
God."[185] And after other remarks he continues, saying,

> How will they be able to prove to us from someplace out of
> the divine Scriptures that there is "one unbegotten and one
> begotten" in the way they themselves have believed "he has

182. First part of Marcellus, *fr.* 121 (40 K./H.) (114,1–5 V.), reporting Pau-
linus of Tyre (= second part of Urk. 9,2f.; III 18,4–7 Op.); see Marcellus, *fr.* 91;
Asterius, *fr.* 54–55 (118 V.); Paulinus of Tyre in Marcellus, *fr.* 122 (84 K./H.) =
Paulinus of Tyre, *ep.* (= Urk. 9,4; III 18,8 Op.).

183. Eusebius of Caesarea, *ep. ad Euphrat. Bal.* (Urk. 3,3; III 5,5–10 Op.).

184. Marcellus, *fr.* 122 (84 K./H.) (114,8–12 V.). Paulinus of Tyre, *ep.* (Urk.
9,4; III 18,8 Op.).

185. Jn 17.3.

been begotten,"[186] given that neither prophets nor evangelists nor apostles have said this?[187]

(53) Thereupon, as if, having drawn up a list of all the contestants in an athletic event, he were simultaneously to start wrestling with them, he turns to Narcissus and says:

> So that if someone should say [this], claiming that there is "a first and a second God," as Narcissus has written in these very words[188] (54) (though neither does he who says, "Let us make man in our image and likeness," agree),[189] "because he [the Son] and his Father are two," we have heard this partly from the testimony of the Lord and from the holy Scriptures. Well then, if because of this Narcissus were to wish "to distinguish the Word from the Father in power," let him know that the prophet who wrote that God said, "Let us make man according to our image and likeness," also wrote, "God made man."[190]

(55) And having turned from Narcissus to Asterius, he writes these things:

> For Asterius declared that "the Father and Son are one and the same only in this respect, that they agree in all things." For so also he said, "Because of their exact agreement in all [their] words and actions [the Savior] says, 'I and the Father are one.'"[191]

And again he attacks Eusebius, saying:

> For they want the Savior to be a man.[192] This is clear from the fact that Eusebius [of Caesarea] slyly twists the words of the

---

186. Asterius, *fr.* 12 (88 V.); see Asterius, *fr.* 9 (86,4f. V.); Marcellus, *fr.* 1 (65 K./H.) and 17 (86 K./H.).

187. Marcellus, *fr.* 123 (32 K./H.) (114,13–16 V.).

188. Excerpt of Narcissus of Neronias (= second part of Urk. 19; III 41,5f. Op.).

189. Gn 1.26.

190. Gn 1.27; Marcellus, *fr.* 124 (80 K./H.) (116,1–9 V.) (= Urk. 19; III 41,6–10 Op.).

191. Marcellus, *fr.* 125 (72 K./H.) (116,10–13 V.); Jn 10.30; Asterius, *fr.* 39 (102 V.). See also Asterius, *fr.* 38.40–41 (102–104 V.); Marcellus, *fr.* 74 (73 K./H.) (62,5–64,14 V.) and 75 (74 K./H.) (64,15–66,27 V.).

192. See in Marcellus, *fr.* 128 (102 K./H.) (120,1–3 V.).

Apostle (56) to serve his own purposes. For wishing to bring
forth great blasphemy as from a certain long-standing labor,
he "brings forth out of his own treasure evil,"[193] according
to the saying of the Savior.[194] (57) For wishing to show that
the Savior is only a man, as if he were revealing to us a great
ineffable mystery of the Apostle, he thus said, "For this reason,
most clearly even the holy Apostle, handing down [to us] the
ineffable and mystical theology, cries out and has proclaimed,
'There is one God'; then after the one God, he says, '[and] one
mediator between God and man, the man Jesus Christ.'"[195]
(58) Now if he says he is man with regard solely to his economy
in the flesh, then he is *de facto* also confessing that he places
no hope in him. For the prophet Jeremiah said, "Cursed is the
man who trusts in man."[196]

(59) You see how the evil blinds [him]. At any rate, having
himself given testimony to one who confessed that the Son is
God, and having laid to this man's blame that he introduces
[the claim that] the Word of God subsists as God in being[197]
and power, now he slanders the same man [= Eusebius himself]
for saying that Christ is a mere man, obviously lying both in
what he has said and in those remarks that he adds again immediately afterwards about him, saying:

> But the aforementioned man [= Eusebius of Caesarea], having
> given little thought to the holy prophets, said, as if expounding
> "an ineffable and secret theology of the Apostle," "there is one
> God and one mediator between God and men, the man Jesus
> Christ."[198] (60) And he who wrote these things and boasts exces-
> sively about his knowledge of the Scriptures did not consider
> that the most holy Apostle who wrote this has also written,
> "He who, though he was in the form of God, did not regard

193. Mt 12.35.
194. See Eusebius of Caesarea (Urk. 3,5; III 6,3f. Op.) and Marcellus, *fr.* 127
(101 K./H.) (118,11–22 V.).
195. 1 Tm 2.5; quotation from Eusebius of Caesarea (= Urk. 3,5; III 6,5–7
Op.).
196. Jer 17.5; Marcellus, *fr.* 126 (100 K./H.) (116,14–118,10 V.).
197. οὐσίᾳ.
198. 1 Tm 2.5; shortened quotation from Eusebius of Caesarea (cf. Urk. 3,5;
III 6,5–7 Op.).

equality with God as something to be grasped at, but emptied himself, having taken the form of a slave, being born in the likeness of men. And (61) being found in human form ..."[199] You see how (as if he saw beforehand in spirit the evildoing of these men) the holy Apostle thus wrote in another passage "as a man" and "being born in the likeness of men," so that he might put a stop to their great blasphemy.[200]

And after other remarks, he slanders the same [= Eusebius of Caesarea] brutally in this way:

How then can Eusebius, who paid no attention to these passages, wish the Savior to be only (62) a man?[201] For even if he does not dare to say this openly, he is convicted from his own writings of wanting to do so.[202]

And he who said this blamed the same man for proclaiming that the Son is God, writing in this way:

... Into what great blasphemy he fell, having dared to separate the Word from "the" God and to call the Word another God, who is separated from the Father in being[203] and power.[204]

(63) Marcellus, having laid out such great enormities and ones greater by far than these, not against the bishops alone, but even against the wholesome and ecclesiastical faith, would clearly himself be guilty of such a heresy. That the man cared nothing for truth, you would learn if you read the letters themselves of the bishops, in which you would find him mutilating the overall sense of their statements and hiding all the connections between them, seizing upon individual phrases (64) and contriving evil slander out of these. At any rate he abuses Eusebius quite openly, as having said that Christ is a mere man, when he should have compared his own letter with the apostol-

---

199. Phil 2.6–7.

200. Marcellus, *fr.* 127 (101 K./H.) (118,11–22 V.).

201. See Eusebius as given in Marcellus, *fr.* 126 (100 K./H.) (116,14–118,10 V.).

202. Marcellus, *fr.* 128 (102 K./H.) (120,1–3 V.).

203. οὐσία.

204. First part of Marcellus, *fr.* 117 (82 K./H.) (110,1–3 V.).

ic statement, through which the Apostle himself said, "There is one God and one mediator between God and men, the man (65) Jesus Christ."[205] Therefore, this most wise fellow has slandered this apostolic statement, as if it belonged to Eusebius, not having understood that he was slandering the Apostle. But the statements of his that are brought out in the same letter, as well as those that have been composed in the remaining treatises of his concerning the divine Scriptures, which indeed have been passed around in every place,[206] (66) he has delivered over to silence, having hidden in silence the things that he did not want to slander. One would find that he has done something similar, too, with the remaining writings he has slandered.

Having a care for the proportion of the text, we will leave a closer examination of these things to those who wish, while we ourselves strive zealously to uncover the still remaining outlandish statements of Marcellus himself about the Son of God, so that it might become obvious to all the manner in which he himself thought about the Son of God.

---

205. 1 Tm 2.5.

206. Eusebius refers here to his own numerous theological treatises and scriptural commentaries, accusing Marcellus of making the case for his accusations of heresy against the bishop of Caesarea by quoting Eusebius out of context and highly selectively.

BOOK TWO

FTER IDENTIFYING those [bishops] whom he slandered, we now have the opportunity to bring to light the faith of the Galatian, or rather his lack of faith in the Son of God, and to lay bare the evil belief that lurked within the man for a long time, now that the pretext of the letter has been dealt with briefly, and to show to all through the testimony of his own statements what sort of man it is who leads the Church of Christ. He believes that the Son neither is nor pre-subsists nor ever wholly existed with God before the birth through the Virgin, but says he is only a word, connatural with God, eternally coexisting and united to him, just as the word in a human being would also be. For he himself uses this example, having said that there is a word internally in God himself, which at one time is quiet but at another time is active for the purposes of communication, and comes forth from the Father in activity alone, just as we also, in giving some command, would be active in saying and uttering something. But that no one, at any rate in this sense, would say that the communicating and active word is a son is obvious to all.

Although he [Marcellus] grants this in the case of God, I do not know in what sense he says that the Word, which has not subsisted, assumed the flesh and was active in it (3) and at that time became Christ, Jesus, King, Image of God, and beloved and glorified Son, yes, even "firstborn of all creation,"[1] [and] that the one who did not exist previously, then came to be, although he did not subsist. But his most incredible statement is that he [the Son] took his beginning, yes, not even four hundred whole years ago and that when all these ages [have passed]

1. Col 1.15.

117

he will cease [to exist] after the time of the judgment, when the Word is united to God, so that he will no longer be another besides God, while the flesh that he assumed will be left behind, empty of the Word, with the result that at that time neither the Son of God nor the Son of Man whom he assumed will subsist.

(4) Further, he [Marcellus] goes to this extreme, as if he had been made deaf and [did] not hear the angel Gabriel, announcing to the Mother of God clearly and speaking distinctly about him who would be born from her and issue forth "from the seed of David according to the flesh,"[2] stating, "Behold, you will conceive in your womb and bear a son, and you will call his name Jesus. He will be great, and will be called Son of the Most High; and the Lord God will give to him the throne of his father David, and he will reign over the house of Jacob forever; and of his kingdom there will be no end."[3] Nor did he understand the statements of Daniel the great prophet, who put his seal upon these same things through the prophecies he made in the divine Spirit, saying, "And behold, with the clouds of heaven there came a Son of Man, and he came to the Ancient of Days (5) and was presented before him. And to him was given dominion and honor and kingship, and all peoples, nations, and languages will serve him; his dominion is an everlasting one that shall not pass away, and his kingdom will not be destroyed."[4] But neither did Isaiah convince him about the unending kingdom of the Son of Man even when he prophesied in this way: (6) "for to us a child is born, to us a Son is given; and the government will be upon his shoulder, and his name will be called angel of great counsel, wonderful counselor, mighty God of power, prince of peace, father of the age to come. For he will bring in peace and healing (7) with him. His rule [will be] great, and of his peace there will be no end, for the throne of David and for his kingdom he will establish it, and uphold it with justice and righteousness from this time forth (8) and forever more."[5] Indeed, those things that Gabriel announced

2. Rom 1.3.
3. Lk 1.31–33.
4. Dn 7.13–14.
5. Is 9.6–7.

to the Virgin were in agreement with these statements, considering that he said that he [who would be born] from her would reign "forever" and "of his kingdom" there would be no end.

But how Marcellus dared to write things that are contradictory to all these statements, you would learn from his pronouncements, through which he denied the divinity along with the humanity of the Son of God, a novelty that surpasses every godless (9) heresy. For those who claimed that the Son of God neither was before nor pre-existed belong to the heterodox, some of whom, having supposed that he is a man from a man like the rest of men, said that he has been honored with adoption as a son, and having granted this, have confessed that he has an immortal and everlasting honor, glory, and eternal kingdom. But there are others who, denying the man, have proposed that the Son of God is the pre-existing God.[6] Well, those who are foreign to the Church were driven to this great error, but he who ruled over the Church of God for such a long time destroys the existence of the Son of God. Having served at his altar, he believes that he himself, I suppose, will obtain for himself presently an eternal and immortal life, while he deprives (10) the High Priest of this. But we have "a great High Priest," according to the Apostle, "who has passed through the heavens, Jesus, the Son of God,"[7] who, he dares to say, neither pre-existed nor pre-subsisted, but will neither be nor coexist with the saints of God according to that very promise of the kingdom of heaven. For at that time when all those saints will participate in the kingdom of God in incorruptible and immortal bodies, he deprives Christ alone and the body that he assumed (11) of it. He also does not find it disturbing that the originator of the resurrection,[8] the cause of eternal life for all, will be deprived not only of the kingdom, but he even declares

6. On the early history of "docetism," to which Eusebius seems to refer here, see Markus Vinzent, "'Ich bin kein körperloses Geistwesen': Zum Verhältnis von Kerygma Petri, 'Doctrina Petri' und IgnSm III," in *Monarchianismus im 2. Jahrhundert, VCSup* 50, ed. Reinhard Hübner and Markus Vinzent (Leiden: Brill, 1999), 241–86.

7. Heb 4.14.
8. See Rv 3.15.

that he will be deprived of life itself—just as if someone were
to give their eyes, but take away the light that provides illumi-
nation to these. And neither the great angel of God Gabriel
nor the great prophet Daniel, about whom it was said, "You are
not wiser than Daniel, are you?"[9] nor the great Isaiah nor the
remaining (12) chorus of the prophets induced the man either
to write or think these sorts of things, nor did [the] Jews themselves [induce him], among whom it is hoped that the Christ
(who is even now still expected, [and] whom they were accustomed to call "[the] Anointed") will have the undying and immortal kingdom. But [Marcellus] has become even worse than
these [the Jews] because he dared to profane both the beginning and the end of the Son of God, against whom the divine
Apostle himself did not blush to prohibit [anyone] from uttering such blasphemies, on the contrary saying, "The saying is
worthy of belief: if we have died with him, we shall also live
with him; if we endure, we shall also reign with him,"[10] and that
we shall be heirs of God, but certainly not without Christ, for
(13) he says, "heirs of God and fellow heirs with Christ, provided we suffer with him in order that we may also be glorified
with him."[11] And again he [the Apostle] says, "But if we have
died with Christ, we believe that we shall also live with him.
For we know that Christ, once raised from the dead, will never die again; death will no longer have dominion over him,"[12]
(14) and again, "but the free gift of God is eternal life with
Jesus Christ our Lord."[13] Therefore, eternal life will be provided to us in no other way than "with Jesus Christ our Lord,"[14]
and our hope [will be] not simply to live, but to be glorified
together with him and to be heirs together with him and to
rule together with him. For we will acquire all things from (15)
communion with him. The same [Apostle] teaches this, having
said, "God is worthy of belief, by whom you were called into the

9. Ezek 28.3.
10. 2 Tm 2.11–12.
11. Rom 8.17.
12. Rom 6.8–9.
13. Rom 6.23.
14. Ibid.

communion of his Son, Jesus Christ our Lord."[15] But he shows what [this] communion [will be], saying, "and raised [us] up" and "made [us] sit with him in the heavenly places in Christ Jesus, that in the coming ages, he might show the immeasurable riches of his grace (16) in kindness towards us in Christ Jesus."[16] But the same [Apostle] also taught these things about the Savior when he said, "But he holds his priesthood permanently, because he continues forever. Consequently he is able for all time to save those who draw near to God through him, since he always lives (17) to make intercession for them."[17] And truly [he not only said this] but also said that Melchizedek remains a priest "forever" because of his resemblance to "the Son of God."[18] But that Marcellus dared to write things contrary to all these claims will be shown a little later. For now, let us first examine what he thought about the fact that there was neither a source nor did the Son of God subsist.[19]

Chapter 2

(1) Having denounced those who have said that the Son of God was truly a Son, living and subsisting, he lays down his own stated opinion in these very words, writing as follows:

Therefore, before the descent and birth through the Virgin, he was only Word. For before the assumption of the human flesh, what else was "that which came down 'in the last days'"[20] as he [Asterius] himself also wrote, "and that which was born from the Virgin"? It was nothing other than Word.[21]

(2) Then proceeding on, he next says that he is eternal, asserting thereby that he is ingenerate. He writes this way:

15. 1 Cor 1.9.
16. Eph 2.6–7.
17. Heb 7.24–25.
18. Heb 7.3.
19. περὶ τοῦ μηδὲ τὴν ἀρχὴν εἶναι μηδ᾽ ὑφεστάναι τὸν τοῦ θεοῦ υἱὸν ...
20. Heb 1.2.
21. Marcellus, *fr.* 5 (48 K./H.) (8,19–22 V.).

You hear, then, the consistent testimony of the Holy Spirit, giving witness through many and diverse persons to the eternity of the Word. (3) And because of this he [John] begins from the eternity of the Word, saying, "In the beginning was the Word, and the Word was with God, and the Word was God."[22] Using three successive testimonies, he wishes to show the eternity of the Word.[23]

And after some other remarks, he adds:

For previously, as I have said many times, he was nothing other than Word.[24]

(4) And he adds that he was not "image of the invisible God,"[25] saying:

Therefore, it is absolutely clear that before the assumption of our body the Word in and of himself was not "image of the invisible God."[26]

And again after some other remarks he adds:

Well then, what was this "which came down"[27] before the Incarnation? Surely, I suppose, he [Asterius] says, "Spirit."[28] For if he would like to say something besides this, the angel will not agree with him, because he said to the Virgin, "The Holy Spirit will come upon you."[29] But if he will say that he is Spirit, let him listen to the Savior, who says, "God is Spirit."[30]

(5) For this reason, clearly, since the Savior said, "God is spirit," about the Father, Marcellus is convicted of saying that the Father himself was incarnated. And he dares to write still more in this manner:

22. Jn 1.1.
23. Marcellus, *fr.* 6 (53 K./H.) (10,1–6 V.).
24. Last part of Marcellus, *fr.* 52 (91 K./H.) (46,8–9 V.).
25. Col 1.15.
26. Ibid.; first part of Marcellus, *fr.* 53 (92 K./H.) (46,10–48,1 V.).
27. Asterius, *fr.* 58 (120,1 V.).
28. Asterius, *fr.* 58 (120,2 V.).
29. Lk 1.35.
30. Jn 4.24; Marcellus, *fr.* 61 (54 K./H.) (54,1–5 V.).

Well, then, let him learn that the Word of God came, not "being called Word figuratively,"[31] as those men say, but being true Word.[32]

(6) And again he adds these things to what has been said:

If one were only to consider the Spirit, the Word would rightly appear to be one and the same with God. But if one were to consider the addition of the flesh to the Savior, the divinity seems to extend itself only by virtue of its activity, so that, as is to be expected, the monad is truly indivisible.[33]

(7) And he adds still more to the argument through what he wrote in the remarks immediately following in this way:

Therefore, to have said that "he has been begotten before the ages"[34] seems a logical statement: for that which has come forth from the Father who sent it forth becomes an offspring. But the other statement has no longer been taken in a sound or pious sense by him [Asterius].[35] (8) For to have said that he who has come forth from him [the Father], and that this is the true manner of begetting, is not the Word, but [that] "he is simply only son"[36] has usually provided a certain justification for those listening who are inclined to take a human perspective.[37]

And [that] in these words he brazenly denied the Son, introducing a mere word that commands what must be done, is clear from what he adds, saying,

(9) ... whom all the divine Scriptures proclaim in this way. For David said concerning him, "By the Word of the Lord, the heavens were made,"[38] and the same again: "He sent forth his

---

31. Marcellus's statement is based on Asterius, *fr.* 71 (130 V.); see also Marcellus, *fr.* 94 (46 K./H.) (84,1 V.).

32. Marcellus, *fr.* 65 (45 K./H.) (56,1–2 V.).

33. Marcellus, *fr.* 73 (71 K./H.) (62,1–4 V.).

34. Prv 8.23, 25; excerpt of Asterius, *fr.* 17 (90,1–2 V.).

35. See Asterius, *fr.* 17 (90 V.).

36. See Asterius, *fr.* 53 (116 V.); see also Asterius, *fr.* 27 (96,2–3 V.).

37. Marcellus, *fr.* 66 (36 K./H.) (56,3–8 V.).

38. Ps 32.6 (RSV 33.6).

Word and healed them."[39] And Solomon said, "Evil men will
seek me, and they will not find me. Because they hated wisdom
and did not choose the Word[40] of the Lord."[41] And Isaiah said,
"The Law will go forth from Zion, and the Word (10) of the
Lord from Jerusalem."[42] And again Jeremiah says, "The wise
men shall be put to shame; they shall be dismayed and taken
because they rejected the Word of the Lord."[43] And Hosea[44]
the prophet also said, "They hated him who reproves in the
gate, and despised a pious Word."[45] Micah himself, likewise
mindful of the Word, said, "The Law will go forth from Zion,
and the Word of the Lord from Jerusalem."[46]

(11) Bringing together these many remarks about the word
of command, Marcellus says that even the Word-God that "was
in the beginning with God"[47] was of this sort. For this reason
he carries on, claiming:

> But the holy apostle and also disciple of the Lord, John, teach-
> ing clearly and explicitly at the beginning of the gospel, as
> something previously unknown among men, calling him Word
> of the Almighty, thus said, "'In the beginning was the Word,
> and the Word was with God, and the Word was God."[48] Not
> making use of [only] a single testimony, he reveals the eternity
> of the Word.[49]

(12) And he builds on these comments, adding immediately
afterwards:

> ... So that by saying, "In the beginning was the Word,"[50] he
> might show that the Word was in the Father by power (for

39. Ps 106.20 (RSV 107.20).
40. LXX = "fear."
41. Prv 1.28–29.
42. Is 2.3.
43. Jer 8.9.
44. The quotation in fact derives from Amos.
45. Am 5.10.
46. Mi 4.2; Marcellus, *fr.* 67 (47 K./H.) (56,9–58,5 V.).
47. Jn 1.2.
48. Jn 1.1.
49. Marcellus, *fr.* 68 (51 K./H.) (58,6–10 V.).
50. Jn 1.1.

God, "from whom are all things,"[51] is the source of all things that have come to be), and by saying, "And the Word was with God,"[52] [he might show] that the Word was with God by activity ("for all things (13) were made through him, and without him not one thing was made"),[53] and by having said that "the Word was God,"[54] [he might show us] not to divide the divinity, since the Word is in him and he himself is in the Word (for [the Word] says, "The Father is in me, and I am in the Father").[55]

And he adds still [more] to these remarks, laying bare [his] peculiar opinion through those remarks he carries on with immediately afterwards, saying:

Well then, the holy apostle and disciple of the Lord, John, calling to mind his eternity, became a true witness to the Word,[56] saying, "In the beginning was the Word, and the Word was (14) with God, and the Word was God,"[57] making no mention here of a generation of the Word,[58] but using three testimonies, one right after another, he confirmed that the Word was in the beginning.[59]

And he adds to these remarks, saying:

We know to refer the economy according to the flesh to the man, but we believe that the eternity according to the Spirit is united[60] to the Father.[61]

(15) Proceeding to these remarks, he next adds these statements:

51. 1 Cor 8.6.
52. Jn 1.1.
53. Jn 1.3.
54. Jn 1.1.
55. Jn 10.38; Marcellus, *fr.* 70 (52 K./H.) (60,3–9 V.).
56. See Jn 21.24.
57. Jn 1.1.
58. See Asterius, *fr.* 74 (124–128 V.).
59. Marcellus, *fr.* 71 (33 K./H.) (60,10–14 V.).
60. Technically, aorist tense and so "was united."
61. Marcellus, *fr.* 72 (70 K./H.) (60,15–16 V.).

If then [the Savior] himself says these things, "I proceeded and came forth from the Father,"[62] and again, "And the word that you hear is not mine, but the Father's who sent me,"[63] and, "All that the Father has is mine,"[64] it is clear that it makes sense for him also to have said that "the Father is in me, and I am in the Father."[65] So that the Word who says this is in God, (16) while the Father is in the Word, because the Word is a power of the Father. For a witness most worthy of belief has said he is "the power and wisdom of God."[66] Thus the Savior says, "I and the Father are one,"[67] not because of the "exact agreement in all [their] words and actions," as Asterius said,[68] but because it is impossible either for the Word to be separated from God or for God to be separated from his own Word. Thus if Asterius thinks that the Savior said this "because of [their] agreement in all things," and does not wish to learn the truth by taking into consideration the second economy, it is necessary to remind him that sometimes an apparent (17) disagreement is to be seen [between the Father and Son]. For so [the following] words of [Scripture] teach us. For what sort of agreement is this at the time of the Passion when he [the Son] says, "Father, if it is possible, let this cup pass,"[69] and then adds, "But not as I will, but as you will"?[70] For the first statement, "let this cup pass," was not characteristic of one who was in agreement. And even the addition appears to give no indication of agreement, (18) for he says, "Not my will, but your will, Father, be done." You hear how the text shows an apparent disagreement between the one who wills [and the one who does not will]. For it is clear that the Father willed [the Passion] from the fact that what he wanted happened. But that the Son did not will [the Passion] is clear from the fact that he begged [the Father to

62. Jn 8.42. The biblical text actually reads "from God," not "from the Father."

63. Jn 14.24.

64. Jn 16.15.

65. Jn 10.38.

66. 1 Cor 1.24.

67. Jn 10.30.

68. Asterius, *fr.* 39 (102 V.).

69. Mt 26.39.

70. Ibid.

"let this cup pass"]. Again, he [the Son] says, "I do not seek my
own will but the will of the Father who sent me."[71] (19) How
then does [Asterius] say that "the Savior said, 'I and the Father
are one,' because of [their] agreement in all things"?[72]

And after a bit he adds:

How can the Son be in agreement with the Father or the
Father be in agreement with the Son, when the Son says, "All
that the Father has is mine"?[73] For the statement "All that the
Father has is mine" was, on the contrary, that of a Son greedily taking what belonged (20) to the Father. For this reason,
having omitted to say that all that the Father has is held in
common, he said, "All that the Father has is mine." And yet it
was not characteristic of one who was in agreement to speak in
this way, but [to say]: "All that the Father has is held in common." For if the Acts of the Apostles, praising the agreement
of those coming to the faith at that time, declared, "They had
all things in common,"[74] and if one ought to think that among
men who are capable of agreement all things are held in common, how much more necessary was it for the Father and the
Son to have things in common, since they have been divided
into two hypostases? But now, by saying, "All that the Father has
is mine," the Son appears to take greedily what belongs to the
Father. But by alleging that he is not Lord of his own word, but
that the Father is [Lord] even of this (21) (for he [the Savior]
says, "The word that you hear is not mine but the Father's who
sent me"),[75] he indicates that the Father has taken the property
of the child. But each of these statements, which correspond to
Asterius's opinion, (22) seems to be illogical. For it was necessary for the one who was in agreement not to take from another the things that rightfully belong to him, for this is indeed
greedy, but to think that those things that belong to each are
held in common. So whenever we look at the human flesh, we

71. Jn 5.30.
72. See Asterius, *fr.* 39 (102 V.); Marcellus, *fr.* 74 (73 K./H.) (62,5–64,14 V.).
73. Jn 16.15.
74. Acts 4.32.
75. Jn 14.24.

will thus find that the Savior said, "I and the Father are one,"[76] not as Asterius has written, for it was not "because of their exact agreement in all [their] words and actions," as he has written, that (23) the Savior said, "I and the Father are one." For if this were the case, he would surely have said, "I and the Father are in agreement with one another in all things." But in this instance he said, "I and the Father are one." Therefore, if there was some disagreement in those matters, and if the Lord must speak the truth, it follows that the Savior knew precisely that when he said, "I and the Father are one," he said this at that time not with regard to the man whom he assumed, but with regard to the (24) Word who came forth from the Father. For if there should seem to be a certain disagreement, this ought to be referred to the weakness of the flesh, which the Word assumed, not having it before. But if the oneness were to be spoken of, this appears (25) to apply to the Word. For this reason, he rightly said not only, "I and the Father are one," but also, "Have I been with you so long, Philip, and you say, 'Show us the Father'?"[77] (clearly not to these eyes, but to the eyes of the mind that are capable of discerning intellectual things). For what the Father and his Word are is invisible to the eyes of the flesh. [Christ] did not say this to Philip "because of [their] agreement in all things."[78]

(26) Having said all these things [and] having taken up the argument anew, he lays down [his] teaching in this way:

For before the fashioning of all, there was a certain silence, as one might expect, since the Word was in God. For if Asterius has believed that "God is Maker of all things,"[79] it is clear that even he himself will confess along with us that the one [God] has always existed and never received a beginning of his existence, while the other things have both come to be by him and have come to be out of nothing. For I do not think to someone who says that there also are certain things that are ingenerate [he would say that he also believed this, but] that he is firmly

76. Jn 10.30.
77. Jn 14.9.
78. Marcellus, *fr.* 75 (74 K./H.) (64,15–66,27 V.).
79. Asterius, *fr.* 21 (92 V.).

convinced that the sky and earth and everything in the sky
and upon the earth came to be from God. Well now, (27) if
he were to believe this,[80] it would be necessary for him also to
confess that there was nothing other than God. Thus the Word
possessed his own glory, since he was in the Father.[81]

(28) And having said these things, he carries on after some
other remarks:

Asterius calls the authority[82] given to him "glory," and not only
glory, but also "pre-cosmic glory,"[83] not understanding that
when the cosmos did not yet exist, there was nothing other
than God alone.[84]

(29) Marcellus, having said these things and having blatantly denied the Son, so that he might persuade us of precisely the
sort of Word of God he has in mind, exhibits his conception
more clearly to our understanding, representing it through
these remarks he wrote:

For just as all the things that have come into existence have
come into existence by the Father through the Word, so also the
things that are said by the Father are communicated through
the Word. Because of this, even the most holy Moses called the
Word an angel,[85] at that time when he appeared for no other
reason but so that he might announce to Moses these very
things that he believed would benefit the sons of Israel. (30)
And [the Word] believed that it would benefit [them] to believe
that there was one God. For this reason, he also said to him
[Moses], "I am who am,"[86] so that he might teach [them] that
there was no other God apart from himself. This is easy to know,
I think, for those who ponder well a small and humble example
from our experience. (31) For it is not possible to separate the
word from a human being in power and hypostasis. For the word

80. See Asterius, *fr.* 21; 27; 29 (92; 96 V.).
81. Marcellus, *fr.* 76 (103 K./H.) (68,1–10 V.).
82. See Mt 28.18; Jn 17.2; 5.21–22.
83. Asterius, *fr.* 36 (100 V.).
84. Marcellus, *fr.* 77 (104 K./H.) (68,11–13 V.).
85. Ex 3.2.
86. Ex 3.14.

is one and the same with the man, and is separated [from him] in no other way than by the activity alone of the deed.[87]

And he gives yet another illustration exhibiting his opinion, when he says these sorts of things next:

For God was in need of no other preparatory material, such as matter or any other human [material] for [the] establishment, but this which (32) he had ready in his own mind. Since, then, it was impossible for God to contemplate the establishment of the heavens apart from [the] Word and the wisdom that belongs to the Word, he [the prophet Solomon] rightly said, "When he established the heavens, I was present with him."[88]

And he adds again, likening [the Word] of God to the human word, so as to show that he is non-subsistent,[89] and writes in this way:

To be sure, the Father in this passage says to Moses, "I am who am,"[90] (33) but he clearly says it through the Word. For whatever the Father says, in every case he appears to say it through the Word. This is clear even from our own experience, insofar as one can compare small things with great and divine ones. For whatever we wish both to say and do according to our capacity, we do by means of our word.[91]

(34) Then, after some intervening remarks, he says in addition:

How then did Asterius, pretending "to follow the holy Scriptures simply and scrupulously,"[92] not know this passage, which says, "The Lord your God, this is God in heaven above and on earth beneath, and there is no other beside him,"[93] and that "he is one," and that "there is no other beside him"?[94]

---

87. Marcellus, *fr.* 87 (61 K./H.) (74,12–76,10 V.).
88. Prv 8.27; Marcellus, *fr.* 88 (59 K./H.) (76,11–15 V.).
89. ἀνυπόστατον.
90. Ex 3.14.
91. Marcellus, *fr.* 89 (62 K./H.) (76,16–78,4 V.).
92. Asterius, *fr.* 50 (114 V.); see also Asterius, *fr.* 9 (86 V.).
93. Dt 4.39.
94. Dt 4.35; last part of Marcellus, *fr.* 92 (78 K./H.) (82,8–12 V.).

(35) And proceeding, he again affirms [this] confidently, claiming:

Not "having been called Word figuratively,"[95] even if those who teach differently burst asunder with their lies, but being chiefly and truly Word.[96]

And he adds:

For what mystery was hidden other than that concerning the Word? And so this mystery was previously hidden "in God,"[97] so that none of the earlier people knew clearly the truth about the Word, but we now enjoy the riches of the glory[98] and of the hidden mystery.[99]

(36) And after these remarks, he has again made use of a human image, writing in this way:

For who, either of the holy angels or of just men, was so trustworthy as to undo the punishment ordained for him by the mouth of God,[100] (37) if not the Word himself, who coexisted and who formed along [with him], to whom the Father said, "Let us make man in our image and likeness,"[101] since there was no other god who was capable of forming along with him? For he says, "I am the first and I am the last; besides me there is no god."[102] Therefore, neither was there any "newer god," nor was there "another god" after these,[103] (38) who was capable of working together with God. But if, using a small human example from our experience, one were to explain the divine activity as through an image, it would be as if some man knowledgeable in making statues, wishing to form a statue, first considers within himself its type and character and then figures out how

95. Section of Asterius, *fr.* 71 (130 V.).
96. Marcellus, *fr.* 94 (46 K./H.) (84,1–2 V.).
97. Eph 3.9; Col 1.26.
98. Eph 3.16.
99. Marcellus, *fr.* 96 (50 K./H.) (84,9–13 V.).
100. See Asterius, *fr.* 37 (100 V.); Marcellus, *ep. ad Lib.* 6; Gn 3.19; Rv 1.5.
101. Gn 1.26.
102. Is 44.6.
103. See Asterius, *fr.* 55 (118 V.), and Paulinus of Tyre in Marcellus, *fr.* 122 (84 K./H.) (114,8–12 V.) (= Paulinus of Tyre, *ep.* = Urk. 9,4; III 18,8 Op.).

much width and height would be suitable for it. He scrutinizes the proportion of the whole in each part, and after having prepared the right amount of bronze[104] and outlined beforehand in his mind the future statue with a clear mental picture of it, he is conscious of the cooperation of his reason,[105] with which he makes his calculations and with which he is accustomed to do everything (for nothing beautiful comes to be without reason).[106] When he begins this perceptible work, which he sees in his mind's eye, he exhorts himself as he would another, saying, "Come now, let us make, let us form a statue." Just so does God, the Lord of the universe, in making a living statue from earth, exhort himself with nothing but his own Word, saying, "Let us make man … ,"[107] although not in the same way as the other creatures. For the whole creation came into existence by [the] Word.[108]

(39) And in addition to these remarks, after some other comments, he says:

But now I believe the divine Scriptures, that God is one, and the Word of this [God] on the one hand came forth from the Father, so that "all things" might come to be "through him,"[109] but on the other hand, after the time of the judgment, the restoration of all things, and the destruction of all opposing activity, "then he will be subjected to him who put all things under him,"[110] "to [his] God and Father,"[111] so that in this way the Word might be in God, just as he also was previously before the cosmos existed. For there was nothing else before but God alone; but when all things were going to come into existence through the Word, the Word came forth in active energy, being [the Word] of the Father.[112]

104. See Prv 8.27.
105. Literally, "word."
106. Again, λόγος in the sense of rationality.
107. Gn 1.26.
108. Marcellus, *fr.* 98 (58 K./H.) (88,11–90,8 V.).
109. Jn 1.3.
110. 1 Cor 15.28.
111. 1 Cor 15.24.
112. The last part of Marcellus, *fr.* 109 (121 K./H.) (102,13–21 V.).

(40) And again he makes the same idea plainer when he says:

Before the world existed, the Word was in the Father. But when
Almighty God resolved to make everything in heaven and on
earth, the generation of the world required active energy. And
because of this, there being nothing else besides God (for
all things are confessed to have come to be by him), at that
moment, the Word, having come forth, (41) became maker of
the cosmos, he who even beforehand was preparing it within
his mind.[113]

And again, after all these [statements], he carries on, saying:

And because of this he does not name himself "Son of God,"
but everywhere calls himself "Son of Man," so that through this
sort of confession he might enable the man through fellowship
with him to become by adoption Son of God, and so that after
the completion of the deed, he might again, as Word, be united
to God, fulfilling that which was said by the Apostle: "Then he
himself will be subjected to him who put all things under him,
so that God may be all in all."[114] For then he will be what he was
before.[115]

Through all these statements Marcellus brazenly blasphemes
against the Son of God. (42) For if God and the Word within
him were one and the same, he could never himself become
his own father, just as he could not become his own son, since
he would be a single entity. But if the same God himself was a
single entity with his own Word, clearly he neither was a Father
(since he did not have a Son), nor was he Son (since he did not
have a Father).

(43) Therefore, then, we know from the foregoing what sort
of things the fellow recounted concerning the claims that the
Son of God neither exists nor pre-exists, but exists as a mere
word within God himself, at one time silent and then at another exerting himself in active power. And having presented
these same things in many and various ways in his writing, he

113. First part of Marcellus, *fr.* 110 (60 K./H.) (104,1–6 V.).
114. 1 Cor 15.28.
115. Marcellus, *fr.* 111 (41 K./H.) (104,12–18 V.).

gathered together in the treatise a great heap of superfluous statements. But in any case, content with refutations of him provided by himself out of those statements he proposed, we will not dignify the irrationality of this Jewish dogma with a counter-refutation.

(44) Henceforth, having turned to his statements about the flesh, which he says the Word within God assumed only by virtue of activity, come, let us see how he applies to the flesh the theology brought forward in the divine Scriptures concerning the only-begotten Son of God, on the one hand denying that he is the truly pre-existing Son of God, but on the other applying the theology to the flesh,[116] which the impious fellow asserted would a little later be abandoned by the Word.

Chapter 3

(1) For "the Word" "was in the beginning,"[117] as nothing other than Word. But once the man who had not existed previously was united to the Word, it [the Word] became man, as John teaches us, saying: "And the Word became flesh."[118] Well now, because of this he certainly mentions only the Word. For if the divine Scripture should mention the name of Jesus or Christ, it appears so to name the Word of God when he existed with the human flesh. But if someone should proclaim that even before the New Testament the name of Christ or Jesus can be shown to apply to the Word alone, he will find that this has been said prophetically, as is also clear from this statement: "The kings of the earth stood up, and the rulers gathered themselves together, against the Lord and against his Christ."[119]

(2) And after other remarks, he continues:

Rightly, therefore, before the descent he was this, which we said many times: Word. But after the descent and the assump-

116. What Eusebius means here is to attribute divinity to the assumed flesh, in effect, an accusation of Christological adoptionism.
117. Jn 1.1.
118. Jn 1.14.
119. Ps 2.2; Marcellus, *fr.* 7 (42 K./H.) (10,7–17 V.).

tion of the flesh he also acquired different titles, since "the Word became flesh."[120]

Note that through these statements Marcellus does not wish the name[s] of Jesus and Christ and the remaining titles to apply to the Word, but to the flesh that he has assumed. But we need to note this so that when he [Marcellus] rejects the flesh again,[121] he will be convicted of impieties against the very Christ of God. Then, after what was said before, proceeding on, he next writes these sorts of things about the body of the Savior:

> (3) And let Asterius not think this implausible that, although it was of more recent origin, his [Christ's] body was able to obtain such great antiquity. But let him reflect that even if it is the case that the human flesh is most certainly of more recent origin, nevertheless, the Word, having deemed it right to assume this [flesh] through a pure virgin, and having united what belonged to himself to this [flesh], not only made the man who was created in himself "firstborn of all creation,"[122] but also wants him to be a beginning of all things, not only of those on earth, but also of those in heaven.[123]

(4) Having said all this, after other remarks, he refers to the flesh the apostolic statements through which [the Apostle] gives the theology regarding the Son of God (saying, "He is the image of the invisible God, firstborn of all creation, for in him all things were created, in heaven and on earth ... whether thrones or dominions or principalities or authorities—all things were created through him and for him. He is before all things, and in him all things hold together"),[124] unashamedly applying these sorts of statements of the Apostle to the flesh. Concerning this, Marcellus himself proceeds to write these things:

120. Jn 1.14; Marcellus, *fr.* 8 (49 K./H.) (10,18–12,2 V.).
121. As Marcellus does when he suggests that the Word will cast off the assumed flesh at the consummation of salvation history in *fr.* 106.
122. Col 1.15.
123. Marcellus, *fr.* 11 (8 K./H.) (12,17–14,5 V.).
124. Col 1.15–17.

Therefore, if he [the Savior] confesses that the flesh does not benefit him, how is it possible that the flesh, which is of earth and is of no avail, will also coexist with the Word even in the ages to come—as if it did offer some benefit to him?[125]

(5) And again he adds further about the same flesh:

… How would it still be possible for the "form of a slave,"[126] which the Word assumed, since it is the form of a slave, to continue to coexist with the Word?[127]

But having said these sorts of things about the flesh, he now says it is "image of God"[128] and "firstborn of all creation,"[129] and that since it is before all things, "all things in heaven and on earth—whether thrones, dominions, (6) principalities, authorities—were created" in it.[130] And he writes as follows:

Therefore, if on the one hand he is himself "firstborn of all creation," but on the other, "All things were created in him,"[131] it is fitting for us to know that the Apostle in this instance is speaking of his economy in the flesh.[132]

And he confirms the remark, adding next:

Thus he [Christ] was named "firstborn of all creation"[133] because of the fleshly birth and not "because of the first creation,"[134] as those men think.[135]

(7) And he adds:

125. A middle section of Marcellus, *fr.* 106 (117 K./H.) (96,9–12 V.).

126. Phil 2.7.

127. A later section of Marcellus, *fr.* 106 (117 K./H.) (98,20–22 V.).

128. Col 1.15; Marcellus, *fr.* 53 (92 K./H.) (46,10–48,3 V.) ("image of the invisible God").

129. Col 1.15; Marcellus, *fr.* 13 (4 K./H.) (14,14–16 V.).

130. Col 1.16–17, reporting Marcellus's interpretation of this passage, which belongs to Marcellus, *fr.* 11 (8 K./H.) (12,17–14,5 V.).

131. 1 Cor 1.16.

132. Marcellus, *fr.* 13 (4 K./H.) (14,14–16 V.).

133. Col 1.15.

134. See Asterius, *fr.* 13–14; 23; 25; 30; 35 (90; 94; 96; 100 V.).

135. Marcellus, *fr.* 14 (5 K./H.) (14,17–16,1 V.).

Well then, this most holy Word before the Incarnation was not called "firstborn of all creation"[136] (for how is it possible for him who always exists to be firstborn of someone?), but the first "new man"[137] in whom God wanted "all things to be gathered up"[138]—this man the divine Scriptures call the "firstborn of all creation."[139]

And again he adds:

You hear how not only these things, but also the things that pre-existed "in the heavens and on the earth" happen to "have been created in him"[140] according to the new creation.[141]

(8) And so he has said that these statements through which he was called "firstborn of all creation" [were made] because of the flesh. But observe that he also refers the statement "The Lord created me as the beginning of his ways for his works,"[142] again to the flesh, paying no attention to the divine Scripture that speaks in this way, from the person[143] of Wisdom in the Proverbs: "I, Wisdom, live with prudence, and I attain knowledge and discretion.... By me kings reign, and rulers (9) decree what is just."[144] The same Wisdom adds next: "I walk in the way of righteousness; I am directed along the paths of justice, endowing with wealth those who love me, and filling their treasuries with good things. If I should announce to you the things that happen by day, (10) I will remember to recount the things of the age. The Lord created me as the beginning of his ways for his works. Before the age, he founded me, at the first, before the making of the earth,"[145] and what follows after these. Not having wished to apply his mind to these [statements], since there is [for him] only one goal, that is, not to confess

136. Col 1.15.
137. Eph 2.15; 4.24.
138. Eph 1.10.
139. Col 1.15; Marcellus, *fr.* 15 (6 K./H.) (16,2–6 V.).
140. Col 1.16.
141. Marcellus, *fr.* 16 (7 K./H.) (16,7–9 V.).
142. Prv 8.22.
143. ἐκ προσώπου.
144. Prv 8.12, 15.
145. Prv 8.20–24 (RSV 8.20–23).

the Son of God, Marcellus applies the foregoing theology to the flesh, and having turned aside from the straight road, he contrived a dead-end for himself, writing literally in this way:

(11) Therefore, since this passage of Proverbs did not intend to show the beginning of the divinity of our Savior, as those men think, but [to show] the second economy according to the flesh, [the prophet] said, "The Lord created me."[146] For this reason he fittingly mentions the creation of the human flesh.[147]

(12) And next he adds:

Accordingly, the "creation" refers to the fact that he is a man. For this reason he says, "The Lord created me as the beginning of his ways for his works";[148] "created me," that is, through the Virgin Mary, through whom God chose to unite the human flesh to his own Word.[149]

(13) And after other remarks, he continues, saying:

Therefore, since this is so, it follows that we should closely investigate the passage, which was stated in proverbial fashion: "The Lord created me as the beginning of his ways for his works."[150] For the Lord our God, having made that which did not exist previously, truly created. For he created not the existing flesh, which the Word assumed [but the non-existent flesh].[151]

And he carries on again, saying:

Therefore, this is [the meaning of] the statement: "The Lord created me as the beginning of his ways for his works."[152]

(14) And he adds:

"Before the age, he founded me,"[153] calling this foundation his foreordained fleshly economy, as the Apostle also says, "For no

146. Prv 8.22.
147. Marcellus, *fr.* 26 (9 K./H.) (30,1–4 V.).
148. Prv 8.22.
149. Marcellus, *fr.* 28 (10 K./H.) (30,9–12 V.).
150. Prv 8.22.
151. Marcellus, *fr.* 29 (11 K./H.) (30,13–32,2 V.).
152. Prv 8.22; Marcellus, *fr.* 34 (126 K./H.) (34,3–4 V.).
153. Prv 8.23.

other foundation can anyone lay than that which is laid, which is Jesus Christ."[154] Here [the prophet or the Apostle] calls to mind one age in which he said the dispensation of Christ was founded.[155]

(15) And again he confirms the same statement, claiming:

... The prophet rightly said, "Before the age, he founded me,"[156] that is, the [foundation] according to the flesh, because of the communion with his true Son, the Word.[157]

And he next says in addition:

Then [Wisdom] says, "At the first, before the making of the earth."[158] What sort of earth was this, other than, obviously, our flesh, which again became earth after our disobedience? For [Scripture] says, "You are earth, and to earth you shall return."[159] For it was necessary that this [flesh] obtain healing, by having communion in some way with the holy Word.[160]

(16) Observe that Marcellus in these remarks trips himself up. At any rate [he stumbles] in another [passage],[161] [when,] having said that the flesh, having been created, is the "beginning of the ways"[162] of God, and again that the same is a "foundation,"[163] he adds, "before the making of the earth."[164] Then again he interprets the earth as the flesh, not seeing that it does not follow at all to say the flesh was created before the flesh and to name the flesh again after the creation of the flesh. (17) But he adds still more to these [reflections], saying next:

154. 1 Cor 3.11.
155. Ps 54.20 (RSV 55.19); Marcellus, *fr.* 35 (17 K./H.) (34,5–10 V.).
156. Prv 8.23.
157. The last part of Marcellus, *fr.* 38 (20 K./H.) (36,8–9 V.).
158. Prv 8.24.
159. Gn 3.19.
160. Marcellus, *fr.* 39 (21 K./H.) (36,10–13 V.).
161. See Marcellus, *fr.* 28 (10 K./H.) and 29 (11 K./H.) (30,9–32,2 V.).
162. Prv 8.22; the text refers to Marcellus, *fr.* 29 (11 K./H.) (30,13–32,2 V.).
163. 1 Cor 3.11; Marcellus, *fr.* 38 (20 K./H.) (36,6–9 V.).
164. Prv 8.23.

Then [the prophet] says, "Before the making of the depths."[165]
Here the prophet says in proverbial fashion that the depths are
the hearts of the saints, which have in their depths the gift of
the Spirit.[166]

(18) And in these remarks, note that, having taken the phrase
"the Lord created me"[167] as having been said with regard to the
flesh, then having been boxed in by the Scripture that says "before he made the depths," on the one hand he interprets the
depths, saying they are the hearts of the saints, but on the other, he does not see that the hearts of the saints—to be sure, of
Abraham and of Isaac and of Jacob and Moses and Elijah and
Melchizedek and the rest of the prophets—(19) have come into
existence before the flesh of the Savior. Therefore, how is it possible for the statement "before the making of the depths" to
apply to the flesh? And yet after other remarks, he again adds
more, saying:

> Therefore, what is one to make[168] of this central passage:
> "Before the springs abounding with water came forth"?[169]
> [Scripture] says these are the holy apostles. The text of Exodus
> reveals this mystery to us, having proclaimed long ago the
> types of the apostles. For since the number of the apostles is
> twelve, it mentions twelve springs.[170]

(20) And he adds further, writing the same thing in this way:

> Therefore, in all likelihood, the Master spoke about the birth
> in the flesh through the prophet Solomon, when the latter
> said, "Before the springs abounding with water came forth."[171]

(21) Next, then, having gone through other things, he carries on:

---

165. Prv 8.24.
166. Marcellus, *fr.* 40 (22 K./H.) (38,1–3 V.).
167. Prv 8.22.
168. Klostermann's addition "likewise" in harmonizing this passage with
the earlier quotation is not needed.
169. Prv 8.24.
170. Ex 15.27; Marcellus, *fr.* 41 (23 K./H.) (38,4–8 V.).
171. Prv 8.24; Marcellus, *fr.* 42 (24 K./H.) (38,9–11 V.).

Therefore, since we have spoken concerning the foregoing, it follows next that we also complete [our interpretation of] what remains. And that passage remains that speaks of the mountains and hills. [The prophet] says, "Before the mountains had been shaped, before all the hills, he begets me."[172] [The prophet] calls the apostles and the successors of the apostles mountains and hills, so that he might indicate in proverbial fashion the [apostles'] upright way of life in comparison to that of other men.[173]

(22) Having proposed certain interpretations of this sort, he again turns to the apostolic statements, making claims that contradict the Apostle. For the one [the Apostle] who taught the pre-existent Son of God also [taught] that he is "firstborn of all creation,"[174] testifying in a loud voice that "all things" were created "through him and in him" and that he is "before all things."[175] But the other [Marcellus] drags down this theology, too, to the level of the flesh, a little later (23) denying even this. So he says in this way:

Because of this he rightly adds "who is the image of the invisible God."[176] When did he become an image other than when he assumed the form "in the image and likeness"?[177] For previously, as I have said many times, he was nothing other than Word.[178]

And he continues, clarifying the same point still more openly through what he says:

Therefore, it is absolutely clear that before the assumption of our body the Word in and of himself was not "image of the invisible God."[179] For it is natural for the image to be seen, so that through the image that which has hitherto been invisible might be seen.[180]

172. Prv 8.25.
173. Marcellus, *fr.* 45 (27 K./H.) (40,3–8 V.).
174. Col 1.15.
175. Col 1.16–17.
176. Col 1.15.
177. Gn 1.26.
178. Marcellus, *fr.* 52 (91 K./H.) (46,6–9 V.).
179. Col 1.15.
180. Marcellus, *fr.* 53 (92 K./H.) (46,10–48,3 V.).

(24) And again he adds, saying:

> How, then, has Asterius written that the Word of God is an
> "image of the invisible God"?[181] For images reveal those things
> of which they are the images even when they are absent, so
> that even he who is absent seems to appear through them. If it
> is the case that while God is invisible the Word is also invisible,
> how can the Word be in and of himself "image of the invisible
> God,"[182] seeing as he, too, is invisible? For it is impossible for
> that which is invisible ever to appear through [another] invisi-
> ble thing.[183]

(25) But in these remarks, too, Marcellus does not see that
if we should grant that the flesh is the image of God, we will
then have to say that the flesh even of all human beings and the
outward appearances of [their] bodies are images of God, with
the result that the Savior had nothing extraordinary in and of
himself. But he [Marcellus]—as if he had forgotten the things
he wrote after these about the flesh, having said it is "the form
of a slave"[184] from the apostolic comparison and because of this
is not (26) able to coexist with the Word because it is "the form
of a slave," but also [having] openly said:

> … How is it possible that [the flesh], which is of earth and is
> of no avail, will also coexist with the Word even in the ages to
> come?[185]

—insists that the flesh in the present is the image of the invisible God, maintaining obstinately:

> … that before the assumption of our body the Word itself was
> not "image of the invisible God."[186]

(27) And again, after the things that were presented, he carries on, saying:

---

181. Asterius, *fr.* 11 and 13 (88 V.).
182. See also ibid.
183. Marcellus, *fr.* 54 (93 K./H.) (48,4–10 V.).
184. Phil 2.7.
185. Middle passage of Marcellus, *fr.* 106 (117 K./H.) (96,10–12 V.).
186. Col 1.15; section of Marcellus, *fr.* 53 (92 K./H.) (46,10–48,1 V.).

For this reason in every way it is clear that the flesh that was added to the Word was spoken of by the holy Apostle as the "image of the invisible God,"[187] so that through the visible, that which is invisible might also appear. Hence the Apostle says, "He is the image of the invisible God." Clearly now he became a true image of the invisible God at that time when he assumed the flesh that was made "in the image"[188] of God. (28) For if through this image, we were made worthy to know the Word of God, we ought to believe the Word himself when he says through the image, "I and the Father are one."[189] For it is impossible for anyone to know either the Word or the Father of the Word without this image.[190]

(29) And again he adds:

And so the Apostle also says in this way, as we mentioned a little while ago, "He emptied himself, having taken the form of a slave,"[191] indicating to us through "the form of a slave" the human flesh, which the Lord our God formed with his own Wisdom when he said, "Let us make man in our image and likeness,"[192] rightly calling the human flesh "image." For he knew exactly that a little later it would be an image of his own Word.[193]

(30) After these remarks he attempts to argue that even [the statement] "From the womb before the morning star I begot you"[194] was made about the flesh, and writes as follows:

Well then, because the star that reveals the day was rightly called the morning star by the prophet David, it is no longer appropriate to seek out what the morning star is. For this was the star that appeared at that time, which moved ahead and showed (31) the day to the Magi. Therefore, it is entirely clear

187. Col 1.15.
188. Gn 1.26.
189. Jn 10.30.
190. Marcellus, *fr.* 55 (94 K./H.) (48,11–19 V.).
191. Phil 2.7.
192. Gn 1.26.
193. Marcellus, *fr.* 56 (95 K./H.) (50,1–6 V.).
194. Ps 109.3 (RSV 110.3).

that the verse "Before the morning star, I begot you"[195] was spoken by the Lord Almighty concerning the Word who was born together with the human flesh through the Virgin. The gospel also clearly shows this, insofar as our Lord was first born through the Virgin[196] and then later, the star appeared that revealed the day.[197]

(32) Proceeding on to these remarks, he again adds:

For the man received not only authority over things on earth but, naturally, also over [things] in heaven.[198] For if, when he became "man" as well as "mediator between God and men,"[199] [and] then "in him all things were created," as the Apostle said, "in heaven and on earth,"[200] it follows to know exactly that authority has been given to him, not only over [things] on earth, but also over [things] in heaven.[201]

And again, after other remarks, he continues:

For if the holy gospel speaks about a certain glory that was given to him by the Father,[202] the man appeared to have received this through the Word. For having become "the mediator between God and men,"[203] according to the holy Apostle, he glorified the God-fearing human beings with the glory that was given to him by the Father.[204]

(33) And again he adds these remarks:

And he deemed the man who fell through disobedience worthy to be united through the Virgin to his own Word. For what other sort of glory among human beings could be greater than this glory? Having said, "I have glorified you," [the Father]

---

195. Ibid.
196. Mt 1.25.
197. Mt 2.2; Marcellus, *fr.* 59 (31 K./H.) (52,4–12 V.).
198. See Jn 17.2; 5.21–22; Mt 28.18.
199. 1 Tm 2.5.
200. Col 1.16.
201. Marcellus, *fr.* 78 (105 K./H.) (70,1–6 V.).
202. See, for example, Jn 17.5.
203. 1 Tm 2.5.
204. Marcellus, *fr.* 79 (106 K./H.) (70,7–11 V.).

continues, saying, "And I will glorify [you] again,"[205] so that, because of his abundant lovingkindness in the second glory after the resurrection of the flesh, he might make immortal the man who was previously mortal and glorify him with such great glory that he is not only delivered from his previous enslavement but is even made worthy of superhuman glory.[206]

(34) And again he adds further:

… So that, as I said, he might enable the man himself who was previously deceived by the Devil to conquer the Devil again. Because of this, he assumed the man, so that as a result of this he might enable him to receive the first fruits of authority.[207]

And he adds still more, saying:

For this is the beloved,[208] the man united to the Word, of whom the evangelist recorded, "This is my beloved Son, with whom I am well-pleased."[209]

(35) And again he continues:

That the Word of the invisible God[210] was going to be born through a virgin and assume human flesh, and so also that through it, having condemned the Devil, who had previously prevailed over the man, he might enable him to become not only incorruptible and immortal, but also enthroned together with God in heaven.[211]

(36) It is necessary to hold all these things in memory because of the things that are going to be brought forward by Marcellus himself against the flesh that the Word of God assumed. For as if he had forgotten all these things that he presented, he pursues a goal neither auspicious nor pious with regard to the saving body. In addition to all of these, as of those

---

205. Jn 12.28.

206. See Rom 8.21; Marcellus, *fr.* 80 (107 K./H.) (70,12–19 V.), directed against Asterius, *fr.* 36–37 (100 V.).

207. Marcellus, *fr.* 81 (108 K./H.) (72,1–4 V.).

208. See Ps 44.1 (RSV 45).

209. Mt 3.17; Marcellus, *fr.* 82 (109 K./H.) (72,5–7 V.).

210. See Col 1.15.

211. Marcellus, *fr.* 83 (110 K./H.) (72,8–12 V.).

previous things that were brought forward by him, he attempts
to show that even the statement "The Lord reigns; let the earth
rejoice"[212] is (37) to be referred to the flesh. And he says in
this way:

> At any rate, he who came down and took to himself the flesh
> through the Virgin was established king over the Church,[213]
> clearly so that the man who had previously been deprived of
> the kingdom of heaven might be able to obtain the kingdom
> through the Word. For this reason, God devised this economy,
> since he wished that this man, who had previously been de-
> prived of the kingdom because of disobedience, might become
> Lord and God. Therefore, the most holy prophet David says
> prophetically, "The Lord reigns; let the earth rejoice."[214]

(38) And after other remarks, he carries on:

> For this reason, just as Christ our Lord received a beginning
> of his kingdom at a certain time, the prophecy says, "And I was
> established as king by him."[215]

And again he continues:

> For because of this he will also rule as king after he has come
> in human flesh, and having been established through the
> Word as king,[216] the man who was previously deceived will de-
> stroy "every rule" of the Devil and "authority and power."[217]

(39) Having said all these things about the flesh of the Savior
and still more things than these, and having said that it is the
image "of the invisible God,"[218] the "firstborn of all creation,"[219]
the king, Jesus, Christ, the beloved, and all the other things he
laid down, having claimed that the Word was called all of these

212. Ps 96.1 (RSV 97.1).
213. See Ps 2.6.
214. Ps 96.1 (RSV 97.1); Marcellus, *fr.* 99 (111 K./H.) (90,9–15 V.).
215. Ps 2.6; Marcellus, *fr.* 100 (112 K./H.) (92,1–3 V.).
216. See Ps 2.6.
217. 1 Cor 15.24; the first part of Marcellus, *fr.* 101 (113 K./H.) (92,4–6 V.).
218. Col 1.15.
219. Ibid.

things because of it [the flesh], the time has already[220] now come to consider the sort of end he confers on it [the flesh].

Chapter 4

(1) For because of this he will rule as king after he has come in human flesh, and having been established through the Word as king,[221] the man who was previously deceived will destroy "every rule" of the Devil and "authority and power."[222] For [Paul] says, "For he must reign until he has put all enemies under his feet."[223] Thus the holy Apostle says that this [is] the end of the kingdom of our Lord Christ, namely, when he puts all things under his feet.[224]

And after a bit, he says in addition:

Here the Apostle reveals the greatest mystery to us, declaring that there will be an end of the kingdom of Christ; and this end will be when he puts all things under his feet.[225]

(2) And developing still further the same argument, he writes in this way:

We have said in our foregoing remarks, using proofs out of the divine Scriptures, that our Lord Jesus Christ received a beginning of [his] kingdom. There is one [passage] that says, "I was established as king by him over Zion, his holy mountain,"[226] (3) and another is, "The Lord reigns; let the nations rage,"[227] and again, "The Lord reigns; let the earth rejoice."[228] And

220. Marcellus implies that because of Christ's resurrection the time has "already" come to talk about the fate of Christ's resurrected body, because the power of Christ's resurrection is already at work in salvation history, though obviously incomplete at the time Marcellus is writing.

221. See Ps 2.6.

222. 1 Cor 15.24.

223. 1 Cor 15.25.

224. Marcellus, *fr.* 101 (113 K./H.) (92,4–10 V.).

225. Marcellus, *fr.* 102 (114 K./H.) (92,11–13 V.).

226. Ps 2.6.

227. Ps 98.1 (RSV 99.1).

228. Ps 96.1 (RSV 97.1).

altogether there is abundant testimony consisting of myri-
ad statements to show that the man received a beginning of
[his] kingdom through the Word. Therefore, if he received a
beginning of [his] kingdom no more than four hundred years
ago all told, it is nothing paradoxical if the Apostle says that
he who obtained this kingdom such a short time ago will hand
over the kingdom, to be sure, to God who established him as
king, as Scripture says.[229]

(4) And after other statements, he writes as follows:

Therefore, [the Word] appears to have been separated from
the Father by activity alone because of the flesh, until the
approaching time of judgment appears, so that according to
the prophecy, when those who once pierced [him] look upon
the one whom they have pierced,[230] in this way the (5) rest
may also take place in proper order. For since all things are
going to be subjected to Christ in the end time, as the Apostle
said, then, "He will be subjected to him who put all things
under him."[231] Well then, what do we learn about the human
flesh, which the Word assumed for us, not four hundred whole
years ago? Will the Word have this even then in the ages to
come or only until the time of judgment? For it is necessary
that that which was said by the prophet be confirmed in deed.
For [Zechariah] says, "They will look on him whom they have
pierced."[232] But clearly they pierced the flesh.[233]

(6) And he adds [to this] after other comments, saying:

For that the Word assumed our flesh not for his own benefit, but so that the flesh might attain immortality because of
its communion with the Word, is also clear from the same
statement of the Savior. For concerning the flesh, through the
possession of which he associated with the disciples, he thus
said, "Do you take offense at this? Then what if you were to
see the Son of Man ascending where he was before? It is the

229. Marcellus, *fr.* 103 (115 K./H.) (92,14–94,9 V.).
230. Jn 19.37; Zec 12.10; Rv 1.7.
231. 1 Cor 15.28.
232. Jn 19.37; Zec 12.10.
233. Marcellus, *fr.* 104 (116 K./H.) (94,10–21 V.).

Spirit that gives life; the flesh is of no avail."[234] Therefore, if he
confesses that the flesh does not benefit him, how is it possible that the flesh, which is of earth and is of no avail, will also
coexist with the Word even in the ages to come—as if it did
offer some benefit to him? (7) For it seems to me also because
of this that the Lord Almighty says to him, "Sit at my right
hand, until I make your enemies your footstool."[235] Seeming to
distinguish him by activity alone because of [the] human flesh,
and determining, as it were, a certain specified time for him to
sit at his right hand, he thus says to him, "until (8) I make your
enemies your footstool."[236] The holy Apostle, interpreting for
us even more clearly this prophetic statement of David, thus
said somewhere, "He must reign until he has made his enemies
his footstool."[237] Thus the human economy and kingdom seem
to have a certain limit. For this which was said by the Apostle,
"until he has made his enemies his footstool," conveys nothing other than this. (9) Therefore, whenever he has made his
enemies his footstool, he [will] no longer need this partial
kingdom, since he will be wholly king of the universe. For
he will reign together with [his] "God and Father,"[238] whose
(10) Word he was and is. For the Word himself did not receive
a beginning of kingdom for himself, but the man who was
deceived by the Devil has become king through the power of
the Word, so that, having become king, he might conquer the
Devil, who had deceived [him] previously. Because of this, the
Acts of the Apostles also teaches us regarding this man, whom
the Word of God assumed and whom, having assumed, he sets
at the right hand of the Father, when it says: "whom heaven
must receive until the time of restoration."[239] And these [Acts]
[speak in this way], determining, as it were, a certain limit and
appointed time during which it is fitting for the human
(11) economy to be united to the Word. What else does the
phrase "until the time for restoration" wish to convey to us

234. Jn 6.61–63.
235. Ps 109.1 (RSV 110.1).
236. Ibid.
237. 1 Cor 15.25.
238. 1 Cor 15.24.
239. Acts 3.21.

than [the] coming age, in which all things must be completely restored? Well then, if Paul said that in the time of the restoration of all things even creation itself will pass from bondage to liberty (for he says that "the creation itself will be set free from its bondage to decay and obtain the glorious liberty of the (12) sons of God"),[240] how would it still be possible for the "form of a slave,"[241] which the Word assumed, since it is the form of a slave, to continue to coexist with the Word? Therefore, the divinely inspired Paul said clearly and distinctly that in a certain short span of time within past as well as future ages the fleshly economy of the Word has occurred for our sakes and that as this economy has a beginning, so also it has an end, having thus said, "Then comes the end, when he delivers the kingdom to [his] God and Father."[242]

(13) After other remarks, he adds to these:

Therefore, he assumed the human flesh not for his own sake, but for ours. But if it is obvious that he has assumed it for our sake, and [if] everything that pertains to us by his providence and activity will come to an end in the time of judgment, then there will no longer be a need for this partial kingdom.[243]

Having said these things, Marcellus, then perceiving that he had fallen into an absurdity of his own making, adds these statements to what was said:

But if someone should say that the human flesh is worthy of the Word because he made it immortal through the resurrection, let him know that not everything that is immortal is worthy of God. (14) For God, who is able by his own will to make even things that come from nothing immortal, is greater even than immortality itself. That not everything that is immortal is worthy of being united with God is also clear from the fact that the principalities, powers, and angels, although immortal, in no way belong to the oneness of God.[244]

240. Rom 8.21.
241. Phil 2.7.
242. 1 Cor 15.24; Marcellus, *fr.* 106 (117 K./H.) (96,4–100,3 V.).
243. Marcellus, *fr.* 107 (119 K./H.) (100,4–7 V.).
244. Marcellus, *fr.* 108 (120 K./H.) (100,8–14 V.).

(15) Having said these things and as if becoming aware that he himself had fallen into the depth of absurdity, he attempts to call [himself] back from it, confessing in some way that he knew nothing about what he had said. For this reason, he continues, saying:

> But if someone should ask about this flesh that has become immortal by the Word, what are we to say to him? [We would say] that we think it is dangerous for us to expound dogma about things of which we have no exact knowledge from the divine Scriptures. (16) For how is it (17) possible for those who overturn even the dogmas of others to do this? But we will say to those who wish to learn from us the accurate truth about this that, convinced by the holy Apostle, we know that it is fitting for us to see the hidden mysteries in this way, as he himself said. "For now we see," he says, "in a mirror dimly, but then face-to-face. Now we know in part; then we shall know fully, even as we have been known."[245] So do not ask me (18) about things about which I have no clear knowledge from the divine Scripture. Well then, because of this, I will not be able to speak clearly about that divine flesh that acquired communion with the divine Word. But now I believe the divine Scriptures, that God is one and that, on the one hand, the Word of this [God] came forth from the Father, so that "all things" might come to be "through him,"[246] but that, on the other hand, after the time of judgment, the restoration of all things, and the destruction of all opposing activity, "then he will be subjected to him who put all things under him," "to [his] God and Father,"[247] so that in this way the Word might be in God, just as he also was previously.[248]

(19) This wonderful author proposed this sort of end for the flesh of our Savior, having forgotten what he said about it in the previous remarks. (20) Then, having declared clearly in this way that the saving body would be bereft of the Word after the time

245. 1 Cor 13.12.
246. Jn 1.3.
247. 1 Cor 15.28, 24.
248. With the exception of a missing small final passage, this is Marcellus, *fr.* 109 (121 K./H.) (102,1–19 V.).

of judgment, he feigns piety and says he does not know [how]
to answer if someone should ask him about the flesh, but would
say to the one who asks, "Do (21) not ask me about what I have
not learned." But someone who came across him could well say
to him, "Why then do you mock yourself, man? Why indeed do
you rush down [the] cliffs,[249] offering definitive statements in
writing things about which you have not learned? Why do you
not preserve the things you have received from both the fathers
and the teachers of the Church? But you innovate recklessly,
introducing into [its] life a new and alien distortion, granting
a beginning, both circumscribed in time and more recent, to
the kingdom of Christ, and having determined an end of this,
and denying the truly only-begotten Son of God and assuming
[that he is] a mere word, without being and non-subsistent,[250]
which you say is nothing other than one and the same with
God, which indeed even everyone would say with good reason
if he were denying the Son of God. (22) For the Word that does
not subsist is not a Son, just as neither would the word that is in
man ever be said [to be] a son of man, having arisen within the
one speaking by virtue of activity alone. Again and again, you
say that this [Word] has become Son of God from the Father
not four hundred whole years ago through the assumption of
the flesh and was called "Jesus" and "Christ," and designated
image "of the invisible God" and "firstborn of all creation,"[251]
and then that at that time he became a king who ruled over all
these things from the time indicated, [but] then he will cease
[to exist] completely at the time of the consummation of all
of these things. (23) From where then have you learned these
things? Who is your authority for teaching these things—which
of the bishops, what sort of synods, what sort of book of ecclesiastical men? Where do you think the immortal body of the
Savior would go? For confessing that it is immortal and calling
it divine, you will suppose, I think, that it is altogether both
incorruptible and indissoluble, and having a nature of this sort
it remains, to be sure, solid and indissoluble. But (24) you took

249. Mk 5.13; Mt 8.32; Lk 8.33.
250. ἀνούσιαν καὶ ἀνυπόστατον.
251. Col 1.15.

away the Word from it [the assumed flesh] and united it to God. Therefore, will the body stand alone without [the] Word in immortal and incorruptible irrationality[252] and inactivity? And how will the Word itself return into God and be united again with him after its separation from the flesh? Consequently, was he [the Word] not in God when he coexisted with the flesh, although he was in him in every respect, being both co-eternal with him [and] one and the same with God?[253] How, then, did he come to be in the body? If indeed he dwelt in it in place of a soul, he will consequently be in a hypostasis distinct from the Father, (25) both living and subsisting in the flesh that he assumed. What, therefore, hindered [Marcellus from] confessing that he was the living Son of God even before the constitution of the world? But he [Marcellus] would say that he has come to be in the body likewise by activity alone and not by the hypostasis of being.[254] For he says that, coexisting with the body by active energy alone (by moving it and doing all the things related in the gospels), he was united by virtue of being[255] to God, existing as a Word inseparable and indistinguishable from him. (26) If, then, he should say these things, let him answer us who have asked whether the activity of the Word has come to this flesh alone, but not also to the other holy men of God. Is not the same Word also active with regard to all the remaining things fashioned by the Word? And surely we have learned that "by the Word of the Lord, the heavens were made,"[256] and "all things were made through him, and without him not one thing was made."[257] (27) Therefore, he is active even with regard to all things. We know from the divine Scriptures also that "the Word of the Lord came to Hosea the Son of Beeri,"[258] and "the Word of the Lord came to Isaiah the son of Amoz,"[259]

---

252. Literally, "wordlessness."
253. Klostermann's punctuation of the text here is incorrect.
254. οὐχὶ δὲ οὐσίας ὑποστάσει.
255. οὐσίᾳ.
256. Ps 32.6 (RSV 33.6).
257. Jn 1.3.
258. Hos 1.1.
259. Is 2.1.

and "the Word of the Lord came to Jeremiah." [260] And the same Word of God also worked in every prophet. Consequently then, all those prophets had a value equal to that of the only-begotten Son of God, and the Savior had nothing more, if indeed he was moved only in activity by the Word that was united with God.[261] (28) But neither does Marcellus grant to the Christ of God to bear [honors] equal to those of the prophets. For those men will receive an eternal life both immortal and everlasting; they will live unto all ages in the proclaimed kingdom of heaven and will enjoy goods of which "no eye has seen, nor ear heard, nor the heart of man conceived."[262] But the Christ of God himself, the common Savior of all, "the firstborn of the dead,"[263] the hope of the resurrection of the saints, he alone consequently will at that time be left behind, his kingdom will come to an end, and the life-giving flesh will be abandoned, alone, and irrational,[264] so that he neither pre-exists as Son of God nor endures into infinity (29) according to the teaching of Marcellus.

Rightly, therefore, these claims roused the emperor, as one truly God-loving and thrice-blessed, against the fellow, and yet countless flatteries and many praises of the emperor appear in his treatise. These things forced even the holy synod that assembled in the royal city from diverse provinces of Pontus, Cappadocia, Asia, Phrygia, Bithynia, Thrace, and the regions beyond to censure the man through the decree against him even though it was unwilling [to do so]. These matters forced even us to proceed to the investigation at hand, at one and the same time supporting the opinions of the holy synod and trying (30) to do this to the best of our ability at the command of our fellow servants. But I think it was especially necessary for me that the treatise has been written because of those who have thought the fellow was treated unjustly. For it is necessary

260. Jer 1.2.
261. So the position of Asterius, *fr.* 47 (112 V.), which, as Eusebius shows in the next sentence, is even superior to that of Marcellus.
262. 1 Cor 2.9.
263. Col 1.18.
264. Literally, "without the Word."

to assuage the suspicion of our brothers through presenting clearly his lack of belief in the Son of God that has been quietly circulating for a long time, but which now had been spoken through that treatise of his; although no one called for it, he came along, bearing it unbidden, and having given it into the hand of the emperor, he deemed [him] worthy to discern the things that had been written [in it]. I suppose that he probably hoped that, because of the praises directed at [the emperor], [in it] he would find protection from the emperor himself, and that he might (31) take vengeance on the bishops who had been slandered by him. But, to be sure, his escape did not turn out as he had hoped. For the judge of these events was God and Jesus Christ himself, the one who is denied by [this] writer, who indeed, seeing the secrets of the fellow, made him become both his own accuser and prosecutor, with no one coming to his aid. For this reason the one man [Marcellus], priding himself on [his] treatise, approached the emperor, while the other [Constantine] left the judgment of this book to the synod, and the holy synod of God rejected the treatise as unfit, and rightly so, because it confesses neither a beginning nor a pious end of the Son of God.

ON ECCLESIASTICAL
THEOLOGY

BOOK ONE

Dedication

TO THE MOST honorable and beloved fellow minister Flacillus, Eusebius sends greetings in the Lord.

It is no wonder if those things written by us in brief against the garrulous and long-winded writing of Marcellus were sufficient. For indeed there is no need of many words for the refutation of those things that are immediately obvious to their readers. Because of this, then, in the previous two books,[1] I produced a clear refutation of them, having used only the citation of the man's words without providing an entire counterargument. But now, in addition to those excerpts, I have produced by my own hands[2] another refutation of those words in three books. For the man who composed a single large and error-riddled treatise says that "he has done this so as to make

---

1. The *Against Marcellus*.

2. Eusebius is clearly at pains to insist that he did not employ the assistance of an episcopal "ghost writer" on the project. Deacons, in particular, often served as theological advisors, secretaries, and draft writers; for example, Athanasius served Alexander in this capacity. Asterius himself seems to have advised Dianius and other Eusebian bishops (see *Lib. syn. ad synod. Antioch. anno 341* [Mansi II, col. 1350]; see on this W. Kinzig, *In Search of Asterius: Studies on the Authorship of the Homilies on the Psalms*, Forschungen zur Kirchen- und Dogmengeschichte 47 [Göttingen: Vandenhoeck & Ruprecht, 1990], 18–19), and, of course, Marcellus had Photinus as his deacon and theological advisor—who produced the first commentary on Marcellus's creed (the only one used by Rufinus for his credal commentary). On this see Markus Vinzent, *Der Ursprung des Apostolikums im Urteil der kritischen Forschung*, FKDG 89 (Göttingen: Vandenhoeck & Ruprecht, 2006), part IX. When Eusebius insists that he wrote this book by himself, he is, indeed, indicating that he did not use any assistant(s), perhaps indicating from the beginning that Marcellus's and Athanasius's claims that "the Eusebians" are all inspired by their theological advocate Asterius are not true for what follows.

known the one God,"[3] lest, having divided up the text,[4] he unwittingly give the Son of God the rank of a hypostasis. But honoring the all-holy and thrice-blessed Trinity, we have brought
together in a corresponding number of books the entire subject, having sworn off wordiness, and also presenting the true
theology as concisely as possible. Therefore, you yourself are
to be the judge, when you read [them], of whether these remarks are sufficient to the task. But if they leave anything out,
it will fall to you, both to provide for these omissions, since it is
clearly the duty of a brother to provide for the deficiencies of a
brother, and if they are in need of revision in any place, to put
it right through correction.

I pray that you may fare well and remember me to the Lord
in all things.

[*Preface*]

(1) I thought that the citations of Marcellus's own words that
I assembled in the previous books were sufficient for their refutation. For they contained so clear and indisputable a denial
of the Son of God that even without any counter-argument, the
thought contained in these words had to be rejected by those
who are nourished by the Church of God. (2) But because I
became concerned lest by chance some might later be drawn
away from the Church's theology by the frequent citations [of
Scripture][5] that the man has used in order to make them be-

---

3. Fragment from Marcellus, *fr.* 1 (128 K./H.) (2,1–2 V.), derived from the
preface of his book or from the letter of dedication.

4. Marcellus used one book to stress one hypostasis in God; Eusebius is,
therefore, going to use three books because he believes in three hypostases
in God.

5. With Migliore (p. 45) we think that the second "juxtaposition" means
"scriptural citations," although our translation is slightly different from his.
This interpretation is supported by the number of scriptural texts Marcellus
had gathered, and the way Eusebius in *CM* 1–2 juxtaposes them with more
scriptural texts. In addition to the more theological arguments in *ET*, Eusebius again devotes much attention (e.g., *ET* 1.20) to the proper interpretation of
various scriptural passages, so as to argue that these do not support Marcellus's position.

lieve what he thought would agree with his views, I judged that it was necessary under the present circumstances to expand the refutation of these remarks, so that every person might learn that not a single one of his quotations of the inspired Scripture provides a testimony that agrees with him [Marcellus] when he denies the Son of God; rather, all his quotations completely and incontrovertibly state the opposite and correct his erroneous interpretations of the divine Scriptures. And indeed, using the same method [the quotation of Scripture], I will bring to bear on that matter the theology concerning our Savior. I will have nothing new to say, nor will I relate any brilliant discovery of my own; rather, I offer the uncorrupted teaching of the Church of God. This teaching the Church now preserves, since it received it from those who from the beginning personally saw and heard the Word from heaven.

Chapter 1

(1) Before embarking on the close examination of these matters, since in the middle of [Marcellus's] treatise[6] I found that Sabellius[7] was being criticized by him, astonished at that man's stupidity, because he did not refrain from speaking ill of one whom he ought to have praised more than all because he held beliefs and ideas similar to his, I resolved not to pass over that remark in silence, but to offer a refutation[8] of this [man— namely, Sabellius] too in the present treatise. For, on the one hand, his [Marcellus's] disparagement of the ministers of God (even if it led to censure for him, but good reputation for those who are freeing themselves from communion with him)[9]

6. This could also be translated as "book," as Marcellus's treatise consisted of only one book. We prefer "treatise" because Eusebius is talking about a text, not necessarily a physical object, which "book" suggests. "In the middle" seems to reflect what is reflected in the surviving fragments. In *fr.* 69 (44 K./H.) (58,11 V.), roughly the middle of the book, Marcellus talks about Sabellius.

7. For Sabellius, see the introduction, pp. 35–36.

8. Eusebius promises to "kill two birds with one stone": to refute Marcellus, but in showing Marcellus's kinship with Sabellius, to refute the latter too.

9. Although a bit vague, it is clear that Eusebius is not talking about Atha-

(2) is only to be expected since it seems natural for one to denigrate ideas that are displeasing to him; but on the other hand, his [Marcellus's] unwitting attack on himself through the condemnation of one who thinks as he does seems to me to have its cause in both want of perception and shameless impudence. But since this is the case, he would become his own accuser, introducing God as a "Son-Father," just as Sabellius does, even if not [using] the term himself, but in the true sense, by taking away the hypostasis of the Son, and by defining God as one and calling him Father of himself and again Son of himself too. (3) Having granted that the one who is in God is Word, and having defined him as one and the same with him, he said that he is to be called the Father of this one, and that the Word is his Son, not truly as a Son in the hypostasis of being,[10] but literally and truly as Word. Hence, he indicates that he is not Word in a figurative sense,[11] but that he is literally and truly Word, and nothing (4) other than Word. But if he is nothing other [than Word], it is clear he was not Son literally and truly but, as far as the term and name go, was called this in a figurative sense. Saying that the Word is one and the same with God, he clearly stated that the one who was made flesh and was born from the Virgin is God himself. Long, long ago the Church of God rejected this when Sabellius said it, after counting him among the godless heretics.

---

nasius, but perhaps about other bishops like Theophronius of Tyana, who seems to have had some sympathy with Marcellus's theology, but then—under pressure from Eusebius of Nicomedia—at the Dedication Council of 341 distanced himself from it. See Markus Vinzent, "Die Entstehung des römischen Glaubensbekenntnisses," in *Tauffragen und Bekenntnis, Studien zur sogennanten "Traditio Apostolica," zu den "Interrogationes de fide" und zum "Römischen Glaubensbekenntnis,"* ed. Wolfram Kinzig, Christoph Markschies, and Markus Vinzent (Berlin: Walter de Gruyter, 1999), 282–92, 304.

10. ἐν οὐσίας ὑποστάσει. See Heb 1.3.

11. See Asterius, *fr.* 71 (130 V.), according to Marcellus, *fr.* 65 (45 K./H.) (56,1 V.), 94 (46 K./H.) (84,1 V.).

Chapter 2

The children of the Jews first received the confession of the one God in opposition to the polytheistic error of the Greeks. But the saving grace of recognizing that the same [God] is also Father of an only-begotten Son has been given to the Church as a special privilege. For as Son it knows Jesus Christ alone and no other, not according to the generation of the flesh that he assumed (for it has been taught to call this flesh the "form of a slave" and "Son of Man"),[12] but according to his [generation] before all ages from God himself and the Father, [which is] unknowable to all. According to this [generation from God] the fullness of the paternal divinity also made him, the Son, God, and so as a result he possesses a divinity that is not his own, one separated from that of the Father, nor one that is without source and that is unbegotten, nor one that is foreign, from somewhere else, and different from the Father's. Rather, he is filled with divinity by participating in the paternal [divinity] itself, which pours into him as from a fountain. For the great Apostle taught that "in him alone dwells all the fullness" of the paternal "divinity."[13] For this reason, then, one God is proclaimed by the Church of God, "and there is no other besides him,"[14] but also one only-begotten Son of God, the image of the paternal divinity, who, because of this, is God.

Chapter 3

So then, not having succeeded in understanding this theology, many contrived various pathways of error:

1) those who granted that the Son is God, but who denied the man whom he has assumed;

2) those who have supposed that [Christ] is a mere man, but did not recognize that God was in him;[15]

---

12. "Form of a slave," Phil 2.7; "Son of Man," for example, Mk 8.31.

13. Col 1.19; 2.9.

14. Dt 4.35; 32.39.

15. Eusebius seems to play heresiological extremes against each other, the

3) those who, from fear of seeming to have introduced a second God, defined Father and Son as the same [God].[16]

The Church of God, having rejected these men, glories in the
gospels' proclamation of the truth. On the one hand, it boasts
that there is one God who is over all; on the other, it affirms
one only-begotten Son, God from God, Jesus Christ. It confesses that the same became Savior and Son of Man, being Son of
God before he also became Son of Man, and that he became
this, which he was not, because of the ineffable abundance of
the Father's love for humankind.

Chapter 4

The word of truth, indeed, proclaims this through the voice
of the Church. As for those who deny the Son of God, however,
alleging that there is one God and no other, why do they even
flock into the Church at all, when they should associate with
the synagogues of the Jews? And why do they also spit on them
[the Jews] with blasphemous words, slandering the one God
with two names,[17] if indeed they suppose the same is Father
and the same is Son? For of whom will [the Father] be Father,
if no Son subsists? And of whom will the Son be Son, if the one
who has begotten him does not exist prior to him? But if [the
Father][18] is entirely one, I suppose he himself will be the one
who was incarnated and suffered and ended mortal life among
men.[19]

---

first reducing the human side of the Incarnate (e.g., Docetism), the second a
form of psilanthropism.

16. Another allusion to the modalism of Sabellius.

17. I.e., God as Father and Son.

18. The reference, we assume, is not to "God," but to "Father," as this name
was the last to appear. In addition, Eusebius just discussed what happens if
the Father is one: as a consequence, the Father (not God the Son) would be
incarnate.

19. Eusebius broaches the Patripassianist charge here. If Father and Son
are not distinguished, then the one who is incarnate is the Father.

Chapter 5

(1) But the Church of God expelled Sabellius for saying these things, as one who dared [to make] godless and impious [claims]. Marcellus, however, tries to revive these views in veiled form, not through persuasive arguments. For although he correctly defines God as one, he says that this God has the Word itself within himself, united and joined to him. And then he calls one aspect of the one God "Father" and the other "Son," as if there were a certain twofold and composite being[20] (2) in him. And inasmuch as the one [Sabellius] who does not divide the power that is without source, unbegotten, and divine, but openly confesses it as the same, is better than this man [Marcellus] in his choice of evil views, by so much more is the Jew better than either of these, since he does not divide the one God into Father and Son as Marcellus does, nor does he introduce the same as "Son-Father" in the manner of Sabellius, but he reveres God and acknowledges his Christ, and looks for him whose coming is proclaimed by the prophets. But since they [the Jews] did not receive the latter when he came, they underwent and will undergo a penalty for their lack of faith in him.

Chapter 6

(1) But those who can believe in the one who has come acknowledge through prayer[21] these three:

• the one from "the seed of David"[22] and from the holy Virgin,

• and the Son of God who has taken up his dwelling in the latter, who pre-exists and subsists substantially,[23]

• and God who is Father of this latter, by whom he [the Son] constantly confesses that he has been sent.[24]

20. οὐσίαν.
21. Eusebius is probably referring to some kind of doxological or credal formula with this reference to "prayer."
22. Rom 1.3.
23. οὐσιωδῶς ὑφεστῶτα.
24. Jn 5.30; 6.57; 14.24.

Therefore, according to the Apostle, there is "for us one God, the Father, from whom are all things, and one Lord, Jesus Christ, through whom are all things,"[25] the pre-existing only-begotten Son of God, and thirdly the Son of Man according to the flesh, whom the Son of (2) God assumed for us. But neither should the body that he assumed be thought of as the same thing as the Son of God who assumed it, nor should the Son of God himself be thought of as one and the same with the one who begot him. Hence, since these three truths are foundations,[26] those who, while granting the two, dismiss the third, ought to be cast out of the Church.[27]

Chapter 7

(1) Thus certain godless men belonging to the heterodox, having rejected the flesh of the Savior, and having said that he has appeared on earth in a kind of phantom-like appearance,[28] were the first completely to miss the mark of truth. But those who have accepted the fleshly economy but have denied the pre-existence of the Son of God have contrived for themselves, as I said, various "dead-ends."

Some men have said that he became a mere man, better than the common nature of all men in no respect except in the advantages of virtue;[29] others, having declared that the God of

25. 1 Cor 8.6.

26. 1 Cor 3.11: "For no other foundation can anyone lay than that which is laid, which is Jesus Christ" (RSV).

27. Eusebius obviously has no clear trinitarian structure in his mind, as the third here, of course, is not the Spirit, but the assumed man, which also shows the early state of the debate that focused on Father-Son-man/body, rather than Father-Son-Spirit. As a result, the three foundations Eusebius is talking about here are fundamentally binitarian and Christological in reference. He does, however, address the Spirit in *ET* 3.4–6. This is more proof that theologians early on are sensitive to the Christological implications of Marcellus's trinitarian theory.

28. Another reference to Docetism, perhaps with Marcion(ites) in mind, as "phantom" was regarded as one of the catch terms of this "heresy." See, for example, Tertullian, *Adv. Marc.* 1.22.

29. Certainly a charge against his colleague Asterius. See Asterius, *fr.* 31; 34; 35 (98, 100 V.).

the universe himself dwelt in the body, explained that he himself was called Son of himself on account of the human economy that he endured. These men,[30] granting the two, God and man, deprived themselves of the third, having denied that the Savior is himself the only-begotten Son of God.

(2) Long ago Sabellius and now Marcellus, having been carried away together by their view of these matters, boasted [first] that they knew full well, just like the faithless Jews, the God over all,[31] and together they confessed, second, the flesh taken from the holy Virgin; but third, the Son of God, who is light and truth, the very culmination of the salvation of us all, they threw overboard and were shipwrecked together by their denial (3) of the Son and of the light of truth. Thus one will hear these men confessing the one God and honoring the flesh of the Savior, but though they confess the Son of God who dwelt in the flesh with their words and their lips, they in fact reject him.

For it is necessary to search for the Son of God, who is truly living and subsisting, and who is neither the same as the body that he assumed nor the same as the God and Father. For neither would anyone be pious who said that the God who is beyond the universe is "Son" (for of whom will the one who has encompassed the divinity that is without source and unbegotten be Son?), nor will anyone who said that the only-begotten Son of God is the same as the Father escape from the punishment leveled at the blasphemous.

Chapter 8

(1) For this reason, then, the Church of God, rightly discerning[32] the straight and imperial way, rejected the other ways that diverge [from this one], and hands over to its children [this] knowledge of inspired grace, teaching them to confess in the very mystery of rebirth,[33] namely, to believe in one God the Fa-

30. Namely, Asterius and Marcellus.
31. See Rom 9.5; Eph 4.6.
32. This is possibly an allusion to 2 Tm 2.15.
33. The term refers to baptism, although it is interesting that despite

ther who rules over all, giving them to know that in this way the theology is perfect and exact and complete in all its parts, which hands down

- one God in contradistinction to the polytheistic error of the Greeks,
- but knows that he is Father in opposition to the teaching of the Jews,
- and confesses that he is ruler over all, turning away from the impiety of the godless heterodox.

(2) In any case, none of the heterodox would say that the Father of Christ is the same as the God who rules over all,[34] nor would any of the Jews confess that God is a Father since they do not know the only-begotten Son, nor would a Greek say that he recognized one God alone.

For this reason, then, purifying itself of the error of all of these, the Church proclaims the one God, teaching that he is both Father and Ruler over all, on the one hand Father of the one and only Christ, and on the other, God and Creator and Lord of all the remaining creatures. So also the Church hands down [the] only-begotten Son of God, Jesus Christ, who has been begotten before all ages from the Father, but who is not the same as the Father, but who exists in himself and lives and truly coexists as Son, God from God and light from light and life from life, who has been begotten from the Father for the salvation of the universe by means that are unspeakable and

---

talking of a "handing over of knowledge of inspired grace," what follows does not seem to refer to a known and traceable credal formula, but again points directly to the discussion in the text above on "Sabellianism." The variations of Eusebius's formulae indicate that he is simply trying to answer questions about the catechumens' belief that were part of the baptismal liturgy. And yet this is another example of how important the liturgical argument was for the development of theological and later trinitarian thinking during the fourth century.

34. Eusebius likely has various Gnostic mythologies in mind here. This is an important, although difficult, statement, as the term "ruler over all" (*pantokrator*) is somewhat mysterious. As noted elsewhere (see Markus Vinzent, "Die Entstehung des römischen Glaubensbekenntnisses," in *Tauffragen und Bekenntnis*, 254), the term *pantokrator* is very rarely used in early Christian literature.

ineffable and altogether unknowable and incomprehensible to us, and he subsists not in the same way that the remaining begotten beings do, nor does he live a life that resembles that of the creatures that have been begotten through him, but he alone (3) was born from the Father himself and is life itself.

For it was also fitting for the God of all before any creation and before all ages to bring forth this only-begotten offspring as a certain basis and unbreakable foundation of those things that were going to come into existence through him. For this reason, then, before all the things that were going to come into existence, he begot the Son as the ray of a certain light and fountain of life and treasure chest of goods, "... in whom are hidden all the treasures of wisdom and knowledge,"[35] according to the (4) divine Apostle. For out of such great goods the Father, who alone is good, caused the Son to subsist, so that being life itself, he might give life to the universe, and being light itself, the "true Light,"[36] he might also illuminate every intellectual and rational being,[37] and as Word and Wisdom itself, he might bring into existence and govern everything in a wise and rational manner. On account of these things, then, he alone and no other has been proclaimed and is only-begotten Son of God.

Chapter 9

(1) For this reason, one might[38] rightly censure those who have dared to represent him as a creature, which came into existence out of nothing, like the remaining creatures. For how will he still be Son? And how will the one who assumes the same na-

35. Col 2.3.
36. Jn 1.9.
37. οὐσίας.
38. Although Eusebius is writing against Marcellus, he at least sees that Marcellus was right to attack his opponent Asterius, who had dared to call the Son a creature who, like other creatures, was created out of nothing. Unfortunately, because this work by Eusebius has been rarely used to interpret Asterius, these notions of Asterius's have been overlooked for a long time. As in the previous chapter, it is obvious that Eusebius distances himself not only from Marcellus, but also from Asterius.

ture as the remaining creatures be only-begotten of God? For by virtue of the latter he would instead be the brother of these [creatures],[39] but not the Son of God, and he will be one of the many creatures,[40] since he would have a share in the fellowship of the creation out of nothing just as they have. (2) But the divine oracles do not teach in this way concerning him. Rather, when they teach about the origin of creatures, they consistently give witness that all things came into existence through him. For "all things were made through him, and without him not one thing was made,"[41] and "in him all things were created in heaven and on earth, visible and invisible,"[42] and "all things were created through him and for him. He is before all things, and in him all things hold together,"[43] according to (3) the apostolic teachings. When [the Scriptures] introduce the theology concerning him, they distinguish him from all the remaining [creatures], and acknowledge him as Lord and Master and Fashioner and God and Savior of all, and reveal him alone and no other as the only-begotten Son of God, and call him alone Wisdom and Word and Life and Light and "image of the invisible God"[44] and "radiance of eternal light."[45] And they teach [us] to think countless other things akin to these about him, thus revealing the unique relation of the paternal divinity to him alone as to an only-begotten Son. (4) For this reason, the Father's voice also proclaimed him alone beloved Son by the river Jordan, testifying with a great cry, "This is my beloved Son, with whom I am well pleased."[46] It[47] gives this testimony a second time when it confirms the same statement during the transfiguration on the mountain.[48] (5) Thus

39. Asterius, in fact, taught this. See Asterius, *fr.* 31 (98 V.). Eusebius accepts Marcellus's criticism of Asterius in this respect, also to counteract Marcellus's claim that he, Eusebius himself, was simply a follower of Asterius.

40. See Asterius, *fr.* 45; 34; 23; 44 (110; 100; 94; 108 V.).

41. Jn 1.3.

42. Col 1.16.

43. Col 1.16–17.

44. Col 1.15.

45. Wis 7.26.

46. Mt 3.17.

47. The Father's voice.

48. Mt 17.5.

since the God of the universe himself has provided this testimony for him, and the evangelist expressly teaches that he is the only-begotten Son, in that passage where he said, "No one has ever seen God, the only-begotten Son (or only-begotten God)[49] who is in the bosom of the Father, he has made him known,"[50] [and] even the Savior himself in the teachings concerning him confirms this, when he said, "For God so loved the world that he gave his only-begotten Son, that all who believe (6) in him might have eternal life,"[51] the man who, after these statements, defines the Son as something that came into being out of nothing, and as a creature that came forth from the non-existent, unwittingly grants only the name to him, but denies that he is truly the Son. For that which has come into existence out of what is not could not truly be the Son of God, because he would be nothing other than one of the creatures.

Chapter 10

(1) The true Son of God, seeing as he has been born from him, that is to say, from the Father, would rightly be called both the only-begotten and beloved [Son] of the Father. So he would also be God. For what would an offspring of God who has been made like the one who has begotten him be [other than a true Son]? Therefore, on the one hand, a king creates but does not beget a city, while on the other, he is said to beget, but not create, a son. And the craftsman would be a fashioner but not a father of that which is crafted by him, nor would he be called fashioner of the son who came forth from him. All the more, the God of the universe would be said to be Father of the Son, but (2) also rightly creator and maker of the cosmos. And if once somewhere in Scripture someone were to find it said, "The

49. The addition in parentheses (so in the critical edition, reflecting Eusebius's argument) is another instance of Eusebius distancing himself from Asterius, who confessed the Son as "only-begotten God." See Asterius, *fr.* 9 (86 V.), quoted in Marcellus, *fr.* 1 (65 K./H.).

50. Jn 1.18.

51. Jn 3.16.

Lord created me as the beginning of his ways for his works,"[52] it is necessary to scrutinize the sense of the statement, which I will set out a little later,[53] but not to undermine on the basis of one statement, like Marcellus, the most important dogma of the Church. For that man, having once heard that the Son is Word, stumbled on the man and eliminated his existence.[54] (3) Indeed, how is it pious to compare the Son, who is given witness to by both himself and the Father, with the rest of the creatures? How will he be only-begotten if he is counted together with the multitude of creatures? And surely from the name itself, the Son shows [his] natural relationship to the Father, just as, again, the name "only-begotten" encompasses both his nature and his birth itself and the fact that he is an only [Son] and that no other has a share with him in the sonship.

But (4) these people, too, seem to have suffered the same illness as Marcellus. For one man, fearing to say that there were two gods, put forth a denial of the Son, setting aside his hypostasis.[55] But others, having granted two hypostases, one ingenerate and the other created out of nothing, assert one God.[56] But for those men the Son will no longer be the only-begotten or indeed Lord or God, since he will not share in the divinity of the Father, but will be placed on a level with the remaining creatures because he came to subsist out of nothing.

(5) But the Church does not teach this. It proclaims the Son of God to be God and Lord and teaches that he is truly Son and God, not as many men have been called in name sons and

52. Prv 8.22, obviously one of the scriptural texts debated between Asterius and Marcellus; see Asterius, *fr.* 17; 48 (90; 114 V.); Marcellus, *fr.* 23–46 (24–40 V. = *fr.* 125; 123; 124; 9; 12; 10; 11; 13; 14; 15; 16; 126; 17; 18; 37; 38; 39; 22; 23; 24; 25; 26; 27; 89 in K./H.).

53. Specifically, in *ET* 3.1–3; see pp. 275–304 below.

54. ὕπαρξιν. When Eusebius speaks about "stumbling on the man," he may have in mind Marcellus's willingness to attribute a hypostasis distinct from that of the Father's to the assumed humanity of God, even though he will not attribute a hypostasis to the pre-existent assuming Word himself. See *fr.* 85 (74,1–5 V.).

55. It is unclear to whom Eusebius refers here, but he clearly has supporters of Marcellus in mind.

56. See Asterius, *fr.* 52–56 (116–118 V.)—as the edition shows, texts that are quoted by both Marcellus and Eusebius.

gods,[57] concerning whom it has been said, "I said, you are gods and sons of the most High, all of you,"[58] but because the one who alone was begotten from the Father himself "existed in the form of God"[59] and was "image of the invisible God and first-born of all creation."[60] For this reason, the Church has learned to honor and revere and worship him alone as Lord and Savior and its God.

Chapter 11

(1) If the notion of proclaiming two gods makes them afraid,[61] let them know that even when the Son is confessed by us to be God, the former [namely, the Father] would still be the one and only God, the only one without source and unbegotten, the one who possesses the divinity as his own,[62] and who has become the cause of being and of being in such a way[63] for the Son himself.

Even the Son himself confesses that he lives because of [him],[64] saying outright, "As the living Father sent me, and I live because of the Father,"[65] and, "For as the Father has life in

57. So Asterius, *fr.* 31; 45; 72 (98; 110; 132 V.).

58. Ps 81.6 (RSV 82.6).

59. Phil 2.7.

60. Col 1.15.

61. Eusebius is referring to the debate between Marcellus and Asterius. See Marcellus, *fr.* 97 (76 K./H.) (86–88 V.), in which he is reacting to Asterius. See Asterius, *fr.* 55 (118 V.).

62. Note that Eusebius is not only saying that the Father has "his own divinity," but the "divinity as his own," which is a subtle but important difference. The Son also has his own divinity, but does not possess it as his own, but as a divinity that is given to him by the Father, whereas the Father alone has the divinity out of himself. In this respect, Eusebius accepts Asterius's position that what the Son is (and does) has been given to him by the Father. See Asterius, *fr.* 36; 38 (100; 102 V.). Eusebius's counter-argument against Marcellus reflects the debate between Marcellus and Asterius. See Asterius, *fr.* 51 (116 V.), Marcellus, *fr.* 92 (78 K./H.) (80,13–82,12 V.).

63. αὐτῷ τε τῷ υἱῷ τοῦ εἶναι καὶ τοῦ τοιῷδε εἶναι γεγονὼς αἴτιος.

64. I.e., the Father.

65. Jn 6.57. Again with this scriptural quotation and the next one, Eusebius reflects the discussion between Marcellus and Asterius that Eusebius encountered in Marcellus's work against Asterius. See Asterius, *fr.* 38–42 (102; 104;

(2) himself, so also he has given to the Son to have life in himself."⁶⁶ For this reason, he also teaches that the Father is both
our God and his God, when he says, "I go to my Father and to
your Father and to my God and to your God."⁶⁷ The great Apostle teaches that God is the head of the Son and the Son is the
head of the Church, in one place saying, "the head of Christ is
God,"⁶⁸ and in another asserting about the Son, "and he made
him head over all things for the Church, which is his body."⁶⁹
(3) Therefore, he himself would be the originator and head of
the Church while the Father would also⁷⁰ be his head. In this
way the Father of the only-begotten Son is one God, and the
head of even Christ himself is one. Since there is one source⁷¹
and head, how could there be two gods, and not

one, that one alone,

who acknowledges no higher being nor other cause than
himself,

who possesses the divinity of monarchical authority as his
own, without source and unbegotten and

who has given a share of his own divinity and life to the Son,

who through him [the Son] has brought all things into existence,

who sends him,⁷²

---

106 V.); Marcellus, *fr.* 74 (73 K./H.) (62,5–64,14 V.). Asterius had used these
scriptural texts to underline the power of the Father and the fact that the Son
was on the receiving side of the Father's creative activity (although the first
of the creatures to receive the Father's power and divinity). Asterius does this
in order to differentiate Father and Son and to work out his soteriology. In
contrast, Marcellus asserts against Asterius that the Son is not just the one who
received the Father's power, but is himself the Father's power and Logos.

66. Jn 5.26.
67. Jn 20.17.
68. 1 Cor 11.3.
69. Eph 1.22–23.
70. Klostermann's addition of a second "head" is incorrect and misleading, which is proven by the next sentence ("of even Christ"). Eusebius wants to
express that the Father is head of both, the Son and the Church, and that the
Son's headship (as with his divinity) is not a second one, but is the headship
of the Father.
71. ἀρχῆς.
72. See Jn 6.57; Mk 9.37.

who gives commands to him,[73]
who enjoins,[74]
who teaches,
who hands over all things to him,[75]
who glorifies him,[76]
who exalts him in the highest,[77]
who revealed him as king of the universe,
who gives all judgment to him,[78]
who wishes that we also obey him,[79]

who encourages him to take up his throne at the right hand of his magnificence (4) when he addresses him and says, "Sit at my right hand,"[80] the one

who, for all these reasons, also exists as God of the Son himself,

in obedience to whom his only-begotten child
"emptied himself,
humbled himself,
took on the form of a slave and
became obedient unto death,"[81]
to whom he [the Son] also prayed,[82]

73. See Jn 14.31.

74. See Jn 8.28.

75. 1 Cor 15.24. See Marcellus, *fr.* 103 (115 K./H.) (94,8 V.); 106 (117 K./H.) (100,2 V.); Jn 5.22; Mt 11.27; Lk 10.22—all passages that are addressed by Asterius. See Asterius, *fr.* 74 (134–136 V.). Eusebius must have known this text of Asterius, as can be seen from the scriptural texts that follow in Asterius, ibid.

76. Jn 12.28. See the debate between Marcellus and Asterius on this topic, Asterius, *fr.* 36; 74 (100; 134–138 V.); Marcellus, *fr.* 80 (107 K./H.) (70,12–19 V.).

77. Phil 2.9.

78. Jn 5.22.

79. Mk 9.7; Mt 17.5; Lk 9.35.

80. Ps 109.1 (RSV 110.1). See the debate on this topic in Marcellus, *fr.* 106 (117 K./H.) (96,4–100,3 V.).

81. Phil 2.7, 8. Eusebius is referring here to Marcellus's criticism of Eusebius's interpretation of this biblical verse; see Marcellus, *fr.* 127 (101 K./H.) (118,11–22 V.).

82. See Jn 17.11, 20–23; on this, Asterius, *fr.* 41 (104 V.); with regard to Mt 26.39, see Asterius, *fr.* 74 (136,21 V.).

to whom he renders obedience when he [the Father] commands,[83]

to whom he also gives thanks,[84]

whom he also teaches us to consider the "only true God,"[85]

whom he confesses to be greater than himself,[86]

whom, in addition to all these features, he wishes all of us to know is also his God?[87]

(5) And when he glorified his Father in this way, the Father, glorifying him in return,[88] revealed him as Lord and Savior and God of the universe and co-regent of his kingdom.

Well then, having been taught these things by her own God, the Church deems it right to recognize him as God, Lord, and Savior, but also as the only-begotten Son of the God who is over all, and to address no other creature as God,[89] but knows (6) this one alone as God, whom alone the Father begot from himself, just as he himself indicates, speaking through Solomon, "Before the mountains had been shaped, before all the hills, he begets me,"[90] thus in some way hinting at the divine and transcendent powers by the terms "mountains" and "hills."[91]

Chapter 12

(1) Well then, if someone should also inquire about a matter he has no business inquiring into and should question both

83. See Mk 14.35–36; Mt 26.39; Lk 22.42.

84. See Jn 11.41.

85. Jn 17.3.

86. See Jn 14.28; on this, Asterius, *fr.* 42 (106 V.).

87. See Jn 17.20–23; 20.17; see Asterius, *fr.* 41 (104 V.).

88. See Jn 12.27–28; 13.32; 17.1. On this, see Asterius, *fr.* 74 (136 V.).

89. The latter argument is directed against Asterius's reading of Prv 8.22–31 as discussed between him and Marcellus. See Asterius, *fr.* 17; 48 (90; 114 V.); Marcellus, *fr.* 23–46 (24–40 V.).

90. Prv 8.25.

91. Eusebius equally distances himself from Marcellus's position and exegesis, which did not read into Prv 8.22–31 the pre-cosmic birth of the Son, but referred this biblical text to the Logos's Incarnation, the second economy, and his birth from Mary, and which equated the "mountains" and "hills" of Prv 8.25 with the "apostles" and their successors, the bishops. On this, see Marcellus, *fr.* 26 (9 K./H.) (30,3–4 V.); 28 (10 K./H.) (30,9–12 V.); 45 (27 K./H.) (40,3–8 V.).

how God could beget and how he who is beyond the universe
will be Father, the audacity of this question will be silenced by
the one who made this statement: "Do not inquire into those
things that are deeper than you, nor scrutinize those things
that are higher than you. Meditate on the commandments you
have been given; what has been hidden is no concern of yours."[92]
And let Paul, who said, "O the depth of the riches and wisdom
and knowledge of God! How unsearchable are his judgments
and how inscrutable his ways!"[93] convince the man who dares
to go further not to reach for things that are unattainable. Or
let him rather say regarding those things that he also says have
come into existence out of nothing, how and in what way they
came to subsist, (2) since they did not exist at all previously. For
indeed he [God] did not construct everything in the way that
craftsmen among us do, having taken matter as a pre-existing
substrate in his hands. Just as so great a thing was impossible
by nature for men (I mean bringing into being from nothing
that which does not exist at all), but was possible for him, he
also became maker of the universe not in a human way, but by
means that are ineffable and inexpressible to us. (3) So in this
way and much more would the begetting of his only-begotten
be unsearchable and inscrutable, not only by us alone, as one
might say,[94] but also by all the powers that are greater than we
[are]. For how could those things that are greatly subordinate
by nature, far lower and distant from the ineffable and divine
being,[95] comprehend what is transcendent and highest? And
how could those things that did not exist previously and that
were brought into being through him out of nothing (which
would render the one who brought them into being the cause
of their existence)[96] obtain knowledge of the first creation? Or
how then will we, men of yesterday, clothed in "skin and flesh,"

92. Sir 3.21–22.
93. Rom 11.33.
94. Eusebius is referring back to Rom 11.33.
95. οὐσίας.
96. "Cause" is the translation for αἴτιος, "existence" that for ὑπάρξεως. The
idea that creating things makes the creator the cause of their existence is an
important idea in Eusebius, linked to his defense of his own monotheism in
the face of Marcellus's contention that the assertion of two hypostases com-

strung together "by bones and sinews,"[97] and not even understanding our own affairs, conduct without danger an inquiry
about the ineffable, curiously trying to find out how the Father
begot the Son?

That even countless things that are right at our feet escape
our knowledge (4) should be self-evident. For who would be
able to say how the soul was enclosed in the body, how it will
leave it, how it penetrated [the body] in the first place, what
the form of the soul is, what is its appearance, what is its shape,
what is its being?[98] The man who troubles himself over demons,
the being[99] of angels, the principalities, thrones and poten-
tates, authorities, (5) and ruling powers has not yet [been able
to explain these things] to me. If we are at a loss in all these
matters, what need is there for investigating the knowledge concerning the divinity that is without source and ingenerate? Why
inquire into the things that are unattainable, how God subsists
as Father of an only-begotten Son, as if the Father's voice were
not enough for us as a testimony to the beloved, whom he proclaimed, having said, "This is my beloved Son, (6) with whom I
am well-pleased; listen to him."[100]

If indeed it is commanded that we listen to him, being obedient to the imperial law, let us listen to the beloved Son. What
he wishes us to know about him, he will show, having said, "For
God so loved the world that he gave his only-begotten Son, so
that everyone who believes in him might have eternal life."[101]
Of course, then, we should believe him, so that we might obtain
eternal (7) life, for "he who believes in him," he says, "has eternal life,"[102] not he who knows how [the Son] was begotten from
the Father, for then no one would have a share in eternal life,
since indeed this has been said, that "no one knows the Father,

---

promises it. For Eusebius, there is only one God because there is only one
cause.
    97. Jb 10.11.
    98. οὐσία.
    99. οὐσίας.
    100. Mt 17.5.
    101. Jn 3.16.
    102. Jn 3.36.

except the Son, nor does anyone know the Son" except the "Father" alone who begot him.[103]

And therefore faith is sufficient for us for salvation, which allows [us] to know God as [the] Father who rules over all, and to acknowledge his only-begotten Son as Savior, who indeed, in addition to other things, also handed over these statements in this way: "That which has been begotten of flesh is flesh, and that which has been begotten of the spirit is spirit,"[104] (8) but "God is spirit."[105] Thus it follows that one must also think that what has been begotten of God is God.

By as much, however, as God who transcends the universe was differentiated and separated by nature from earthly flesh, by so much is it necessary to think that the manner in which the Father begot the Son is differentiated from the generation of fleshly things. For neither by sending something forth, nor by being altered, nor by being moved by passion, nor (9) by enduring anything whatsoever of those things that we normally experience, did he cause him to subsist. For he was not a body so that one could attribute emanation, or diminution, or extension,[106] or change, or turning, or flux, or partition, or suffering to him. In contradistinction to all these kinds of change, he brought into existence the work of generation in a way ineffable and incomprehensible to us, or rather, unsearchable and inscrutable to every generated nature.

Therefore, as the sun begets the ray, so also the Son is said to be [the] "radiance of eternal light"[107] and "radiance of glory,"[108] though surely not like a perceptible image of light, for in a manner beyond any analogy, he [the Father] made him [the

103. Mt 11.27.
104. Jn 3.6.
105. Jn 4.24.
106. This is obviously directed against Marcellus's view that the divine Monad (Oneness) had been broadened into a *Trias* (Trinity) during the soteriological economy. See Marcellus, *fr.* 48 (67 K./H.) (42,10–11 V.); 73 (71 K./H.) (62,3 V.). Marcellus uses the verb πλατύνεσθαι for this "broadening." As shown in the introduction, both Asterius and Arius were keen to stress the non-materialistic nature of the Son's begetting.
107. Wis 7.26.
108. Heb 1.3.

Son] subsist by means that are ineffable and incomprehensible, and this as the one and only-begotten [Son].

(10) Let every mouth reject the impious and godless men who have suffered the error of polytheism, those men who, having cast down into the multitude the special and unique begetting of the only-begotten Son, have addressed him as Father "of gods and men,"[109] both mixing together men with gods, and introducing the same Father as being of one nature with the former. But with demonic energy they uttered this impious and godless statement, proposing gods that have similar natures and similar sufferings to [those of] the mortal, passible, and sinful race of human beings, and the common Father of these as almost in every way likened to his children. But the ecclesiastical herald proclaims to all one only-begotten Son of one God, whom he [the Father] made to subsist for the salvation of and providence over all creatures.

Chapter 13

(1) Since the nature of generated things, while different in corporeal and incorporeal things, animate and inanimate, rational and irrational, and mortal and immortal, was not capable of drawing near to God, who transcends all and is over all, nor of having a share in the brilliance of his divinity, because the superior nature [of God] surpasses its deficiency, but would have, because of the weakness of its nature, been totally and utterly lost, had it not encountered God's help in the form of the Savior, the Father's love of humanity fittingly established his only-begotten child for all, who moves through all, supports all, and who showers upon all those the guidance[110] that comes from him. (2) For the Father who begot him has revealed him alone as shepherd and Savior, guardian, protector, healer, and governor of all things in heaven and on earth taken together, having entrusted to him alone the direction of the constitution and government of the universe, which he [the Son] himself teaches, saying, "All things have been given to me by my Fa-

109. Homer, *Il.* 8.1.52.
110. Literally, "abundance of means."

ther,"[111] and again, "For the Father loves the Son and has given all things into his hand."[112] (3) Such a wise governor, having taken up [this] inheritance from the Father, taking his stance upon the whole cosmos and looking up to his Father, leads and carries out the governance of everything, neither neglecting the smallest of those things that are in need of his leadership nor overlooking the most humble. Therefore, indeed, he comes to the assistance of all, distributing to each the things that are fitting for it, and for the care of the universe providing like a physician those (4) things that conduce to its salvation. For this reason he rightly did not overlook human life, but even long ago he provided his aid to human beings who from of old were beloved by God, at one time appearing in human form to the forefathers of the Hebrews, and at another, ordaining fitting laws for the descendants of these, and even then, too, to those who would come afterwards he gave out through prophets oracles of his coming (5) epiphany, which would illuminate all human beings. And when the time of these [human beings] passed, he brought to fulfillment in deeds the ancient oracles and then became present, having further been mingled with mortal life, the shepherd becoming one of the sheep,[113] although he himself was the only-begotten Son of God, in, as it were, a divine statue, the instrument of the body,[114] conversing from above with the human race through [his] (6) teachings,

111. Mt 11.27; Lk 10.22.

112. Jn 3.35.

113. Either an allusion to Paul's statement in Phil 2.6–11 that the Son took on the form of a slave, or, more likely, to Johannine literature indicating that the shepherd became one of the sheep, an idea that is close to Asterius's Christology.

114. I.e., the mouth or voice. Given Eusebius's Christology, which is proto-Apolinarian and based on a Word-Flesh model, the incarnate Son is like a god taking up residence in a statue, while being the statue's (= body's) mouth or voice. The Son becomes present in the world, being—as Asterius had already stated in *fr.* 46 and *fr.* 47 (112 V.)—one among those to whom he speaks. Yet in Eusebius the Son is more than just the first creature as in Asterius. The Son, although in the statue (hence among the people), talks from above to the people who are looking at the statue from below. The image used here is that of a colossal statue, as, for example, the statue of Constantine in the Capitoline in Rome.

healings, and ineffable lessons of inspired wisdom. Soon, however, and at the Father's prompting out of surpassing love for humanity, he drove right up to the very gates of death, so that he might render even those here worthy of his own grace, having drawn them up to life with him. Thus "God was in Christ reconciling the world to himself."[115] And he underwent the fleshly economy, although he was and pre-existed before it, having been honored with the divinity of the paternal glory. For indeed, not thinking it "robbery to be equal with God," but thus having emptied himself and "having taken on the form of a slave, he humbled himself, becoming obedient" to the Father "even unto death,"[116] so that "just as death" came "through one man's sin" and gained dominion over the entire race,[117] so also eternal life "through his grace" might rule over those who [believe] in him and through him are acknowledged by his God and Father.

Chapter 14

(1) Thus the Church rightly proclaims these things, and rejected Sabellius like a certain counterfeit coin stamped with the denial of the Son of God, because he, too, said that he knew one God and there was none other besides him—just like Marcellus.

The first heralds of our Savior himself, however, called those who said they knew one God and did not deny the body of the Savior, but did not know the divinity of the Son, "Ebionites";[118] that is to say, they called them in the Hebrew language "poor" with respect to their understanding. (2) The Church fathers[119]

115. 2 Cor 5.19.
116. Phil 2.6–8.
117. Rom 5.12, 16, 17.
118. Eusebius discusses the Ebionites in his *Historia ecclesiastica* 3.27.
119. Eusebius's *On Ecclesiastical Theology* with its "Church theology" is an important source for a) the development of a Christian/Church theology, b) the development of a Church-related (and soon owned and distinguished from non-Church-related) philosophical discipline, and c) the development of an orthodoxy that is based on references to a tradition of Church fathers and their pupils/descendants, distinct from philosophical school traditions. As we

also exposed the Samosatene as one foreign to the Church of God, because, although he taught that Jesus was the Christ of God, and confessed that there was one God over all just as Marcellus does, he did not also confess that Christ both is the Son of God and was God before the fleshly birth. But on the one hand this man was driven far away from his [Christ's] Church as one who was irreverent toward Christ, (3) while on the other, Sabellius, because he offended the Father himself, whom he dared to call Son, underwent the same judgment as the godless heretics. Marcellus, however, suspecting that he would suffer the same fate as Sabellius, invented a more novel subterfuge for his error, determining that God and the Word in him were one, but granting him two labels, namely, Father and Son. Indeed, he did not hide (4) nor did he escape, but sometime later he himself was caught with his own nets.[120] But even before he was caught, having been struck by conscience, he began to slander Sabellius to deflect suspicion from himself.

Chapter 15

(1) Listen to how he slandered the man, having mentioned him by name, writing these things about him in these very words:

> For Sabellius, who himself had also slipped from the right faith, had accurate knowledge neither about God nor about his holy Word. For the one who did not know the Word was also ignorant of the Father. For he [the Word] says, "No one knows

---

have noted in the introduction, this aspect of Eusebius's theology was inspired by the debate between Asterius and Marcellus, wherein Asterius tried to defend Eusebius's letter with reference to Paulinus (who himself had written a letter that ended with a quotation from Origen), while Marcellus distinguishes between the teaching of the gospel and the philosophical school tradition, placing Origen in the latter. See Asterius, *fr.* 5; 7; 9 (84; 86 V.); Marcellus, *fr.* 17–22 (86; 87; 37; 38; 39; 88 K./H.) (16–22 V.).

120. This is another indication that Marcellus was active on the anti-Arius and anti-Asterius side of the early trinitarian debates, and, as such, an early opponent of Eusebius's, but in the early stages of these debates had enough support to survive opposition to his views and efforts to depose him. See the introduction, pp. 13–18.

the Father except the Son,"[121] that is, the Word. For the Word
through himself provides the knowledge of the Father. For
he also said in this way to those of the Jews who at that time
thought they knew God, but who rejected his Word, through
whom alone God is known: "No one knows the Father except
the Son and him to whom the Son revealed him."[122] For since
it was impossible to know God in any other way, he [the Word]
teaches human beings to know him through his [God's] own
Word, so that that man [Sabellius] has erred who does not
know accurately the Father and his Word.[123]

(2) Marcellus wrote these things in an effort to clear himself
of the suspicion of "Sabellianizing" as far as his speech and writing went, but surely by virtue of his intent and the similarity of
his thinking to that man's [Sabellius's], he is caught by the same
arrows that pierce that man from all sides, as for me ...[124] and
through prayer, there would be an avoidance of the same fate.
But now he appears to have erred to a greater degree than that
man. For the one was in large part ignorant when he erred, I
suspect, but the other, acknowledging that the man was in error, and yet casting himself off the notorious cliff of the same
impiety, would be worthy of no forgiveness. But let us thorough-
ly scrutinize the things that have been said.

Chapter 16

(1) Therefore, in the first place, since he said that neither
Sabellius nor the Jews knew God because they did not acknowledge the Word, it is necessary to examine what sort of Word
he [Marcellus] proposes, for if the Son of God is the only-
begotten, who subsists and lives, he [Marcellus] nevertheless
does not acknowledge him. Thus to begin with, our Savior mentioned the "Son" in different ways and called him many times
"only-begotten Son" and never spoke of himself as "Word," but
through all of the gospels, taught that he is Son of God (on

121. Mt 11.27.
122. Ibid.
123. Marcellus, *fr.* 69 (44 K./H.) (58,11–60,2 V.).
124. The text is corrupt here.

account of which he also blesses Peter when he said, "You are the Christ, the Son of the living God,"[125] and he testifies that the knowledge has come to him [Peter] through a revelation of the Father, having said, "Blessed are you, Simon bar Jonah, because flesh and blood did not reveal this to you, but my heavenly Father").[126]

This wondrous man [Marcellus], as if his ears were blocked, writes these things, in these very words.

> And because of this he does not name himself "Son of God," but everywhere calls himself "Son of Man," so that through this sort of confession he might enable the man through fellowship with him to become by adoption Son of God.[127]

(2) See how he [Marcellus] does not dare to confess that he is "Son of God," lest he deviate from the teaching of Sabellius, but calls him "Son of Man" on account of the flesh that he assumed. Indeed, throughout the whole of his own treatise, he calls him "Word," indicating repeatedly that "he was nothing other than (3) Word."[128] And, again, in the remarks in which he disparages Sabellius, he refers to the statement of the Savior, in which he said, "No one knows the Father (4) except the Son and him to whom the Son revealed him,"[129] and as if he were correcting this statement, he again calls the Savior "Word" instead of "Son," thus saying:

> For he [the Word] says, "No one knows the Father except the Son,"[130] that is, the Word.[131]

And he adds:

> For the Word through himself provides the knowledge of the Father.[132]

---

125. Mt 16.16.
126. Mt 16.17.
127. Marcellus, *fr.* 111 (41 K./H.) (104,12–15 V.).
128. A rephrasing of Marcellus, *fr.* 7 (42 K./H.) (10,7 V.).
129. Mt 11.27.
130. Ibid.
131. Marcellus, *fr.* 69 (44 K./H.) (58,13–14 V.).
132. Marcellus, *fr.* 69 (44 K./H.) (58,14–15 V.).

And he adds:[133]

> It was impossible to know God in any other way than through
> his own Word.[134]

And again he puts "Word" instead of "the Son" and calls
him "his own Word." Even in the briefest of remarks he mentions the "Word" several times, but the "Son" not once. And he
even (5) alters the saying itself of the Savior, introducing "that
is, the Word,"[135] instead of "the Son," as if the reference to the
Son would not harmonize better with the title of the Father.
For this reason, on the one hand the Savior rightly and appropriately matches the title of the Son[136] to that of the Father, but
on the other, he who declined to call him the Son above is always talking about the "Word" below, and although he accuses
Sabellius of denying the Son, he makes a spectacle of himself
doing the same thing as he, hoping that by casting aspersions
on him [Sabellius] he will avoid the suspicion of evil doctrine.
Therefore, if he blames Sabellius for denying the Son of God,
he should first put the blame on himself. But if (6) Sabellius
was ignorant of the Word, as [Marcellus] himself defined it,[137]
he was not rightly accused for this. For no one would say that
either Sabellius or the Jews themselves, although they deny the
Christ of God, were ignorant of the fact that there is a word
(which Marcellus says is "in God"),[138] through whom [God]
gave oracles to Moses and the prophets, but rather that they
acknowledged [this word] correctly—and not only the Jews,

133. This example shows that when Eusebius states about Marcellus that
the latter "adds," it does not follow from this reference that the text that Eusebius then is quoting followed immediately the former quotation in Marcellus's
book.

134. Marcellus, *fr.* 69 (44 K./H.) (58,18–19 V.).

135. Ibid. (58,14 V.).

136. Literally, "fits the yoke of the Son to that of the Father."

137. According to Eusebius, Marcellus defined the Word much as Sabellius
defined the Son, namely, as identical with the Father; hence Marcellus is not
right to accuse him. Eusebius thinks that even Marcellus would admit that Sabellius, as the Jews had done, had accepted the existence of the Word spoken
to Moses and the prophets.

138. Marcellus, *fr.* 76 (103 K./H.); 109 (121 K./H.) (68,1–2; 102,18 V.).

but also the Greeks. For what person would not admit that God is rational,[139] just as he is wise, good, and powerful? Sabellius would not deny knowing this. But because he did not also confess that the Son of God lived, subsisted, (7) and pre-existed the flesh, [and] because of this agreement with Marcellus, he was driven from the Church of God just as he [Marcellus] was.

It would be clear how Marcellus thought the same things as Sabellius from those remarks in which he asserted that "God and his Word are one and the same,"[140] when he said in these very words:[141]

Chapter 17

(1) If one were only to consider the Spirit, the Word would rightly appear to be one and the same with God.[142]

Later, however, comparing the (Word) of God to the human word, he also adds:

The word in a man is[143] one and the same with him, being separated [from him] by nothing other than the activity alone of the deed.[144]

Therefore, he soon explained that before the establishment of the cosmos there was nothing else except God, and again said in these very words that

When the cosmos did not yet exist, there was nothing other than God alone.[145]

139. This passage plays upon the double meaning of the Greek word λό-γος—which can mean *rationality* as well as *word*.

140. See below, n.142.

141. It is interesting to note that Eusebius carefully chooses the next quotations from Marcellus's book, always cutting out and leaving aside the biblical references of Marcellus.

142. Marcellus, *fr.* 76 (103 K./H.); 109 (121 K./H.) (68,1–2; 102,18 V.).

143. Although there is a variance in the wording from how Eusebius quotes Marcellus, *fr.* 87 (61 K./H.) (76,9 V.), shortly afterward the translation harmonizes the text for the sake of a smoother reading.

144. Marcellus, *fr.* 87 (61 K./H.) (76,8–10 V.).

145. Marcellus, *fr.* 77 (104 K./H.) (68,11–12 V.).

(2) Whereas later[146] he compared the Word of God to the word by which we communicate, in those remarks in which he wrote in this way:

> For just as all the things that have come into existence have come into existence by the Father through the Word, so also the things that are said by the Father are communicated through the Word.[147]

And having called him the communicating word in these remarks, he proceeds in what follows to present him as one and the same, inseparable in hypostasis from the Father, saying somewhere in this way:

> And this is easy, I think, for those who reflect well upon a small (3) and humble example from our experience. For it is impossible for anyone to separate the word of a man in power and hypostasis. For the word is one and the same with the man, and is separated [from him] in no other way than by the activity alone of the deed.[148]

And again he has used the same image when he said:

> For whatever the Father says, in every case he appears to say it through the Word. This is clear even from our own experience, insofar as one can compare small things with great and divine ones. For whatever we wish both to say and do according to our capacity, we do by means of our word.[149]

(4) It would be fitting to think one hears Sabellius more than Marcellus saying these things, if Marcellus had not mocked Sabellius for these ideas, because he shamelessly dared to call "Son" the communicating word in God, as he himself [Marcellus] thinks [Sabellius had done]. For again Sabellius was not so stupid as to attribute to God who is over all a word like the one in men, nor was he so unintelligent as to call the word that does not subsist "Son of God." (5) For this reason, Sabellius, having

---

146. Eusebius combines here two Marcellan passages, *fr.* 76/77 (103/104 K./H.) and 87 (61 K./H.), which he uses by alternating between them.

147. Marcellus, *fr.* 87 (61 K./H.) (76,8–10 V.).

148. Marcellus, *fr.* 87 (61 K./H.) (76,5–10 V.).

149. Marcellus, *fr.* 89 (62 K./H.) (76,17–78,4 V.).

said that there is one God, but having denied the Son, following the proposition that was attributed to him, alleged that the Father and the Son were the same. Marcellus, however, admitting, as that man did, that God and the Word in him are one and the same thing, blames Sabellius in vain, but not (6) himself as well. For either he [Marcellus] must approve of that man, or censure him, and, in censuring him, he must give up that evil doctrine that is like his and not imagine God after the manner of a statue-maker deliberating with himself and not speak of him as engaging in a dialogue with his own reason and being exhorted by himself:

> "Come, let us make, come, let us form (7) a statue" (for he said that in such a way as God said, "Let us make man"),[150]

nor suppose that the Word is in God at one time in mental thought, as in man, [and] at another time communicated as it is in speech among us. For one could tolerate hearing Sabellius or one of the Jews, who undisguisedly deny the Son of God, say these things, rather than a Christian. (8) But this one [Marcellus], like one taking pride in Jewish teaching, introduces into the Church of Christ this impious and godless dogma concerning the non-existence of the Son of God, maintaining through the whole treatise he labored over that before the world came into existence "there was nothing other than God alone,"[151] so that he might bar the means of approach to the Son. (9) But he is also arrogant, boasting that he knows one God, as if we too do not say this, since we have received that the Son of God is truly "Son," and having learned from him to acknowledge one God,[152] and that he is God and at the same time Father of the only-begotten Son, [himself] truly existing as a Son, begotten before all ages from him [the Father], and who before the assumption of the flesh was not only called "Word," which that venerable man asserts, but also countless other things. This

---

150. Gn 1.26, but also part of Marcellus, *fr.* 98 (58 K./H.) (90,4f. V.).

151. Last part of Marcellus, *fr.* 77 (104 K./H.) (68,12–13 V.).

152. Eusebius clearly refers to Marcellus's letter to Constantine that introduced his work to the emperor. See Marcellus, *fr. Praef.* (128 K./H.) (3,1f. V.); see also above Eusebius of Caesarea, *ET praef.* (60,10–12 K./H.), pp. 160–61.

190   EUSEBIUS

one [Marcellus], however, would falsify[153] the divine Scripture, flatly denying that before the coming in the flesh he was called anything other than Word.

Chapter 18

(1) Listen at any rate, then, as he maintains [this] obstinately, writing in this way in these very words:

> So that it is clear in every way that no other name befits the eternity of the Word than this very one that John, the most holy disciple of the Lord and apostle, uttered in the beginning of the gospel. For since after the assumption of the flesh he is proclaimed both "Christ" and "Jesus," as well as "life"[154] and "way"[155] and "day"[156] and "resurrection"[157] and "door"[158] and "bread"[159] and whatever else he is called by the divine Scriptures, besides these it is not fitting for us to be ignorant of the first name, which was Word. For because of this, too, the most holy evangelist and disciple of the Lord, much roused in spirit, recalling the origin[160] from above, and not a more recent one, said, "In the beginning was the Word,"[161] and, "the Word was with God, and the Word was God,"[162] so that he might show that if there is any new and more recent name, it exists as a result of his new and recent economy according to the flesh.[163]

(2) And he adds in what follows:

153. Eusebius is accusing Marcellus of presenting a false picture of the Scriptures, suggesting they only refer to the preexistent Christ as Word, when in fact that is not the case. So Marcellus is in effect presenting a "skewed" picture of the scriptural evidence.
154. Jn 11.25; 14.6; 1 Jn 1.1–2; 5.20.
155. Jn 14.6.
156. Jn 9.4.
157. Jn 11.25.
158. Jn 10.7, 9.
159. Jn 6.35.
160. ἀρχῆς.
161. Jn 1.1.
162. Ibid.
163. Marcellus, *fr.* 3 (43 K./H.) (4,19–6,11 V.).

Therefore, before the descent and birth through the Virgin, he was only Word. For before the assumption of the human flesh, what else was "that which came down 'in the last days,'"[164] as he [Asterius] himself also wrote, "and that which was born from the Virgin"?[165] It was nothing other than Word.[166]

And again he carries on:

For previously, as I have said many times, he was nothing other than Word.[167]

(3) And yet again he continues, alleging:

For "the Word" "was in the beginning,"[168] as nothing other than Word. But once the man who had not existed previously was united to the Word, it [the Word] became man, as John teaches us, saying: "And the Word became flesh."[169] (4) Well now, because of this he certainly mentions only the Word. For if the divine Scripture should mention the name of Jesus or Christ, it appears so to name the Word of God when he existed with the human flesh. But if someone should proclaim that even before the New Testament the name of Christ or the Son can be shown to apply to the Word alone, he will find that this has been said prophetically.[170]

And after other remarks, he adds, saying:

Rightly, therefore, before the descent he was this, which we said many times: Word. But after the descent and the assumption of the flesh he also acquired different titles.[171]

These, therefore, are the statements through which Marcellus is caught denying the Son of God, who is and lives and is truly Son, and (5) introducing a mere word. And it has been shown through his remarks presented above, of what sort of

164. Heb 1.2.
165. Asterius, *fr.* 57 (118 V.).
166. Marcellus, *fr.* 5 (48 K./H.) (8,19–22 V.).
167. Last sentence of Marcellus, *fr.* 52 (91 K./H.) (46,8–9 V.).
168. Jn 1.1.
169. Jn 1.14.
170. Marcellus, *fr.* 7 (42 K./H.) (10,7–14 V.).
171. First part of Marcellus, *fr.* 8 (49 K./H.) (10,18–12,2 V.).

word he supposed him to be, using as an example the human word and saying that he is one and the same with God. And then, having established this starting point, it happened accordingly that on the basis of his assumptions, he proceeded to falsify the divinely inspired Scripture and to manufacture distorted interpretations of it.[172]

Chapter 19

(1) It seems to me opportune here to scrutinize briefly some of these [distortions] and to show to those who are ignorant that no Scripture is in accord with that man who innovates and turns away from those with pure faith, but, on the contrary, that all [Scriptures] state and testify the opposite of the statements that have been wrongly maintained by him.

It was especially necessary to show this to those who honor the man,[173] lest as a result one of them, because of his ignorance of the divine readings, might ever think that he [Marcellus] hit the target of truth.

(2) And therefore this [claim] must first be considered, which indeed he has also dared to assert,[174] namely, that before the birth through the Virgin the Son of God was not called by any other name than "Word." For [Marcellus] alleges that neither was he anything but "Word" before the coming of the flesh, nor was he called otherwise, except prophetically, for he both was and was called Word and nothing else, but that after [his] coming in the flesh he acquired additional different names.

172. Klostermann did not recognize the grammatical structure of the sentence and misleadingly added an unnecessary πρῶτον.

173. This passage gives an insight into the agenda and also the reason why Eusebius had to compose this second attempt to refute Marcellus. Despite his first attack on Marcellus in *CM,* there still must have been bishops who honored Marcellus at the time when Eusebius wrote *ET,* according to this passage, because they thought that Marcellus's use of Scriptures "hit the target of truth." This latter sounds as if Eusebius is quoting from his opponents. Unfortunately it escapes our knowledge whether he did so directly from their writings or as part of a letter from his own supporting colleagues.

174. Again, Klostermann, ignoring the dramatic content of the sentence before, unnecessarily and misleadingly adds a πρῶτον.

Chapter 20

(1) Therefore, then, this must be shown first: that [Marcellus] has shown himself [to be] unlearned and ignorant of the divine Scriptures.

[1] For the divine evangelist John himself first called him "Word."

[2] Not long after, but right away and immediately afterwards, he called him "God," having said, "And the Word was God."[175] Although he could have said, "and the Word was *of* God," he did not say this, lest anyone say that he was like the word in human beings. No, he calls him "God," thus showing the extraordinary nature of the honor befitting his status as God.

[3] (2) Moving on to a different aspect of the honor accorded him, [John] calls him "Light," having shown that he existed prior to the assumption of the body (3) in accordance with this same statement, in which he says concerning the Baptist: "He was not the light, but came to bear witness to the light that enlightens every man coming into the world. He was in the world, and the world was made through him, yet the world did not know him. (4) He came to his own home, and his own people did not receive him."[176] You see how in these lines he [John] called him not only "Word," as Marcellus thinks, but also "God" and "Light," and he taught that he pre-existed and that the world came into existence through him. For just as he said before that all things came into existence through the Word of God and "without him"[177] nothing was made, so also [these things were made] through the light: (5) for "the world," he says, "was made through him,"[178] so that the light and God the Word are one and the same. In saying at one time that the world and at another time all things were made through him, he reveals the helper of God. In any case, the evangelist could have said, "All things were made by him," and again, "And the world was made by him," but he did not say "by him" but

175. Jn 1.1.
176. Jn 1.8–11.
177. Jn 1.3.
178. Jn 1.10.

"through him," so that he might refer us to (6) the sovereign
power of the Father that makes the universe. But he also says,
"The world did not know him."[179] All human beings by virtue
of notions implanted by nature confess the God of all, and the
children of the Jews were first led by the hand by the prophetic
writings, as even Marcellus himself shows, (7) proceeding to his
next remarks. Therefore, this was another [besides the God of
all], whom "the world did not know," God and Word, existing
as and having been called "Light." But [he was not] a perceptible light, nor one that illuminates the eyes of the flesh like the
sun. For in this way, even the nature of the irrational animals
would participate in it. But now he [John] teaches what sort
of light this light was, saying, "He was the light that enlightens
every man coming into the world."[180] Consequently, this light
was the (8) rational light of human beings alone. Therefore,
by its intellectual and rational power, it rendered the souls that
have been made "in his image and likeness"[181] intellectual and
rational. And since that light did not happen to be perceptible,
neither was the light that transcends the universe, God himself. For "God is light, and in him is no darkness,"[182] and the
light was unapproachable, as the divine Apostle teaches, saying
"dwelling in (9) unapproachable light, which no one has seen
or is able to see."[183] "He," however,[184] "was in the world" "en-
lightening every man coming into the world."[185] But the world
too, he says, was made through this sort of light, of the one who
is greater—to be more specific, of the Father, who established
everything through the Son. Thus these three respectful and
pious titles—"Word," and "God," and "Light," which are as one
in conformity with the powers of the Son of God—were placed
by the Theologian at the beginning of his gospel.

179. Ibid.
180. Jn 1.9.
181. Gn 1.26.
182. 1 Jn 1.5.
183. 1 Tm 6.16.
184. The "δέ" indicates that Eusebius is here differentiating between the
light = "the" God, and his noetic and rational light = the Son, through which
the original light shines and creates, as is developed in the next sentence.
185. Jn 1.10, 9.

[4] (10) Shortly thereafter the same [evangelist John] also adds a fourth [title], calling the same "Only-begotten" when he says, "And the Word became flesh and dwelt among us, and we saw his glory, glory as of an only-begotten from the Father, full of grace and truth."[186] Therefore, he was already called the "Only-begotten" of God before assuming the flesh. For even if, he says, "The Word became flesh"[187] especially for us, nevertheless we, to whom he deemed it right to reveal his divinity, "saw his glory,"[188] not looking at the flesh (for it was the "form of a slave"),[189] but at his glory, which is contemplated apart from the body but with a pure mind, a glory that is ineffable and surpasses all the rationality of mortals, the sort of glory that one might imagine belongs to the only-begotten Son of God. (11) It was, however, a glory [that came] "from the Father."[190]

You see that he [John] did not say, "And we saw his glory, glory as 'of a word,'" although he had said before, "the Word became flesh."[191] Rather, in order to teach what sort of word he had in mind (because it was not a communicating word; for how could this sort of word be one capable of becoming flesh?), he instead necessarily called him "Only-begotten." (12) And he teaches that his glory is that according to which he is conceived as only-begotten Son of God.[192] And he says that the glory comes to him from no other source than from the Father. For he did not possess a glory that is ingenerate or without source or acquired by himself, but [one that is] received "from the Father." Indeed, even he [Christ] himself indicates this when he says, "Father, glorify me with the glory which I had with you before (13) the world was."[193] And the Father answers him, saying,

186. Jn 1.14.
187. Ibid.
188. Ibid.
189. Phil 2.7.
190. Jn 1.14.
191. Ibid.
192. The point here is that, after having praised the Son's glory, Eusebius wants to make sure that the reader understands the character of this glory, which, by nature, is the Father's and belongs to him as its sole source, as Eusebius makes clear in the next sentence.
193. Jn 17.5.

"I have glorified you, and I will glorify you again."[194] And still further, the same evangelist establishes his hypostasis, adding, "John bore witness to him, and cried out, saying, 'This was he who comes after me, who ranks before me, for he was before me.' And from his fullness (14) we have all received."[195] But the new Sabellius does not listen to John when he cries out that "He was before." And yet according to the flesh John the Baptist was before the birth of the Savior; so how then can he give witness that he [Christ] was before him? For it was not by virtue of the birth according to the flesh (15) that the Savior was before him; thus it was by virtue of the fact that he was only-begotten of God that he was before John and existed before him. Therefore, does he [Marcellus] admit that these things refer to the Father and God of the universe, or to a word in God, one that is without being and non-subsistent,[196] that is the same as God? And how would it be possible to say concerning the word that does not subsist, "He was before"? Who would be so insane as to think John the Baptist spoke about the God of the universe [when he said], "He was before me," and, "Because before me he was." (16) Therefore, the one who is acknowledged as divine and who existed before him has been shown through these statements to pre-exist the birth of John, and before the coming in the flesh existed as and was called not only "Word," but also "God" and "Light" and "Only-begotten."

[5] From what source the knowledge of these things came to the evangelist he himself will show, saying in what follows: "The only-begotten Son who is in the bosom of the Father, he has made him known."[197] You see from whom he has learned the theology concerning the Son. (17) For neither does Moses say this, nor any of the prophets after Moses, nor yet any of the angels or of the greater powers, but "the only-begotten Son" himself, "he has made this known." Therefore, the invisible God did not make it known, but the only-begotten Son, having become visible, made the Father known to human beings, clearly

194. Jn 12.28.
195. Jn 1.15–16.
196. ἀνούσιον καὶ ἀνυπόστατον.
197. Jn 1.18.

existing as another beside the invisible God. But because he also pre-existed, he was neither in the thought of the Father, as it appeared to Marcellus, but in his bosom. Indeed, just as the Savior promised that we would rest in the bosom of Abraham, Isaac, and Jacob, so also the Son was in the bosom of the Father, without having been one and the same with the Father, since neither will we be the same (18) as the holy patriarchs [when we rest in their bosom].

For in addition to these, observe that, after once naming him "Word," addressing the same as "God," calling him "Light," revealing him as "Only-begotten," and confessing him as "Son of God," he [John] no longer calls him "Word," but later also depicts him as the Savior who did not call himself "Word," but "Son," "Only-begotten," "Light," "Life," "Truth," and many other things, just as it is possible to hear him teaching somewhere in this way: "For God so loved the world that he gave his only-begotten Son, so that everyone who believes in him might not perish,"[198] and again: "For God did not send the Son into the (19) world to judge the world,"[199] and once more: "He who does not believe has already been judged, because he has not believed in the name of the only-begotten Son of God."[200] And here again God gave and "sent the Son as the Savior of the world,"[201] the one who was sent being clearly another besides the one who sent. For this reason it seems to me that our Savior himself through the following said—written, as it were, against Marcellus and those who are jealous of the Son's nature—"Has it not been written in (20) the law that I said, 'You are gods'? If he said those men are gods to whom the Word of God came, and Scripture cannot be set aside, are you saying of the one whom the Father sanctified and sent into the world, 'You blaspheme,' because I said, 'I am the Son of God'?"[202] You hear how many times the Savior himself called himself not "Word," but "Son," and added that he was "Only-begotten," (21) and how

198. Jn 3.16.
199. Jn 3.17.
200. Jn 3.18.
201. 1 Jn 4.14.
202. Jn 10.34–36.

he taught that he was sent and was sanctified before being sent by the Father, and that he is ashamed of those who hesitate to confess him "Son of God," teaching from the divine Scripture that men mortal by nature were called not only sons of God but even gods. For this reason one must not think it blasphemy to confess him both "Son of God" and "God," (22) "whom the Father sanctified and sent into the world."[203]

Therefore, why should we tolerate the man who dared after these sorts of remarks to say,[204] "For he was Word and nothing else,"[205] and who said in his own words [the following]?

> And because of this he does not name himself "Son of God," but everywhere calls himself "Son of Man," so that through this sort of confession he might enable the man through fellowship with him to become by adoption Son of God.[206]

When Marcellus said these things, I do not know with what eyes he was able to look at nor with what lips he was able to contradict these sorts of (23) testimonies. And that he himself is also "Light," the Savior shows, when he says in agreement with what has been recounted before concerning light: "I am the light of the world,"[207] and again: "I am the light, and the truth and the life,"[208] and once more: "Because the light has come into the world and men loved (24) the darkness rather than the light."[209] And if someone were to ask where he has come from, he will give an answer by saying, "He who comes from above is above all,"[210] and, "He who comes from heaven … bears witness to what he has seen and heard."[211] But who was "He who comes

---

203. Jn 10.36.

204. The implied addition to "tolerate the man" is *in episcopal ranks.* Eusebius is talking about past events—i.e., justifying Marcellus's deposition in Constantinople in 336 for his refusal to recant his views, which, according to Eusebius, clearly contradicted Scripture.

205. See Marcellus, *fr.* 7 (42 K./H.) and 52 (91 K./H.) (10,7–17; 46,6–9 V.).

206. Marcellus, *fr.* 111 (41 K./H.) (104,12–18 V.); the same fragment has already been quoted above.

207. Jn 8.12.

208. Jn 14.6 (quoting "light" instead of "way").

209. Jn 3.19.

210. Jn 3.31.

211. Jn 3.31–32.

from heaven"? Was it the flesh that the Savior assumed? Not at all! But he himself, that is to say, the "Light," the "Word," "God," the "Only-begotten," and "Son," he, who himself is all these things, gives witness, he says, to the things "he has seen and heard." (25) Therefore, he both has seen and heard before he came to earth. Whom has he seen other than the Father? Whom did he hear other than the Father?

Therefore, he taught that he himself was not a communicating word, but a Son truly living and subsisting, so as to say, "the Father loves the Son, and has given all things into his hand. He who believes in the Son has eternal life."[212] Let us believe, then, that "the Father," "loving the Son," (26) "has given all things into his hands."[213]

Accordingly, one must pay careful attention to "all things," since it includes the existence of all creatures, and through this term one can see the greatness of the power of the Son of God, if one has reflected with how great a hand he received from the Father the (27) existence of all beings. For if the whole heaven and world are great, and those things that are beyond the visible, subsisting in incorporeal and incorruptible intellectual and divine powers, are still far greater and more excellent than these, and all such great things in transcending our minds escape our knowledge, in grasping all of these the one hand of the only-begotten Son of God (28) reveals the superiority of his infinite power. Indeed, the Son himself shows this, too, in another remark, when he says, "All things have been given to me by my Father."[214]

If, then, we are at a loss as to who the one was who has received this sort of commission and how great he is, do not seek, he says, or inquire! For he does not have a nature capable of being known by men, nor even is an accurate comprehension of the Son of God by the greater and more divine powers possible. (29) For this reason, having said before, "All things have been given to me by my Father," he adds, "And no one knows the Son

212. Jn 3.35–36.
213. Jn 3.35.
214. Mt 11.27.

except the Father."[215] Well then, let every forbidden word concerning the Son of God be silenced, and let the knowledge of
his generation from him [the Father] be granted to the Father
alone, nor let anyone in seeking the ineffable nature and being[216] probe any further,[217] but let his teaching about himself be
secured for us only by the grace of faith, which teaches clearly
that all things were given to him by the Father. (30) Therefore,
God gave and bestowed these things, making them something
to be handed down for [our] betterment and benefit, to one
who was, as it were, a Savior and healer and helmsman of the
universe. The Son, however,[218] received them as a faithful keeper of a deposit, and accepted them,[219] not as a word that is without being and non-subsistent,[220] but as one who is truly a Son,
only-begotten and beloved of the Father.

[6] (31) Further, in addition to these titles, he also called
himself the "Bread of life," saying, "I am the bread of life,"[221]
[and] "I am the living bread that came down from heaven."[222]
And that he existed as a living being,[223] he made absolutely

215. Ibid.
216. οὐσίας.
217. Eusebius is forbidding the advancement of the search into the nature
of God. "Probing" suggests the notion that to press on or advance further
would be intrusive and inappropriate—which obviously Eusebius thinks it
would be.
218. This distinction, despite all the praise of the Son, may highlight Eusebius's subordinationist thinking of the Son.
219. The role of the Son is astonishingly passive: keeper of a deposit.
220. ἀνούσιος καὶ ἀνυπόστατος.
221. Jn 6.48.
222. Jn 6.51.
223. καὶ ὅπως ὑπῆρχε ζῶν. This is a slightly difficult argument, but Eusebius wants to make clear that the "living" from John 6.51 does not mean, as
Marcellus would have had it according to Eusebius, that the Logos exists indistinguishable from the Father. Eusebius adds John 6.57 to draw the parallel
between the two distinguishable hypostases of the living Father and the living
Son with the different hypostases of the living Son and the creatures who live
through the Son. Life according to Eusebius means life and existence as a hypostasis, distinguished and different from one's source and origin of life. The
idea of an origin seems to be less important than that of difference of hypostases and existence. See also the beginnings of the next and the next-but-one
paragraph, which start: "Therefore, then, he was the bread of *life and existed* in

clear, articulating this in the remarks where he says, "As the living Father sent me, and I (32) live because of the Father, so he who eats me will live because of me."[224] He also taught this in other statements, having said, "For as the Father has life in himself, so also he has given to the Son to have life in himself."[225]

Therefore, he was the bread of life and existed in heaven, refreshing the angelic powers and nourishing them with the power of his divinity, and was such before he came to earth and was the Son who has life (33) "in himself,"[226] just as the Father has life "in himself."[227] For the excellent and unique character of the ingenerate and divine life of the Father, on account of which "he alone has immortality,"[228] as was said by the holy Apostle, the Son alone could have, seeing as he was the image of the Father even in this respect. But he has the aforementioned life not like the Father, not without source nor ingenerate nor (34) acquired by himself, but has received [this immortal life] from the Father. For thus he says, "For as the Father has life in himself, so also he has given to the Son to have life in himself."[229] Therefore, the one has given, the other received.[230] And he alone received this privilege, to have life provided to him not like the remainder of living things from some place or another from without, but to have it springing forth in himself just like the life that is in the Father.[231] For this reason all things that

---

heaven …" and, "You see how, even *existing in heaven,* he was the bread of *life.*" Emphasis added.

224. Jn 6.57.

225. Jn 5.26.

226. The Son's being and existence here refer to his pre-existence in heaven.

227. Jn 5.26.

228. 1 Tm 6.16.

229. Jn 5.26.

230. After Eusebius has made it clear that there is a hierarchy between Father and Son, in what follows he is going to distinguish what makes the Son privileged over and above the creatures—a differentiation that recalls Asterius's wording of the Son who is only born/only-begotten, i.e., the only one that is created solely (μόνος) by the Father, whereas all the other creatures received life through the Father and the Son simultaneously with all others, namely, the multitude of creatures. On this, see Asterius, *fr.* 23–37 (94–100 V.).

231. This idea that life in the Son is life that springs forth from within

participate in life live because of the additional help of the Son. But he alone has life springing forth in himself, the Father having given this to him for the benefit (35) of those beings that were going to be brought to life through him. He himself, then, also teaches this, saying, "As the living Father sent me, and I live because of the Father, so he who eats me will live because of me. This is the bread that came down from heaven."[232]

You see that even when he was in heaven, he was the bread of life. For this reason, somewhere it has been said: "Man ate the bread of angels."[233] And consequently, before he was sent by the Father, he was in heaven and lived because of (36) the Father, not as a communicating word or as if he were one and the same with God, but he subsisted and had his own life, which the Father (37) has given to him.

Progressing further, and revealing the transcendence of the Father's glory, he said, "Just as the Father taught me, these things I speak. And he who sent me is with me. He has not left me alone, for I always do what is pleasing to him."[234] Observe carefully that he said (38) "always." For he says not only "now," when he associated with men on earth through the flesh,[235] "do I accomplish those things that are pleasing to the Father," but "always." And[236] he gives witness that he speaks these things that he has learned from the Father as from a teacher.[237] There-

---

himself while being life from the Father makes one wonder why Eusebius was so opposed to Marcellus, who thought precisely of this intrinsic in-being of the Logos in God and God in the Logos. This is one of the important passages that show that despite all the invective, Eusebius and Marcellus shared more than they were willing to admit on the battlefield of opposition.

232. Jn 6.57–58.

233. Ps 77.25 (RSV 78.25).

234. Jn 8.28–29.

235. See Bar 3.36–39, one of the key passages of early monarchianism, which is also used by Marcellus against Asterius. See Marcellus, *fr.* 93 (79 K./H.) (82,13–15 V.); R. Hübner/M. Vinzent, *Der Paradox Eine, VCSup* 50 (Leiden: Brill, 1999), 231.

236. Marcellus used the idea of eternity ("always" in the sentence before) to refute Asterius's example of the Son being taught by the Father, hence being a second, subordinate hypostasis. See Asterius, *fr.* 34 (100 V.).

237. Again, with this idea of the teacher, Eusebius takes sides with Asterius in this debate between Marcellus and Asterius. See Asterius, *fr.* 34 (100 V.): "As

fore, he also acknowledges the Father as [his] teacher, clearly as another besides him, since surely everyone who is a pupil of someone else is other than (39) the teacher.

But if the Word was in God, on account of which he was also said to be rational,[238] as someone who communicates the thoughts of the Father, how could he become teacher of himself? How, then, being inseparable from God, did he say that he himself was sent? How, existing as one and the same with God, did he affirm that he did things pleasing to the latter?

If in response to these things Marcellus were to say that the Word made these statements when he was in the flesh, what will we say with regard to this failure to confess that he is Son, (40) [while claiming that he is] only Word? How was he [the Word] in the flesh when he said these things? Was he, therefore, living and subsisting and existing outside of the Father? And who was the Father, then, since he did not possess his own Word in himself, but subsisted without a Word? If the Word, while dwelling in the flesh when he was teaching upon the earth, was outside the Father, living, subsisting, and moving the flesh in place of a soul, he was clearly another besides the Father, and again he and the Father existed as two hypostases, (41) and so every effort of Marcellus has been proven to be in vain, because he has defined the one who has come in the flesh as the substantial,[239] living, and subsisting Word. For if the Word who dwelt in the body existed outside of God, but was united and joined to God so as to be one and the same with him, he [Marcellus] must of necessity admit that either it is the Father himself in the flesh, or the Son who subsists in himself and acts in the body, or the soul of a man,[240] or if none of these, that the flesh[241] moves itself

---

from a teacher and craftsman, he (the Son) has learned to create and thus he serves God (the Father) who has taught him." In what follows, Eusebius may even have preserved the conclusion that is missing in the shortened fragment of Asterius that Athanasius preserved.

238. Λογικός.

239. οὐσιώδη.

240. The soul existing on its own in the body, separate from the Father and the Son.

241. The flesh existing on its own as flesh, separate from the Father, the Son, and the soul.

spontaneously, being without soul (42) and without rationality.[242]

If, however, he were to say [it is] the Father, the Father will be for him the one who was begotten and who suffered and who has undergone every trial involved in human suffering, which view indeed the Church of God decreed was impious when Sabellius expressed it.

If it is, however, not lawful to say that the Father was incarnate, it is necessary for those who are taught [Marcellus and his pupils][243] by the one [Sabellius] who teaches this, to confess the Son. (43) And if Marcellus denies that this [Son] subsists, the cause must be that he supposes him to be a mere man, composed of body and soul, in no way different from the common nature of human beings. But this teaching, too, has been cast out of the Church. Indeed, long ago the Ebionites and lately the Samosatene and those called Paulinians after him, because they thought this, (44) paid the penalty for their blasphemy.

What, then, is left after these but to introduce the flesh alone devoid of any inner life, which moves itself like the self-moving statues of wonderworkers?[244] And how could the flesh and the body itself without the one acting [within] have said by itself: "Just as (he) taught me, these things I speak"?[245] And how could the flesh have said, "For I always do what is pleasing to him"?[246]

And how did the flesh say that it was itself sent by the Father? Is it pious, then, to say that God is the Father of the flesh, or rather of the one who indwells and acts in it? Who, then, was this? Was it the Word in God, who himself is God according to Sabel-

242. In fact, without "word" or λόγος—thus suggesting that the indwelling Word is the mover of the assumed body in Christ.

243. This is an indication that Eusebius is obviously not thinking of Marcellus alone, but also of people supporting him or following him, for example, Marcellus's deacon Photinus, who soon after the publication of Eusebius's text enters the debate.

244. Eusebius likely has in mind here the statues of the ancient figure of Daedalus, which were reported to be able to move on their own, as Plato mentions at *Meno* 97d–e. On this, see Jan N. Bremmer, "The Agency of Greek and Roman Statues: From Homer to Constantine," *Opuscula* 6 (2013): 7–21.

245. Jn 8.28.
246. Jn 8.29.

lius, or is it (which is pious and true to say) the living and subsisting (45) only-begotten Son of God? But if he [Marcellus] should say neither of these, of necessity he will suppose that it is the soul of a man, and for him Christ will be a mere man. And our novice author[247] will no longer be a Sabellian but a Paulinian. But if he were to say that the Word in God dwelt in the flesh as (46) nothing other than Word, namely, a communicating or active word, how also could this Word have said that it lived its own life alongside the Father? How was it sent, having always been joined and united to God? And how did it say that the Father was its teacher? And how did it say that it always did "what was pleasing to the Father"?[248] For these remarks would be explicitly characteristic of a Son who subsists and lives, and throughout the entire gospel the one who prays to the Father, who glorifies the Father, who is deemed worthy to be glorified by the Father; what else does he show but that he himself subsists, and especially (47) when he says, "The testimony of two men is true. I bear witness to myself, and the Father who sent me bears witness to me"?[249]

Through all these remarks, the Savior himself, having shown that he himself lives, nowhere called himself "Word," but "Son" and "Light" and "Only-begotten" (48) and "Bread of life" and anything rather than "Word." He teaches that he also possesses a word, when he says, "If a man loves me, he will keep my word,"[250] but he does not say that he himself is "Word."

How, then, after all this does the man who has declared that [the Savior] is Word alone and nothing else not blush with shame? Listen, then, to how he wrote, saying:

So that it is clear in every way that no other name befits the eternity of the Word than this very one that John, the most holy disciple of the Lord and apostle, uttered in the beginning of the gospel.[251]

247. Eusebius, the experienced writer and author of many works, seems to hint at the fact that Marcellus's opus was the first he had ever written.
248. Jn 8.29.
249. Jn 8.17–18. This is a key passage for Eusebius, wherein he sees the teaching of two hypostases unambiguously affirmed.
250. Jn 14.23.
251. The beginning of Marcellus, *fr.* 3 (43 K./H.) (4,18–6,1 V.).

(49) And again:

So that he might show that if there is any new and more recent name, it exists as a result of his new and recent economy according to the flesh.[252]

(50) And again:

Therefore, before the descent and birth from the Virgin, he was only Word. For before the assumption of the human flesh what else was "that which came down 'in the last days,'"[253] as he [Asterius] himself also wrote, "and that which was born from the Virgin"?[254] It was nothing other than Word.[255]

(51) Marcellus had to say and to declare all these things in order not to confess the Son of God. Against him, the evangelist would have said, crying out in a loud voice, "Why do you say this, man? I did not say that he was only Word, but also God,[256] and 'the light that enlightens every man coming into the (52) world,'[257] and the only-begotten Son who is 'in the bosom of the Father.'"[258] Let no one, then, misrepresent the Theologian, but listen to him carefully, [as he explains] how he understood "Word," having added right next to it: "And the Word was God,"[259] and added: "All things were made through him."[260] He was not called "Word" once by the Savior of the world himself, but "Son of God," "Only-begotten," "Light," "Life," "Truth," and everything other than "Word."

[7] (53) If he [Marcellus] were to say that these [views of his] were taken from the New Testament, it will be said to him that even the statement "In the beginning was the Word"[261] came from no other source than from it. Well then, one and the

---

252. Ibid. (6,9–11 V.).
253. Heb 1.2.
254. Asterius, *fr.* 57 (118 V.).
255. Marcellus, *fr.* 5 (48 K./H.) (8,19–22 V.).
256. Cf. Jn 1.1.
257. Jn 1.9.
258. Jn 1.18.
259. Jn 1.1.
260. Jn 1.3.
261. Jn 1.1.

same gospel and the same evangelist, having said he was Word, also ascribed to him all the remaining [titles].

[8] (54) And even Paul the divine Apostle, who says, "For us there is one God, the Father, from whom are all things, and one Lord, Jesus Christ, through whom are all things,"[262] clearly speaks of the Son of God, "through whom all things were made," before his coming in the flesh, not as "Word," but as "Lord," "Jesus," and "Christ." But if, according to Marcellus, God and the Word in him were one and the same, it would have been sufficient for the Apostle to declare, "for us there is one God, (55) the Father, from whom are all things." For the thought made full sense, and the statement was complete in itself because it described God as maker of the universe. But even a Jew could say this. But the herald of the Church teaches us that in addition to the first clause [of his statement] we should (56) also not be ignorant of the second. And what was this? "And one Lord Jesus Christ." For this reason he adds the second statement, saying next, "For us (for even if not for all, but for us, he says)[263] there is one Lord Jesus Christ." For what reason after the "one God" does this man also present "for us there is one Lord," saying in addition "through whom are all things"? For since "all things were made through him," it is fitting for us who have come to this conviction, to believe that he is Lord (57) of the universe after the God who is over all. And that he [Paul] did not say this regarding the flesh, but concerning God the Word, is clear from the addition of "through whom are all things." For he says, "For us there is one God, the Father, from whom are all things, and one Lord, Jesus Christ, through whom are all things." This indeed was also said about the light and the pre-existent Word. Therefore, Jesus Christ was himself the light and the Word "through whom all things" came into existence, but not the flesh. For it would have been totally incoherent for him [Paul] to say "through whom are all things" about the flesh.[264]

262. 1 Cor 8.6.
263. That is, even if not for Jews and radical unitarians like Marcellus.
264. In view of everything Eusebius has said about creation happening through the pre-existent Son and Word and not the incarnate man Jesus, it

[9] (58) The same Paul knows to call the Son of God who pre-existed the flesh "Christ," in the same way as he addresses him as "rock," in the remarks he wrote concerning those who sojourned in the desert with Moses, saying, "For they drank from the spiritual rock that followed them, and the rock was Christ";[265] and the same point is confirmed after other statements when he claims, "We must not put Christ to the test, as some of them did (59) and were destroyed by serpents."[266] And he reiterates this same point once more, saying, "By faith Moses, when he was grown up, refused to be called 'Son of Pharaoh's daughter.' … He considered abuse suffered for Christ greater wealth than the treasures of Egypt."[267] He reveals this still further in the clearest fashion in those remarks in which he declares, "Have this mind among yourselves, which was also in Christ, who, though he was in the form of God, did not count equality with God a thing to be grasped at, but emptied himself, having taken the form of a slave, … (60) and being found in human form."[268]

You see altogether that before emptying himself and taking the form of a slave, he existed and pre-existed and existed "in the form of God." And who was this? None other than Jesus Christ.

Therefore, God the Word himself was Jesus Christ even before (61) assuming the flesh. For one must listen carefully to the divine Apostle when he says, "Have this mind among yourselves which was also in Christ," and when he makes quite clear in the following who this Jesus Christ then was, in those additional remarks in which he says, "who, though he was in the form of God, did not count equality with God a thing to be grasped at, but emptied himself, having taken the form of a slave."[269] (62) Thus could such a statement apply to the flesh? Is

---

is clear that he thinks the attribution of the phrase "through whom are all things" to the flesh that the Son assumes is nonsensical.

265. 1 Cor 10.4.
266. 1 Cor 10.9.
267. Heb 11.24, 26.
268. Phil 2.5–7.
269. Phil 2.5–6.

it suitable to say the words "who" and "existed" concerning the flesh? Did the flesh "empty himself, having taken on the form of a slave"? But this is ridiculous.

Come then, let us examine in what sense it was said, "Who, though he was in the form of God, did not count equality with God a thing to be grasped at, but emptied himself." If, then, the Word was without existence,[270] in no way subsisting outside of God, but being within him, at one time in rest and silence (63) and at another in activity, how was he also in the form of God, since as power for God he was himself "God"?[271] And how did he "not count equality with God a thing to be grasped at," being himself God? How did he "humble himself, becoming obedient"[272] to the Father? For being obedient, one [person] to another, would have to be (64) indicative of two persons.[273]

And since Marcellus has used the word within men as an image, one should inquire if it is possible to apply the statement[274] to the human word: "who being in the form of man, did not count equality with man a thing to be grasped at, but emptied himself, becoming obedient to man." And how could the word that is by nature in man, do these things, being one and the same with the man? Consequently "the one who was in the form of God" will not be a mere word that is non-subsistent[275] but truly an only-begotten Son of God, who "did not count equality with God a thing to be grasped at, but emptied himself, having taken the form of a slave," whom the divine Apostle

---

270. ἀνύπαρκτος.

271. Klostermann, who misunderstood this difficult passage, incorrectly deleted the "for God." Of course, Marcellus would not have entertained Eusebius's thought that the Logos is God as "power for God"; on the contrary, he maintained that the Logos is God as God, but he added that he was this God's power. Using Marcellus's thinking, Eusebius sharpens and overstresses the differentiation that Marcellus was also willing to make within God, and to deduce from there that such differentiation presupposes difference between two divine persons, as Eusebius further explains. Hence, Klostermann deleted a most important element of the text—against the manuscript.

272. Phil 2.8.

273. προσώπων.

274. I.e., Phil 2.7.

275. ἀνυπόστατος.

also called Jesus Christ, knowing correctly that he pre-existed the flesh.

[10] (65) In addition to these [titles], the same Apostle called him a "Mediator of God," having said that the law of Moses was given into his hand, in that passage where he says, "The law was ordained through angels by [the] hand of a mediator. Now a mediator implies more than one; but God is one."[276] You hear that he individually refers to God and names angels, and introduces between them the mediator, saying, "Now a mediator implies more than one." Consequently, he existed even before the Incarnation because he acted as a mediator at the time of Moses for the giving of the Law.

[11] (66) The same Apostle also calls him "High-priest," saying, "We have a great high-priest, who has passed through the heavens, Jesus, the Son of God."[277]

[12] (67) Not only [this], but the same Apostle also knows the same to be the "Radiance of the glory" and "Exact Imprint of God" and "Son" and "Heir," since he says, "In these last days he has spoken to us by a Son, whom he appointed the heir of all, through whom he also made the ages. He is the radiance of glory and the exact imprint of his hypostasis,"[278] and, just as above it was said concerning the Word, "All things were made through him,"[279] and concerning the light, "He was in the world, and the world was made through him,"[280] and concerning Jesus Christ, "For us there is one Lord Jesus Christ, (68) through whom are all things,"[281] see here how in similar fashion it is said concerning him: "through whom he also made the ages."[282]

[13] It is worthwhile with these remarks to pay careful attention to the sense in which he was called "Radiance." For I think the title is indicative of the begetting of the Son from the

276. Gal 3.19–20.
277. Heb 4.14.
278. Heb 1.2–3.
279. Jn 1.3.
280. Jn 1.10.
281. 1 Cor. 8.6.
282. Heb 1.2.

Father. Because, when the Son has been referred to and when God has been addressed as Father, we often imagine something along the lines of the generation of animals,[283] the Apostle has used an image that is (69) more befitting God, having said about the Father, "He dwells in unapproachable light,"[284] and having defined the Son as the radiance of the paternal light, so that the radiance is the offspring of the first light, not in the manner of generation that pertains among mortal animals, but according to the model just described. Therefore, he [Paul] also fittingly calls him "image of the invisible God"[285] because he existed "in the form of God,"[286] and because (70) he is the radiance and "exact Imprint of the hypostasis."[287]

For because of all these [truths], writing about him, he said, "He is the image of the invisible God, firstborn of all creation, for in him all things were created, in heaven and on earth, visible and invisible, whether thrones or dominions or principalities or authorities—all things were created through him and for him. He is before all things, and in him all things hold together."[288] (71) For these things were said concerning the divinity of the Son of God, even if Marcellus does not think so. For the divine Apostle would not have said all these things concerning the flesh. For this is stupid and unintelligible in addition to being an incoherent interpretation of the phrase. For how was it fitting to say concerning the flesh, "*who* is the image," when one should rather say, "*it* is the image"?

[14] (72) And in another passage, the same [Apostle] also

---

283. The optative (ὑπολάβοιμεν) already indicates that Eusebius is thinking hypothetically and also acknowledging the longstanding tradition of the (Neo-Platonic) discussion about the Father-Son relationship in connection with birthing. On this, see more in M. Vinzent, *Pseudo-Athanasius, Contra Arianos IV*, 353. The addition, however, of Klostermann (without manuscript basis) is misleading and removes Eusebius from the Neo-Platonic tradition within which he himself stands. We translate "animals" to draw further the contrast between the messy corporeal birth of animals and the spiritual reflection of the Son as the proper analogy for his birth.

284. 1 Tm 6.16.
285. Col 1.15.
286. Phil 2.6.
287. Heb 1.3.
288. Col 1.15–17.

named him "Image of God," saying, "And even if our gospel
has been veiled, it has been veiled to those who are perishing.
In their case the god of this world has blinded the minds of
the unbelievers, to prevent the light of the gospel of Christ,
(73) who is the image of God, from shining in their hearts."[289]
We should also investigate the meaning here, since the divine
Apostle brought forth a defining statement concerning Christ,
having said he was the "Image of God," lest anyone suppose
there are two gods, rather than the one who is over all. For if
"there is one God, and no other besides him,"[290] he would be
the one who is also recognized through the Son as through
an image. (74) Therefore, the Son is also God, because of the
form of the Father that is in him as in an image. The divine
Apostle indeed shows this when at one time he says, "He was in
the form of God,"[291] and at another defines him as the "Image
of God." Therefore, the Son both was and was addressed together with [these] other titles also as "Image of God" before
his coming in the flesh. But these [testimonies] from the New
Testament have been assembled by us, a few from myriads, for
the sake of the due proportion of the treatise.

[15] (75) In addition,[292] the prophets of God who lived long
ago honored him with different theologies.[293] For one called
him "Spirit of God," saying, "There shall come forth a shoot
from the stump of Jesse, and a branch shall grow out of his
roots. And the Spirit of God shall rest upon him, the Spirit of
wisdom and understanding,"[294] and so forth. For through these
words the one who is "from the seed of David according to the
flesh"[295] and God, the Word, who dwelt in him, became clearly
apparent. For this reason the divine Apostle at one time said,
"The Lord is the Spirit,"[296] and at another, "Christ the power of

289. 2 Cor 4.3–4.
290. Dt 4.35.
291. Phil 2.6.
292. This awkward break of paragraphs indicates that these paragraph
breaks in the edition do not derive from Eusebius.
293. I.e., divine titles.
294. Is 11.1–2.
295. Rom 1.3.
296. 2 Cor 3.17.

God and the wisdom of God."[297] And another [prophet] likewise calls him "Spirit," saying, "the Spirit before us, Christ the Lord."[298] Also in the gospel it was said clearly concerning him: "Behold, my servant[299] whom I have chosen, my beloved with whom my soul is pleased. I have put my Spirit upon him, and he shall proclaim justice to the Gentiles."[300]

[16] (76) Another one of the prophets called him "Life" and "Light" in addressing God and saying, "For with you is the fountain of life; in your light we shall see light."[301] For who was the fountain of life from God and the light, other than he who said in the gospels, "I am the light of the world,"[302] and, "I am the way and the truth and the life"?[303] For this reason again, approaching God as a suppliant in prayer, the prophet says, "Send out your light and your truth; they will lead me."[304]

[17] Even Zerubbabel, having proclaimed him as "Truth," was deemed worthy of the prizes of victory when he was summoned before the King of the Persians, saying, "The (77) truth endures and is strong forever, and lives and prevails forever and ever. With her there is no favoritism, but she does what is just instead of anything that is unjust or wicked."[305] To this he adds, "To her belong the strength and the kingship and the power and the majesty of all the ages."[306] For having said that the truth lives and conquers and rules, he revealed in the clearest possible fashion [the Truth's] hypostasis. And in accordance with these statements even the Savior himself, in calling himself truth, confirmed the testimony of Zerubbabel.

[18] (78) And he also called him a "River" who said, "There is a river whose streams make glad the city of God."[307]

297. 1 Cor 1.24.
298. Lam 4.20; note that Eusebius varies from the LXX, adding πρό and changing the case of κύριος from genitive to nominative.
299. Literally, "behold my child" (παῖς).
300. Mt 12.18; cf. Is 42.1.
301. Ps 35.10 (RSV 36.9).
302. Jn 8.12.
303. Jn 14.6.
304. Ps 42.3 (RSV 43.3).
305. 1 Esd 4.38–39.
306. 1 Esd 4.40.
307. Ps 45.5 (RSV 46.4).

[19] (79) And already he addressed him as "Mountain" who said, "the mountain in which God is pleased to dwell."[308] For this reason also in Daniel [we read] the stone cut "from the mountain" "without hands"[309] and again the same had been seen, having been restored to the lofty mountain, the mountain signifying the pre-existence of his divinity,[310] and the stone his humanity.

[20] (80) And the prophets[311] called him "Justice," such as the one who said, "Who roused justice from the east?"[312]

[21] And [they called him] "Sun of justice"; for example, the one who said, "But for those who fear me, the sun of justice will rise, and healing will be on its wings,"[313] and another [prophet] says, "The sun will go down on the prophets," "those who lead my people astray."[314] For indeed these statements would not be suitably applied to the visible sun, but neither would they be so to the incarnate Word.

[22] (81) Solomon in Proverbs calls him "Wisdom," too, saying, "Wisdom built her house, and set up seven pillars,"[315] and so forth. And that wisdom pre-existed the world, living and subsisting, he himself taught from the mouth of wisdom herself, having uttered these words: "I, wisdom, live with prudence, and I attain knowledge and discretion,"[316] and adding in what follows, "By me kings reign, and rulers decree what is just; by me the great are magnified, and rulers govern the land through me."[317]

[23] (82) But Solomon addresses him also as both "Tree of life" and "Lord," saying, "[This] is a tree of life to all who lay hold of it, and steadfast for those who lean upon it as upon the Lord."[318]

308. Ps 67.17 (RSV 68.16).
309. Dn 2.34.
310. As Eusebius already suggests in the conclusion to *ET* 1.11.
311. The reference to "the prophets" indicates, again, that the next paragraph is an integral part of the logical structure.
312. Is 41.2.
313. Mal 4.2.
314. Mi 3.6, 5.
315. Prv 9.1.
316. Prv 8.12.
317. Prv 8.15.
318. Prv 3.18.

[24] (83) And the father of Solomon, David, in the Psalms, named him "Lord" together with "Priest," in one passage, saying, "The Lord said to my Lord: Sit at my right hand,"[319] and in another claiming, "The Lord has sworn and will not change his mind. You are a priest forever after the order of Melchizedek."[320]

[25] (84) And the same [David] knew to confess him as "God," proclaiming, "Your throne, O God, endures forever and ever; your royal scepter is a scepter of equity. You loved justice and hated wickedness. Because of this, God, your God, anointed you with the oil of gladness above your fellows."[321] For if in these lines God is anointed by God, who else would he be but the very one who was proclaimed Christ ["Anointed One"] because of the paternal anointing?

[26] (85) And this same [Christ] was also the "Beloved by God," which indeed the title of the Psalm shows, which says, "An ode for the beloved."[322]

[27] (86) Isaiah calls him "Arm," saying, "The Lord will reveal his holy arm before the eyes of all the nations."[323]

[28] And David knew him to be "Justice" together with "Salvation," and so he said, "The Lord made known his salvation; before the nations (87) he revealed his justice";[324] and again: "Tell of his salvation from day to day";[325] and again: "Who will render out of Zion the salvation of Israel?"[326] and, "Show to us your mercy, Lord, and grant us your salvation."[327]

[29] And what need is there for me to take up each example, when for the one who is eager to learn it is possible to gather together these sorts of examples from throughout the divinely inspired Scripture, through which the men of God, illuminated by the divine Spirit, reveal the knowledge of the only-begotten

319. Ps 109.1 (RSV 110.1).
320. Ps 109.4 (RSV 110.4).
321. Ps 44.7–8 (RSV 45.6–7).
322. Ps 44.1 (RSV 45).
323. Is 52.10.
324. Ps 97.2 (RSV 98.2).
325. Ps 95.2 (RSV 96.2).
326. Ps 13.7 (RSV 14.7).
327. Ps 84.8 (RSV 85.7).

Son, which at that time was a secret from and escaped the notice of the majority of the Jewish people? For this reason, they also proclaimed him in various ways with forms of address that have been concealed. For the grace of the proclamation of the theology concerning him was preserved for his coming, by which his Church throughout the world, as if receiving some mystery that was long ago kept hidden in silence, (88) is exalted.

Indeed, the divine Apostle also teaches this when he says, "According to the divine office which was given to me for you, to make the word of God fully known, the mystery hidden for ages and generations, but now made manifest to his saints. To them God chose to make known how great among the Gentiles are the riches of the glory of this mystery, which is Christ in you, the hope of glory."[328]

You see that the Son of God was the mystery that was previously hidden, but now (89) has been made manifest. For this reason the prophets of God wrote their mystical theology about him in the prophetic spirit while the majority of the Jewish nation remained in ignorance of the hidden mystery—as a result of which they were taught to know one God because they were repeatedly being dragged down by polytheistic error, but were ignorant that God was Father of the only-begotten Son. For this mystery was preserved for the Church [to be formed] from the Gentiles, (90) according to [the] excellent grace granted to it, for in him are, according to the Apostle, "hidden all the treasures of wisdom and knowledge."[329]

But through all these passages the Word of God, who "in the beginning was with God,"[330] was shown to have been called not only "Word," as Marcellus thinks, but also "Son," "Only-begotten," "Light," "Bread," "Jesus," "Christ," "Lord," "High Priest," "Radiance," "Character," "Image," "Firstborn of all creation," "Font of life," "Truth," "River," " Justice," "Sun of justice," "Wisdom," "Tree of life," "Lord," "God," "Beloved," "Priest," "Arm," "Justice," and "Salvation." And he was and was called all these things even when he pre-existed the flesh, just as the

328. Col 1.25–27.
329. Col 2.3.
330. Jn 1.1.

(91) Scriptures cited have shown. Well now, for what reason, having disregarded all these truths, does Marcellus insist upon "the Word" alone, not even passing over to the remaining names, but alleging that he is only Word of God and the communicating Word, who at one time rests in silence in God and at another speaks or acts in activity alone, other than that he openly Sabellianizes, and does not believe in the Son of God nor acknowledge the mystery that pre-existed long ago, and which was made manifest only to the Church (92) of Christ through his grace?

But if he were to say that the fact that God has the Word within himself and uses [this] Word is the mystery that is unknown (for this seems to Marcellus himself to be the case when he writes in this way:

> For what mystery was hidden other than that concerning the Word? And so this mystery was previously hidden "in God,"[331] so that none of the earlier people knew clearly the truth about the Word),[332]

well then, if he should say this, let him learn that every one of the Jews who have not acknowledged the Christ of God would even confess that (93) God has the Word and is not irrational.[333] Even Sabellius himself and every Greek and barbarian who supposed there was a God would unambiguously say this. For as soon as one mentions God, one thinks of him as wise, rational, powerful, righteous, and good. Therefore, what sort of mystery was hidden, which is confessed by all? For who would *not* say that there is in God wisdom, power, life, light, truth, justice, word, and everything that is noble and good? Rather, one would say that he is all these things and whichever of these is higher and better and unknown to us. For nature without the need of a teacher compels every human being to confess these things about God.[334] (94) For this reason we are also taught that the Son is all these things, seeing as he is the only-begotten Son

---

331. Eph 3.9; Col 1.26.

332. Marcellus, *fr.* 96 (50 K./H.) (84,9–11 V.).

333. Literally, "without a word": ἀλόγος.

334. For the philosophical background to Eusebius's discussion here of "natural notions" about God, see St. Basil of Caesarea, *Against Eunomius,*

and heir of the Father and also possesses whatever the Father possesses.[335] For this reason he has been said to be in the form of God and image of God, according to the divine Apostle, who said, "who, though he was in the form of God, did not count equality with God a thing to be grasped at,"[336] and again, "who is the image of God."[337] (95) Consequently, that God is rational was not "the mystery, which was hidden for ages and generations,"[338] nor was this mystery "now made manifest,"[339] having been acknowledged by all men by means of natural notions; for if someone were to ask what sort of mystery it is, the Apostle answers, saying "[the mystery] now made manifest to his saints. To them God chose to make known how great among the Gentiles are the riches of the glory of this mystery, (96) which is Christ in you."[340]

Christ, therefore, was the mystery, and it is clear that he is the Son of God. For this reason the prophets of God previously glorified him mystically with various forms of address, concealing his ineffability and dispensing[341] by his grace his revelation to all.

Well now, when after so many scriptural testimonies Marcellus affirms that in the beginning before the assumption of the flesh the Word was nothing other than Word and was called by no other name, but then acquired other titles when "the Word became flesh"[342] (before this being nothing other than Word), how could he not be convicted as unlearned and devoid of understanding of the divine Scriptures? But since this is so, bring on the rest, so that we might examine further the new Sabellius come back to life.

---

trans. Mark DelCogliano and Andrew Radde-Gallwitz, FOTC 122 (Washington, DC: The Catholic University of America Press, 2011), 108, n. 77.

335. A possible allusion to Jn 16.15?
336. Phil 2.6.
337. Col 1.15.
338. Col 1.26.
339. Ibid.
340. Col 1.26–27.
341. The idea expressed here is that the mystery of Christ's identity is given out bit by bit over time.
342. Jn 1.14.

BOOK TWO

OW THAT THE testimonies from the divine Scriptures have been presented, in which it was shown that the Son of God was called not only "Word" before his coming in the flesh (as Marcellus thought) but also many other things, come now, let us consider the remaining idol of Sabellius, which has, as it were, popped up out of the earth.[1] For he dared to say that the God who is over all,[2] the Father of our Lord Jesus Christ, has himself been born from the holy Virgin and has himself suffered, having written in this way:

> Well then, what was this "which came down"[3] before the Incarnation? Surely, I suppose, he [Asterius] says, "Spirit."[4] For if he would like to say something besides this, the angel will not agree with him, because he said to the Virgin, "The Holy Spirit will come upon you."[5] But if he will say that he is Spirit, let him listen to the Savior, who says, "God is Spirit."[6]

(2) Through these remarks, he said that the God of the universe (concerning whom our Savior and Lord taught, having said, "God is spirit, and those who worship him must worship in spirit and in truth"),[7] is the Spirit that came upon the Vir-

---

1. The remaining idol's "popping out of the earth" recalls the figure from Greek mythology, Cadmos, who, at Athena's request, sowed dragon's teeth in the ground, from which popped up the so-called *Spartoí* (the "sown"). They subsequently fell upon one another, and only a few survived, who then were used by Cadmos to build the new town of Thebes.
2. Rom 9.5; Eph 4.6.
3. Asterius, *fr.* 58 (120 V.).
4. Ibid.
5. Lk 1.35.
6. Jn 4.24; Marcellus, *fr.* 61 (54 K./H.) (54,1–5 V.).
7. Jn 4.24.

gin, (3) in this way openly bringing Sabellius back to life. And proceeding on, he refers to the Father the statement of Jeremiah the prophet, who clearly said concerning the Incarnation of the Savior,

> "After these things he appeared on earth and lived among men,"[8]

claiming in these very words:

> But the Father must be in the Word, even if it does not seem so to Asterius and to those who think the same things as he does.[9]

(4) But he also does the same thing with regard to the Passion of the Savior. For having brought forth from the Lamentations of Jeremiah the passage that says,

> "The Spirit before us, Christ the Lord, was taken in their destructive snares,"[10]

he adds:

> And here likewise, the prophet speaks of the Word who has assumed our flesh.[11]

And he continues, saying:

> A spirit could never become the maker of a shadow.[12] But that God himself is [Spirit], the Savior said, "God is Spirit."[13] And that God is light, he himself teaches us, saying, "I am the light."[14]

You see how he transfers that which has been said about the Savior to the divinity (5) of the Father. And again, he shame-

---

8. Bar 3.38; Klostermann did not recognize that this was a quotation of Marcellus, *fr.* 93 (79 K./H.) (82,17–18 V.).

9. Marcellus, *fr.* 95 (55 K./H.) (84,3–4 V.).

10. Lam 4.20. The LXX has "the Lord's anointed," not "Christ the Lord." For the first time recognized as a fragment of Marcellus by K. Seibt, *Die Theologie des Markell,* 353; Marcellus, *fr.* 62 (55 K./H.) (54,6–8 V.).

11. Marcellus, *fr.* 63 (56 K./H.) (54,8–9 V.).

12. See Lam 4.20.

13. Jn 4.24.

14. Jn 8.12; Marcellus, *fr.* 64 (57 K./H.) (54,10–12 V.).

lessly eliminates the hypostasis of the Son, alleging that before the fashioning of the creatures there was nothing other than God alone. Therefore, he writes as follows in this literal statement.

> Asterius calls the authority[15] given to him "glory," and not only glory but also "pre-cosmic glory,"[16] not understanding that when the cosmos did not yet exist, there was nothing other than God alone.[17]

And again, he confirms the same point, saying:

> ... The sky and earth and everything in the sky and upon the earth came to be from God. Well now, if he were to believe this,[18] it would be necessary for him also to confess that there was nothing other than God.[19]

Chapter 2

(1) You see, a Jew openly denies the only-begotten Son of God, "through whom all things" came to be.[20] For if there was nothing other than God before the generation of the world, the Son would not have then existed. And how could [it be that] "all things came to be through him, and without him not one thing came to be"?[21] Therefore, on the one hand, the Jew, denying the Christ of God, before the generation of the world knows nothing except God alone, with Marcellus giving witness in support of him, while on the other hand, the Church of Christ is proud to say with all candor, "We have one God, the Father, from whom are all things, and (2) one Lord, Jesus Christ, through whom are all things."[22] But when she says "through whom are all things," she acknowledges that he

15. See Mt 28.18; Jn 17.2; 5.21–22.
16. Asterius, *fr.* 36 (100 V.).
17. Marcellus, *fr.* 77 (104 K./H.) (68,11–12 V.).
18. See Asterius, *fr.* 21; 27; 29 (92; 96 V.).
19. Marcellus, *fr.* 76 (103 K./H.) (68,7–10 V.).
20. 1 Cor 8.6; Jn 1.3.
21. Jn 1.3.
22. 1 Cor 8.6.

is before all things. And therefore the man who says that before the generation of the world there was nothing other than
God alone falsifies the truth. For the Son, his only-begotten,
was also with the only God before the establishment of the
world and coexisted with the Father. For he also taught her [the
Church] this, who said, "In these last days, he spoke to us in a
Son, whom he appointed as heir of all, through whom he also
(3) made the ages."[23] And in Proverbs, the Son himself teaches
about himself through Solomon, saying, "When he established
the heavens, I was present with him."[24] But he himself also "was
the light that enlightens every man coming into the world,"[25]
because "he was in the world, and the world was made through
him."[26] But if "the world was made through him," (4) it is clear
that he pre-existed the world. Thus God was not alone before
the establishment of the world, but his only-begotten Son was
present with him, and looking upon him the Father rejoiced,
as he himself [the Son] as Wisdom teaches, saying in Proverbs,
"I was daily his delight."[27] And the Son himself, contemplating
the Father's thoughts, was filled with joy, for which reason he
says, "I rejoiced before him always."[28] The Church of Christ,
having received these pious and divine mysteries, preserves
[them]. But the man who says,

> When the cosmos did not yet exist, there was nothing other
> than God alone,[29]

(5) shows himself to be wrapped in the mantle of either a Jew
or a Sabellius.[30] For if right from the start he denies the Son

23. Heb 1.2.
24. Prv 8.27.
25. Jn 1.9.
26. Jn 1.10. The whole chain of scriptural quotations forms one argument
in Eusebius.
27. Prv 8.30.
28. Ibid.
29. Marcellus, *fr.* 77 (104 K./H.) (68,11–12 V.).
30. The conjecture by Klostermann goes against the sense—Eusebius does
not want to portray Marcellus slipping into the mantle of himself, a Sabellian,
but into that of his models, either Jew or Sabellius, which is also confirmed by
the argument that directly follows.

and introduces God alone, he will be a Jew who rejects Christ; on the other hand, if he accepts the title of the Son insofar as he is Word, but claims that the one God is he, Son together with Father, he will bring Sabellius back to life. For if before the world there was nothing other than God, either he [God] will himself be Father and Son, or he will not have a Son.

Chapter 3

(1) But Marcellus seems to say that the Son is this, [namely,] the Word in God himself, by which he is thought to be rational, so that he is father of himself, and again son of himself. Listen, then, to his words, in which he writes in this way:

> For before the fashioning of all there was a certain silence, as (2) one might expect, since the Word was in God. For if Asterius has believed that "God is Maker of all things,"[31] it is clear that even he himself will confess along with us that the one [God] has always existed and never received a beginning of his existence, while the other things have both come to be by him and have come to be out of nothing.[32]

You see that, having posited that God is without beginning,[33] he said that the Word that was in him was in silence prior to the fashioning. And proceeding on, he adds:

> Well now, if he were to believe this,[34] it would be necessary for him also to confess that there was nothing other than God. Thus the Word possessed his own glory, since he was in the Father.[35]

(3) Consequently, as is only reasonable, he says that the Word is also eternal, that is to say, ingenerate, writing as follows:

31. Asterius, *fr.* 21 (92 V.).

32. Marcellus, *fr.* 76 (103 K./H.) (68,1–5 V.).

33. "Beginning" (ἀρχή) can also sometimes be translated "origin" or "source" in Eusebius, depending on whether he wants to emphasize the logical start of existence or the source from where this start takes its beginning.

34. See Asterius, *fr.* 21; 27; 29 (92; 96 V.).

35. Marcellus, *fr.* 76 (103 K./H.) (68,8–10 V.).

You hear, then, the consistent testimony of the Holy Spirit, giving witness through many and diverse persons to the eternity of the Word.[36]

And again:

And because of this he [John] begins from the eternity of the Word, saying, "In the beginning was the Word, and the Word was with God, and the Word was God."[37] Using three successive testimonies, he wishes to show the eternity of the Word.[38]

(4) And it is possible to hear how he claimed that the Word is united to God and is likewise unbegotten[39] with him, when he says in this way somewhere:

We know to refer the economy according to the flesh to the man, but we believe that the eternity according to the Spirit is united[40] to the Father.[41]

Chapter 4

(1) Well then, having asserted that the Word is in the Father in this way, he next declares that he is one and the same thing with him, writing in these words as follows:

If one were only to consider the Spirit, the Word would rightly appear to be one and the same with God. But if one were to consider the addition of the flesh to the Savior, the divinity seems to extend itself only by virtue of its activity, so that, as is to be expected, the monad is truly indivisible.[42]

(2) And proceeding on again, he says:

Thus the Savior says, "I and the Father are one,"[43] not because of the "exact agreement in all [their] words and actions," as

36. Marcellus, *fr.* 6 (53 K./H.) (10,1–2 V.).
37. Jn 1.1.
38. Marcellus, *fr.* 6 (53 K./H.) (10,2–6 V.).
39. συναγέννητον.
40. Technically, aorist tense and so "was united."
41. Marcellus, *fr.* 72 (70 K./H.) (60,15–16 V.).
42. Marcellus, *fr.* 73 (71 K./H.) (62,1–4 V.).
43. Jn 10.30.

Asterius said,[44] but because it is impossible either for the Word to be separated from God or for God to be separated from his own Word.[45]

Therefore, then, if God and the Word within him were one and the same thing, as it seems to Marcellus, the one who came to be within the holy Virgin and was made flesh and became man and suffered what has been recorded and who died for our sins was himself the God who is over all[46]—indeed, a view for which the Church of God reckoned Sabellius among atheists and blasphemers when he dared to say this.

Chapter 5

So, if Marcellus were to say that the Word of God was the one who was incarnated, but determined that he was inseparable from God, having asserted that the monad is indivisible, and that there is one hypostasis of God and of the Word within him, according to him one would have to think that the one who was incarnated was none other than the God who is over all.[47] But if the monad is indivisible, God and the Word within him are one and the same thing, and who, then, would someone say is the Father and who is the Son, since the underlying reality[48] is one? And so in this way, Marcellus, introducing him who is one and the same, a Son-Father, renewed [the error of] Sabellius.

Chapter 6

(1) But the Church of God also acknowledges that the monad is indivisible, confessing one source, the one God who is unbegotten and without source, but also deems the only-begotten Son who is born from him, truly existing and living and subsisting,

44. Asterius, *fr.* 39 (102 V.). Marcellus emphasizes that the one source of will and action cannot be divided, but also that neither can they go separate ways, and hence disagree.

45. Marcellus, *fr.* 74 (73 K./H.) (62,11–14 V.).

46. Rom 9.5; Eph 4.6.

47. Ibid.

48. τοῦ ὑποκειμένου.

as Savior, although he is neither without source nor unbegotten
(so as not to posit two sources and two gods), but begotten from
the Father himself and having the one who has begotten him as
source. (2) For this reason, it has received the belief in one God
the Father, who rules over all, and in Jesus Christ our Lord, the
only-begotten Son of God, this holy and mystical faith providing regeneration in Christ to those who are enlightened through
it. But Marcellus says that the monad extends itself in activity,
which takes place in bodies, but not at all in the incorporeal,
ineffable, and indescribable being.[49] (3) For it is neither extended in activity, nor contracted in inactivity, nor does it act in any
way as human beings do, nor does it move in any way as human
beings do. But God, being an indivisible monad, begot his only-
begotten Son from himself, neither being divided nor undergo-
ing alteration, (4) change, flux, or any suffering. For neither by
commanding nor by being commanded nor by laying down the
law does he do these things, speaking as human beings do by
the tongue and lips. Nor, when looking to the ordering of the
universe, did he contemplate [it] by making use of eyes as we
do, but having anticipated things that do not exist[50] beforehand
by means of his ineffable and divine power, he sees even those
as if they already existed (5) and subsisted. But neither does he
construct [the universe] by making and fashioning as craftsmen
among us do, having taken pre-existing material in his hands
and fingers, but again, by means of his ineffable and incomprehensible power he brought into existence from nothing the
being[51] of all creatures. Therefore, then, if he made all things
by means that are ineffable and unfathomable to us, why, then,
should it be controversial if we say that no passion has occurred
within him in the begetting of the Son, as there is in the generation of mortal animals, because [the begetting of the Son] took
place beyond all things and before all things, in a way completely
unlike things commonly acknowledged to be mortal by nature,
but rather in the manner that is known to him alone?

49. οὐσίας.
50. Rom 4.17.
51. οὐσίαν.

Chapter 7

(1) But are you afraid, man, lest, having confessed that there are two hypostases, you introduce two sources and cast aside the monarchical divinity? Well then, learn that because there is one God who is without source and unbegotten, but the Son has been begotten from him, there will be one source and a single monarchy and kingship, since even the Son himself acknowledges his Father as source. (2) "The head of Christ is God,"[52] according to the Apostle. But are you anxious that one might have to accept that there are two gods if you confess that there are two hypostases of Father and Son?[53] But know this too: that the man who grants that there are two hypostases of Father and Son is not compelled to say there are two Fathers, nor that there are two Sons, but will grant that one is the Father and the other is the Son. Thus, in the same way, it is not necessary for the man who posits two hypostases to grant that there are two gods. (3) For we neither deem them equally worthy of honor, nor both without source and unbegotten, but deem the one [hypostasis] as unbegotten and without source, while [we deem] the other as begotten and having the Father as his source. For this reason, even the Son himself teaches that his Father is also his God, when he says, "I go to my Father and to your Father (4) and to my God and to your God."[54] Thus God is shown to be both Father and (5) God of the Son himself. For this reason, then, the God of the Son is proclaimed by the Church to be one. And the Son, when he is compared to the Father, will not also be God of the Father himself, but only-begotten Son, his "beloved,"[55] "image of the invisible God,"[56] and "radiance"[57] of the paternal glory; and he reveres, worships, and glorifies his own Father, acknowledging him as God even of himself, to whom he has been reported

52. 1 Cor 11.3.
53. Klostermann's addition of εἴη is unnecessary.
54. Jn 20.17.
55. Mt 3.17.
56. Col 1.15.
57. Heb 1.3.

also to pray, to whom he also gives thanks, and to whom he also became "obedient unto death."[58] (6) And he confesses that he lives "because of the Father"[59] and is able to do nothing without the Father and that he does not do his own will but the will of the Father. Indeed, he says explicitly, "I have come down from heaven not to do my own will but the will of him who sent me,"[60] and again, "I am able to do nothing of myself. But as I hear, so I judge, and my judgment is just, because I do not seek my own will but the will of the one who sent me."[61] And yet that the one who sent him was another besides himself he shows right afterward, when he says, "If I bear witness to myself, my testimony is not true; (7) there is another who bears witness to me."[62] Then, having called to mind the Baptist, he teaches that the Father is his witness, saying, "And the Father who sent me has himself borne witness to me."[63] And he adds, "If you loved me, you would have rejoiced, because I go to the Father; for (8) the Father is greater than I."[64] Through all of these statements he shows that he himself is other than the Father. And he shows the superiority of the Father's glory when he speaks of the one who has sent and of himself as having been sent and having come down from heaven "not to do my own will but the will of him who sent"[65] him.

And what would Marcellus say to these things, listening to the one who has come down from heaven teaching these things? For he will not even now, I think, say that the flesh of the Savior says these things; (9) for the flesh has not come down from heaven. Well then, who will he say is the one who has come down from heaven and teaches these things? Will it be God himself or the Word who has been united to him? But if he should say the Father, having exposed his naked Sabellianism, the Savior himself will denounce him as a liar, saying,

58. Phil 2.8.
59. Jn 6.57.
60. Jn 6.38.
61. Jn 5.30.
62. Jn 5.31–32.
63. Jn 5.37.
64. Jn 14.28.
65. Jn 6.38.

"I have come down from heaven not (10) to do my own will but the will of him who sent me,"⁶⁶ and, "I am able to do nothing of myself, but as I hear, so I judge,"⁶⁷ and, "I do not seek my own will but the will of the one who sent me,"⁶⁸ and, "the Father is greater than I."⁶⁹ For to think that the (11) Father says these things would be the height of madness. But if he says that the foregoing statements apply to the Word that is connatural⁷⁰ with God and to his reasoning by which he reasons and reflects within himself, how, then, could the thought of God and the reasoning within him also have come down from heaven? And how, having come to be in the flesh that it assumed, did it recount these things? How will the Word, who is in God, say that he has come down "not to do [his] own will, (12) but the will of him who sent"⁷¹ him? Through these statements the Son of God shows his own reverence for the Father. And since he [the Son] leads all creatures that have come to be through him, as he is Savior and Lord and Fashioner of all (for "all things came to be through him and without him not one thing came to be"),⁷² then he can also be addressed as God, (13) Master, Savior, and King. For this reason his Church has been taught to revere and worship and honor him as God, (14) having learned to do this from him. Thus the Savior himself says, "The Father judges no one, but has given all judgment to the Son, that all may honor the Son, just as they honor the Father,"⁷³ clearly commanding [the Church] to honor him not like the prophets nor like the angels or the powers that are distinct from these, but very nearly like⁷⁴ the Father himself. For the Father himself, having wished this, "has given all judgment to the Son, that all may honor (15) him, just as they honor the Father."⁷⁵

66. Ibid.
67. Jn 5.30.
68. Ibid.
69. Jn 14.28.
70. συμφυᾶ.
71. Jn 6.38.
72. Jn 1.3.
73. Jn 5.22–23.
74. τῷ πατρὶ παραπλησίως.
75. Jn 5.22–23.

Indeed, Thomas the Twin also, knowing these things correctly, seeing as he was one of the band of the twelve disciples, acknowledged him as both God and Lord with crystal-clear words, saying, "My Lord and my God!"[76] For this reason, then, it is also fitting for us to revere the Son alone and no other with divine honor, just as we honor the Father, (16) and in this way the Father is honored through the Son. And indeed, [the Son] teaches this very thing too, when he says, "He who honors the Son honors the Father who sent him."[77]

For just as in honoring an image of an emperor that had been sent [to us], we would honor the emperor himself who is the archetype of the image, in the same way the Father would be honored through the Son, just as (17) he is also seen through him. For "he who has seen" the Son "has seen the Father,"[78] seeing the unbegotten divinity impressed in the Son as in an image and mirror. "For he is [the] radiance of eternal light, [the] spotless mirror of the activity of God, and [the] image of his goodness."[79] And having received all these things from the Father, he has received the glory from him [the Father] and from the divinity, as a genuine and only-begotten Son would receive it. But the Father has not also received [it] from anyone, and since he himself is source, fountain, and root of all good things, he would rightly be addressed as [the] one and only God.

Chapter 8

(1) But since Marcellus is ignorant of these matters, he does not want the Son to have been truly begotten from the Father, as a living and subsisting Son, but contends that the Word came forth from God like [that] very word that communicates or commands something. Listen, then, to him as he frankly says even this in these words:

76. Jn 20.28.
77. Jn 5.23.
78. Jn 14.9.
79. Wis 7.26.

Therefore, to have said that "he has been begotten before the ages"[80] seems a logical statement: for that which has come forth from the Father who sent it forth becomes an offspring. But the other statement has no longer been taken in a sound or pious sense by him.[81] For to have said that he who has come forth from him [the Father] is not the Word, but [that] "he is simply only son,"[82] and that this is the true manner of begetting, has usually provided a certain justification for those listening who are inclined to take a human perspective.[83]

(2) Then, after showing that the Word has not been begotten from the Father, he thus says in these exact words:

Well then, the holy apostle and disciple of the Lord, John, calling to mind his eternity, became a true witness to the Word,[84] saying, "In the beginning was the Word, and the Word was with God, and the Word was God,"[85] making no mention here of a generation of the Word.[86]

And so, denying in this way the Son of God, he alleged that at one time the Word who is in God was within God, but at another time came forth from God and (3) at still another time will return again into God and will be in him as he also was before. Listen to how he says these things in these words:

But now I believe the divine Scriptures, that God is one and that, on the one hand, the Word of this [God] came forth from the Father, so that "all things" might come to be "through him,"[87] but that, on the other hand, after the time of judgment, the restoration of all things, and the destruction of all opposing activity, "then he will be subjected to him who put all things

80. Prv 8.23, 25, quoted by Asterius; see Asterius, *fr.* 17 (130 V.).

81. See Asterius, *fr.* 17 (130 V.).

82. See Asterius, *fr.* 53 (116 V.).

83. Marcellus, *fr.* 66 (36 K./H.) (56,3–8 V.).

84. See Jn 21.24.

85. Jn 1.1.

86. See Asterius, *fr.* 74 (124–128 V.); Marcellus, *fr.* 71 (33 K./H.) (60,10–13 V.).

87. Jn 1.3.

under him,"[88] "to [his] God and Father,"[89] so that in this way the Word might be in God, just as he also was previously.[90]

(4) And again, he proposes the same idea more plainly, writing in this way:

Before the world existed, the Word was in the Father. But when Almighty God resolved to make everything in heaven and on earth, the generation of the world required active energy. And because of this, there being nothing else besides God (for all things are confessed to have come to be by him), at that moment, the Word, having come forth, became maker of the cosmos, he who even beforehand was preparing it within his mind.[91]

(5) And again, after all these remarks, he continues on, saying:

And because of this he does not call himself "Son of God," but everywhere he calls himself "Son of Man," so that through this sort of confession, he might enable the man through fellowship with him to become by adoption Son of God, and so that after the completion of the deed, he might again, as Word, be united to God, fulfilling that which was said by the Apostle: "Then he himself will be subjected to him who put all things under him, so that God may be all in all."[92] For then he will be what he was before.[93]

Having said so many things about the Word that is in God, by which we think he is rational, Marcellus has fallen upon treacherous ground, having dared to say that the Word that is in him has been at one time outside of God and again within him after the time of the judgment, so that in this way he might be in God, united to him just as he also was before.

88. 1 Cor 15.28.
89. 1 Cor 15.28, 24.
90. With the exception of a missing, small, final passage, this is Marcellus, *fr.* 109 (121 K./H.) (102,1–19 V.).
91. Marcellus, *fr.* 110 (60 K./H.) (104,1–6 V.).
92. 1 Cor 15.28.
93. Marcellus, *fr.* 111 (41 K./H.) (104,12–18 V.).

Chapter 9

(1) Well then, it is now time for him to answer our questions. Therefore, what should we think of that intermediate period when the Word was outside of God? And how did he come forth? And in what sort of state, then, was God when he did not have his own Word within himself? For if the Word will be in God at the consummation of the universe, just as he also was prior to the time of consummation, how will he be the Word who *came forth* from God? For if, on the one hand, subsisting in himself, he became other than God, the effort of Marcellus will be in vain; but if, on the other hand, having also come forth from God, like the spoken word in our own experience, he remained inseparable from the Father, he was therefore always and through everything (2) in God, even when he was active. How, then, at the time of the judgment does he [Marcellus] send him back, saying that at that time he will be united to God and will be just as he also was before? For if at that time he will be just as he also was before, the Word who came forth from God will not be such as he was before, but even God himself will be unlike himself, formerly having the Word within himself and receiving him back at the consummation of the universe and [only] then becoming as he also was before, but in the meantime being dissimilar. And the Word, having become, so to speak, outside of God, will not before the consummation of the universe be such (3) as he was previously. And which of these would be the more impious statement?

For altogether, [the expressions] "was" and "be" and "has once come to be" and again "about to be," which are indicative of a change in time, would be foreign to the being[94] that is timeless, without source, ingenerate, and immutable, concerning which it is fitting to think that it alone exists and always exists unchangeably and in exactly the same way, being neither diminished, nor contracted, nor extended, nor expanded, nor having anything outside or inside itself, nor becoming one thing at one time and another thing at another, nor being one

94. οὐσίας.

thing before and becoming something else afterward and then again (4) being restored to its former state.

Indeed, Marcellus dared to propose these ideas, saying that long ago there was God and a certain quiet together with God, sketching out for himself the views of that very founder of the godless heretics who made a spectacle of himself promulgating atheism, saying, "There was God and silence,"[95] and that after the silence and quiet, the Word of God came forth in the beginning of the making of the universe in active energy, so that he is no longer such as he was when he was previously resting in the silent God, but, (5) upon coming forth from God, becomes active. And how, then, did he come forth? Altogether, I suppose, like the expression of the articulate voice, that is, God speaking and talking just as human beings [do]. At any rate, this is what seemed to him to be the case when he wrote in this way:

> For just as all the things that have come into existence have come into existence by the Father through the Word, so also the things that are said by the Father are communicated through the Word.[96]

(6) And again:

> For whatever the Father says, in every case he appears to say it through the Word. This is clear even from our own experience, insofar as one can compare small things with great and divine ones. For whatever we wish both to say and to do according to our capacity, we do by means of our word.[97]

(7) Therefore, then, if the Word came forth in this way from the Father, [that is,] in active energy, for what reason did it occur to Marcellus to set a limit to the activity of the Word, [namely,] the time of the consummation, during which he says that

---

95. On Simon Magus, see Theodor Zahn, *Ignatius von Antiochien* (Gotha: Friedrich Andreas Perthes, 1873), 390.

96. Marcellus, *fr.* 87 (61 K./H.) (74,12–13 V.).

97. Marcellus, *fr.* 89 (62 K./H.) (76,17–78,4 V.). When Marcellus uses the term "word" at the end of this statement, he uses it in the sense of our fundamental rationality.

the Word will be in God, just as he also was before (he granted that beforehand he was resting in God's silence)? Therefore, after the consummation, too, there will be a certain quiet, since the Word will intend no activity. But before the establishment of the creatures there was nothing, he says, except God, and since there was nothing, (8) it is fair enough [to say] that he [God] was silent. But Daniel the prophet prophesies that at the time of the consummation, there will be tens of thousands before the throne of God, saying, "a thousand thousands served him; and (9) ten thousand times ten thousand stood before him,"[98] and all in some degree will be sons of the age that is to come then, namely, the blessed souls of patriarchs, prophets, apostles, and all holy spirits of the martyrs, and sheep of our Savior, who will stand at his right hand and will hear: "Come, O blessed of my Father, inherit the kingdom prepared for you from the foundation (10) of the world."[99]

Well now, given that all these will exist and live an immortal life after the time of the judgment, why won't the Word of God be active even then? For what reason did it occur to Marcellus to declare that God will then no longer speak to the saints nor use his active Word, but will be, as he also was before, that is, silent and at rest?[100] For he makes this point, having said several times that he will then be as he also was before—and he was before, as [Marcellus] himself said, at rest. (11) Thus at that time God will cease to speak, though before this time [he was] speaking and using his active Word, but afterward [will] deprive his saints of [his] own Word and the Wisdom in him in the promised kingdom of heaven itself.

You see over what sort of cliff he [Marcellus] has gone, having employed no guide—surely not the divine Scriptures. At any rate, he contrived for himself all these ideas (12) on the basis of one statement, which he nevertheless has not understood.

98. Dn 7.10.
99. Mt 25.34.
100. Eusebius is not very accurate here, as he blends the Word and God and speaks as if Marcellus talked of both the Word's and God's (the Father's) changing between silence and speaking, inactivity and activity.

Once[101] he had confronted the evident proofs of the Young[102] and New Testament, he was driven into a corner from all directions, and having discovered a single passage that supports his evil belief, and lighting upon it as upon a windfall, he put together [that belief] on the basis of this single passage, and not on that one that had been spoken from the mouth of our Savior but [on one spoken] from the mouth of the evangelist, in which he called him [Word], having said, "In the beginning was the Word, and the Word was with God, and the Word was God."[103] And so, having taken his start from there, he denied the Son as if he were nothing other than a word like the one recognized [to exist] in us.

Chapter 10

(1) And yet the great and divine evangelist himself has called [him] not only "Word," as has been said many times by us,[104] but also "God"[105] and "Light"[106] and "Son"[107] and "Only-begotten."[108] And he recounts that the Savior himself nowhere in the Scripture calls himself "Word," but throughout the gospel "Life"[109] and "Light"[110] and "Only-begotten"[111] and "Son of God"[112] and "Truth"[113] and "Resurrection"[114] and "Bread of

101. Klostermann's "but" is unnecessary.

102. Eusebius here ridicules how Marcellus turns a "New" Testament into a "Young" Testament with his claim that only the New Testament can give witness to the "active Word" that became incarnate in the relatively recent past ("not four hundred years ago"), as he says in his *fr.* 103 (105 K./H.).

103. Jn 1.1.

104. The phrase "as has been said many times by us" might refer to the tortuous survey of *ET* 1.20.

105. Jn 1.1.

106. Jn 1.4; 1.5; 3.19; 8.12; 11.9; 12.35–36.

107. Jn 1.34; 1.49; 3.18; 5.25; 10.36; 11.4, 27; 17.1; 19.7.

108. Jn 1.14, 18; 3.16, 18.

109. Jn 11.25; 14.6.

110. Jn 8.12; 12.46.

111. Jn 1.18; 3.16.

112. Jn 10.36.

113. Jn 14.6.

114. Jn 11.25.

life"[115] and "Vine"[116] and "Shepherd"[117] and countless other things, as (2) has already been shown. Why on earth, then, given that these titles are so numerous, does he [Marcellus] not stop [when he encounters] all the remaining titles in the text, and inquire carefully into the sense of those things that are said, but instead says that he is chiefly designated by the [title of] "Word" alone,[118] as if he were nothing other than Word? Thus he writes in these very words, saying,

> Not "having been called Word figuratively,"[119] even if those who teach differently burst asunder with their lies, but being chiefly and truly Word.[120]

(3) And again:

> Well then, let him learn that the Word of God came, not "being called Word figuratively,"[121] as those men say, but being true Word.[122]

And again:

> For previously, as I have said many times, he was nothing other than Word.[123]

And again:

> Therefore, before the descent and birth through the Virgin, he was only Word. For before the assumption of the human flesh,

115. Jn 6.35.

116. Jn 15.1, 5.

117. Jn 10.11. It is surprising that Eusebius leaves out three more self-descriptions of Jesus according to John: Christ (Jn 4.26), the one who is from above (Jn 8.23), the door (Jn 10.7), and the way (see Jn 14.6). He obviously reacts against Marcellus, *fr.* 3 (43 K./H.) (4,18–6,11 V.), where this list of titles in John has been taken to refer to the Word incarnate.

118. See Marcellus, *fr.* 3 (43 K./H.) (4,18–6,11 V.).

119. Section of Asterius, *fr.* 71 (130 V.).

120. Marcellus, *fr.* 94 (46 K./H.) (84,1–2 V.).

121. See Asterius, *fr.* 71 (130 V.).

122. Marcellus, *fr.* 65 (45 K./H.) (56,1–2 V.).

123. Last sentence of Marcellus, *fr.* 52 (91 K./H.) (46,8–9 V.). Marcellus often says that before the creation of the cosmos, there was nothing other than God. But the context here indicates he is talking about different titles for Christ, which he refuses to apply to the second person before the Incarnation.

what else was "that which came down 'in the last days,'"[124] as he [Asterius] himself also wrote, "and that which was born from the Virgin"?[125] It was nothing other than Word.[126]

It would be right to bring this sort of inquiry before Marcellus when he says these things: (4) for what reason, my good man, do you add for us [the words] "nothing other" and "only"? For we correctly know that statement, "In the beginning was the Word,"[127] without the qualification "only," but also the statement that "the Word was God"[128] and that "he was the light that enlightens every man"[129] and "only-begotten Son"[130] and all the other statements that have been proposed. But no one would be able to show that it has been said that he was "only" Word and "nothing other" than Word. (5) From where, then, comes the audacity of this addition ["only"]? For why shouldn't one rather say that he was only Son and nothing other than Son? Why shouldn't one say that he was God and nothing other than God? Why not "Light of the world"[131] and nothing other than this? Why not "Life"[132] and nothing other [than this]? And one could in all justice extend the same line of reasoning to similar [statements]. (6) But just as anyone, if he were to say this, would be accused of making a mistake (for he is all these things together, being one Son of God, and even if one rates one of these as more important than others,[133] according to each conception of the different divine powers in him and titles), (7) so also the man who said of the Word that he is only Word and nothing else would rightly be said to be in error. For since only the evangelist John called him "Word" and not only this, but also other things, while the Savior addressed himself as "Light"

124. Heb 1.2.
125. Asterius, *fr.* 57 (118 V.).
126. Marcellus, *fr.* 5 (48 K./H.) (8,19–22 V.).
127. Jn 1.1.
128. Ibid.
129. Jn 1.9.
130. Jn 1.18.
131. Jn 8.12.
132. Jn 14.6.
133. Marcellus, *fr.* 3 (43 K./H.) (4,18–6,11 V.), claims that "Word" would be the proper, not the improper or metaphorical, title of (the incarnate) Christ.

and "Truth" and "Life" and "Only-begotten Son" and the rest, but nowhere as "Word,"[134] how could it not be absurd to say with regard to those things he called himself that he is one of these and no other, and with regard to the evangelist's title for him, which addressed him as Word, to confirm that he is nothing other (8) than Word? But "chiefly and truly" he [the evangelist] also says "he is" "God."[135] For there was not one man who addressed him as Word and another man who called him God, but one and the same evangelist taught at the same time that he was God and Word, having said, "and the Word was God,"[136] and the same evangelist also called him "Light." Therefore, has not the Master and Savior himself <through>[137] the evangelist given witness concerning himself that he is chiefly and truly the only-begotten Son and all the other things? But the one who disregarded all [these] things says that he is chiefly and truly only Word, and he adds that he would consequently be only Word, and from that point he stumbles upon the analogy of the human word.

Chapter 11

(1) And hearing him [called] "Light," he does not fall to [the level of] the corporeal light, nor does he say he is like the splendor of the sun, but with regard to the Word, he proposes that he is a communicating [word] and like the human word, so that he says that at one time he rests in God and at another comes forth from God, and becomes inside and outside him, just like

134. This is an accurate remark, as the self-descriptions of the Lord in the New Testament do not include the title "Word."

135. Second part of Marcellus, *fr.* 94 (46 K./H.) (84,2 V.). Here is one of Klostermann's most extensive corrections of the manuscript text, deriving from a misunderstanding of the argument. He has overlooked that Eusebius combines (deliberately or not?) a quotation from Marcellus (to which the first part is referring) with John—as the following argument highlights—from whom "God" is taken (John 1.1) to contradict Marcellus. See Marcellus, *fr.* 94 (46 K./H.), where this fragment ends not in the Johannine predication of "God," but "Logos/Word." Klostermann's entire addition has to be deleted.

136. Jn 1.1.

137. These brackets indicate a manuscript emendation.

the word in our own experience, the word that is called "interior" and the word that is (2) heard expressed by means of the voice. Thus he says in these very words:

> For whatever the Father says, in every case he appears to say it through the Word. This is clear even from our own experience, insofar as one can compare small things with great and divine ones. For whatever we wish both to say and to do according to our capacity, we do by means of our word.[138]

And again he says these things:

> For before the fashioning of all there was a certain silence, as one might expect, since the Word was in God.[139]

Then he continues:

> For there was nothing else before but God alone; but when all things were going to come into existence through the Word, the Word came forth in active energy.[140]

(3) Having said such things about the Word, listen to how he attempts to interpret the gospel saying, writing as follows:

> But the holy apostle and also disciple of the Lord, John, teaching clearly and explicitly at the beginning of the gospel, as something previously unknown among men, and calling him Word of the Almighty, thus said, "'In the beginning was the Word, and the Word was with God, and the Word was God."[141] Not making use of [only] a single testimony, he reveals the eternity of the Word.[142]

(4) And again he says,

> Using three successive testimonies, he wishes to show the eternity of the Word.[143]

And again, he adds,

138. Marcellus, *fr.* 89 (62 K./H.) (76,17–78,4 V.).
139. First sentence of Marcellus, *fr.* 76 (103 K./H.) (68,1–2 V.).
140. Excerpt from Marcellus, *fr.* 109 (121 K./H.) (102,19–20 V.).
141. Jn 1.1.
142. Marcellus, *fr.* 68 (51 K./H.) (58,6–10 V.).
143. Last sentence of Marcellus, *fr.* 6 (53 K./H.) (10,4–5 V.).

So that by saying, "In the beginning was the Word,"[144] he might show that the Word was in the Father by power (for God, "from whom are all things," is the source of all things that have come to be);[145] and by saying, "And the Word was with (5) God,"[146] [he might show] that the Word was with God by activity ("for all things were made through him, and without him not one thing was made");[147] and by having said that "the Word was God,"[148] [he might show us] not to divide the divinity, since the Word is in him and he himself is in the Word (for [the Word] says, "The Father is in me, and I am in the Father").[149]

Marcellus, denying the hypostasis of the only-begotten Son of God through these many statements, calls the divine evangelist to witness to his evil belief, as if he knew nothing other than the Word, which at one time is active and at another rests in God, and was nothing other than God himself.

Chapter 12

(1) And yet the great man who is at once both evangelist and theologian, having mentioned the Word three times in this passage, has not only said that he is Word of God. For he did not say, "In the beginning was the Word *of God*," but indefinitely, "In the beginning was the Word,"[150] having left it to us to investigate what sort of Word he was. And again, he said, "And the Word was with God,"[151] when he could have said, "And the Word *of God* was *in* God." But he also said, "the[152] Word was God,"[153] and not "the Word was *of* God," lest we assume that he is a certain activity of God (2) that communicates or makes something. And indeed Marcellus, having thought that the Word of God is

144. Jn 1.1.
145. 1 Cor 8.6.
146. Jn 1.1.
147. Jn 1.3.
148. Jn 1.1.
149. Jn 10.38; Marcellus, *fr.* 70 (52 K./H.) (60,3–9 V.).
150. Jn 1.1.
151. Ibid.
152. Klostermann's addition of "and" is superfluous.
153. Jn 1.1.

himself eternal, that is to say, unbegotten, asserted this many times, not comprehending that if, on the one hand, he should say that the Word is other than God, there will be two eternal beings (the Word and God) and no longer one source, but that if, on the other, he should say that there is one eternal one, asserting that God is the same as the Word, he will blatantly agree with Sabellius, introducing (3) that entity that is one and the same, a Son-Father. Therefore, for him the Father will be begotten and have suffered, and he himself will be the one who prays to himself and says that he has been sent by himself and that he is Son and only-begotten of himself; here Marcellus does not speak truly, but lies with dissimulation through his ignorance. And what other statement could be more impious than this? But come, let us see what sort of Word the evangelist announces to us when he says, "In the beginning was the Word, and the Word was with God, and the Word was God."[154]

Chapter 13

(1) Thus the term "word," as it has been utilized in the Greek tongue, admits of various meanings:

1) That which has been placed in the rational soul, by which it is possible for us to reason, has been called "word."

2) And besides this, there is another meaning: that which communicates something through the tongue and articulate speech.

3) And in a third (2) sense, ["word"] refers to that which has been laid down by an author in writing.

4) And already we have also been accustomed to call "word" that seminal or vegetative power, by which those things that are not yet growing but will soon come forth in actuality into the light are stored up in potentiality in seeds.

5) And besides these, we have otherwise been accustomed to call "word" that knowledge of a certain skill or science, which also comprehends all the basic principles of these sorts of things, such as medicine or architecture or geometry.

154. Ibid.

Chapter 14

(1) Well now, since the different senses of the term "word" have been presented, and the evangelist has said without qualification, "In the beginning was the Word, and the Word was with God, and the Word was God,"[155] it is fitting [for us] to consider the sense intended [here], whether in the present instance the evangelist conveys a certain peculiar use of the term "word" besides those known to us, on the one hand having said without qualification "word," while on the other having added some strange and paradoxical sense of the power unique to him [the Word] in the statement "and the Word was God."[156] (2) For do not think, he says, that this, too, belongs to those things that are in relation to something else, such as the word that is in the soul or that is heard through the voice, or that which is in physical seeds, or which subsists in mathematical theorems. For all of these, belonging to those things that are in relation to something else, are thought to exist in another pre-existing being.[157] But the God-Word is in need of no other pre-existing thing so that, having come to be in it, he might subsist, but he is in himself (3) living and subsisting, since he is God. For "the Word was God."[158]

And hearing that he is God, he [the evangelist] says, lest you suppose that he also is without source and unbegotten like his Father, learn that this God-Word was "in the beginning."[159]

And what beginning he attributes to him, he [John] clarifies immediately afterward, not having said, "and the Word was *the* God," with the addition of the article, lest he assert that [the Word] was the God who is over all. But neither [did he say] the Word was "in God," lest he compare him to the likeness of a human [word], but he said, "and the Word was (4) with God."[160] For if he had said, "and the Word was in God," having

155. Ibid.
156. Ibid.
157. οὐσίᾳ.
158. Jn 1.1.
159. Eusebius is using ἀρχή here in the sense of "source."
160. Jn 1.1.

proposed that he is like an accident in a subject and one thing
that is in another thing, he would have introduced, as it were, a
composite God, supposing that he [God] is a (5) being[161] without rationality, while he renders the Word an accident in th[at]
being.[162] Having thought this very thing, Marcellus causes the
Father and Son to become the same thing, calling the being[163]
Father, and the Word within him the Son, without realizing
that he who grants this, having supposed that God is without
[his] Word, would fall into the godless and impious claim of asserting that God is irrational,[164] having the Word as an accident
within himself while not being himself (6) rational.[165]

But it is necessary to confess that that which is beyond the
universe is one single thing, divine, ineffable, good, simple, incomposite, something of one form, that is God himself,[166] Intellect itself, Word itself, Wisdom itself, Light itself, Life itself,
Beauty itself, Goodness itself, and whatever one could think is
greater than these, and rather beyond (7) all knowing and beyond all thought and conceiving. And [one must also confess]
the only-begotten Son of this [God], as if he were the image
of the Father who has been brought forth from him and [is]
altogether and in every way most like the one who has begotten him, and [one must confess that] he, too, is God and Intellect and Word and Wisdom and Life and Light and Image
of the Good and the Beautiful itself; not that he himself is the
Father, but that he is the only-begotten Son of the Father; not
that he himself is the one who is, who is unbegotten and without source, but the one who has been brought forth[167] from the
latter and who acknowledges as source the one who has begotten him.

(8) But if, denying these arguments, Marcellus should allege that God and the Word within him were the same, defin-

---

161. οὐσίαν.
162. οὐσίᾳ.
163. οὐσίαν.
164. I.e., literally, "without his word," or "without his rationality."
165. Literally, "not being himself Word."
166. See below, *ET* 3.17.
167. φύντα.

ing God as incomposite and simple, see, then, how he confesses neither the Father nor the Son, but openly either professes what Jews believe or introduces Sabellianism, because he alleges that the same is Father and Son. As a result, according to him, the statement "In the beginning was the Word" is equivalent to the statement "In the beginning was the God," and the statement "and the Word was with the God" is equivalent to the statement "and the God was with the (9) God," and likewise, too, the third statement is the same as the statement "and God was the God," which statement indeed would, in addition to being incoherent, also be most illogical.

In addition, how can there be scope for the statement "and all things came to be *through* him," since the underlying reality is one? For he [the evangelist] does not say that all things have come to be "by" him or "from him" but "through him." Now the addition of the preposition "through" indicates that which is of service, as the same evangelist further on shows, saying, "The Law was given through Moses; grace and truth came through Jesus Christ";[168] for as the Law, since it is not of human invention nor comes from Moses himself, but from God, designated Moses as servant and helper for the giving of the Law to human beings, and because of this it has been said, "The Law was given through Moses," so also, "grace came through Jesus Christ,"[169] the (10) Father having effected it through Christ. Therefore, in the same way it has also been said, "All things came to be through him,"[170] since there was one who did the making, himself having been assisted, so that one must seek the maker of the universe as another, the one who caused all things to subsist through the one who has been spoken of as divine. And (11) who would this be? But he [Marcellus] could not say. Since these things are so, it is necessary to confess that the one who is spoken of as divine by the evangelist is neither the God who is over all[171] nor the Father himself, but the only-begotten Son of the latter, who is not an accident in the Father,

168. Jn 1.17.
169. Ibid.
170. Jn 1.3.
171. Rom 9.5; Eph 4.6.

nor something that exists in him as in a subject, nor as one and
the same thing with God, but truly as Son, living and subsisting, existing in the beginning and being with God and being
God, (12) through whom he fashions all things, so that it would
be correct, if one were to clarify and to say instead of "in the
beginning was the Word," "in the beginning was the Son," and
instead of "and the Word was with God," "and the Son was with
the Father," and instead of "and the Word was God," "and the
Son was God." And likewise that statement that follows right
after would also agree with these: for "all things came to be
through him, and without him not one thing came to be."[172]
(13) Well then, rightly did the divine evangelist say that he was
in the beginning, having attributed to him a source, that is to
say, the begetting from the Father. For everything that is begotten from something has the one who has begotten him as
source. And surely likewise he added, not "and the Word was in
God," but "and the Word was with God," teaching that the one
who was begotten, having also possessed the Father as source,
is not somehow far from the Father, nor has he been separated
or moved to some great distance from him, but that he is present to him and exists together with him.

(14) And indeed, he [the Son] also taught this in Proverbs,
having said previously, "before all the hills, he begets me,"
having added afterwards, "when he established the heavens, I
was present with him."[173] Thus the Word, that is to say the only-
begotten Son, was with God, his own Father; he coexisted with
him and (15) was always and everywhere present with him.

And indeed [John] also shows this, when he says, "And the
Word was with God." But since it was fitting for us to know also
to what rank he belonged, he necessarily added, "and the Word
was God." For how was he who was begotten from the one and
only unbegotten God not going to be God? For if "that which
has been begotten of the flesh is flesh, and that which has been
begotten of the spirit is spirit,"[174] according to the saving teaching, it would follow, too, that that which has been begotten

172. Jn 1.3.
173. Prv 8.27.
174. Jn 3.6.

from God (16) would be God. For this reason also "the Word was God," even God [the] maker and fashioner of all things. And indeed this same point the evangelist also showed immediately afterwards, having added "all things came to be through him."

Therefore, the Law, which was a tutor [given] through Moses, introducing God as maker of all in the story of the making of the universe, in transmitting the elements and principles of godly piety, taught, "In the beginning God made the heavens and the (17) earth,"[175] and what follows. And guiding the Jewish people through them [these principles and elements], the Law exhorted [them] to believe that the cosmos is created, so that they might not worship the creation (18) instead of the "one who created it."[176] But how and through whom God fashioned all things, Moses had not yet handed over to those under him, but "grace and truth came through Jesus Christ,"[177] proclaiming the mystery that had been hidden in silence by Moses, and initiating the newer and mystical teaching for the Church of God. Having shouted openly for all to hear, "In the beginning was the Word, and the Word was with God, and the Word was God,"[178] and "All things came to be through him, and (19) without him not one thing came to be,"[179] and having added still to these, "In him was life, and the life was the light of human beings. The light shines in the darkness,"[180] and the things that follow these, through [these] [the Church] teaches the Son of God and the excellence of the divine light and of the life that is in him, and how everything that has been said by Moses and even that which is beyond these were established through him. But Marcellus, grasping none of these things, is convicted now of Judaism and then of Sabellianism: (20) as a Jew, claiming that before the establishment of the cosmos there was nothing except God alone (while the Church confesses that before

175. Gn 1.1.
176. Rom 1.25.
177. Jn 1.17.
178. Jn 1.1.
179. Jn 1.3.
180. Jn 1.4–5.

the establishment of the cosmos there were the Father and the Son), while as Sabellius, declaring that Son and Father are one and the same thing, and introducing him [the Son] as at one time an interior word and at another as an expressed word. (21) For although he pretends not to allow these terms, he clearly [means them] when he says that [the Word] is at one time in God and at another comes forth in active energy, and through these statements he likens him to the human word.

To be sure, the divine evangelist established that the one who was spoken of as God by him was Word in none of the ways that have been recounted, but such as it was fitting to think of the only-begotten Son of God: namely, that he was Word in such a way that all things were established by the Word and without the Word nothing came to be, but God and only-begotten in such a way that he alone was truly Son of the God who is over all—really a genuine and beloved Son, (22) who is made like his Father in all things. For this reason he was also truly light in such a way that he sheds intellectual and rational light upon the souls made in his image. For this reason he [John] says that he is the light not of all things, but only of human beings. For he [John] said, "He was the light that enlightens every man coming into the world."[181] Likewise, he was also truly life, in the sense that he provides to all living things the stream of living water that flows from him. And if you considered each conception of the divine powers in him, you would find that they also were true names of him. For in all things the Son of God was truth, which indeed he himself shows, saying, "I am the truth."[182]

Chapter 15

(1) But this novice author neither understands nor knows these things, nor is he aware that he is ignorant of them, although he indeed even boasts that he knows how they are. Come then, having taken these matters up again, let us listen to how he likens [the Word] to the word in human beings, to

181. Jn 1.9.
182. Jn 14.6.

the word in thought and the word in expression, writing in this way:

And this is easy to know, I think, for those who ponder well a small and humble example from our experience. For it is not possible for anyone to separate the word from a man in power and hypostasis. For the word is one and the same with the man, and is separated [from him] in no other way than by the activity alone of the deed.[183]

(2) Indeed in these remarks he has used the expressed word as an image, while he [has used] the interior word as an image in the following remarks when he says:

For God was in need of no other preparatory material, such as matter or any other human [material] for [the] establishment, but this which he had ready in his own mind. Since, then, it was impossible for God to contemplate the establishment of the heavens apart from the Word and the wisdom that belongs to the Word, he [the prophet Solomon] rightly said, "When he established the heavens, I was present with him."[184]

(3) Then, proceeding right on, he shows that the Word of God is also at the same time interior, writing in this way:

For who either of the holy angels or of just men was so trust-worthy as to undo the punishment ordained for him by the mouth of God, if not the Word himself, who coexisted and who formed along with [him], to whom the Father said, "Let us make man ..."[185]

(4) And immediately after this, he clarifies what sort of Word he is, introducing [it] when he says:

But if, using a small human example from our experience, one were to explain the divine activity as through an image, it would be as if some man knowledgeable in making statues, wishing to form a statue, first considers within himself its type and character and then figures out how much width and

183. Last part of Marcellus, *fr.* 87 (61 K./H.) (76,5–10 V.).
184. Prv 8.27; Marcellus, *fr.* 88 (59 K./H.) (76,11–15 V.).
185. Gn 1.26; first part of Marcellus, *fr.* 98 (58 K./H.) (88,11–14 V.).

height would be suitable for it. He scrutinizes the proportion of the whole in each part, and after having prepared the right amount of bronze[186] and outlined beforehand in his mind the future statue with a clear mental picture of it, he is conscious of the cooperation of his reason, with which he makes his calculations and with which he is accustomed to do everything (for nothing beautiful comes to be without reason).[187] When he begins this perceptible work, he exhorts himself as he would another, saying, "Come now, let us make, let us form a statue." Just so does God, the Lord of the universe, in making a living statue from earth, exhort himself with nothing but his own Word, saying, "Let us make man …"[188]

Through these remarks [Marcellus] clearly attributes to God both an interior word with which someone calculates and an expressed word with which he converses, having supposed that the Word that is in God is also like the one in us.

Chapter 16

(1) Therefore, there is no need to reconsider how all these statements serve to deny the Son of God. I think that it is enough to ask this much: if indeed there was one God and nothing else, neither Father nor Son, why did Scripture fabricate such names? And why does even Marcellus himself dissimulate, calling the Son not Son, but Word? And since he has used that word that is in human beings as a model, it should be said that while not every man has a son, every man *is* rational and has within himself a connatural reason. (2) Therefore, a son is something other than [a man's] reason. Thus, if he [Marcellus] were to allege that God has within himself a word and nothing else, [a word] by which he both thought and conversed with himself, saying, "Let us make man,"[189] why does he also call him unnecessarily Son? Why does he mislead the Church? Why does he pretend to believe in the Son of God when he

186. See Prv 8.27.
187. Again, λόγος in the sense of rationality.
188. Gn 1.26; middle part of Marcellus, *fr.* 98 (58 K./H.) (88,18–90,7 V.).
189. Gn 1.26.

does not, making a show of calling the Word that is in God "Son," while the image clearly teaches us to make a great distinction between the word that is implanted in the soul and the Son who was begotten from someone [else] and who himself (3) subsists and lives and is active? But "not I," he will say, as is to be expected, "but the divine evangelist addressed him as Word; from this it follows that we too should make this confession [with him]." And even I myself say yes [to that].

Chapter 17

(1) Nevertheless, I do not think it fitting to take the expression in any other sense than that in which the evangelist himself defines the "Word" when he teaches the disciples. And clearly he showed what sort of word this was, adding this immediately afterwards when he says, "And the Word was God."[190] Indeed, he could have said, "And the Word was *the* God," with the addition of the article, if indeed he thought that the Father and the Son were one and the same and that the (2) Word himself was the God who is over all[191]—but he did not write in such a way. For it would have been necessary to have said either that the Word was *of* God or that the Word was *the* God, with the addition of the article, if he were going to make what he wrote agree with the thought of Marcellus. But now he also shows that the Word himself is God in a similar way as the God with whom he was. For, having said before, "and the Word was with God," he continues, saying, "and the Word was God," not only teaching us more clearly to think first that the Father of the Word, with whom the Word was, is God, the one who is beyond all,[192] and then not to be ignorant that, in addition, after him his Word, the only-begotten Son, was not himself (3) the God who is over all,[193] but was also himself God. For the conjunction "and" connects the divinity of the Son to the Father. For this reason he [John] says, "And the Word was God" so that we might

190. Jn 1.1.
191. Rom 9.5; Eph 4.6.
192. Ibid.
193. Ibid.

see that he who is over all,[194] with whom the Word was, is God, and hear that the Word himself is God, as an image of *the* God, and an image not as in inanimate material but as in a living son, who also has been made like, in the closest way possible, to the archetypal divinity of the Father. (4) But since it seemed a good idea to Marcellus to compare the Word of God to the human word, we will also say it is better by far, if one uses the human word as an image, to have used instead this example and to say that the mind is the father of the word in our experience, being other than the word. For no man ever has come to know what the mind is in its being,[195] but it is like a king, who, seated within his secret treasures, takes counsel as to what things must be done; and his word, having been begotten from [his] innermost chambers as from a father, (5) is made known to all outside. Therefore, they may partake of the benefit of the word, but no one ever knows the unseen and invisible mind, which indeed is the (6) father of the word. In the same way, then, but rather beyond every image and example, the perfect Word of God, the all-powerful king, not being composed of syllables and words and names like the expressed word of men, but living and subsisting like an only-begotten Son of God, goes forth from the paternal divinity and kingship, and he refreshes the entire world with the gifts of his abundance, causing all creatures to overflow with life and reason and wisdom and light and participation in every good. The Father and God of the universe, who is transcendent, however, is unapproachable and unfathomable to all because of his ineffable and invisible intelligence, for which reason he has also been said to dwell in "unapproachable light."[196] (7) But the one who is unapproachable and unfathomable to all would be the Father, while there is the other, who is nearer to all since indeed he governs all things with the Father's consent (for which reason it has been said, not of the Father, but of the Son, that "he was in the world, and the world was made through him"),[197] and the one was beyond

194. Ibid.
195. οὐσίαν.
196. 1 Tm 6.16.
197. Jn 1.10.

the universe and over all things, "dwelling in unapproachable light,"[198] while the other is omnipresent through all things and [is] in all things by his careful providence—thus only in this way can the image of the human word be compared to him. But since these things have been shown by us, it is fitting for somebody who wants to learn to ask:

Chapter 18

(1) Why at the beginning of his book did the evangelist proclaim the only-begotten Son of God as Word? To this, we will answer: because of the hidden prophecies about him of long ago. For to each prophet, it was said, "the Word of the Lord that came"—for example, "to Isaiah,"[199] and "the beginning of the Word of the Lord in Hosea,"[200] and "the Word of the Lord that (2) came to Joel,"[201] and "The Word of the Lord came to Jonah,"[202] and likewise "to Micah."[203] And to the remaining prophets as to each one that expression *came* was added (for the divine Scripture correctly and necessarily indicates that [the Word] was in none of the prophets but came to each, to the extent that the power of each was capable of admitting [it], coming to it and providing to the soul of each the appropriate spirit from [him]). And understandably, in the present case, the evangelist was about to announce the intelligible economy of the Word. He no longer teaches that he came as one to another, as he came to the ancients, but that he assumed flesh and became man. And since he was going to announce to all his saving advent to human beings, when he says next, "and the Word became flesh and dwelt among us," he necessarily goes back to the beginning,[204] showing of what sort the (3) Word was who just recently became incarnate, and he describes him

198. 1 Tm 6.16.
199. Is 2.1.
200. Hos 1.2.
201. Jl 1.1.
202. Jon 1.1.
203. Mi 1.1.
204. Jn 1.14. Eusebius uses ἀρχή here to mean "source" or "origin."

as God, announcing at the same time the knowledge of him
and of his divine appearance among human beings. Then,
since the ancients knew beforehand from the divine Scriptures
that the Word had come to each prophet, he himself [the evan-
gelist] announces the more divine and excellent source of him,
which none of the prophets (4) proclaimed to human beings
so obviously and explicitly. For this reason, in handing over the
mystery concerning the Word that had been unknown and hidden, he shouted in a great voice to all, saying, "In the beginning
was the Word, and the Word was with God, and the Word was
God; all things came to be through him, (5) and without him
not one thing came to be."[205] For he says that if, having been
taught by the earlier holy writings, you have previously learned
in times long ago that the Word of the Lord came now to this
prophet and likewise again to another and yet again to another, even so now it must be proclaimed to all not that he came,
but that he "was in the beginning" and that he "was God" and
that "all things came to be" through him, and that that very
God-Word through whom all things came to be, by the Father's
love for humankind, (6) "became flesh and dwelt among us."[206]

John, the great disciple and apostle of Christ, announced
these things, instructing all human beings in the new and recent mysteries of the Savior: not that God was rational,[207] nor
that he himself ponders within himself and converses with himself, saying, "Let us make man,"[208] nor that he has used words
that command what he wishes to be done. For every man who
denied (7) the Son of God would say these things. And indeed,
Marcellus does just this when he flees to the ancient Scripture
as to a place of refuge and tries to bring together those things
that were enjoined upon the Jewish people in their infancy regarding the prohibition against worshiping idols and the ob-
ligation to acknowledge and revere only one God. And there
were many instances of teaching available to him concerning
the one God, it having been handed over for their [the Jews']

205. Jn 1.3.
206. Jn 1.14.
207. λογικός.
208. Gn 1.26.

benefit then and in times since, whenever the Jews fell into idolatry. Indeed then, fleeing to this position and having barricad-
ed himself in by his Jewish hardness of heart as in a fortress, he
proposed the denial of the Son of God.

Chapter 19

(1) In any case, listen to how he has used such words, writing
in this way in these words:

> Well, then, who does Asterius think it is who says, "I am who
> am,"[209] the Son or the Father? For he said that "there are two
> hypostases of the Father and of the Son," looking at the human
> flesh that the Word of God assumed and because of it imagin-
> ing that this is so, in this way separating the Son of God from
> the Father, just as someone might separate the son of a man
> from [his] natural father.[210]

(2) And he immediately adds:

> Well then, if [Asterius] will say that the Father said these things
> to Moses while separating himself from the Son, he will con-
> fess that the Son is not God. For how is it possible for the one
> who says, "I am who am," not to confess at the same time that
> "the one who is" is himself in contradistinction to him who is
> not? But if he were to allege that the Son said this "I am who
> am" while separated in hypostasis, he will be thought to say
> the same thing again concerning the Father [namely, that the
> Father is not]. And each of these is impious.[211]

(3) And again, trying to show that the Father and Son are
one, he writes in this way:

> For [Christ] himself confesses, "The Father is in me, and I
> am in the Father."[212] And that he said this neither simply nor
> carelessly is also clear from another apostolic statement. For
> he who said, "one Lord, one faith, one baptism," said, "one

209. Ex 3.14.
210. See Asterius, *fr.* 52 (116 V.); Marcellus, *fr.* 85 (63 K./H.) (74,1–5 V.).
211. Marcellus, *fr.* 86 (64 K./H.) (74,6–11 V.).
212. Jn 10.38.

God and Father," "who is over all and through all and in all."[213] You see that he does not deviate here from the agreement [of Scripture], but here, too, has thought the same thing. For having said "one Lord," he said "one God,"[214] so that whenever he calls to mind the one Lord, he might also include the Father, and so that whenever he speaks about the Father, he might give testimony that the Word is not outside of God.[215]

(4) Having said these things, Marcellus then brings together more Scriptures from the Old (5) Testament to show that God has no Son. In any case, alleging that God is an indivisible monad, he shows that the same is Father and the same is Son, writing in this fashion:

What then? Unless, taking note of the Spirit, we were to think that the monad is indivisible in power, would we not commit an error, since the Word clearly teaches us, "You will worship the Lord your God, (6) and you will serve him alone"?[216] He also proclaims the same thing through the gospel according to Mark. For when one of the scribes came to him and asked him which was the first of the commandments, he answered him in this way, having said, "The first of all is 'Hear, O Israel, the Lord our God, the Lord is one, and you shall love the Lord your God with all your soul and all your strength.' This is the first commandment. And the second one is like this—'you will love (7) your neighbor as yourself.' There is no other commandment greater than these." "And the scribe said to him, 'You are right, teacher; you have truly said that God is one and there is no other beside him.'"[217] (8) But the scribe, who seems to have learned piety through the Law, appears to praise the response of the Savior when he says, "Hear, O Israel, the Lord your God is one," and to confirm by an oath that he spoke well, for he says, "You have truly said that God is one and that there is no other beside him." But those who boast that they know the mysteries of the New Testament, these men also wish to

213. Eph 4.5–6.
214. Ibid.
215. Marcellus, *fr.* 90 (75 K./H.) (78,5–13 V.).
216. Mt 4.10; cf. Lk 4.8; Dt 6.4–5.
217. Mk 12.29–32.

invent a second god, divided in hypostasis and power from the Father.[218]

(9) He adds to these remarks, making out that God is one and that there is no Son in these comments:

But that the divine Scripture knows to call the monad "Lord" and "God" has also already become clear from what has been said before, in what God said to his servant Moses. "God said again to Moses, 'Speak thus to the sons of Israel: the Lord, the God of your fathers, the God of Abraham, and the God of Isaac, and the God of Jacob has sent me to you.'"[219] You see how [Scripture] addresses the same as Lord and God, demonstrating to us, (10) then, one person.[220] Again, Scripture likewise says, "And the Lord spoke all these words, saying, 'I am the Lord your God, who brought you out of the land of Egypt, out of the house of bondage. You shall have no other gods besides me.'"[221] You hear how through the pronoun ["I"], [Scripture] declares that there is only one God. (11) And again, a little later [God] says, "I am the Lord your God,"[222] saying that he himself is Lord and God. What do we learn through another Scripture? [Scripture] says, "Know this day, and do not be confused in your mind, that the Lord your God, this is God in heaven above and on the earth beneath, and there is no other beside him."[223] And again, in the same [book] of Deuteronomy, it says, "Hear, O Israel, the Lord our God is one Lord, and you shall love the Lord your God with all your heart, and with all your (12) soul, and with all your mind."[224] And again, in the same [book]: "See, see that I am, and there is no God beside me; I kill and I make alive; I wound and I heal."[225] How, then, did Asterius, pretending "to follow the holy Scriptures simply and scrupulously,"[226]

218. Asterius, *fr.* 55 (118 V.); Marcellus, *fr.* 91 (77 K./H.) (78,14–80 V.).
219. Ex 3.15.
220. πρόσωπον.
221. Ex 20.2–3.
222. Ex 20.5.
223. Dt 4.39.
224. Dt 6.4–5.
225. Dt 32.39.
226. Asterius, *fr.* 50 (114 V.); see also Asterius, *fr.* 9 (86 V.).

not know this passage, which says, "The Lord your God, this is God in heaven above and on earth beneath, and there is no other beside him,"[227] and that "He is one," and that "there is no other beside him"?[228]

(13) And after other statements, he again adds to these, saying,

Then how will the holy prophet Jeremiah not openly refute [Asterius] for teaching otherwise? For, prophesying to us regarding the Savior, he said as follows: "This is God; no other can be compared to him! He found the whole way to knowledge and gave it to Jacob his servant and to Israel whom he loved. After these things he appeared on earth and lived among men."[229]

(14) And again he adds, saying,

But the Father must be in the Word, even if it does not seem so to Asterius and to those who think the same things as he does. For this is the opinion of the divine prophet Isaiah, who says through the Holy Spirit, "And they will bow down to you, and they will make supplication to you; because God is in you, and there is no other beside you. For you are God."[230] You see how completely he refutes the crafty malice of those who teach differently.[231]

(15) And he continues:

And if you wish to hear still another prophecy from the same [prophet] that confirms for us that there is one God, he [the prophet] says, "I am God, the first, and to the last; I am."[232] For the "I" is indicative of one person,[233] for the two words show one person[234] to us. For having said "I," [the Lord] also adds

227. Dt 4.39.
228. Dt 6.4; 4.35, 39; Marcellus, *fr.* 92 (78 K./H.) (80,13–82,12 V.).
229. Bar 3.36–38; Marcellus, *fr.* 93 (79 K./H.) (82,13–18 V.).
230. Is 45.14–15.
231. Marcellus, *fr.* 95 (55 K./H.) (84,3–8 V.).
232. Is 41.4.
233. προσώπου.
234. πρόσωπον.

"am," so that through the two parts of the statement, pronoun and verb, the monad of the divinity (16) might be attested to. And if one should need yet another testimony, I will again present to him the same prophet saying, "I am the first, and I am the last; besides me there is no god."[235] If Asterius thinks that the Son, "being separated in hypostasis from the Father, is like a son of man,"[236] being scandalized by the human flesh that he assumed for our sake, let him show us who says these things. (17) For the text here also speaks of one person.[237] Therefore, who is the one who says, "There is no god besides me"? Let him also hear still another prophecy, which states, "A righteous god and a savior, there is none besides me."[238] If he were to think that there were two gods,[239] it would be necessary for him to confess that the other one was neither righteous nor a savior. But if [that other god] is neither righteous nor a savior, how can he still be God? For there is declared to be one who is righteous and a savior. And again, [the prophet] says, "Before me, there was no other god, and after me there shall be none. I, I am God, and besides (18) me there will be no savior."[240] If [Asterius] wishes to hear yet another prophetic saying, which was perhaps in some way spoken with regard to him and those disposed [to think] as he does regarding the divinity, let him hear the same Isaiah saying, "Repent, those who have gone astray, return in [your] heart, and remember the former things of old; for I am 'the' God, and there is no other besides (19) me."[241] [Isaiah] did not say, "I am a God," so that through the addition of the article he clearly demonstrated that there is one God. What also [did] Hosea the prophet [say]? Doesn't he also testify to the same things, when he says, "I led you out of Egypt, and you shall know no other god besides me, and besides me there is no savior"?[242] And again, Malachi says, "Did not one God (20) create you, and is there not one Father of you

235. Is 44.6.
236. Asterius, *fr.* 54 (118 V.).
237. προσώπου.
238. Is 45.21.
239. See Asterius, *fr.* 55 (118 V.).
240. Is 43.10–11.
241. Is 46.8–9.
242. Hos 13.4.

all?"[243] But Asterius will probably say that David said nothing about this, even though he is the oldest of all the prophets next to Moses, and that because of this, it is doubtful whether or not it is right to think there are "two gods divided in hypostasis."[244] Therefore, so that [Asterius] might not say this, I think it logical to show to him [David] saying the same things as those aforementioned holy men. He says, "Hear, my people, and I will speak to you; [hear,] Israel, and I will give witness to you. If you listen to me, there will be no (21) strange god among you; you shall not bow down to a foreign god. For I am the Lord your God."[245] Does not the one who reveals himself and says "I am" clearly say that there is only one God, that is, himself?[246]

Chapter 20

(1) Marcellus was gathering together all these [quotations] and still more than these for the purpose of denying the Son, not having realized, because of his ignorance, that this sort of teaching was provided to those [prophets] on account of the hardness of heart of the Jewish people. For the Holy Spirit was not able (2) to hand down through the prophets of God the perfect rule of reverence toward God to human beings who were imperfect in [their] hearts. And for this reason he thus commanded them by law to perform sacrifices and bodily circumcision and the keeping of the Sabbath and abstinence from certain sorts of meat, and physical ablutions and corporal blessings, [which included,] yes, to be sure, promises of a land flowing with "milk and honey,"[247] but *not* a kingdom of heaven. But our Savior and Lord himself, when asked why Moses commanded the man who wished to dismiss his wife to give her a bill of divorce,[248] commands the opposite, and gave the universal teaching, having said, "For your hardness (3) of heart,

243. Mal 2.10.
244. See Asterius, *fr.* 54–55 (118 V.).
245. Ps 80.8–10 (RSV 81.8–10).
246. Marcellus, *fr.* 97 (76 K./H.) (86,1–88,10 V.).
247. Ex 3.8.
248. See Mt 19.7.

Moses wrote this; but from the beginning it was not so."[249] Thus he also would have said the same thing if someone had asked, "Why do you suppose Moses and the prophets after him, having at one time commanded [the Israelites] to worship one God, did not teach [them] the knowledge of the Son?" For since they were continuously being led astray by the error of polytheism, they were not capable of receiving the grace of the gospel. For this reason, then, on account of their hardness of heart, they [Moses and the prophets] gave them the teaching about the one God, instructing them to turn away from thinking that there were many gods, to turn instead toward belief in one God. (4) Thus Moses provided an incomplete teaching to those who were with him because of their incomplete understanding, just as he made no mention of the creation of angels in the account of the making of the world, and yet the prophets who came after these mention not only angels but also divine powers and holy spirits and the super-celestial servants of God, teaching about whom Daniel said, "A thousand thousands served him, and ten thousand times ten thousand stood before (5) him."[250] But Moses handed down his account in silence about all of these—and yet he did so not because he was ignorant of them, having in fact received beforehand accurate knowledge of all things by the divine Spirit; even so, he made no (6) mention at all of those things as having been made by God in the making of the world. And one would say that the reason for this was none other than the people's hardness of heart, just as the Savior himself taught. And you would also learn from the writings of the New Testament that there are countless other things in the constitution of the universe that are not conveyed at all in the writings of Moses. Hence he made no mention of the principalities or powers or world rulers or "spiritual hosts of wickedness,"[251] with which (7) the divine Apostle says we have to take up battle. Why then? Since one cannot clearly learn from either Moses or the remaining prophets the accounts concerning these, should we disbelieve the Apostle? Or whenever

249. Mt 19.8; Mk 10.5.
250. Dn 7.10.
251. See Eph 6.12.

the same [Apostle] recalls once again the rank of the greater powers, saying that Christ is seated at the right hand of God "in the heavenly places, far above all rule and authority and power and dominion, and above every name that is named, (8) not only in this age but also in that which is to come,"[252] and again, whenever he names thrones and dominions and principalities and authorities, saying, "for in him all things were created, in heaven and on earth, visible and invisible, whether thrones or dominions or principalities or authorities,"[253] is it not therefore fitting to accept these things, even though neither Moses nor the remaining prophets had received anything about these beforehand? Or will we also say the same thing about these—that those who were "stiff-necked and uncircumcised in heart and ears"[254] were not able to believe what was said about them?

The prophets of God did not reveal anything to them of the Jerusalem above, as Paul, disclosing it plainly to the Church of Christ, proclaimed even about it, saying, "But the Jerusalem above is free; and she is our mother,"[255] and, "You have come to Mount Zion and to the city of the living God, the heavenly Jerusalem, and to innumerable angels in festal gathering, and to the assembly of the firstborn who are enrolled (9) in heaven."[256] Let Marcellus respond to these, if he is able to produce the teaching about them from the ancient Scriptures. (10) But if he should not find [anything to say], let him give the reason on account of which the prophets of God were silent regarding all these matters and countless others akin to these, concerning which the same Apostle implored God on our behalf, "that we may have power to comprehend with all the saints what is the breadth and length and height and depth, and to know the (11) love of God, which surpasses knowledge."[257] But even our Savior himself revealed the greatest mysteries concerning the kingdom of heaven, the consummation of the universe and

252. Eph 1.20–21.
253. Col 1.16.
254. Acts 7.51.
255. Gal 4.26.
256. Heb 12.22–23.
257. Eph 3.18–19.

the promises, at one time through parables and at another through the secrets [he revealed] to his disciples, to whom he said, "To you it has been given to know the mysteries of God."[258] One would not be able to discover (12) their equivalent from Moses or from the remaining prophets. What then? Since these things were not given to the Jewish people, but were reserved until the opportune time for the Church of Christ, is it necessary in addition to this that we put aside the grace that was given to us, or rather that we give thanks to him who deemed us worthy of this sort of knowledge? For the same reason, therefore, it would be appropriate to accept the teachings about the Son from his New Testament, not concerned if the men of God did not reveal the knowledge of him to the people of hardened hearts, dispensing at the proper (13) time the teaching concerning him. For it did not seem advantageous to hand over the mystery concerning the Father and Son at that time to men who were weighed down with the error of polytheism, to whom neither did he reveal the words concerning the subordinate powers, lest on this pretext those who imagine that their God is father of "gods and men"[259] fall into Greek polytheism. (14) For this very reason, the Word, protecting them from this sort of error, announced the one God, although he surely did not deny that the same was Father. And he taught them to worship the true [God], and he commanded them to acknowledge none but him, while he, to be sure, did not deny that he is a father. And if he called him Lord and God and just and savior, it still would not prevent anyone from thinking that he is Father of his only-begotten and beloved (15) Son. Therefore, if the Father or the Son should say, "I am who am,"[260] the statement would be true of each. For the Father would be "He who is," being himself alone "God who is over all and through all and in all,"[261] as the divine Apostle taught. And the Son himself would also speak the truth, calling himself "He who is" since he alone is the only-begotten Son of "He who is." But since he also

258. See Mt 13.11.
259. Klostermann: Homer, *Il.* 8.1.52.
260. Ex 3.14.
261. Eph 4.6.

exists as image of the invisible God, in this way he would be image of him, with respect to the fact that [God] himself alone is "He who is."[262] For this reason [as sole image of the invisible God who is "He who is"], he also calls himself "He who is," since throughout the divinely inspired Scripture he calls himself both God and Lord just as the Father was.

Chapter 21

(1) It is also possible to know this from the oracle given to Moses. Thus Scripture says, "And God spoke to Moses and said to him, 'I am the Lord. I appeared to Abraham, to Isaac, and to Jacob, as their God.'"[263] You see how he said that he himself appeared to the fathers. And when he appeared, Scripture again gives witness, saying, "And the Lord God appeared to Abraham by the oak of Mamre, as he sat at the door ..."[264] And how did he appear but in human form? And whom should one believe this to be other than the Son of God? Indeed, [Christ] also showed this in the gospels, saying to the Jews, "Your father Abraham rejoiced that he was to see my day, (2) and he saw [it] and was glad."[265] And as his listeners wondered, he added to the statement: "Before Abraham was, I am,"[266] showing in the clearest fashion possible his own pre-existence. What, then, does the statement convey other than that he is the Son of God, who gave the oracle to Moses and said, "I am who am"?[267] For he taught that he himself appeared to Abraham. And how (3) he was "He who is" has been stated.

And the great Apostle Paul knew the Son of God was the mediator of the giving of the Law through Moses, which he taught, saying, "The Law was ordained through angels by [the]

262. I.e., the Son and nobody else. This means that the Father "alone was," while the Son "was the alone begotten" (begotten without a helper), whereas all others are begotten with the help of the Son; hence the "alone" marks the Son as sole "image" of the Father; see Asterius, *fr.* 10 (86 V.).

263. Ex 6.2–3.

264. Gn 18.1.

265. Jn 8.56.

266. Jn 8.58.

267. Ex 3.14.

hands of a mediator. Now a mediator implies more than one."[268] Therefore, the one who spoke to Moses was the mediator, mediating by means of that [law] for (4) the salvation of human beings even before the assumption of the flesh. The same Apostle showed that this was Jesus Christ, having said, "There is one God, and one mediator between God and men, the man Jesus Christ."[269] Therefore, whether the statement "I am who am" was made to Moses from his own person[270] or the Father was the one who uttered this statement through him, in each case (5) the statement would be true. Well, then, let Marcellus not be puzzled, using, as he thinks, an irrefutable syllogism, when he says,

> Well then, who does Asterius think it is who says, "I am who am,"[271] the Son or the Father?[272]

then implying next that if the Father were "He who is," the Son will not be God, because

> ... he [Asterius] says that the "one who is" is himself in contradistinction to him who is not? But if he were to allege that the Son said this, "I am who am," while separated in hypostasis, he will be thought to say the same thing again concerning the Father [namely, that the Father is not]. And each of these is impious.[273]

(6) Saying these things, the same man has fallen into each of these absurd claims, on the one hand asserting that the "one who is" is one, while on the other hand denying the other. And who this is, he should know. For he will either, having granted the Father, deny the Son, or having accepted the Son alone, he will dismiss the Father. Rather, he will be convicted of knowing neither the Father nor the Son, because in granting one alone he tosses the other aside.

And if he should hear God saying, "I am the Lord your God, who brought you out of the land of Egypt, out of the house of

---

268. Gal 3.19–20.
269. 1 Tm 2.5.
270. προσώπου.
271. Ex 3.14.
272. First part of Marcellus, *fr.* 85 (63 K./H.) (74,1–2 V.).
273. Second part of Marcellus, *fr.* 86 (64 K./H.) (74,6–11 V.).

bondage. (7) You shall have no other gods before me,"[274] again, let his soul not be troubled at this, but let him listen to those things that follow immediately afterwards. For having said, "You shall have no other gods before me," he continues, "You shall not make for yourself a graven image, or any likeness of anything that is in heaven above, or that is in the earth beneath, or that is in the water under the earth. You shall not bow down to them or serve them. For I (8) the Lord your God am a jealous God."[275] You see how he gave the command, lest [the people] be led astray by the polytheistic error of the Gentiles, that they should acknowledge him alone as God and Lord. And who was this? The Son, who had the image of the Father within himself, and ordered these things on his own authority for those who were sick with idolatry. For as "all things were made through him,"[276] the Father having caused to subsist the being[277] of all creatures through the Savior, so the Father himself handed over to human beings the knowledge of (9) and piety toward him through the Son as a mediator. And the Apostle taught this, writing in these very words to the Galatians, in which he said, "The Law was ordained through angels by [the] hand of a mediator. Now a mediator (10) implies more than one; but God is one."[278] And if he should say, "See, see that I am, and there is no God beside me,"[279] again it was the Father claiming this through the Son as through an image and mediator. For if, then, Isaiah the prophet says, "Sons I have reared and brought up,"[280] and again, "Israel does not know me, and my people do not understand me,"[281] and again, "I commanded the stars, and by my hand I made firm the heavens,"[282] and everything else of this sort, will we not say that Isaiah said these things, but that God was speaking through him and in him [the prophet]? Will it, then, not be fitting also with regard to

274. Ex 20.2–3.
275. Ex 20.4–5.
276. Jn 1.3.
277. τὴν τῶν γενητῶν ἁπάντων οὐσίαν ὑποστησαμένου.
278. Gal 3.19–20.
279. Dt 32.39.
280. Is 1.2.
281. Is 1.3.
282. Is 45.12.

the only-begotten Son of God [to say] that the Father needed to confirm these things through him for those who stood in need of these sorts of commandments? These men were idolaters, as the same Scripture teaches, saying, "And the Lord said, 'Where are [their] gods, in whom they trusted, of whose sacrifices you eat the fat and of whose libations you drink the wine? Let them arise and help you, and let them become your protectors.'"[283] For to these remarks was added the statement "See, see that I am, and there is no God beside me."[284]

Chapter 22

(1) Well now, if pronouncing countless times through the prophet he proclaimed, "Besides me there is no God,"[285] and, "A righteous God and a savior, there is none besides me,"[286] and, "You shall know no other god besides me, and besides me there is no savior,"[287] and all the other remarks akin to these that are referenced in the other prophets, God was also on that basis "in Christ reconciling the world to himself,"[288] and it was the Father himself who was saying these things to human beings through the only-begotten Son as through an interpreter.

And indeed, the Son himself handed down in the gospels, teaching [the people] to acknowledge only one God, when he said, "And this is eternal life, that they know you, the only true (2) God, and Jesus Christ, whom you have sent."[289] Therefore, he himself was the true God, who alone is one and besides whom there is no other, who enjoined these things upon the Jewish nation when they had fallen into idolatry, not only through the prophets but [also] through his own Son.

Thus when Isaiah (or rather, when God through him) said, "Besides me there is no God; who is like me?"[290] and right after,

283. Dt 32.37–38.
284. Dt 32.39.
285. Is 44.6.
286. Is 45.21.
287. Hos 13.4.
288. 2 Cor 5.19.
289. Jn 17.3.
290. Is 44.6–7.

"You are witnesses if there is a god besides me," he continued, "and there were none then. All who make idols and graven images [do so] in vain, creating shame (3) for themselves."[291] And throughout the whole of his prophecy you would find the inanimate statues struck down, and in each prophet you will likewise find the one God proclaimed for the purpose of quashing the error of believing in many gods. Thus even we were accustomed, when confronted by the superstitions of the Greeks in conversations with them, to dispense [only] at the opportune moment the teaching concerning Christ, in the meantime producing for them refutations of their idolatrous error and defending with convincing arguments the claim that God is one.

(4) Well now, let Marcellus learn, if, having grown old in the episcopate of the Church of Christ, he even now has not yet learned that the knowledge of the hidden mystery regarding the Son of God was in no way granted to the people of old, who had slipped into idolatry, and that the "mystery hidden for ages and generations"[292] was dispensed to his Church alone through his grace, in which mystery the teaching of the holy Trinity of Father and Son and Holy (5) Spirit was included. But the fellow [Marcellus] who has gathered together all these statements, as many as even a teacher of Jews could utter concerning circumcision while conversing in a synagogue of the Jews, thinks himself so high and mighty because he casts these things before the disciples of Christ, not knowing that one who is a Jew in his flesh could say more than he. And so he boasts of these things, making a spectacle of himself while he distorts the true divine teaching regarding our Savior.

Chapter 23

(1) Therefore, then, since he does not understand the statements of the holy Apostle, who taught in various ways that he is the image of God, through those remarks of his that I have been laying out, it is necessary from this point forward to understand that the Church of God does not proclaim two gods.

291. Is 44.8.
292. Col 1.26.

For it does not introduce two unbegottens or two things with-out source, as has been said many times by us, nor does it introduce two beings[293] parallel to one another because of their equal glory, and for this reason not two gods, but it teaches one source and God and that the same is Father of the only-begotten and beloved Son, just as it also teaches one image of the "invisible God,"[294] which is the same as his only-begotten and beloved Son. And even if the Apostle in speaking of God should call the Father "the blessed and (2) only Sovereign,"[295] and again, "who alone has immortality and dwells in unap-proachable light,"[296] and again, "the king of ages, immortal, invisible, the only God,"[297] and again, "to the only wise God be glory for evermore through Jesus Christ! Amen,"[298] and even if still more things than these should be said for the glorification of the God who is one and over all,[299] it is necessary to think that the only-begotten Son of God is the image even of all of these, not as if he were an image that has been formed in inan-imate matter but as one in a living Son. And even if the Savior himself teaches that the Father is the only true God, saying, "that they may know you, the only true God,"[300] one should not hesitate to confess that he [the Son] is true God and that he has this status as in an image, so that the addition of the word "only" applies to the Father alone as to [the] archetype of the image. Just so, the divinely inspired Paul taught (3) most clearly that he [the Son] is the image[301] and radiance[302] of the Father and is "in the form of God,"[303] as has been shown through what has gone before. Therefore, just as when one father subsists and one son is brought forth from the father, one would not correctly think of saying there were two fathers or two sons,

293. οὐσίας.
294. Col 1.15.
295. 1 Tm 6.15.
296. 1 Tm 6.16.
297. 1 Tm 1.17.
298. Rom 16.27.
299. Rom 9.5; Eph 4.6.
300. Jn 17.3.
301. Col 1.15.
302. Heb 1.3.
303. Phil 2.6.

and just as when one king has come to power whose image
is borne throughout the earth, not wisely would one say that
there were two rulers, but that there is one who is honored also
through the image, in the same way (as we have often said) the
Church of God, having undertaken the worship of one God,
(4) continues to worship the same also through the Son, as
through an image. Indeed, not understanding these things,
Marcellus claimed that the image "of the invisible God"[304] is
the flesh of the Savior, which the Apostle has called the "form
of a slave,"[305] not having considered that even all human beings
have been formed in the likeness of the flesh of the Savior. Yet
he declares that the body that the Savior assumed is an image
of the ingenerate and ineffable paternal divinity, but he denies
that the only-begotten Son of God, through whom all things
were established (for "all things were made through him, and
without him not one thing was made"),[306] is the image of God,
saying in these very words:

> Therefore, it is absolutely clear that before the assumption of
> our body the Word in and of himself was not "image of the
> invisible God."[307]

(5) You see the tremendous distortion he has forced upon the
apostolic interpretation. Thus John the evangelist announced
the mystery that was known (although in a hidden way) to Moses
and the remaining prophets, and revealed it by crying in a loud
voice, "In the beginning was the Word, (6) and the Word was
with God, and the Word was God. All things were made through
him."[308] He gave witness that "he was the light that enlightens
every man coming into the world. He was in the world, and
the world was made through him, yet the world did not know
him,"[309] and clearly demonstrated his sonship when he said of
the Father, "No one has ever seen God," and of the Son, "The

304. Col 1.15.
305. Phil 2.7.
306. Jn 1.3.
307. Col 1.15; first part of Marcellus, *fr.* 53 (92 K./H.) (46,10–48,1 V.).
308. Jn 1.1, 3.
309. Jn 1.9–10.

only-begotten Son who is in the bosom of the Father, he has made him known."[310]

Chapter 24

(1) This wondrous teacher of the words of Christ, bringing together out of the divine Scripture the commands of God and the exhortations as to what must be done, defines the Word who was "in the beginning"[311] as something of this sort. Hear how he attempts to understand these things, writing in this way:

> Of those who teach them as if they were ashamed to mention the Word, whom all the divine Scriptures proclaim in this way. For David said concerning him, "By the Word of the Lord, the heavens were made,"[312] and the same again: "He sent forth his Word and healed them."[313] And Solomon said, "Evil men will seek me, and they will not find me. Because they hated wisdom and did not choose the Word[314] of the Lord."[315] And Isaiah said, "The Law will go forth from Zion, and the Word of the Lord from Jerusalem."[316] And again Jeremiah says, "The wise men shall be put to shame; they shall be dismayed and taken because they rejected the Word of the Lord."[317] (2) And Hosea[318] the prophet also said, "They hated him who reproves in the gate, and despised a pious Word."[319] Micah himself, likewise mindful of the Word, said, "The Law will go forth from Zion, and the Word of the Lord from Jerusalem."[320]

Having brought together these passages and others like these, he [Marcellus] thinks that through them he can provide

310. Jn 1.18.
311. Jn 1.1.
312. Ps 32.6 (RSV 33.6).
313. Ps 106.20 (RSV 107.20).
314. LXX = "fear."
315. Prv 1.28–29.
316. Is 2.3.
317. Jer 8.9.
318. The quotation in fact derives from Amos.
319. Am 5.10.
320. Mi 4.2; Marcellus, *fr.* 67 (47 K./H.) (56,9–58,5 V.).

further support (3) for his belief. See how, having mixed together the witnesses from the divine Scripture, he at the same
time confused the Word that is sent out from God, the saving
and healing Word, and the one that exhorts persons as to what
must be done. For the statement "they hated him who reproves
in the gate, and despised a pious word"[321] presupposes a sort
of word that altogether, I suppose, exhorts one to pious and
just deeds, and purports to confess anything rather than the
Son of God, just as if one were ashamed to mention the Son.
For we know that the Son of God is son in the most primary
sense[322] and truly only-begotten Son of God, and we correctly
know that he is Word, not like the word among men, but such
as it is fitting to think the Word of God is, one who is a living
and subsisting Son. But it makes sense that the man who introduces a word that communicates and exhorts one to deeds
hesitated to confess the Son, whom he denied in fact.[323]

Chapter 25

(1) And yet he himself does not perceive that he writes things
that contradict himself. For in other passages he boldly affirms
that none of the former people [the Jews] knew anything about
the Word, for the mystery was hidden. He writes as follows in
these very words:

> For what mystery was hidden other than that concerning the
> Word? And so this mystery was previously hidden "in God,"[324]
> so that none of the earlier people knew clearly the truth about
> the Word, but we now enjoy the riches of the glory[325] and of the
> hidden mystery.[326]

And again he adds,

---

321. Am 5.10.
322. Κυριώτατον: perhaps an allusion to Marcellus's *fr.* 94, wherein he asserts that the second person is chiefly and truly Word—*not* Son.
323. Lit., "by the deed itself."
324. Eph 3.9; Col 1.26.
325. Eph 3.16.
326. Marcellus, *fr.* 96 (50 K./H.) (84,9–13 V.).

But the holy apostle and also disciple of the Lord, John, teaching clearly and explicitly at the beginning of the gospel, as something previously unknown among men, calling him Word of the Almighty, thus said, "'In the beginning was the Word.'"[327]

Therefore, in these remarks he asserts that God's having a Word was a hidden mystery, while on the other hand, in the prophetic statements that were just now presented, he asserts that all the divine Scriptures proclaim something about the Word, and he gathers together still more testimonies concerning the Word of God. (2) Consequently [this Word] was not unknown to the former people, for they all knew these sorts of words, since they bore the prophetic statements in their mouth and memory. But this Christian presents himself before us as the scribe of the Jews, not listening to the Savior when he says, "Woe to you, scribes and Pharisees, hypocrites!"[328] and he is amazed at the one who confirms with an oath that "God is one, and there is no other but he,"[329] not (3) knowing that even the "demons believe and tremble."[330]

Note how from the prophetic writings themselves he gathers together those statements about the Word that instruct [us] as to what deeds must be done, which things even the children of the Jews will confess to know, seeing as they have received this before us. But not even (4) Sabellius himself was ignorant of this sort of word. How then, striking down the Jews and Sabellius, did he say that they did not know the Word in those remarks of his that I presented? And since the same man claimed through the previous remarks that no one was able to know God or his Word unless he has received the image of the invisible God, which is clearly the flesh, (5) as he himself said (for he contended that God and his Word are known only through the image, saying that the flesh is the image), it must be remembered through the foregoing that apart from the incarnate presence, all Jews correctly knew the word of God and the

---

327. Jn 1.1; first part of Marcellus, *fr.* 68 (51 K./H.) (58.6–10 V.).
328. Mt 23.13.
329. Mk 12.32.
330. Jas 2.19.

words in the prophetic writings that exhorted them to pious deeds, because they studied these from tender youth onwards, and confessed that God is the maker and fashioner of all, just as even the scribe who confirms this by oath did.

(6) All these things, then, serve to show that the man is a Sabellianizer. Now it remains to proceed also to those distorted interpretations of the divine Scriptures that he has contrived, so that every one of those who admire the man might learn that he causes them to deviate not only from the right faith, but also from the sound reading and interpretation of the divinely inspired Scriptures.

BOOK THREE

HE GREAT evangelist John announced the theology of our Savior in a manner different from the one that had been handed down [previously]. That Marcellus, having denied this, drove headlong into the faithlessness of the Jews, has been shown from what has been said. And in what distorted a fashion he misinterpreted teachings that were clearly pronounced about our Savior, you may learn from a great many of his other statements, but especially, indeed, from this one. In the Proverbs of Solomon, Wisdom, speaking in her own person[1] about herself, introduces these things, explaining in detail: (2) "I, Wisdom, live with prudence, and I attain knowledge and discretion. The fear of the Lord is hatred of evil. Pride and arrogance and the way of evil and the twisted paths of the wicked I hate. (3) I have good advice and sound wisdom; I am insight, I have strength. By me kings reign, and rulers decree what is just; by me the great are magnified, and rulers govern the land through me. I love those who love me, and those who seek me find me. Riches and honor are with me, enduring wealth and righteousness. (4) My fruit is better than gold and precious stones, and my yield is greater than choice silver. I walk in the way of righteousness; I am directed along the paths of justice, endowing with wealth those who love me, and filling their treasuries with good things. If I should announce to you the things that happen by day, I will remember to recount the things of (5) the age. The Lord created me as the beginning of his ways for his works. Before the age, he founded me, at the

---

1. αὐτοπροσώπος. In this section of the work, involving extensive scriptural interpretation, the Greek noun πρόσωπον is consistently translated as "person."

275

first, before the making of the earth. Before the making of the depths, before the springs abounding with water came forth, before the mountains had been shaped, before all the hills, he begets me—when the Lord made fields, uninhabited regions, and the first habitations. When he established the heavens, I was present with him; when he marked out his throne on the winds, when he made firm the clouds above, when he established the springs of water under heaven firmly, and when he made the foundations of the earth, then I was beside him in harmony; and I was daily his delight; I rejoiced before him always, rejoicing to have completed his inhabited world and delighting in the human race."[2]

Chapter 2

(1) Wisdom says these things about herself in Proverbs. I have deliberately laid these out in their entirety out of necessity, having shown that the one who says these is one person, since there is no change of speaker in the middle [of the passage]. Therefore, Wisdom is shown to be teaching these things about herself. And here in the first place it must be noted in what an indefinite way she is called Wisdom. For [the text] says, "I[3] live with prudence";[4] yet it does not say the "Wisdom *of God.*" But just as in the evangelist, the statement "in the beginning was the Word"[5] was written indefinitely, and again, "The Word was with God,"[6] and it was not said, "the Word *of God*," so that no one might think that he is spoken of as something that exists in relation to something else, nor as an accident in God, but as subsisting and living (for which reason [the text] adds, "and the Word was God,"[7] and did not say, (2) "the Word was *of* God"); the same also applies in the case of Wisdom. For God,

2. Prv 8.12–31.
3. Klostermann's correction of the text is unnecessary. The "I" is precisely the indefinite way of Wisdom speaking as one person.
4. Prv 8.12.
5. Jn 1.1.
6. Ibid.
7. Ibid.

the Word, and Wisdom are one and the same. For this reason, she is named in Proverbs indefinitely, not only in the previously cited words, but also, to be sure, through remarks like this: "Happy are those who find Wisdom,"[8] and, "God by Wisdom founded the earth,"[9] and, "Say to Wisdom, you are my sister,"[10] and, "Proclaim Wisdom so that understanding might attend you,"[11] (3) and, "Wisdom is better than jewels,"[12] and, "Wisdom built her house, and set up seven pillars,"[13] and all the other statements akin to these [that] are presented in the same book. In none of them was Wisdom said to be *of* God, but Wisdom without qualification, so that we might not think it is some accidental thing that is a contingent feature of God, like knowledge in an intelligent man, but subsisting and living Wisdom, the very same as the (4) Son of God.

If, however, someone should suppose that the Wisdom spoken of there is a wise disposition in God, according to which we think God is wise, let him heed the Scripture when it says, "Say to Wisdom, you are my sister."[14] Who would be so insane as to suppose that the God who is over all[15] and the wise disposition in him are said to be "sister" of the types [of wisdom] that belong to those human beings who conduct their affairs wisely? (5) But if you take the statement as applying to the Christ of God (for "Christ is the wisdom and power of God"),[16] there will be no impediment to the understanding, since he does not refuse the sisterhood even among us because of his abundant love for humankind. But if God and the Wisdom introduced in Proverbs are one and the same because Wisdom was a wise disposition in him according to which God is thought to be wise, what prevented [Solomon] from writing "God" instead of "Wisdom"? Yet the statement "Wisdom built her house, and set up

8. Prv 3.13.
9. Prv 3.19.
10. Prv 7.4.
11. Prv 8.1.
12. Prv 8.11.
13. Prv 9.1.
14. Prv 7.4.
15. Rom 9.5; Eph 4.6.
16. 1 Cor 1.24.

seven pillars"[17] and those that follow this are said, but not "God (6) has built his house," and so on; and respectively,[18] "Say to Wisdom, you are my sister,"[19] was said, but not, "Say to God, you are my brother."

You see, however, how this sort of (7) statement strikes the ear as discordant. But if you suppose that these remarks apply to the Son (for he himself was Wisdom), the entire passage will read well, since no impious thought provides an impediment, given that the Apostle Paul gives testimony that agrees with this; with unmistakable clarity he named our Lord and Savior Jesus Christ "Wisdom," having said, "Christ the power and wisdom of God."[20] (8) Since these things are so, it follows from all that has been laid out previously that the statement "The Lord created me as the beginning of his ways for his works"[21] has also been said by him.[22]

If he says, however, that he himself was created, he did not say this as if he had come into being from what is not, nor as if he were like the rest of the creatures and he himself had come into being from nothing, as some have supposed incorrectly,[23] but as if he both subsisted and lived, and was before and pre-existed the establishment of the whole cosmos, having been appointed to rule the universe by the Lord, his Father.

Therefore, the [phrase] "was created" has been said here instead of "he appointed" (9) or "he established." And to give another example, the Apostle called those who rule and lead among men "creation" when he said, "For the Lord's sake accept the authority of every human creation, whether of the emperor as supreme, (10) or of governors, as sent by him."[24] And

17. Prv 9.1.

18. Klostermann's attempts to correct the manuscript reading here are unnecessary. His problem derives from misunderstanding πάλιν; it does not mean "again," but "respective."

19. Prv 7.4.

20. 1 Cor 1.24.

21. Prv 8.22.

22. Literally, "by his person": προσώπου.

23. Eusebius is clearly distinguishing himself here from the position held by Asterius, *fr.* 44 (108 V.).

24. 1 Pt 2.13–14.

the prophet, having said, "Prepare to call upon your God, O Israel,"[25] "Wherefore behold him making firm the thunder and creating the Spirit and proclaiming unto men his anointed (Christ),"[26] and, "Let this be recorded for a generation to come, so that a people that is being created may praise the Lord,"[27] took[28] [the language of] "creating" as applying to that which has come into being from non-existence. For the Lord did not create the Spirit at the time when he proclaimed his Christ to all human beings through it. (11) For "there is nothing new under the sun."[29] But the Spirit was both in existence and pre-existed, but was sent at that time when the apostles had been gathered together, when like thunder "from heaven there came a sound like the rush of a violent wind,"[30] and, "They were filled with the Holy Spirit,"[31] and as a result of this they proclaimed the Christ of God to all human beings in accordance with the prophetic utterance. [In the case of] "Wherefore behold him making firm the thunder and creating the Spirit and proclaiming unto men his anointed (Christ),"[32] the verb *creating* was used for *sending* or *appointing;* "thunder" expressed in another way the gospel proclamation. And the one who says, "Create a clean heart in me, O God,"[33] did not say this as if he had no heart; rather, he prayed that a pure mind (12) might be perfected in him. So also in this way that statement was made "so that he might create in himself one new humanity in place of the two"[34] as equivalent to "so that

25. Am 4.12.
26. Am 4.13.
27. Ps 101.19 (RSV 102.18).
28. Klostermann's correction of the manuscript by adding a "not" is incorrect, as with this sentence. Eusebius is following up his argument about the identification between creation and "endowing," having before made the connection between creation and "appointment." Without the wrongly added "not," Eusebius stresses the "what" (*what* the Spirit was not), instead of taking creation as the beginning of the Spirit (*that* the Spirit was not), as he will explain in the following sentences.
29. Eccl 1.9.
30. Acts 2.2.
31. Acts. 2.4.
32. Am 4.13.
33. Ps 50.10 (RSV 51.10).
34. Eph 2.15.

he might bring together." But note that the same idea is meant in those remarks such as, "Clothe yourselves with the new self, created according to the likeness of God,"[35] and, "If anyone is in Christ he is a new creation,"[36] and if one examined closely the divinely inspired Scripture, he would find that all other [such] statements were made in this sense.

Therefore, do not wonder if metaphorically also in that statement, "The Lord created me as the beginning of his ways for his works,"[37] the verb *he created* was used for *he established* or *he appointed* me to rule, since even in the gospels, when it was said by our Savior, "I confess to you, Father, Lord of heaven and earth, because you have hidden these things from the wise and the intelligent and have revealed them to infants,"[38] we do not say that the confession of sins was shown by the Savior, in the way that it was said in other passages, "Confess your sins to one another,"[39] but the thanksgiving for the infants, the language of confession being used as the equivalent of the statement, "I thank you, Father, Lord of heaven and earth."[40]

(13) And if one searched at one's leisure, one would find myriads of metaphorical statements throughout the whole of the divine Scripture, some of which have a complex meaning, and still others that are predicated univocally of different things, concerning which it would be no small task (14) to pursue at the present time.

Therefore, in this way, even here the statement, "The Lord created me as the beginning of his ways for his works," was used for, "He appointed me to rule over his works." For this reason, [Scripture] did not simply say, "He created me," but added, "as the beginning of his ways for his works."

(15) The Hebrew text explicitly shows this. And so, if some-

35. Eph 4.24.
36. 2 Cor 5.17.
37. Prv 8.22.
38. Mt 11.25.
39. Jas 5.16.
40. Migliore, 166: "but the thanksgiving for the infants, in the sense of 'I thank you, Father …'" This is a little more complicated because of the use of the preposition ἀντί in the sense of "as the equivalent of," which one sees elsewhere in this text.

one should investigate the true meaning of the divinely inspired Scripture, he would find that the Hebrew reading did
not include [the phrase] "He created me," for which reason
none of the remaining translators made use of this wording.
For example, Aquila said, "The Lord acquired me as the head
of his ways," while Symmachus said, "The Lord acquired me as
the beginning of his ways," and Theodotion said, "The Lord
acquired me as the beginning of his way," (16) and the translation seems reasonable.[41]

For he was the head of the whole creation, visible and invisible, its foundation and salvation, whom the Father begot
as [his] only-begotten Son, and having begotten him, he appointed him as Savior of the universe, gathering up within
and through him the constitution of the universe, as the divine Apostle taught, having said, "to gather up all things in
him, things in heaven and things on earth,"[42] so that he not
only sustains all those things that had come into being from
nothing through him, but also so that he takes upon himself
the oversight of the administration of the universe, seeing as
he is Word and Wisdom and Life and Fullness of all Beauty and
Goodness, so that (17) all things are governed and preserved
through him. And he also showed this through the previously
cited statements, through which he said, "By me kings reign,
and rulers decree what is just; by me the great are magnified,
and rulers govern the land through me."[43] (18) Thus all things
are governed by the ineffable laws of the universal wisdom
and providence of the Son of God. He taught this through the
aforementioned statements, and he urged us to cling to him,
saying, "I love those who love me, and those who seek me find
me,"[44] and deterred us from the opposite path when he added

41. Symmachus, Aquila, and Theodotion are three known second-century
translators of the Jewish Bible from Hebrew into Greek. Symmachus and Aquila stand for contrasting approaches: the first for an elegant yet sensible translation, the latter for his literal renderings, as can also be seen in the quotations
that Eusebius gives here.
42. Eph 1.10.
43. Prv 8.15–16.
44. Prv 8.17.

in these words: "the twisted paths of the wicked I hate."[45] (19) Having commanded these and things akin to them, the Son of God (for he himself was Wisdom) next hands over the mystic knowledge concerning himself to those who were previously benefited through them, saying, "If I should announce to you the things that happen by day, I will remember (20) to recount the things of the age."[46] For if, he says, I were going to teach those things that are done by me each day, it is also necessary that I recall my works from the beginning of the age and show how the Father, having begotten me for this, appointed me to rule the universe, so that I might lead his ways and the works that have been made by him through me. For this reason consequently he adds, "The Lord created me as the beginning of his ways for his works,"[47] or, "The Lord acquired me," according to the previously (21) cited translation. For the great acquisition of God was the only-begotten Son, first in that he came into existence from him since he is his Son, and second in that he was appointed the benefactor and Savior of all. And so he is and was named the greatest and most honored acquisition of the Father. For there could be no other acquisition of the Father's more honored than the Son.

For this reason, the first-formed Adam, when he acquired the first son among men, was said also in that passage [to have claimed], "I have acquired a man through God,"[48] since the Hebrew text (22) contains *kanthei* for "I have acquired." Now *kana* is used for "he acquired" in Hebrew. In this way it was said of Abraham, "the field that Abraham acquired (ἐκτήσατο),"[49] for which the Hebrew has *kana*, the same term used in the Hebrew and in [the phrase] "The Lord created (ἔκτισεν) me as the beginning of his ways for his works."[50] For given that the verb *kana* is used here, all the translators are unanimous in rendering it with "he acquired." (23) But the phrase "he created" was reject-

45. Prv 8.13.
46. Prv 8.21a.
47. Prv 8.22.
48. Gn 4.1.
49. Gn 25.10.
50. Prv 8.22.

ed by the Hebrews, which is not found in the Scripture that lies before [us].

There would be a very great difference between "he created" and "he acquired," by which "creation," according to common opinion, shows the passage from nothingness into being, while "acquiring" characterizes the belonging of something that already pre-existed (24) to someone who had acquired [it].

Now, when the Son of God says, "The Lord acquired me as the beginning of his ways for his works,"[51] at one and the same time he revealed his pre-existence and his characteristic belonging to the Father, and also the usefulness and necessity of his own (25) foresight and government with regard to the Father's works. For this reason, he next adds, "Before the age, he founded me, at the first, before the making of the earth. Before the making of the depths, before the springs abounding with water came forth, before the mountains had been shaped, before all the hills, he begets me,"[52] through all of which statements his usefulness and necessity to all is shown, teaching that he both was and pre-existed, and ruled over the whole cosmos, and guided it in accordance with its needs.

For in the [story of] the making of the world [in Genesis], Moses made no mention of invisible powers beyond the universe because of the imperfection of those being instructed by him, but recounted the constitution of the visible cosmos, having recalled four elements in the beginning, heaven and earth, and depths and water, and said that the two have been made by God (for "In the beginning," he says, "God made the heavens and the earth"),[53] but no longer mentioned in a similar way the depths and the water, as if these, too, had been made, but he simply said, "and darkness covered the face of the deep, while a wind from God swept over the face of the waters."[54] Necessarily, then, through the foregoing passages, the Son of God also teaches concerning them that they are created and that he himself exists before them and (26) that all things have been

51. Ibid.
52. Prv 8.23–25.
53. Gn 1.1.
54. Gn 1.2.

made through him. For this reason he says, "Before the age, he founded me, at the first, before the making of the earth. Before the making of the depths, before the springs abounding with water came forth."[55] Calling to mind these three things, the earth and the depths and the water, having saved the greater item, the heavens, he adds it in the fourth and last place. For this reason, he next adds, "When he established the heavens, I was present with him."[56]

(27) Well now, since these things are clearly presented by the divine Scripture and have been treated by us briefly as in an abridgement of the narrative, let us listen to how Marcellus, having cast [his] mind down to earthly things, confidently affirms that all these things were said of the flesh that the Savior assumed, writing literally in this way:

(28) Therefore, since this is so, it follows that we should closely investigate this passage, which was stated in proverbial fashion: "The Lord created me as the beginning of his ways."[57] For the Lord our God, having made that which did not exist previously, truly created. For he created not the existing flesh, which the Word assumed, but the non-existent flesh.[58]

And he adds:

Therefore, if indeed this new mystery appeared most obviously "in the last times,"[59] since for this reason it was foreordained before this age, the prophet rightly said, "Before the age, he founded me ..."[60]—that is, the flesh.[61]

(29) And again he continues, saying:

Then [Wisdom] says, "at the first, before the making of the earth."[62] What sort of earth was this, other than, obviously,

55. Prv 8.23–24.
56. Prv 8.27.
57. Prv 8.22.
58. Marcellus, *fr.* 29 (11 K./H.) (30,13–32,2 V.).
59. Heb 1.2; cf. 1 Pt 1.20.
60. Prv 8.27.
61. Marcellus, *fr.* 38 (20 K./H.) (36,6–9 V.).
62. Prv 8.23–24.

our flesh, which again became earth after [our] disobedience? For [Scripture] says, "You are earth, and to earth you shall return."[63]

You see how far he goes astray, having, on the one hand, deviated from the right [path], and, on the other hand, having contrived for himself instead a path that is rough and (30) impassable to traverse without an exit.[64] Look at how he applied a forced meaning to everything and persisted in uttering a shameless and abominable idea rather than confess that the Son of God himself is Wisdom. (31) Therefore, he refers the clause, "The Lord created me as the beginning of his ways for his works," to the person of the Savior, confessing that he is the one who claims these things in Proverbs. And he says in the same words:

> Therefore, as was fitting, when ancient things had passed in due season and all future things were going to become new through the newness of our Savior, Christ our Lord proclaimed through the prophet, "The Lord created me as the beginning of his ways."[65]

(32) And having said this, he casts his mind down to the flesh of our Savior, adding next:

> For the Lord our God, having made that which did not exist previously, truly created. For he "created as the beginning of his ways" not the existing flesh, which the Word assumed, but the non-existent flesh.[66]

Yet the honorable man does not understand that the one who says, "I, Wisdom, live with prudence,"[67] and, "The Lord created me,"[68] is a certain single voice and one person, such

---

63. Gn 3.19; first part of Marcellus, *fr.* 39 (21 K./H.) (36,10–12 V.).

64. If earth is nothing but flesh that ends in earth, the journey of the divine economy is nothing but a dead end, or a circle that ends where it started from. Eusebius questions here Marcellus's soteriological concept.

65. Prv 8.22; Marcellus, *fr.* 27 (12 K./H.) (30,5–8 V.).

66. A second part of Marcellus, *fr.* 29 (11 K./H.) (30,15–32,2 V.).

67. Prv 8.12.

68. Prv 8.22.

that if one [of these verses] were to be referred to the flesh, the other one would necessarily refer to it also. And Wisdom will be the one who says both. (33) But if the flesh were to say according to Marcellus, "The Lord created me as the beginning of his ways,"[69] it would also be Wisdom, and it will be the flesh that claims, "By me kings reign,"[70] and, "By me the great are magnified."[71] But how could the flesh say, "I will remember to recount the things of the age,"[72] to which it adds, "The Lord created me as the beginning of his ways"?[73]

But he also shows what the ways are, saying next:

> For this one [Christ] became a way of piety for us who were going to walk justly, a beginning of all the ways after these.[74]

(34) And he adds:

> [The author of Proverbs] rightly said that the Lord our Savior was a "beginning of ways" because he also became a beginning of the other ways (after the first way), which we have come to possess, revealing the traditions through the holy apostles who, "with exalted proclamation,"[75] according to the prophecy, proclaimed to us this new mystery.[76]

Yes, Marcellus [said] these things.

Chapter 3

(1) Therefore, if [Marcellus] did not accept the writing both of Moses and of the prophets after Moses, his conclusion would have a certain rationale. But since he is not among those who reject the Old Testament, why then, when he called the apostles and their teachings "ways," did he not pay heed to the prophets of God, who have written countless things concerning the ways

---

69. Prv 8.22.
70. Prv 8.15.
71. Prv 8.16.
72. Prv 8.21a.
73. Prv 8.22.
74. Marcellus, *fr.* 30 (13 K./H.) (32,3–4 V.).
75. Prv 9.3.
76. Marcellus, *fr.* 31 (14 K./H.) (32,5–9 V.).

of God? For in the first place Moses, writing in this way, said, "You should go along the king's highway,"[77] and, "See, I have set before you (2) the way of life and the way of death";[78] and David likewise, "The Lord watches over the way of the righteous, but the way of the wicked will perish";[79] and Jeremiah, "Stand at the crossroads, and ask for the ancient paths of the Lord, and look at what the good way is; and walk in it."[80] And you will find that each of the prophets calls to mind the ways (3) of God differently. Well, then, if our Savior and Lord Jesus Christ [of God] teaches that he himself is the beginning of the ways of God, saying, "The Lord created me as the beginning of his ways for his works"[81] (being altogether, I suppose, more ancient than Moses and the prophets and those who have lived earlier according to the ways of God),[82] but the flesh that he assumed was not older than all of those, the passage has not been rightly understood to refer to (4) the flesh. Thus the Savior did not say these things because of the flesh, but because he pre-existed and led the way as the beginning of all the ways of the Lord, which all the ancient men who loved God traversed.

(5) And since the divine Apostle in saying, "O the depth of the riches and wisdom and knowledge of God! How unsearchable are his judgments and how inscrutable his ways!"[83] proposes certain other ways, those that exercise providence over the universe, through which, by means of his ineffable judgment and incomprehensible calculations, he governs all things with divine power, it follows to say that the one who said, "The Lord created me as the beginning of his ways for his works,"[84] is also the beginning of these ways. And since [Marcellus] did not understand the ways of God, he declared that the (6) flesh of our Savior is the beginning of these [ways]. He also interprets the phrase "for his works," claiming,

77. Nm 20.17.
78. Dt 30.15.
79. Ps 1.6.
80. Jer 6.16.
81. Prv 8.22.
82. Eusebius may have angels in mind here.
83. Rom 11.33.
84. Prv 8.22.

Therefore, [the prophet] says, "He created me as the beginning of his ways for his works."[85] Of what sort of works, however, does he speak? The Savior says about them, "My father
is working still, and I am working."[86] And again he says, "...
having accomplished the work which you gave me to do."[87]

(7) Then, as if clarifying the meaning of those remarks, he
adds,

> For "who" before the revelation of these matters "would have
> believed"[88] that the Word of God, having been born through
> a virgin, would assume our flesh and reveal bodily the entire
> divinity in it?[89]

As if making his meaning complete, he adds,

> Therefore, this is [the meaning of] the statement, "The Lord
> created me as the beginning of his ways for his works."[90]

(8) And he wrote these things, not having been able to lift
up the eyes of his mind "on high" and to say with the prophet,
"When I shall look at your heavens, the work of your fingers,
the moon and the stars that you have established,"[91] nor having recalled the prophetic saying, through which it was said,
"but they do not regard the deeds of the Lord, or (9) comprehend the work of his hands."[92] For if he [Marcellus] had paid
attention to these statements, he would have known that before
the heavens and the earth and before the entire world, and not
only before the visible but also before the intelligible works of
God that have their hypostasis[93] in incorporeal and transcendent powers, the one who says these things both existed and
pre-existed.

---

85. Ibid.
86. Jn 5.17.
87. Jn 17.4; Marcellus, *fr.* 32 (15 K./H.) (32,10–13 V.).
88. Is 53.1.
89. Marcellus, *fr.* 33 (16 K./H.) (32,14–34,2 V.).
90. Prv 8.22; Marcellus, *fr.* 34 (126 K./H.) (34,3–4 V.).
91. Ps 8.4 (RSV 8.3).
92. Is 5.12.
93. ἐν ὑποστάσει.

But [Marcellus], having moved on to that statement, "Before the age, he founded me,"[94] again puts the flesh front and center, saying in this way:

... calling this foundation his foreordained fleshly (10) economy, as the Apostle also says, "For no other foundation can anyone lay than that which is laid, which is Jesus Christ."[95]

And he adds,

Here [the prophet or the Apostle] calls to mind one age in which he said the dispensation of Christ was founded although many ages have passed by, as David said, "He exists before the ages."[96]

(11) And having turned next to the statement, "at the first, before the making of the earth,"[97] he again says that the earth is the flesh [of Christ], writing in this way:

What sort of earth was this, other than, obviously, our flesh, which again became earth after [our] disobedience? For [Scripture] says: "You are earth, and to earth you shall return."[98] For it was necessary that this [flesh] obtain healing.[99]

And he makes these claims, this most wise man, not having recalled how he had said just above that before the making of the earth the flesh was created as the beginning of the ways of God. (12) And if, in short, he indicated the flesh through "the earth," how is it not necessary to confess that the one who says that he was before the making of the earth, pre-existed the flesh? For he says, "Before the age, he founded me, at the first, before the making of the earth."[100] Therefore, the one who says these things existed before the (13) making of the flesh. And if he also called to mind not long ago ages, but [only] the one,[101]

94. Prv 8.23.
95. 1 Cor 3.11; Marcellus, *fr.* 35 (17 K./H.) (34,5–8 V.).
96. Ps 54.20 (RSV 55.19); Marcellus, *fr.* 35 (17 K./H.) (34,8–10 V.).
97. Prv 8.23–24.
98. Gn 3.19.
99. Excerpt of Marcellus, *fr.* 39 (21 K./H.) (36,10–13 V.).
100. Prv 8.23–24.
101. Note that Eusebius accepts here an argument that Marcellus made

which even our Savior mentioned, having said, "The sons of
this age marry and are given in marriage,"[102] so also the flesh
that our Savior assumed did not exist before the present age,
but he himself [God the Son], who taught these things through
Solomon, [did]. You see into what rough terrain [Marcellus]
has fallen, having deviated from the right and imperial (14)
road.

And besides these statements, he adds still more, saying,

[The prophet] says, "Before the making of the depths."[103] Here
the prophet says in proverbial fashion that the depths are the
hearts of the saints, which have in their depths the gift of the
Spirit.[104]

He does not understand that before the incarnate coming
of our Savior, the holy prophets of God partook of the same
Spirit, both Moses and those still more ancient than Moses.
Therefore, if the hearts of the saints were these [depths], it is
necessary that (15) the one who says "before the making of the
depths" be older than all of these depths. How, then, was it possible for these [statements] to be referred to the flesh of the Savior? And surely if he [Marcellus] had knowledge of the divine
Scriptures, he would not so easily have declared that the depths
were the hearts of the holy, having understood that "darkness
covered the face of the deep,"[105] according to the testimony of
Moses, and how complex and difficult it is to interpret the statement in the divine Scripture [as being] about them. For the
Apostle says, "Do not say, 'Who (16) will ascend into heaven?'
(that is, to bring Christ down) or 'Who will descend into the
deep?' (that is, to bring Christ up from the dead)."[106] Thus in
these remarks the regions of Hades seem to have been called
"the deep." But the Lord himself shows this even more clearly

---

against Asterius, who, as one can see in his *fr.* 17 (90 V.), spoke of ages in the
plural. As before, we can see that Eusebius, in his criticism of Marcellus, is also
critical of Asterius.

102. Lk 20.34.
103. Prv 8.24.
104. Marcellus, *fr.* 40 (22 K./H.) (38,1–4 V.).
105. Gn 1.2.
106. Rom 10.6–7.

in the divine oracle made to Job: "Have you entered into the springs of the sea, or walked in the recesses of the deep? Have the gates of death been opened for you in fear, or did (17) the gates of Hades tremble when they saw you?"[107] and the evil powers in the deep, about which it was said, "Praise him [the Lord] from the earth, you sea monsters and all depths,"[108] and still the darkness over the deep, about which Moses said, "Darkness covered the face of the deep."[109] Having learned all of these, if [Marcellus] had been diligent and not inattentive when he read the divine Scriptures, he would not have dared to say that the hearts of the holy were (18) the depths, but he would have known in what sense these statements were made, statements such as, "Deep calls to deep at the thunder of your cataracts,"[110] and again, "The very deep trembled, a multitude of the water's sound,"[111] and again, "The deep is like a garment (19) that covers him."[112]

If he had examined these passages more closely and others akin to them, he would have had some chance of understanding them. But now, having so hastily and incoherently asserted that the hearts of the holy men are the depths, he as a result does not perceive that the one who said, "before the making of the depths,"[113] taught that he himself existed before the holy and God-loving men of the past age, so that it is altogether impossible to refer the foregoing passages to the flesh of the Savior. (20) Having turned to another passage in the same Scripture, he interprets it, too, in this way, saying:

> Therefore, what is one to make likewise of this central passage: "Before the springs abounding with water came forth"?[114] [Scripture] says these are the holy apostles. The text of Exodus reveals this mystery to us, having proclaimed long ago (21) the

107. Jb 38.16–17.
108. Ps 148.7.
109. Gn 1.2.
110. Ps 41.8 (RSV 42.7).
111. Ps 76.17 (RSV 77.16–17).
112. Ps 103.6 (RSV 104.6).
113. Prv 8.24.
114. Ibid.

types of the apostles. For since the number of the apostles is twelve, it mentions twelve springs.[115]

And having said these things, he does not understand that there were also twelve tribes of Israel and twelve patriarchs of these and one book of the twelve prophets, but also twelve hours of the day and twelve months of the whole (22) year. Why, then, would the number twelve pertain more to the apostles than it does to all those other things, [as] if a quantitative number really provided him with a reason for this interpretation of the passage? But it is necessary to comprehend that even the prophets of God, to the extent that they partook of the same Holy Spirit, were no different from [his] springs. For this reason it has been said concerning them in the Psalms: "Bless the Lord God in the assemblies, O you who are of (23) Israel's springs!"[116] And so it is necessary to confess that the one who said, "Before the springs abounding with water came forth,"[117] was the Son of God, even before those springs [came forth]. Listen to how [Marcellus] interprets this, saying,

Therefore, in all likelihood, the Master spoke about the birth in the flesh through the prophet Solomon, when he [the latter] said, "Before the springs abounding with water came forth."[118]

(24) And he adds,

For in this sense the Savior spoke to the holy springs, "Go, make disciples of all nations."[119]

Then, as if he were wrapping up the whole discussion,[120] he adds [this] conclusion to his exposition, saying,

115. Ex 15.27; Marcellus, *fr.* 41 (23 K./H.) (38,4–8 V.).
116. Ps 67.26 (RSV 68.26).
117. Prv 8.24.
118. Ibid.; Marcellus, *fr.* 42 (24 K./H.) (38,9–11 V.).
119. Mt 28.19; Marcellus, *fr.* 43 (25 K./H.) (38,12–13 V.).
120. Eusebius indicates in this statement that he knew of the dialogical, controversial character of Marcellus's work.

From all sides [of the Old and New Testaments] it is clear that the holy apostles were also called "springs" in a figurative sense by the prophet.[121]

He wishes the apostles to be springs, (25) but the prophets do not please him. For what reason [could this be] other than[122] that he was not able to prove that the flesh of the Savior was before them? And yet the Son of God, who teaches [these] things concerning himself in Proverbs, pre-existed even before the springs that are visible by nature, which even Moses called to mind in his account of the making of the world, having said, "But a spring rose from the earth, and watered the whole face of the ground,"[123] and again, "A river flows out of Eden to water the garden."[124] He who converses with Job[125] also recalls the springs of the sea, saying, "Have you entered into the springs of the sea, (26) or walked in the recesses of the deep?"[126] And since Scripture teaches that there are certain waters even above the heavens when it says, "Praise him, you highest heavens, and you waters above the heavens!"[127] it follows that one must think there are certain springs even of those waters (whatever their nature would be), so that he who has said that he pre-existed "before the (27) springs abounding with water came forth"[128] is shown to be more ancient than those waters. Applying his mind to none of these, nor wishing to make the effort, [Marcellus] persists in these same [opinions], since he also makes these claims:

> [The prophet] says, "Before the mountains had been shaped, before all the hills, he begets me."[129] [The prophet] calls the apostles and the successors of the apostles "mountains" and

121. Marcellus, *fr.* 44 (26 K./H.) (40,1–2 V.).
122. Klostermann's textual addition is incorrect.
123. Gn 2.6.
124. Gn 2.10.
125. Above, Christ was mentioned as conversing with Job; see *ET* 3.3.16 (150,9 K./H.).
126. Jb 38.16.
127. Ps 148.4.
128. Prv 8.24.
129. Prv 8.25.

"hills," so that he might indicate in proverbial fashion the [apostles'] upright way of life in comparison to that of other men.[130]

(28) Therefore, the same were also the springs, the same were also the mountains, and the same were also the hills. But just as it is not natural in the case of visible springs and mountains to claim that [they are] the same things (for the springs of the waters have nothing in common with the heights of the mountains in respect of quality), in the same way also in the case of things seen in the mind allegorically, it is necessary to show the difference[s] between these intelligible springs and mountains and hills. But [Marcellus], understanding none of what has been investigated closely, mixes everything up recklessly, so that the springs of the waters and the mountains and the hills appear to be the same things, and he says that all of these are the apostles, having made no distinctions with regard to the ways in which they are different. (29) Why, then, does he not call those who were made perfect in justice and piety even before the Incarnation[131] of our Savior likewise "mountains" and "hills," if not for the reason that[132] he could not let the flesh of the Savior subsist before them? Therefore, only by forcing and twisting the sense can the foregoing statements be said to refer to the flesh of the Savior.

How then, too, could the statement "he begets me"[133] refer to the flesh? For before the springs and before the mountains and before the[134] hills he said he was begotten, having said, "The Lord created me as the beginning of his ways for his works. Before the age, he (30) founded me."[135] If, then, the flesh were to claim these things, as seems to Marcellus to be the case, how

130. Marcellus, *fr.* 45 (7 K./H.) (40,5–8 V.).
131. Literally, "flesh."
132. Again, Klostermann's addition is unnecessary; it is idiomatic for Eusebius to construct in this way.
133. Prv 8.25.
134. Klostermann's later addition, "all" (with Montague), is incorrect; only a little later Eusebius introduces this notion as a second argument. See *ET* 3.3.30 (151,7 K./H.). (It is in the corrections, p. 259.)
135. Prv 8.22.

could the flesh have said, "Before all the hills, he begets me"?[136] For in this case the flesh would be before the apostles. But how can the flesh itself say that it has been begotten by God? For it seemed right to Marcellus to say that (31) the flesh, not existing previously, was created. For he said:

> For the Lord our God, having made that which did not exist, truly created. For he created not the existing flesh, which the Word assumed, but the non-existent.[137]

Thus, on the one hand, we have acknowledged that [the flesh] was created, while, on the other, how it was possible that it was also begotten by God was explained when our Savior said, "That which has been begotten of the flesh is flesh."[138] And the Apostle also says, "born (32) of a woman, born under the law."[139] Therefore, how could the flesh have said concerning the God of the universe, "Before all the hills, he begets me"?[140] Therefore, I think it is evident to all how these passages have this interpretation only by being distorted. But without violence one could say that the Son of God confirmed these even without any allegorical means [of interpretation] since he also pre-existed the earth; he was and pre-existed before the coming forth of the material springs of waters and before the visible depths spoken of and before the composition of the shape of the earth in the heights of the mountains and the hills. For "all things were made through him, and (33) without him not one thing was made."[141]

And if someone should ask why he did not teach that he himself was before the heavens and those things in [the] heavens and the divine and transcendent powers and spirits beyond them, let it be said to him that until that time [the Incarnation] the Word did[142] allude to these things when he imparted

---

136. Prv 8.25.
137. Excerpt of Marcellus, *fr.* 29 (11 K./H.) (30,15–32,2 V.).
138. Jn 3.6.
139. Gal 4.4.
140. Prv 8.25.
141. Jn 1.3.
142. Klostermann's alteration of the text is doubtful. Eusebius did not want to present a tautology (the Son did not teach—and he means teaching

a certain education through the Proverbs to those who were spiritually infants. (34) This is clear from what was said then: "Hear, my child, your father's instruction, and do not reject your mother's teaching,"[143] and then, "My child, be attentive to my laws, and incline your ear to my sayings,"[144] and again, "My child, do not despise the Lord's instruction or dismiss his (35) reproof,"[145] and, "My child, if you do good yourself, you will also be good for your neighbors; but if you become evil, you alone will bear the evil."[146] And you yourself could gather together by yourself countless passages and ones like them from the book of Proverbs, through which the text appears to address those who are spiritually infants. (36) So also Moses, as the teacher of those imperfect in comprehension, alluded to the heaven[s] and the earth and the fashioning of the visible [world], but obviously [did] not also [teach] the creation of the angels or of the divine powers and holy spirits, because his disciples were not yet capable of instruction in these matters. (37) Therefore, consequently the text in Proverbs, too, when it provides instruction to these sorts of men from the mountains around the land and the hills and the springs as from things that are better known, having begun from what is more fundamental, led by the hand those who were being instructed to what is greater, and prepared them to pass over from the lesser things to those that were more divine.

(38) Thus this is the case if one did not inquire needlessly beyond the [literal reading] of the text. But if one wished to reflect more deeply about these things too, he will refer them not to those apostles and all the just and God-loving men who have ever lived, but he will pass from them to the divine and angelic powers, saying that mountains and hills are different ways of speaking figuratively of angels and archangels and divine spir-

---

without using pictures, such as the ones used in Prv 8—and did not call to mind), but what he wants to say is that the Son did not teach these things straightforwardly, but called these contents to mind in the images of Proverbs as a pedagogy for immature people (i.e., the Jews of the Old Testament times).

143. Prv 1.8.
144. Prv 4.20.
145. Prv 3.11.
146. Prv 9.12.

its, and with regard to thrones and (39) dominions and sovereignties and authorities, since indeed the divine Apostle taught that these[147] things, too, were all created "through him and for him"[148] and that he was "before all"[149] these things, beginning from that place, as was right, because it was said in these passages from the person of the Son of God, "Before the mountains had been shaped, before all the hills, he begets me."[150] Therefore, he said that the other things were shaped, while only he was begotten before the (40) establishment of those things mentioned. The same Apostle also knows the heavenly Jerusalem and the heavenly mountain upon which he says Jerusalem is [placed], saying, "You have come to Mount Zion and to the city of the living God, the heavenly Jerusalem, and to innumerable angels in festal gathering, and to the assembly of the firstborn who are enrolled in heaven."[151] And so, pre-existing all of these, the only-begotten Son of God spoke figuratively through the Proverbs, proclaiming in a veiled manner his own ineffable begetting. (41) And that he wanted these things to be understood is clear from what he adds, saying next, "When he established the heavens, I was present with him."[152]

At this point, the honorable interpreter of the Scriptures [Marcellus] came to a stop, having been barred by the Scriptures, and did not proceed further, because he was not able to smooth away [the difficulty] that follows from (42) the thesis advanced by him concerning the flesh of the Savior. For always having called to mind the flesh and having declared that all these things were said about the flesh, he [Marcellus] hastened to the mountains and the hills, having said that these were the apostles, but the things that follow upon these he deliberately handed over to silence, having no longer dared to proceed further with regard to the Scripture.

(43) At this point, then, he puts an end to his argument.

147. The τὰ deleted by Klostermann should be restored.
148. Col 1.16.
149. Col 1.17.
150. Prv 8.25.
151. Heb 12.22–23.
152. Prv 8.27.

After so many things have been said by him at length in the meantime,[153] he now drops the reference to the flesh and confesses that it is the Word of God who said these things. He says this in these very words:

> Before the world existed, the Word was in the Father. But when Almighty God resolved to make everything in heaven and on earth, the generation of the world required active energy. And because of this, there being nothing else besides God (for all things are confessed to have come to be by him), at that moment, the Word, having come forth, became maker of the cosmos, he who even beforehand was preparing it within intellectually, as the prophet Solomon teaches us, saying, "When he established the heavens, I was present with him,"[154] and, "When he established the springs of water under heaven firmly, and when he made the (44) foundations of the earth, then I was beside him in harmony; and I was daily his delight."[155] For rightly did the Father delight in making all things with wisdom and power through the Word.[156]

So Marcellus says. If, therefore, he finally confessed—and this with difficulty—that these things were said by the person of the Word, he should also accept that the entire collection of previous texts is to be referred to that same Word of God. (45) For the one who said, "When he established the heavens, I was present with him,"[157] was the same as the one who said, "The Lord created me as the beginning of his ways for his works."[158] For one and the same person was shown to us from the beginning who was speaking in all the previous passages. And so the same [person] who said, "The Lord created me as the beginning of his ways for his works,"[159] added, "Before the age, he founded me,"[160] and, "At the first, before the making of

153. Of course, relating Prv 8 to the Incarnation of the Lord.
154. Prv 8.27.
155. Prv 8.28–30.
156. Marcellus, *fr.* 110 (60 K./H.) (104,1–11 V.).
157. Prv 8.27.
158. Prv 8.22.
159. Ibid.
160. Prv 8.23.

the earth,"¹⁶¹ and, "before the mountains had been shaped, before all (46) the hills, he begets me."¹⁶² The same added both,
"When he established the heavens, I was present with him,"¹⁶³
and what follows these [words]. If, then, the Word was the one
who said these things, how was he within God, co-ingenerate
with God, and existing as one and the same with him and [yet]
saying that he was created and begotten by him? For one and
the same (47) person, as I said, was shown to be speaking in all
the previous passages.

But even if sometime afterwards, he [Marcellus] confessed
that these things were said by the person of the Word in God,
his conclusions about the flesh of the Savior were forced, and all
those together¹⁶⁴ have been exposed as being outmoded, vain,
and outlandish views. But if the flesh of the Savior was the one
who said, "The Lord created me as the beginning of his ways
for his works,"¹⁶⁵ according to the interpretation given by him,
and if the flesh was established "before the age"¹⁶⁶ and "at the
first, before the making of the earth"¹⁶⁷ (since clearly the flesh is
earth, as he thinks, because of the passage, "You are earth, and
to earth you shall return"),¹⁶⁸ and if it was the flesh that said,
"Before the springs abounding with water came forth, before
the mountains had been shaped, before all the hills, he begets
me"¹⁶⁹ (because [the flesh] was begotten before the election of
the apostles, as that most wise man thinks), it follows that so,
too, the statement, "When he established the heavens, I was
present with him,"¹⁷⁰ was said by the person of the flesh. (48)
But no one would be so out of his mind as ever to accept this

161. Prv 8.23–24.
162. Prv 8.25.
163. Prv 8.27.
164. Namely, the contradictory views of the one verse being interpreted as
relating to the Word of God while the others have been related to the Incarnation.
165. Prv 8.22.
166. Prv 8.23.
167. Prv 8.23–24.
168. Gn 3.19.
169. Prv 8.24–25.
170. Prv 8.27.

interpretation. For the word of truth,[171] giving a great shout, will contradict him, (49) showing who it was at this time who recounts these things. Therefore, that the only-begotten Son, who was begotten by God, living and subsisting, existing even before the establishment of all creatures, was other [than the flesh], he himself shows through those remarks he adds next, saying, "When he established the heavens, I was present with him."[172] For he was together with and present to him [God] even before the creation of the heaven[s] and the things beyond heaven and everything in heaven. Thus this was stated figuratively through the statement, "When he established the (50) heavens, I was present with him."[173]

And how did God establish [the heavens] before he created, if not by making laws for them and designing the way in which it was necessary to establish them? And so the Father designed and made ready, pondering how it was necessary to establish so great a heaven, how much height it would need and the sort of shape its tremendous heights and components [would have] in consideration of those things that would be contained within it and those that would be outside of it and in view of those things being turned over in his [mind]. But he [the Son] who looks intently at the calculations of the Father and alone gains access to the depths within him proceeded on through the works, (51) following the signs of the Father and assisting him. For this reason, it has been said somewhere: "Praise the Lord from (52) the heavens, praise him in the heights! Praise him, all his angels, praise him all his host! Praise him, sun and moon, praise him, all you stars and light! Praise him, you highest heavens, and you waters above the heavens! Let them praise the name of the Lord! Because he spoke, and (53) they came into existence; he commanded, and they were created."[174]

But even before the very heavens and those things that are beyond heaven and all things in heaven came into existence (for all things taken together have been shown to come from

171. By "word of truth" here, Eusebius seems to mean John's gospel.
172. Prv 8.27.
173. Ibid.
174. Ps 148.1–5.

one [source]), the Son of God existed, and was present to and together with the Father when he was still contemplating the establishment of all these things. For this reason he says, "When he established the heavens, I was present with him."[175] Thus like a good scribe taking the archetypal ideas from the Father's calculations, he transferred them to the substances[176] of the works, sculpting and giving specific shape to such things, (54) just as he had seen them stored beforehand in the Father's mind. And that he himself would be a worthy witness of these things, he teaches in the gospels in this way: "Truly, truly, I say to you, the Son can do nothing of his own accord, but only what he sees the Father doing; for whatever he does, that (55) the Son does likewise. For the Father loves the Son and shows him all that he himself is doing."[177]

With regard to this passage, one would quite rightly ask why the Son makes for a second time the things that have already been made by the Father. But he himself resolved that problem, having said, "For whatever the Father does, that (56) the Son does likewise."[178] Therefore, the things that are made by the Son are copies of the archetypal works that pre-exist in the ineffable calculations of the Father. Observing them closely in the mind of the Father, then, the Son made copies of the things he had seen. He shows that [this ability] to look into the Father's depths is a work of the paternal love in the next passage where he also says clearly, "For the Father loves the Son, and shows him all that he himself is doing."[179] Consequently, when the Father revealed his secrets, the Son, seeing them, completed the works of the paternal will through his [own] works. Therefore, coexisting in this way with the Father and being present to him when he was preparing the heavens and the things within them, he [the Son] taught this, saying, "When he established (57) the heavens, I was present with him."[180] The Father rejoiced even before the mak-

---

175. Prv 8.27.
176. οὐσίας.
177. Jn 5.19–20.
178. Jn 5.19.
179. Jn 5.20.
180. Prv 8.27.

ing of the world, looking at his own only-begotten Son himself and discerning himself in him as in an image. For this reason, Wisdom says, "I was daily his delight."[181] But the Son was also filled with joy, being gladdened at the sight of the Father. He himself teaches this when he says, "… I rejoiced before him (58) always, rejoicing to have completed his inhabited world,"[182] the inhabited world here understood as the totality of all creatures in which, having been called into being from nothing through the Son, the God of all rejoiced.

Therefore, the true interpretation, which has been shown from the divine Scripture as in a short and abbreviated explanation, would be something like this. But he [Marcellus], being brought down from on high, has run his mind aground on the flesh of our Savior, misconstruing and misinterpreting the (59) true sense of the divinely inspired Scripture.

But even having passed over to the Word, he says that it is [the Word] within the Father who (60) prepared the heavens as in calculation and deliberation. And he said this in these very words:

> Before the making of the world, the Word was in the Father. But when Almighty God resolved to make everything in heaven and on earth, the generation of the world required active energy. And because of this, there being nothing else besides God (for all things are confessed to have come to be by him), at that moment, the Word, having come forth, became maker of the cosmos, he who even beforehand was preparing it within his mind, as the prophet Solomon teaches us, saying, "When he established the heavens, I was present with him."[183]

(61) In these remarks, it is fitting to observe the completely irrational way in which he [Marcellus] willfully pays no heed to the statement, "I was present with him," which expressly shows the presence of the Son with the Father,[184] but he declares in

---

181. Prv 8.30.
182. Prv 8.30–31.
183. Prv 8.27; see Marcellus, *fr.* 110 (60 K./H.) (104,1–7 V.).
184. Klostermann addition <συν> is incorrect, as Eusebius only works towards this argument.

opposition to Scripture that before the creation there was nothing else besides God. And he did not shudder at having unleashed this statement, though it denies the Son, nor was he troubled [by the fact that] the divine Scripture testifies that before the creation of the heavens he [the Son] alone was present alongside the Father. For it says, "When he established the heavens, (62) I was present with him."[185] For the prefix *syn*, added to the verb "to be present with," shows the presence of the same *together* with the other. Therefore, he [the Son] does not teach simply that he was with the Father but that he himself was *together with* the Father. And the Father did not simply rejoice, but he rejoiced in the presence of the (63) Son. For this reason he [the Son] says, "I was daily his delight."[186] But how could the claim that he was the Father's delight in his presence apply to a Word that did not subsist, one that was in God himself and that acted for the purpose of communication, contrary to the claims that he delighted, and was in the presence of, [the Father], both of which indicate his hypostasis? But Marcellus, not having given a rational account of any of these statements, denies the Son, and says that he is the Word in God who at one point comes forth in active energy, but at another is within [God] not doing anything. And he [Marcellus] does not see that to speak of something being inside and outside of God suggests something composite and a kind of physical change, which is not (64) lawful to accept with regard to the ingenerate and incorporeal nature.

And how, having come forth, did the Word also become the maker of the world? Did God make use of tongue, voice, and[187] even language? And with whom did he also converse, given that there was no one else together with him? And with whom did he join company, there being no one besides him? But did God himself converse with himself, making use of speech and discussion so as also to make the Word come forth from him? (65) And why was God unable to bring into existence the things

185. Prv 8.27.
186. Prv 8.30.
187. Again, Klostermann's "improvement" of the text is incorrect. The brachylogic omission of ἤ after πότερα is typical for Eusebius.

he wanted unless the Word was within him as active power, when even among men, most craftsmen are silent when they are bringing their projects to completion and especially when no one is present with them while they are working? Thus what prevented even God from establishing all things in this sort of way, having the Word within himself? But [Marcellus] also proposed the simile of a sculptor discussing with himself and saying to himself,

> Come now, let us make, let us form a statue.[188]

For he says in this way that even "God, the Lord of the universe, said to himself, 'Let us make man,'"[189] as he showed already many times before through previous remarks, through which, I think, his denial of the Son of God (66) has been made plain. For to allege that God himself, having his own Word within himself, conversed with himself, would be characteristic of a certain Jewish way of thinking. And [to allege] that the Father of the Word within him and the Word within him, his Son, are the same was a feature of Sabellius's evil belief,

Chapter 4

(1) and again, to say that the three, Father, Son, and Spirit, are [the same] is[190] also characteristic of Sabellius's point of view. And Marcellus endorses this same claim when he writes somewhere:

> For it is impossible that the three, being hypostases, could be united in a monad, unless the Trinity were previously to take its beginning from the monad. For the holy Paul said that those things are gathered up[191] in [the] monad, which in no way belong to the oneness of God; for only the Word and the Spirit belong to the oneness of God.[192]

---

188. A small section of Marcellus, *fr.* 98 (58 K./H.) (90,4–5 V.).

189. Gn 1.26; last part of Marcellus, *fr.* 98 (58 K./H.) (90,5–7 V.).

190. If we take out the wrong paragraph break here, the construction does not need Klostermann's addition of <ἓν>.

191. Eph 1.10.

192. Marcellus, *fr.* 47 (66 K./H.) (42,1–4 V.).

(2) Then he tries to bolster this [point] by proceeding to say next:

> Well then, if the Word were to appear to have come from the
> Father himself and to have come to us,[193] and "the Holy Spirit"
> (as even Asterius confessed) "proceeds from the Father,"[194]
> and again the Savior says concerning the Spirit that "he will
> not speak on his own authority, but whatever he hears he will
> speak, and he will declare to you the things that are to come.
> He will glorify me, for he will take what is mine and declare it
> to you,"[195] doesn't the monad in this ineffable statement appear
> clearly and obviously to broaden into a Trinity without in any
> way suffering division? (3) For if the Word proceeds from the
> Father, and the Spirit himself is also confessed to proceed
> from the Father,[196] and again if the Savior says concerning
> the Spirit, "He will take what is mine and declare it to you,"[197]
> is it not, then, obvious that some hidden mystery has been
> revealed?[198] For how, unless the monad, being indivisible, were
> to broaden into a Trinity, would it be possible for him to say
> at one time concerning the Spirit that he proceeds from the
> Father,[199] and at another to say, "He will take what is mine
> and declare it to you,"[200] and again [to say] when he breathed
> upon the disciples, "Receive the Holy Spirit"?[201] (4) For if [the
> Spirit] proceeds from the Father, how is he declared to receive
> this service from the Son?[202] For if there were "two separate

193. See Jn 16.27–28; 8.42.
194. Jn 15.26; Asterius, *fr.* 59 (120 V.).
195. Jn 16.13–14.
196. See Jn 15.26.
197. Jn 16.14.
198. See Eph 3.9; Col 1.26.
199. Jn 15.26.
200. Jn 16.14.
201. Jn 20.22.

202. The service that the Spirit receives is the "giving" of him to the apostles. Marcellus believes (with all others and the gospel) that the Spirit was not given by the Father, but by the Son to the apostles. Now, if Father and Son were two separate persons, the breathing out of the Spirit (Jn 20.22), as with actors wearing masks in the ancient theater, would not be one breathing, but two different persons behind two different masks. Hence it would no longer be the breathing out of Spirit by the Father, but that of the Son. Alternatively,

persons,"²⁰³ as Asterius said, either it is necessary that the Spirit
in proceeding from the Father does not need the service that
comes from the Son (for everything that proceeds from the
Father is necessarily perfect, and in no way in need of the help
of another), or it is necessary that if he [the Spirit] receives
from the Son and from his power bestows grace, he no longer
proceeds from the Father.²⁰⁴

(5) And after some other remarks, he adds:

But if the gospel [says] that, having breathed upon the disciples, [Christ] said, "Receive the Holy Spirit,"²⁰⁵ it is clear that
the Spirit came forth from the Word. How, then, if the Spirit
came forth from the Word, "does" the same "proceed from the
Father"?²⁰⁶

And he adds after other remarks:

Therefore, neither rightly nor appropriately did he [Asterius]
say (and that not once but even a second time) that "there are
three hypostases."²⁰⁷

So through these statements and [others] like these, this
most wise fellow tries to argue that the Father, the Son, and the
Holy Spirit are one and the same, the three names being laid
upon a single hypostasis. (6) For in these matters neither has
he understood how the Son is said to proceed from the Father
and likewise the Holy Spirit, nor has he been able to grasp in
what sense the Savior said concerning the Holy Spirit, "He will
take what is mine and declare it to you,"²⁰⁸ nor in what sense,
having breathed upon his disciples, he said, "Receive the Holy
Spirit."²⁰⁹ Those who reflect piously will easily find the solution
to [these questions], if one were to consider how the Son, al-

---

the Son would not have needed to breathe out the Spirit, as the Father had
already done so.

203. Asterius, *fr.* 56 (118 V.). The term used here is πρόσωπα.
204. Marcellus, *fr.* 48 (67 K./H.) (42,5–44,8 V.).
205. Jn 20.22.
206. Jn 15.26; Marcellus, *fr.* 49 (68 K./H.) (44,9–12 V.).
207. Asterius, *fr.* 61 (120 V.); Marcellus, *fr.* 50 (69 K./H.) (44,13–14 V.).
208. Jn 16.14.
209. Jn 20.22.

ways coexisting and being present with the Father, deep within as if in the most profound and inaccessible recesses of the paternal kingdom, but then being sent forth from the Father for the salvation of the human race, said that he himself came forth from the Father.

And at another time he revealed this about himself through a parable, (7) saying, "A sower went out to sow."[210] For from what place did he go forth, if not from the inmost realms of the paternal divinity? According to the same line of reasoning, the Holy Spirit, too, having always stood by the throne of God, since even "a thousand thousands"[211] stood by it according to Daniel, was himself also sent out, at one time in the form of a dove upon the Son of Man,[212] at another upon each of the prophets and apostles. (8) For this reason [the Spirit] was also said to proceed from the Father. And why do you wonder at this? [Since] it has been said even of the Devil, "So the Devil went forth from the Lord,"[213] and again a second time it was said, "So the Devil went forth from the Lord."[214] You will also find Scripture saying about Ahab, "An evil spirit came forth and stood before the Lord and (9) said, 'I will entice him.'"[215] But now is not the time to trouble ourselves with how and in what ways [Scripture] has spoken about these opposing spirits. The only-begotten Son of God teaches that he himself has come forth from the Father because he is always together with him, and likewise about the Holy Spirit, who exists as another besides the Son. The Savior himself shows this clearly when he says, "He will take what is mine and declare it to you."[216] For this would be unmistakable proof that the Son and the Holy Spirit are not one and the same. For that which takes from another is thought to be other than the one who gives.

210. Mk 4.3.
211. Dn 7.10.
212. See Lk 3.22.
213. Jb 1.12.
214. Jb 2.7.
215. 3 Kgs 22.21 (RSV 1 Kgs 22.21).
216. Jn 16.14.

Chapter 5

(1) And that the Holy Spirit is other than the Son, our Savior and Lord himself taught clearly and distinctly in the plainest of words, when he said to his disciples, "If you love me, you will keep my commandments. And I will pray the Father, and he will give you another Counselor, to be with you forever, even the Spirit of truth, whom the world cannot receive."[217] You see that he says that the Spirit is "another Counselor" and other than himself. And if, having breathed upon the disciples, he said, "Receive the Holy Spirit,"[218] one must not be ignorant that the breath was in some way purifying of the soul of the apostles, rendering them fit for the (2) reception of the Holy Spirit. For he is not said to have breathed upon their faces either the breath of life or the Holy Spirit, as it is written of Adam, "God breathed into his face the breath of life,"[219] but he was said to have breathed first and then said, "Receive the Holy Spirit."[220]

His giving the Spirit, again, shows that he is other than (3) the one who is given. For the one who gives and that which is given could not have been the same, but the one who provides [the Spirit] was the Savior, and that which is given was the Holy Spirit, and those who received the Spirit were the apostles, while the breath purified the apostles, as I said, or even effected the giving of their share of the Holy (4) Spirit, for it is possible to interpret this event in either of these ways. Thus from these passages it is shown that the Holy Spirit is another existing alongside [the Son], as is also shown through additional remarks, in which this is again recorded, when [the Son] said, "If a man loves me, he will keep my word, and my Father will love him, and (5) we will come to him and make our home with him."[221] To this he adds, "These things I have spoken to you, while I am still with you. But the Counselor, the Holy Spirit, whom the Father will send in my name, he will teach you all things, and bring to your remem-

217. Jn 14.15–17.
218. Jn 20.22.
219. Gn 2.7.
220. Jn 20.22.
221. Jn 14.23.

brance all that I have said to you."²²² You hear that he has used a
plural verb about himself and the Father,²²³ having said, "*We* will
come to him and make our home with him," and in speaking of
the Holy Spirit as of another, he said, "He (6) will teach you all
things."²²⁴ Of this nature was also the statement, "And I will pray
the Father, and he will give you another Counselor, to be with
you forever, even the Spirit of truth."²²⁵ Therefore, the Counsel-
or was another beside him [Christ], concerning whom he taught
these sorts of things. Therefore, quite rightly again he added,
saying, "These things I have spoken to you while I was still with
you. But the Counselor, the Holy Spirit, whom the Father will
send in my name, he will teach you all things, and bring to your
remembrance all that (7) I have said to you."²²⁶ For I have up to
this time said these things to you, he says, but the Spirit of truth,
whom my Father will also send, he will teach you everything
(8) that you have not learned now because you were not capable of it; but when he has come, I mean the Counselor, he will
complete the teaching, along with calling to your remembrance
even the things now said by me. And again, he adds, "But when
the Counselor, whom I shall send to you from the Father, comes,
the Spirit of truth, who proceeds from the Father, he will give
witness concerning me."²²⁷ Through all of these remarks, he
clearly shows that the one who is sent by him and who is going to
give witness concerning him (9) is another besides himself. He
confirms [this] fact still further by also saying in these words,
"Nevertheless I tell you the truth: it is to your advantage that I
go away, for if I do not go away, the Counselor will not come to
you; but if I go, I will send him to you."²²⁸ In saying that he went
away, he also revealed in these remarks his passion (10) and the
ascension to the Father that occurred after this.

Therefore, after so many statements, who would be so fool-

222. Jn 14.25–26.
223. Lit., "a multiple way."
224. Jn 14.26.
225. Jn 14.16–17.
226. Jn 14.25–26.
227. Combining elements of Jn 14.16–17 and 15.26.
228. Jn 16.7.

ish as to say that the one who says these things and the one
about whom he said them are one and the same, when he listens to him clearly making a distinction [in order] to declare
the truth, and showing what that truth was: that (11) unless he
went away, the Holy Spirit would not come. And if [the Son] declares differently at one time that the Father will send the Holy
Spirit and at another time that he himself will send him, he
does not, I assure you, teach contradictory things; for whatever
"he sees the Father doing," "that the Son does likewise,"[229] and,
"as he hears, so he judges."[230] For this reason, by the judgment
of the Father, when the Father desires, then the Son and Savior through himself[231] sends to his disciples the Spirit of truth,
the Counselor, to counsel them and to comfort them in what
they suffered at the hands (12) of those who were persecuting
them while they were preaching the gospel. And [he sent the
Holy Spirit] not only to counsel them, but also to teach them
the entire truth of the new covenant, which they did not grasp
from the Savior's instruction when he conversed about these
matters with them, because they were still enslaved by their
Jewish (13) education. But he fulfilled [these predictions] with
his actions after his resurrection from the dead. After having
said to Mary, "Do not touch me, for I have not yet ascended
to my Father,"[232] [and] after he was seen by the disciples having ascended to the Father, then the Holy Spirit was sent and
was with him and willingly revealed the service for which he
had been appointed. (14) [Only] then did he allow himself to
be touched.[233] For when "he breathed upon"[234] [them], then he
also gave to them a share in the grace of the Holy Spirit, such
as could effect the forgiveness of sins. For "there are varieties of
gifts,"[235] of which a part was given to [the disciples] when [the
Savior] was with and present to them, but afterwards he filled

229. Jn 5.19.
230. Cf. Jn 5.30.
231. One needs to read δι' αὐτοῦ.
232. Jn 20.17.
233. See Lk 24.39; Jn 20.27.
234. Jn 20.22.
235. 1 Cor 12.4.

them with an [even] greater and more perfect power. He spoke to [the apostles] about this in the Acts of the Apostles: "but you shall receive power from on high when the Holy Spirit has come upon you."[236] And when he promised that they would be baptized with the Holy Spirit, he also then fulfilled that [promise] after his ascension, when the (15) Holy Spirit was sent to them on the day of Pentecost in accordance with his words.

Although the passages on this topic stand in need of greater explanation and clarification, now is not the time to examine them in detail, since that is not the task set before us; instead it was necessary to show that the Counseling Spirit was other than the Son. This was also shown in a different way in those things that the Savior himself taught, in addition to the others and in which he said, "I have yet many things to say to you, but you cannot bear them now. When the Spirit (16) of truth comes, he[237] will guide you into all truth; for he will not speak on his own authority, but whatever he hears he will speak, and he will declare to you the things that are to come. He will glorify me, for he will take what is mine and declare it to you."[238] In these words he promises again that his disciples will learn from the Holy Spirit [these] things that he himself did not teach, saying, as if about another, "when he comes," and, "he will not speak on his own authority," and, "he will glorify me," and, "he will take what is mine."[239] For to suppose that the Savior himself said all these things about himself would be tremendous and (17) irremediable stupidity. For through these [statements] the Savior himself clearly taught that the Holy Spirit exists as another besides himself, outstanding in honor and glory and privileges, greater and higher than any [other] intellectual and rational being[240] (for which reason he has also been received into the (18) holy and thrice-blessed Trinity). Yet he is surely subordinate to [the Son].[241] Indeed, [the Son] showed this when he

---

236. Acts 1.8.
237. Klostermann's addition here of "that one" is unnecessary.
238. Jn 16.12–14.
239. Jn 16.13–14.
240. οὐσίας.
241. Klostermann's erasure of "being" is not necessary.

said, "For he will not speak on his own authority, but whatever
he hears he will speak."[242] He makes clear, however, from whom
he will hear: "He will take what is mine and declare it to you,"[243]
that is, from my treasure. For in him [the Son] are "hidden all
the treasures of wisdom and knowledge."[244] (19) Therefore, he
himself, seeing as he is the only-begotten Son, receives from
the Father and listens to [the Father], while the Holy Spirit sup-
plies [what he receives] from him [the Son]. Hence, [the Son]
says, "He will take what is mine and declare it to you."[245]

Yet the God who is over all is also said to be "spirit," as the
Savior himself taught, when he said, "God is spirit, and those
who worship him must worship in spirit and truth,"[246] and he
will truly be the holy of holies and "dwelling among the holy."[247]
But the Son of God is also spirit, because he is both spirit and
himself holy of holies, if indeed he is [the] image of the (20) invisible. For this reason it has also been said of him, "Now the
Lord is the spirit,"[248] (21) and, "the spirit before us, Christ the
Lord."[249] But given that the Holy Spirit is another alongside
the Father and the Son, the Savior, showing his unique characteristic,[250] has called him "Counselor," distinguishing him
from the common run of similarly titled [spirits] through the
title "Counselor." For the angelic powers also are "spirits." For
it has been said: "He who makes his angels spirits."[251] But none
of these can be equal to the Counseling Spirit. For this reason, (22) only this [Spirit] has been received into the holy and
thrice-blessed Trinity; in no other way did the Savior command
his apostles to hand over the mystery of his regeneration to
those Gentiles who believed in him than by "baptizing them
in the name of the Father and of the Son and of the Holy Spir-

242. Jn 16.13.
243. Jn 16.14.
244. Col 2.3.
245. Jn 16.14.
246. Jn 4.24.
247. See Is 57.15.
248. 2 Cor 3.17.
249. See Lam 4.20.
250. τὸ ἰδίωμα.
251. Heb 1.7.

it."[252] Thus the Father has the ultimate authority and bestows grace, while the Son assists in this [effort] (for "grace and truth came through Jesus Christ"),[253] and the Holy Spirit, to be sure, the Counselor, himself distributes according to the varieties of gifts within him, "for to one is given through the Spirit the utterance of wisdom, and to another the utterance of knowledge according to the same Spirit, to another faith by the same Spirit,"[254] and likewise what has been reckoned among these.

Chapter 6

(1) Therefore, the Holy Spirit by nature loves to dwell only in those holy ones, bestowed through the Son upon whomever the Father selected. And this would be his task, to sanctify all with whom he shares one or even many of the gifts within him, so that prophets and apostles and every God-loving soul, yes, and even the great and divine powers, have a share in his holiness. Since the Son has been honored with the paternal divinity, he would be the maker and fashioner of all created things, both visible and invisible, and surely also of the very existence[255] of the Counseling Spirit. For "all things were made (2) through him, and without him not one thing was made,"[256] and, "in him all things were created, in heaven and on earth, visible and invisible."[257] But the God who is beyond all things and Father of our Lord Jesus Christ, being something ineffably good and greater than any calculation and conception, any speech and consideration, of all things, however many, of whatever type they may happen to be, leading his Holy Spirit besides the only-begotten Son, rightly has alone been declared the God "who is over all and through all and in all" by the Apostle when he says, "one Lord, one faith, one baptism, one God and Father of us all, who is over all and through all and (3) in all."[258] And he

252. Mt 28.19.
253. Jn 1.17.
254. 1 Cor 12.8–9.
255. ὑπάρξεως.
256. Jn 1.3.
257. Col 1.16.
258. Eph 4.5–6.

alone would be called "one God and Father" "of our Lord Jesus Christ,"[259] while the Son would be "the only-begotten God,
who is in the bosom of the Father."[260] But the Counseling Spirit
would be neither God nor Son, since he himself has not also
received his generation from the Father as the Son has, but is
one of those things brought into existence through the Son,
because "all things were made through him, and without him
not one thing was made."[261]

(4) Therefore, all these mysteries are handed over to the holy
and Catholic Church in this way through the holy pronouncements. But Marcellus, having mixed everything together, at one
time descends into the very abyss of Sabellius, and at another
attempts to renew the heresy of Paul of Samosata, and at another has been shown as a bare-faced Jew. For he introduces a
single hypostasis with three faces,[262] as it were, and three names,
saying that the same is God and the Word within (5) him and
the Holy Spirit. And when he has turned from these claims to
the apostolic theology concerning Christ, again, he has made
use of distorted interpretations. For while the divine Apostle
unmistakably theologizes about the Son of God and says, "He
is the image of the invisible God, firstborn of all creation, for
in him all things were created, in heaven and on earth, visible
and invisible, whether thrones or dominions or principalities or
authorities—all things were created through him and for him.
He is before all things, and in him all things hold together,"[263]

Chapter 7[264]

(1) this wondrous fellow, having stumbled again on the
flesh,[265] declares that it is the image of the invisible God, paying
no attention [to the fact that the statement] "he who is the im-

259. Eph 4.6; 2 Cor 1.3.
260. Jn 1.18.
261. Jn 1.3.
262. τριπρόσωπον.
263. Col 1.15–17.
264. Another example of a wrong paragraph break.
265. Klostermann's addition of κατά is unnecessary.

age" has been put forth in the masculine form. For having no idea how the "he who" could apply to the flesh, he [Marcellus] said that this was shown to be itself the image "of the invisible God."[266] And again he says that [the statement], "He is before all things,"[267] was made about the flesh, not being ashamed to take (2) the "he" as referring to the flesh.[268] And he says that [he] has been called "firstborn of all creation"[269] because of the flesh, and he relentlessly persists in claiming that the things "in heaven and on earth,"[270] "visible and invisible,"[271] were created by means of the flesh, nor does he fail [to say the same about] thrones and principalities and dominions and authorities, saying that they were made worthy of the creation by Christ through the flesh of the Savior. Having already laid out in my previous book Marcellus's remarks about these matters,[272] not to let this [treatise] get too long, I will be satisfied with the testimony of those passages. But that this sort of interpretation of the Apostle's statement is distorted and forced, does not require, I think, further support, because the shamelessness of the interpretation is evident to all.

Chapter 8

Nevertheless, having said so many things about the flesh of the Savior, he does not preserve it safe and sound for us. If only he had maintained the pious manner of thinking about it! Now, after he has said all these things about [the flesh], he declares that at the consummation of the ages it [will] be left behind, devoid of the Word, writing in this way:

Therefore, if he confesses that the flesh does not benefit him, how is it possible that the flesh, which is of earth and is of

266. Col 1.15; see Marcellus, *fr.* 55 (94 K./H.) (48,11–19 V.).
267. Col 1.17.
268. Eusebius's argument here rests on the fact that the Greek word for "flesh" is feminine.
269. Col 1.15.
270. Col 1.16.
271. Ibid.
272. See Eusebius of Caesarea, *CM* 2.3 (50 K./H.), pp. 134–47 in the present volume.

no avail, will also coexist with the Word even in the ages to
come—as if it did offer some benefit to him?[273]

Chapter 9

And he repeats the same claim in another passage, claiming,

Well then, if Paul said that in the time of the restoration of all
things even creation itself will pass from bondage to liberty
(for he says that "even the creation itself will be set free from
its bondage to decay and obtain the glorious liberty of the
sons of God"),[274] how would it still be possible for the "form of
a slave,"[275] which the Word assumed, since it is [the] form of a
slave, to continue to coexist with the Word?[276]

Chapter 10

(1) You see what sort of remarks he has dared to advance
against the flesh of our Savior, not having acknowledged that
even before [his] ascension into heaven, when it [the flesh] was
still upon the earth before the Passion, he glorified it in this
way on the mountain, showing [it, that is, the flesh] as an image of his kingdom to only three of his chosen disciples, so that
his face (2) shone and was brilliant with flashes of light (for the
divine Scripture says, "and his face shone like the sun, and his
garments became white as light");[277] but neither did he [Marcel-
lus] comprehend what sort of glorious body Christ would have,
about which the Apostle spoke, and how he taught that our
bodies would be conformed to that body, when he says, "who
will change our lowly body to be like his glorious body."[278] Nor
has [Marcellus] given any thought to the way in which [Paul]
wrote that the mortal will be swallowed up by life, when he pro-

273. Excerpt from Marcellus, *fr.* 106 (117 K./H.) (96,9–12 V.).
274. Rom 8.21.
275. Phil 2.7.
276. Excerpt from Marcellus, *fr.* 106 (117 K./H.) (98,16–22 V.).
277. Mt 17.2.
278. Phil 3.21.

claims, "not that we would be unclothed, but that we would be further clothed, so that what is mortal may be swallowed up by life."[279] Ignorant of all these statements, [Marcellus] stubbornly insists that the Word is going to be one and the same with God, as he also was before, but as for the flesh left behind by the Word, (3) he has no idea where it will be. Listen to how he says these things:

> But if someone should ask about this flesh that has become immortal by the Word, what are we to say to him? [We would say] that we think it is dangerous for us to expound dogma about things of which we have no exact knowledge from the divine Scriptures. For how (4) is it possible for those who overturn even the dogmas of others to do this? But we will say to those who wish to learn from us the accurate truth about this that, convinced by the holy Apostle, we know that it is fitting for us to see the hidden mysteries in this way, as he himself said. "For now we see," he says, "in a mirror dimly, but then face-to-face," and what follows.[280] So do not ask me about things about which I have no clear knowledge from the divine Scripture. Well then, because of this, I will not be able to speak clearly about that divine flesh that acquired communion with the divine Word.[281]

So the one who confesses that he neither is able to say anything nor has learned anything from (5) the Scripture makes these sorts of claims about the flesh, having taken [them] neither from Scripture nor from other [sources], nor having learned [them] from the Church. Instead, he invented for himself and dreamed up out of his own imagination an offspring that is foreign and alien to the truth. Nor has he taken to heart the scriptural passage that says, "Do not add to his words, lest he rebuke you, and you be found a liar,"[282] and, "Woe to the prophets who follow their own heart."[283] (6) See, then, into what great impiety he has fallen. For he, having cast the whole theology concern-

279. 2 Cor 5.4.
280. 1 Cor 13.12.
281. First part of Marcellus, *fr.* 109 (121 K./H.) (102,1–13 V.).
282. Prv 30.6.
283. See Ezek 13.3.

ing the pre-existent only-begotten Son down to the level of the flesh, and having addressed it as the crown of victory in these very words, saying,

> … that the Word of God enabled the human flesh to become immortal through the resurrection and like one who has been crowned with the wreath of victory to sit at the right hand of the Father,[284]

this same man says that [the flesh] will be empty and bereft in the consummation of all thing[s], uniting the Word with the Father while separating the flesh from the activity of the Word and having left it behind, I don't know how, on the one hand immortal and incorruptible and on the other soulless and unmoved by the (7) Word. And again he tries to support these conclusions on the basis of the divine readings, of which he has no understanding. For our Savior said to those who did not understand the teachings about his flesh and blood, "Do you take offense at this? Then what if you were to see the Son of Man ascending where he was before? It is the Spirit that gives life; the flesh is of no avail; the words that I have spoken to you are spirit and life."[285]

Chapter 11

Not having grasped the intention of the statement, he [Marcellus] thought that [the Word] repudiates the flesh that he assumed from the holy Virgin. Then on this basis, he tries to support the claim that after the consummation of all things the Word that is in God will leave behind the flesh, now empty of his own power. He says so in these very words:

> For concerning the flesh, through the possession of which he associated with the disciples, he thus said, "Do you take offense at this? Then what if you were to see the Son of Man ascending where he was before? It is the Spirit that gives life; the flesh is of no avail."[286] Therefore, if he confesses that the flesh does not

284. Marcellus, *fr.* 84 (127 K./H.) (72,13–15 V.).
285. Jn 6.61–63.
286. Ibid.

benefit him, how is it possible that the flesh, which is of earth and is of no avail, will also coexist with the Word even in the ages to come—as if it did offer some benefit to him?[287]

You see how greatly he has distorted the gospel statement because he did not understand in what manner and for what reason the saving utterance of the Word has been stated.

Chapter 12

(1) But you, having taken up the gospel text, see the whole teaching of our Savior [and] how he did not speak about the flesh that he assumed, but about the mystical body and blood. For when he fed the multitudes with the five loaves and provided this great miracle to those who were watching, many Jews, disparaging the deed, said to him, "Then, what sign do you do, that we may see, and believe you?"[288] Then they made a comparison with the manna in the desert, saying, "Our fathers ate the manna in the wilderness; as it has been written, 'He gave them bread from heaven to eat.'"[289] (2) To these remarks the Savior answered, "Truly, truly I say to you, it was not Moses who gave you the bread from heaven; my Father gives you the true bread from heaven."[290] Then he continues, "I am the bread of life,"[291] and again, "I am the bread that came down from heaven,"[292] and again, "The bread which I shall give is my body."[293] And again he adds, "Truly, truly I say to you, unless you eat the flesh of the Son of Man and drink his blood, you (3) have no life in you; he who eats my flesh and drinks my blood has eternal life, and I will raise him up at the last day. For my flesh is true food, and my blood (4) is true drink. He who eats my flesh and drinks my blood abides in me, and I in him."[294] And when

287. Excerpt of Marcellus, *fr.* 106 (117 K./H.) (96,6–12 V.).
288. Jn 6.30.
289. Jn 6.31.
290. Jn 6.32.
291. Jn 6.35.
292. Jn 6.51.
293. Ibid. Instead of "body," the Johannine text has "flesh."
294. Jn 6.53–56.

he had recounted all these sorts of things in a more mystical way, certain of his disciples said, "This is a hard saying; who can listen to it?"[295]—to which the Savior replied, saying, "Do you take offense at this? Then what if you were to see (5) the Son of Man ascending where he was before? It is the Spirit that gives life; the flesh is of no avail; the words that I have spoken to you are spirit and life."[296] Through these remarks he taught them to hear in a spiritual sense what had been said about his flesh and blood. For [he says], "Do not think that I am speaking about the flesh, which I bear, [saying] that it is necessary to eat it, nor suppose that I command [you] to drink sensible and corporeal blood, but know well that 'the words that I have spoken to you are spirit and life,'[297] so that the words themselves and the statements themselves are the flesh and blood; he who partakes of them always, feeding as it were on heavenly bread, (6) will have a share in the life of heaven." Therefore, he [Christ] says, "Take no offense at what I have said to you about the food of my flesh and the drink of my blood, nor let what I have said about the flesh and blood trouble you when at first you hear it. For these things are 'of no avail'[298] when they are heard sensibly, but the Spirit is that which gives life to those (7) who are able to hear spiritually." But since the upstart interpreter of the evangelical teachings understood none of these things, listen to how he writes, saying in [these] very words:

> After he laid hold of his human body and showed it to those who were watching, he said, "Do you take offense at this? Then what if you were to see the Son of Man ascending where he was before? It is the Spirit that gives life; the flesh is of no avail."[299]

(8) To this one must say, "Where do you, my fine man, get [this] addition,[300] which is not contained in the evangelical writ-

295. Jn 6.60.
296. Jn 6.61–63.
297. Jn 6.63.
298. Ibid.
299. Jn 6.61–63; Marcellus, *fr.* 105 (118 K./H.) (96,1–3 V.).
300. That is, the detail (which is not in the gospel text) Marcellus adds about Christ "laying hold of his human body" before he spoke to his disciples.

ing? For you yourself imagine that the Savior, having taken hold of [his] human body and shown it to those who were watching, said, 'Do you take offense at this?'[301] and you dare to make up this addition yourself?" Then, having taken on that dare, he next thinks to support [the claim] that the flesh of the Savior will be left behind, devoid of the power of the Word, by saying,

> Therefore, if he confesses that the flesh does not benefit him, how is it possible that the flesh, which is of earth and is of no avail, will also coexist with the Word even in the ages to come—as if it did offer some benefit to him?[302]

Thus with such stupidity and ignorance, he began to misinterpret the gospel. He also likewise invented distorted interpretations of the apostolic statements.

Chapter 13

(1) Indeed, when early on in the Acts of the Apostles, Peter says concerning our Savior, "whom heaven must receive until the time of restoration,"[303] because he [Marcellus] has not grasped the meaning of the statement, on the basis of it he attempts to circumscribe the kingdom of Christ, alleging that a certain limit and appointed time for his kingdom is shown because of the (2) phrase "until the time of the restoration." He says that this same claim is also supported by the Psalm that says, "Sit at my right hand, until I make your enemies your footstool,"[304] and [he says] that Paul the Apostle said because of this, "For he must reign until he has made his enemies his footstool."[305] For he supposed that the [phrases] "up to" and "until" are indicative of a circumscribed time. Listen now to how he writes this in so many words, saying,

> For it seems to me also because of this that God Almighty, the Lord, says to him, "Sit at my right hand, until I make your ene-

301. Jn 6.61.
302. Excerpt from Marcellus, *fr.* 106 (117 K./H.) (96,9–12 V.).
303. Acts 3.21.
304. Ps 109.1 (RSV 110.1).
305. 1 Cor 15.25.

mies your footstool."[306] Seeing to distinguish him by activity alone because of [the] human flesh, and determining, as it were, a certain specified time for him to sit at his right hand, he thus says to him, "until I make your enemies your footstool." (3) The holy Apostle, interpreting for us even more clearly this prophetic statement of David, thus said somewhere, "He must reign until he has made his enemies his footstool."[307] Thus the human economy and kingdom seem to have a certain limit.[308]

And after some other remarks, he adds,

Because of this, the Acts of the Apostles teaches in this way regarding this man, whom the Word of God assumed and, having assumed him, he sits at the right hand of the Father, as when it says, "whom heaven must receive until the time of restoration."[309] And these [Acts] [speak in this way], determining, as it were, a certain limit and appointed time.[310]

(4) He adds to this after some other statements:

... How would it still be possible for the "form of a slave,"[311] which the Word assumed, since it is the form of a slave, to continue to coexist with the Word? Therefore, the divinely inspired Paul said clearly and distinctly that in a certain short span of time within past as well as future ages the fleshly economy of the Word has occurred for our sakes and that as this economy has a beginning, so also it has an end, having thus said, "Then comes the end, when he delivers the kingdom to [his] God and Father."[312]

Chapter 14

(1) Through such statements, Marcellus both revealed his ignorance of the Son's "glorious body"[313] and denies his unend-

306. Ps 109.1 (RSV 110.1).
307. 1 Cor 15.25.
308. Excerpt from Marcellus, *fr.* 106 (117 K./H.) (96,12–98,1 V.).
309. Acts 3.21.
310. Excerpt from Marcellus, *fr.* 106 (117 K./H.) (98,9–13 V.).
311. Phil 2.7.
312. 1 Cor 15.24; Marcellus, *fr.* 106 (117 K./H.) (96,4–100,3 V.).
313. Phil 3.21.

ing kingdom, not having understood that the term "until" is usually taken according to a certain custom that is characteristic of Scripture. Indeed, it is in this sense that the Savior said to the disciples, "Lo, I am with you always, until the close of the age,"[314] not denying that he would be with them even after the close of the age, but teaching that even now he will be with them "until the close of the age," watching over and protecting all those who are his disciples, and after the close of the age, he will be present to them to an even greater degree, (2) declaring that they will belong to his kingdom. In this sense, then, both the statement, "Sit at my right hand, until I make your enemies your footstool,"[315] and the statement, "whom heaven must receive until the time of restoration,"[316] have been said not as if he would no longer exist after these things, but as if he would, at the time of the close of the age, depart from the Father's throne and make a second descent from heaven, about which the Apostle teaches, saying, "For the Lord himself will descend from heaven with a cry of command, with the archangel's call, and with the sound of the trumpet of God. And the dead in Christ will rise first; then we who are alive, who are left, shall be caught up together with them in the clouds to meet the Lord in the air; and so we shall always be with the Lord."[317] Thus it is necessary that the Savior remain in heaven and sit at the right hand of the Father "until the close of the age,"[318] but at the very consummation of all things, having effected his second, glorious coming, he will take up his holy ones to dwell forever with him, not until a certain time, but unto endless ages. (3) For, he says, "so we shall always be with the Lord."[319] Therefore, the holy ones, always being with him, will enjoy his kingdom in the kingdom of heaven, which has been proclaimed.

But having understood none of these things, when the holy Apostle said about our Savior, "For he must reign until he has

314. Mt 28.20.
315. Ps 109.1 (RSV 110.1).
316. Acts 3.21.
317. 1 Thes 4.16–17.
318. Mt 28.20.
319. 1 Thes 4.17.

made his enemies his footstool. The last enemy to be destroyed is death,"[320] and again, "When (4) all things are subjected to him, then the Son himself will also be subjected to him who put all things under him, that God may be all in all,"[321] this fine man, as is his custom, also misinterprets these [statements], hearing in some sense—I know not what—that the Son's subjection to the Father is the equivalent of the Word being united to God. For when was he *not* united to him, if the Word existed eternally in God? How, then, does he say, "Then he will be subjected" "to his God and Father"?[322]

Chapter 15

(1) It is necessary to understand the meaning both when the Apostle said that all things would be subjected to the Son himself and when he teaches that even [the Son himself] will be subjected to the Father by virtue of the same subjection, saying, "When all things are subjected to him, then the Son himself will also be subjected to him who put (2) all things under him, that God may be all in all."[323] Yet he [Marcellus] pays no attention to the phrase "all in all." For [Paul] does not say that God will be "all" in the Son, but "in all." This statement would rather indicate a certain conjunction and unity of all things, if God were going to be "all in all." But [Marcellus] interprets the subjection of the Son as the unification of the Word, who will be one and the same with the Father, just as he also was before, as [Marcellus] himself (3) said. Well now, if he defines the subjection to the Father as a unification, it would follow also that that subjection of all things to the Son signifies the same unification with him, so that the Son would no longer exist in and of himself, nor would the multitude of saved creatures subjected to him live their own life, but there would be a certain meshing together and commingling of all of them, since the Son and all the rest, (4) and not only they, but also God him-

320. 1 Cor 15.25–26.
321. 1 Cor 15.28.
322. 1 Cor 15.28, 24.
323. 1 Cor 15.28.

self, would be one and the same. For if all things are united with the Son, and the Son is united with the Father by virtue of being subjected to him, look at (5) what results from this line of reasoning. But just as the Apostle did not indicate unification when he said that all things would be subjected to the Son, but the obedience that comes from free choice and the glory and the honor that all things will give to him as to a Savior and king of all, in the same way also, the same subjection to the Father would indicate nothing other than the glory and the honor and the reverence and the magnificent and free obedience, which even [the Son] himself will give to [his] "God and Father,"[324] when he makes all things worthy of the paternal divinity. (6) For in the meantime, seeing as they are not [at present] worthy of this, having taken upon himself, like a common savior of all, the correction of the imperfect and care of those in need of healing, he exercises his kingship, putting the enemies of the kingdom under his feet. Indeed, the Psalm shows this when it states, "The Lord said to my Lord: 'Sit at my right hand, until I make your enemies (7) your footstool.'"[325] When[326] he places the enemies under his feet, he will, however, establish those worthy of his kingdom in everlasting life, for[327] at that time even death, the last enemy of all, will be destroyed. For when no one dies anymore, and those who are worthy of the kingdom will live in eternal life, death, of course, will no longer exist, since it will no longer have anyone (8) to kill. When these [the holy ones] have been suitably prepared, all holy ones will be subjected with a saving subjection to the Son of God. By the life that he is, they will live eternally; by the wisdom that he is, they will be wise; by the rationality[328] that he is, they will be made rational. So also they will become Christs, having been anointed by the Spirit with his sweet perfume, and they will be displayed as stars of the new age, having been supplied with lights from him, and they will be sons of God, having been

324. 1 Cor 15.24.
325. Ps 109.1 (RSV 110.1).
326. Klostermann's addition of δέ is incorrect.
327. Klostermann's erasure of γάρ is incorrect.
328. Lit., "Word."

adorned with the Spirit of adoption, and they will become partakers in all the remaining powers in him when they will have been subjected to him, so as to become both righteous from his righteousness and holy from his holiness. Since (9) "the Word was God,"[329] too,[330] neither will he begrudge them divinity, so as to confirm that Apostle's prophecy that the holy ones would become "heirs of God and fellow heirs with Christ."[331] Yes, surely they will even have heavenly bodies like those of the sun and the moon and the stars, (10) and by virtue of this they will have a share in his glory. The same [Apostle] shows this, having said, "from it [our commonwealth in heaven] we await a Savior, the Lord Jesus Christ, who will change our lowly body to be like his glorious body, by the power that enables him even to subject all things to himself."[332]

You see that by his power to subject all things to himself, he will also effect the transformation of our body, so as to render even our body "like his glorious body."[333] (11) But if our body will be like "his glorious body," why will his glorious body not participate all the more in his kingdom? And if our body will be swallowed up by life, as the Apostle gave witness, having said, "not that we would be unclothed, but that we would be further clothed, so that what is mortal may be swallowed up by life,"[334] why will his body not be all the more swallowed up, not only by life, as our [body] will be, but also by his divinity, since he availed himself of the powerful assistance of his divinity? Surely, then, let no one question or be in doubt about what it is proper to think about the saving body, by listening to Paul, who clearly says that it is necessary for "what is mortal" to be "swallowed up by life" and that our body will be like Christ's "glorious body by the power (12) [that enables him even] to subject all things to himself."[335] Consequently, then,

329. Jn 1.1.
330. Klostermann's δε is incorrect.
331. Rom 8.17.
332. Phil 3.20–21.
333. Phil 3.21.
334. 2 Cor 5.4.
335. Phil 3.21.

he will subject all things to himself, and it is necessary to think that this saving subjection is of such a nature as accords with the passage, "the Son himself will be subjected to him who put all things under him,"[336] imagining a certain unspeakable and ineffable subjection that is fitting for him alone, when he will lead those gathered together by him as in a chorus to [his] "God and Father,"[337] bringing the glory and honor and reverence and esteem to him, seeing as he is indeed the cause of all good things,

Chapter 16[338]

(1) at which time, too, the conclusion of the apostolic teaching will be fulfilled, which says, "so that God may be all in all."[339] Indeed, we will understand the same thing from the other promise, in which it was said by God himself, "I will live among them, and I will walk among them, and I will be their God, and they shall be my people."[340] But now in the present age the promise comes to the worthy alone, in brief and partially, in accordance with [the statement], "We know in part and prophesy in part."[341] But after the consummation of all things, when the new age has come, he will no longer dwell in some few of them, but in all who are then (2) worthy of the kingdom of heaven. Thus in this way he will be "all in all,"[342] to be sure, "dwelling among them and walking among them,"[343] not disdaining to be "their God"[344] and claiming them all as his people. In this way, then, he will be in them, as he is also said to be in the Son himself, just as [the Son] himself teaches, saying, "The Father is in me, and I am in the Father."[345] And he will be

336. 1 Cor 15.28.
337. 1 Cor 15.24
338. Another odd paragraph break.
339. 1 Cor 15.28.
340. 2 Cor 6.16. Cf. Lv 26.12; Ezek 37.27.
341. 1 Cor 13.9.
342. 1 Cor 15.28.
343. Cf. 2 Cor 6.16.
344. Ibid.
345. Jn 10.38.

"all things" in them, by providing himself to all according to
the capacity of each to participate in his divinity. [And] when
the thrice-blessed hope and unending and immortal life have
been established in this end, in which God will be "all in all,"
filling all with the flashes of his divinity as of ineffable light, the
Son, exalting and rejoicing in their victory, having crowned as
with a wreath of victory those made worthy through him of his
blessedness, will bring to completion his undying and eternal
kingdom under the Father's rule, when all those other oracles
about him will also be fulfilled, indeed also those said by the
angel Gabriel to the all-holy Virgin concerning him who would
be born from her, in fact that "he will reign forever ... and (3)
of his kingdom there will be no end."[346] Then, when the Son
rules, he will hand over to his Father all those who are ruled by
him, not ceasing to exercise rule, nor departing from it, for the
holy Apostle did not say that he would cease to exercise [rule]
(for then he would have written the opposite of what the angel
Gabriel prophesied to the virgin [when he said that] "he will
reign forever ... and of his kingdom there will be no end"),[347]
but that he would hand over the kingdom, that is to say, those
who were (4) ruled by him, "to his God and Father."[348] For as
one overjoyed by his victory, he will hand over to the Father all
those who have been brought to perfection by him as if rendering to him a deposit. Indeed, [Christ] himself teaches this,
saying, "All things have been given to me by my Father."[349] For
this reason it follows that, like a good guardian, he will hand
over the deposit to God that he carried safe and sound through
everything, like a high priest showing to him all those who
are made holy by him, white as snow and shining with their
incorruptible bodies of the resurrection like the most brilliant
robes, so that they might not only rejoice in his rule over them,
but also be filled with the (5) ineffable goods of the Father. For
in this way will "God be all in all,"[350] as the Apostle said, with

346. Lk 1.33.
347. Ibid.
348. 1 Cor 15.24.
349. Mt 11.27; Lk 10.22.
350. 1 Cor. 15.28.

the Son bringing to him those who are ruled, so that all of this might take place; I mean that the Father might be "all in all." For as he was before in the Son, according to [the statement], "The Father is in me, and I am in the Father,"[351] so he will then also be in (6) those who are perfected by the Son.

For the Apostle did not say that the Son would cease to rule and that God would rule, but that the Son would hand over "the kingdom to his God and Father,"[352] revealing the deposit safe and sound and fitting for the worship of and priestly service to the Father, and that God would be "all in all"[353] as if God dwelt among them and walked among them and became all things to them. For of some he will be master, of some king, of some something else. But of all taken together he will be God, becoming all things to them by the divine virtues (7) and powers in him. This is the end of the thrice-blessed hope to which the great Apostle subscribed when he said, "so that God may be all in all."[354]

But he will be all in all in a manner proportionate to the capacity of each, distributing different aspects of his divinity to all, but he will preserve exclusively for his only-begotten Son the excellent and paternal glory and honor and kingdom that cannot be shared with all the rest.

Chapter 17[355]

(1) But if it is necessary that these things be confirmed with a prophetic seal, in order to strengthen the trustworthiness of what has been said, I will call to witness the prophetic spirit [that spoke] through Ezekiel the prophet, which indeed proclaims these same things in these sorts of words: "For thus says the Lord: Behold, I, I myself will search for my sheep and will seek them out. As a shepherd seeks out his flock when gloom and clouds are amidst the sheep that have been scattered

351. Jn 10.38.
352. 1 Cor 15.24.
353. 1 Cor 15.28.
354. Ibid.
355. Another odd paragraph break.

abroad, so will I seek out my sheep."³⁵⁶ And after some other
remarks: "I will save my flock, they shall no longer be a prey;
and I will judge (2) between ram and ram. And I will set up
over them a shepherd, and he will shepherd them, my servant
David, and he will be their shepherd. And I, the Lord, will be
their God, and my servant David shall be ruler among them. I,
the Lord, have spoken! I will make a covenant with David."³⁵⁷
And after other remarks, he repeats the same prophecy a second time, saying, "And I will save them from all their lawless
deeds in which they have sinned, and will cleanse them; and
they shall be my people, and I will be their God. My servant David shall be ruler over them; and (3) he will be shepherd over
all of them."³⁵⁸ And again, he adds, "and David my servant shall
be their prince forever."³⁵⁹

Notice that in all these passages it is said that God will be neither shepherd nor ruler but God of those who will be deemed
worthy of the blessed consummation. And of these same it is
prophesied that David will be ruler and shepherd, David here
intimating in a veiled way Christ, because he is "from his
seed."³⁶⁰ (4) And this is clear from the fact that David died before the time when these things were said. Daniel the prophet
proclaims these things even more clearly, calling the Christ of
God "Son of Man" plainly in this way, just as also the text of the
holy gospels was accustomed to call him. He says in this way, "I
saw in the night visions, and behold, with the clouds of heaven
there came one like a Son of Man, and he came to the Ancient
of Days and was presented.³⁶¹ And to him were given dominion
and glory and kingdom, and all peoples, nations, and languages
shall serve him; (5) his dominion is an everlasting one that shall
not pass away, and his kingdom will not be destroyed."³⁶²

You see how in these remarks, too, the prophet shows that

356. Ezek 34.11–12.
357. Ezek 34.22–25.
358. Ezek 37.23–24.
359. Ezek 37.25.
360. Cf. Rom 1.3.
361. Klostermann's addition < αὐτῷ> is not necessary.
362. Dn 7.13–14.

the kingdom that will be indestructible and undying and without end will not be the kingdom of the Word that is in God, but of the Son of Man, and he clearly teaches that the Son of Man is another besides the Ancient of Days, who received the indestructible kingdom from the Ancient of Days, that is to say, from the same Father. (6) But Marcellus asserts that [they are] one and the same, and that one hypostasis underlies [the] two names. And yet he still dares to circumscribe his kingdom and asserts in an utterly shameless way that there will be an end to Christ's kingdom after the time of judgment, writing in this way:

> Here the Apostle reveals the greatest mystery to us, (7) declaring that there will be an end to the kingdom of Christ, and this end will be when he puts all things under his feet.[363]

And he expands upon that remark, saying in this way somewhere:

> We have said in our foregoing remarks, using proofs out of the divine Scriptures, that our Lord Jesus Christ received a beginning of [his] kingdom.[364]

And he adds,

> And altogether there is abundant testimony consisting of myriad statements to show that the man received a beginning of [his] kingdom through the (8) Word. Therefore, if he received a beginning of [his] kingdom no more than four hundred years ago all told, it is nothing paradoxical if the Apostle says that he who obtained this kingdom such a short time ago will hand over the kingdom, to be sure, to God.[365]

(9) And after some other remarks, he continues, saying,

> Well then, what do we learn about the human flesh, which the Word assumed for us, not four hundred whole years ago? Will the Word have this even then in the ages to come or only until the time of judgment?[366]

363. Marcellus, *fr.* 102 (114 K./H.) (92,11–13 V.).
364. First part of Marcellus, *fr.* 103 (115 K./H.) (92,14–94,1 V.).
365. Second part of Marcellus, *fr.* 103 (115 K./H.) (94,4–8 V.).
366. Excerpt from Marcellus, *fr.* 104 (116 K./H.) (94,16–19 V.).

Yes, Marcellus dared to say these sorts of things. But the prophets of God, determining that the kingdom of Christ will be everlasting, say that after the time of judgment he will have the rule over the new age. For notice how the prophet Ezekiel, having presumed the occurrence of the tribunal of the flocks of God, after the judgment of these, appoints David as their (10) shepherd and proclaims that the same will rule over them.[367] And Daniel first said, "And as I looked until thrones were placed, and the Ancient of Days took his seat; his raiment was white as snow, and the hair of his head like pure wool; his throne was fiery flames, its wheels were burning fire. A stream of fire issued and came forth from before him; a thousand thousands served him, and ten thousand times ten thousand stood before him; the court sat in judgment, and the books were opened."[368] Having foreseen these things, he next sees the Son of Man coming on the clouds of heaven to the Ancient of Days and receiving the indestructible kingdom. Therefore, even at that time he will exercise the power of ruling as king over those worthy of blessedness in a manner both different and greater than [the way in which he rules] now. (11) The gospel gives witness by those remarks in which the Savior himself confirms the prophetic utterances, handing over the teachings about the consummation to his own disciples, through what he taught when he said, "When the Son of Man comes in his glory, and all the angels with him, then he will sit on his glorious throne. Before him will be gathered all the nations, and he will separate them one from another as a shepherd separates the sheep from the goats, and he will place the sheep at his right hand, but the goats at the left. Then the king will say to those at his right hand, 'Come, O blessed of my Father, inherit the kingdom prepared for you from the foundation of the world.'"[369]

But note how these statements agree with what has been said in the prophecy about the judgment of the sheep and the goats and how the Son of Man is introduced as king after the judgment of the flocks, (12) and God as his Father. For even he him-

367. Ezek 37.24.
368. Dn 7.9–10.
369. Mt 25.31–34.

self taught this, having said, "Then the king will say to those at his right hand, 'Come, O blessed of my Father,'"[370] just like David, who was mentioned in the prophecy, who, the text teaches, will be a shepherd and ruler over the flocks [and] who under the leadership of God will shepherd and guide the ones God nurtures. (13) And it is necessary for that man to understand the meaning [of this statement]—that the prophecy spoke figuratively what has been said by the Apostle in the passage, "when he has destroyed every rule and every authority and power,"[371] [and] when it said, "and (14) I will banish wild beasts from the land."[372] For what would those beasts that harassed the flocks in ancient times be but the opposing powers? And when they are removed, the new and fresh age, purified of all evil, will have the Son of Man as king (or according to the prophecy that intimated [this] in a veiled way, David as shepherd and ruler, because he [Christ] is "from the seed" of David),[373] but it is not said that it [the new age] would have God as shepherd or ruler, but God himself, who by virtue of a purpose greater than that of a shepherd and ruler and king, [and] in keeping with the magnificence of the divine power, will rule not only the flocks but also the shepherd himself. For "my servant David shall be their shepherd. And I, the Lord, will be their God."[374] And he calls David "servant" because our Savior and Lord assumed "the form of a servant"[375] "from the seed of David."[376]

Chapter 18

(1) And this is the thrice-blessed end, insofar as it is that promised kingdom of heaven our Savior pledged to those who are worthy of it, [in which] the God who is over all, even his Father, will himself bestow the highest good of all, [that is] him-

370. Mt 25.34.
371. 1 Cor 15.24.
372. Ezek 34.25.
373. Rom 1.3.
374. Ezek 34.23–24.
375. Phil 2.7.
376. Rom 1.3.

self, upon all who are ruled by the Son, becoming therein "all in all."[377] Indeed, our Savior and Lord himself again showed this when offering up to "his God and Father"[378] the great prayer on behalf of his intimates, in which he asks, saying, "That they may all be one; even as you, Father, are in me, and I in you, that they also (2) may be one in us, so that the world may believe that you have sent me. The glory that you have given me I have given to them, that they may be one even as we are one. I in them and you in me, that they may become perfectly one, so that the world may know that you have sent me and have loved (3) them even as you have loved me. Father, I desire that they also, whom you have given me, may be with me where I am, to behold my glory, which you have given me."[379]

The great appeal itself of our Savior on our behalf, that we might be with him where he himself is and that we might see his glory and that his Father might love us just as he loves him, and that he might give, even to us, the very thing that was bestowed upon him, and give, even to us, the glory that was given to him, making us all one, so that we might no longer be many but all one, having been united in his divinity and the glory of the kingdom, not by the coalescence (4) of one being,[380] but by the perfection of the highest virtue. For he taught this, having said, "that they may be perfected."[381] For in this way, having been made perfect by his wisdom and prudence and justice and piety and every virtue, we will be joined together to the ineffable light of the paternal divinity and become, yes, even us, lights because of our closeness to him, and sons of God according to our participating in communion with his only-begotten, having been made perfect through [our] participation in the brilliance of his divinity.

---

377. 1 Cor 15.28.
378. 1 Cor 15.24.
379. Jn 17.21–24.
380. οὐσίας.
381. Jn 17.23. RSV has "that they may become perfectly one."

Chapter 19

(1) And so in this way we will all become one with the Father and the Son. For just as [the Son] himself said that he and the Father were one, saying, "I and the Father are one,"[382] so also he prays that we all will participate, by [our] imitation of him, in that same oneness, not in the way Marcellus [thinks], the Word being united to God and joined to [his] being,[383] but just as the truth gave witness, the Savior himself having said, "The glory that you have given me I have given to them, that they may be one even as we are one, I in them and you in me, that they may become perfectly one."[384] For in this way also at that time will the apostolic saying about the end then be fulfilled, which says, "so that God may be all in all."[385]

(2) And since Marcellus and those who "Sabellianize" as he does have customarily used three statements in their attempts to show that the Father and the Son are one, at one time chattering, "I and the Father are one,"[386] and at another, "The Father is in me, and I am in the Father,"[387] and, "he who has seen me has seen the Father,"[388] yet to the statement, "I and the Father are one," must be added the remarks that precede these, in which he prays on behalf of his disciples that they themselves may also all partake of that same unity, (3) and so he says, "that they may be one even as we are one, I in them and you in me, that they may become perfectly one."[389] And with the statement, "The Father [is] in me, and I [am] in the Father,"[390] we will place again that statement of his, through which, in praying for them, [Christ] said, "even as you, Father, are in me, and I in you, that they also may be in us.... the glory that you have given me I have given to them,"[391] through which he clearly shows

382. Jn 10.30.
383. οὐσίᾳ.
384. Jn 17.22–23.
385. 1 Cor 15.28.
386. Jn 10.30.
387. Jn 10.38.
388. Jn 14.9.
389. Jn 17.22–23.
390. Jn 10.38.
391. Jn 17.21–22.

that the Father is in him in the same way as he also wishes to be in us—not that he himself and the Father are one by virtue of one hypostasis, but that since the Father has given to him a share in his own glory, he also, likewise, (4) imitating the Father, gives to his own [a share in it].

For this reason he says, "The glory that you have given me I have given to them, that they may be one even as we are one,"[392] "even as you, Father, are in me and I in you, that they also may be in us."[393] So, then, the Father and the Son are one according to the community of glory; in giving a share of this to his disciples he also made them worthy of the same unity.

Chapter 20

(1) And again in this way the Father was in him, and he was in the Father, just as the holy Apostle also teaches about all who are worthy of the heavenly kingdom, saying, "Then God will be all in all,"[394] as also [the statement], "I will live among them, and I will walk among them,"[395] has been said, but also, "In him we live and move and have our being."[396] And all these things have been said about us, who subsist in our own hypostasis and live (2) and have nothing in common with the paternal divinity. Why, then, is it necessary to wonder, if such statements are also applied to the Son, given that they neither take away his hypostasis, nor teach that the Father and Son are the same, but show the extraordinary honor characteristic of the Father in comparison to him and the glory of the divine communion that belongs to an only-begotten?

Chapter 21

(1) So, then, "he who has seen" him "has seen the Father,"[397] by virtue of the fact that he alone and no other is image "of

392. Jn 17.22.
393. Jn 17.21.
394. 1 Cor 15.28.
395. 2 Cor 6.16.
396. Acts 17.28.
397. Jn 14.9.

the invisible God"[398] and "radiance of the glory [of God] and the exact imprint of his hypostasis"[399] and exists "in the form of God"[400] according to the apostolic teachings. For as also the one who has seen the king's image that has been made like him to the most accurate degree, receiving an impression of the contours of the form through the drawing, imagines the king, in the same way, or rather in a way beyond all reason and beyond any image, the one who with a mind made clear and the eyes of the soul made pure and illuminated by the Holy Spirit, having scrutinized carefully the greatness of the power of the only-begotten Son and Lord, and having reflected that "in him the whole fullness of the Father's deity"[401] dwells and that "all things were made through him,"[402] and, "in him all things were created, in heaven and on earth, visible and invisible,"[403] and having reckoned that the Father begot him alone as only-begotten Son, since he is like him in all things, by that power he will also see the Father himself through the Son, as he is seen by those who have been cleansed in their mind, about which it was said, "Blessed are the pure in heart, for they shall see God."[404]

(2) So let these things be our challenge, [to us] who tried here to be brief, as in an abridgment. But if particular passages stand in need of greatest refinement, he who cares about their accurate comprehension, having applied his mind to the evangelical and apostolic readings, will derive the whole sense from them at his leisure. Surely, given that myriads of other passages have been collected from here and there in Marcellus's treatise, the great majority stated in a way contrary to the intention of Scripture, others distorted, and possessing no coherence, [and] thinking that the common refutation has become manifest among those who think rightly, through what has been examined by us, I will be content with these remarks.

398. Col 1.15.
399. Heb 1.3.
400. Phil 2.6.
401. Col 2.9.
402. Jn 1.3.
403. Col 1.16.
404. Mt 5.8.

INDICES

GENERAL INDEX

Aaron, 4, 87
Abraham, 140, 197, 257, 264, 282
absurdity, 77, 150–51
abundance, 56, 164, 180, 252
Acacius of Caesarea, 62
accident, 36, 244–45, 276
accuser, 100, 155, 162
acorns, 93
acquiring, 283
activity, 27, 30, 57–58, 108, 117,
    123, 125, 130–32, 134, 148–54,
    174, 187–88, 209, 217, 224, 226,
    230–31, 234–35, 241, 249, 318,
    322
Adam, 107, 282, 308
adoption, 89, 119, 133, 185, 198,
    232, 326
adoptionism, 38, 54, 69–70, 134
afterlife, 40
agreement, 46, 113, 119, 126–28,
    187, 198, 224, 256
Ahab, 307
Alexander of Alexandria, 10, 12,
    14–16, 48
all and in all, 256, 263, 313
all in all, 133, 232, 324, 327–29,
    334–36
Almighty, 89, 98, 124, 133, 144, 149,
    232, 240, 273, 298, 302, 321
alteration, 98, 226, 295
ambition, 95, 104
analogical, 97
anathema, 19, 43–44, 62, 66, 68,
    77–78, 82
Ancient of Days, 118, 330–32
ancients, 93, 253–54

Ancyra, 5, 9–11, 13–18, 60, 64, 66,
    109–10, 112
angel, 77–78, 81, 86, 118, 120, 122,
    129, 219, 328; angel of great coun-
    sel, 118
angels, 42, 83–84, 131, 150, 178,
    196, 202, 210, 229, 249, 261–62,
    264, 266, 287, 296–97, 300, 312,
    332; archangels, 296
anointed, 38, 215, 220, 279, 325
Apolinarian, 43, 55–56, 63, 65–66,
    181
Apolinarius of Laodicea, 6, 8, 55–56,
    59, 63–66, 70
the Apostle, 77, 82–84, 86–89, 91–
    92, 95–97, 106–8, 111, 114, 116,
    119–20, 133, 135–36, 138–39,
    141–44, 147–49, 166, 207, 211,
    216, 218, 227, 232, 261, 266,
    269–70, 278, 289–90, 295, 313,
    315–16, 321, 323–26, 328–29,
    331, 333
apostles, 102, 113, 140–41, 176,
    235, 279, 286, 291–97, 299, 305,
    307–8, 311–13
apostolic statement, 89–90, 101, 116,
    255
Aquila, 281
architecture, 242
Arius, 4–5, 9–17, 19–23, 27, 41–43,
    46–47, 62, 64–66, 69, 75, 179, 183
article, 243, 251, 259
Asia, 10, 154
aspersions, 106, 186
Asterius of Cappadocia, 14–15, 17,
    63

341

INDEX OF HOLY SCRIPTURE

INDEX OF ANCIENT SOURCES

Alexander of Alexandria

Apolinarius of Laodicea

Aristotle

Arius

Asterius of Cappadocia

Constantine

ep. Theod. Laod., Urk.
  28: 11
ep. epp., Urk. 20: 12

Cyril of Jerusalem

cat. 15: 64

Epiphanius of Salamis

haer. 72.6–10: 63
haer. 73.12–22: 43
haer. 76.3: 15

1 Esdras

4.38–39: 213
4.40: 213

Eusebius of Caesarea

CM 1.1–2: 24
CM 1.1.1: 34
CM 1.1.9: 34
CM 1.1.10–11: 40
CM 1.1.11–14: 37
CM 1.1.15: 36
CM 1.1.17: 38, 40
CM 1.1.22: 50
CM 1.1.23: 50
CM 1.1.27: 56
CM 1.1.30: 23
CM 1.1.32–33: 42
CM 1.1.32: 36
CM 1.1.36: 34
CM 1.2: 35
CM 1.2.4: 33
CM 1.4: 24–26
CM 1.4.3: 34
CM 1.4.16: 34
CM 1.4.19–28: 30
CM 1.4.23: 41, 47
CM 1.4.30–31: 25
CM 1.4.33–34: 25, 29

CM 1.4.35: 47
CM 1.4.39: 34
CM 1.4.46: 38
CM 1.4.59: 38
CM 1.4.64: 38
CM 2.1.1–3: 39
CM 2.1.2: 50
CM 2.1.9: 38
CM 2.1.10–11: 40
CM 2.2: 26
CM 2.2.1: 37
CM 2.2.2: 48
CM 2.2.4: 31
CM 2.2.5: 38
CM 2.2.8: 36
CM 2.2.11: 36
CM 2.2.15–25: 26
CM 2.2.26–29: 26
CM 2.2.32: 36
CM 2.2.43: 36
CM 2.3: 106, 315
CM 2.3.2: 39
CM 2.3.23–27: 25

CM 2.3.36–2.4.1–28: 40
CM 2.4: 29
CM 2.4.13: 21
CM 2.4.21: 36
CM 2.4.24: 51–52, 55
CM 2.4.25–26: 58
CM 2.4.27–28: 38
CM 2.4.30: 17

dem. ev. 4.2.2: 109
dem. ev. 5.2.21: 109

ep. Alex. Alex., Urk. 7: 10

ep. Euphr. Bal., Urk. 3,3: 112
ep. Euphr. Bal., Urk. 3,4: 109
ep. Euphr. Bal., Urk. 3,5: 114

ep. ad eccl. Caes., Urk. 22: 13

Eusebius of Caesarea (cont.)

ET praef.: 189
ET 1.1.3: 38
ET 1.1.4: 38, 40
ET 1.2: 37, 41–42, 45, 47, 50
ET 1.3: 38, 51, 56
ET 1.3.1: 38, 51
ET 1.5.1: 36
ET 1.5.2: 38, 40
ET 1.6.1: 34, 55
ET 1.6.2: 50
ET 1.7.1: 38, 51
ET 1.7.3: 50, 57
ET 1.8.1: 37
ET 1.8.2–3: 41
ET 1.8.2: 47
ET 1.8.3–4: 46
ET 1.8.3: 42
ET 1.9–10: 41–42
ET 1.10: 27
ET 1.10.3: 45
ET 1.11: 214
ET 1.11.3: 44–45
ET 1.11.4: 45–46
ET 1.12: 41
ET 1.12.8–10: 41
ET 1.12.8: 41, 57
ET 1.12.9: 42
ET 1.13.2: 46
ET 1.13.5: 55
ET 1.14.2: 34, 38
ET 1.16.2: 50
ET 1.17.2: 36
ET 1.17.4: 36
ET 1.17.7: 36–37
ET 1.17.9: 41
ET 1.18.4: 36
ET 1.19.2: 39
ET 1.20.3: 50
ET 1.20.3, section 5: 46
ET 1.20.4, section 11: 36
ET 1.20.4, section 15: 36

ET 1.20.5: 42
ET 1.20.5, section 25: 36
ET 1.20.5, section 30: 36, 46
ET 1.20.6: 47, 53–54
ET 1.20.6, section 36: 36
ET 1.20.6, section 39: 36, 42
ET 1.20.6, section 40: 43–44, 51, 53, 55
ET 1.20.6, sections 41–42: 55
ET 1.20.6, section 41: 54
ET 1.20.6, section 43: 38, 54
ET 1.20.6, section 45: 38, 71
ET 1.20.6, section 46: 36, 46
ET 1.20.8: 40
ET 1.20.8, sections 55–56: 34
ET 1.20.9: 67
ET 1.20.9, section 63: 43, 46
ET 1.20.9, section 64: 36
ET 1.20.12, section 67: 34
ET 1.20.14: 25, 47
ET 1.20.14, sections 72–74: 34, 39, 47
ET 1.20.29, section 87: 49
ET 1.20.29, section 89: 37
ET 1.20.29, section 91: 36
ET 2.1.1: 31, 38
ET 2.2.1: 34, 40
ET 2.2.5: 40

ET 2.3.3: 37, 48
ET 2.4.2: 38
ET 2.5: 21, 35, 38
ET 2.6.1–2: 41
ET 2.6.1: 44
ET 2.6.2–3: 37
ET 2.7.1–2: 43
ET 2.7.1–3: 44
ET 2.7.1: 41, 44
ET 2.7.5–6: 46
ET 2.7.6: 42
ET 2.7.8: 46
ET 2.7.16–17: 47
ET 2.8.1: 36
ET 2.9.12: 35
ET 2.10.4–8: 34
ET 2.11.1: 36, 37
ET 2.12.2–3: 37
ET 2.12.2: 37, 41, 48
ET 2.12.3: 38
ET 2.14: 23, 45, 47, 244
ET 2.14.4: 36
ET 2.14.9: 46
ET 2.14.14: 47
ET 2.14.19–20: 40
ET 2.14.20: 37
ET 2.15.1: 37
ET 2.15.2: 37
ET 2.15.3: 37
ET 2.15.4: 37
ET 2.17.3: 47
ET 2.17.6: 37
ET 2.17.7: 46
ET 2.18.2: 50
ET 2.19: 33
ET 2.19.21: 27
ET 2.20.5: 49
ET 2.21.1–4: 46
ET 2.21.4: 43
ET 2.22.1–2: 45
ET 2.22.5: 40
ET 2.23: 25, 39
ET 2.23.1–2: 44
ET 2.23.1: 44, 47

(Marcellus?)

Narcissus of Neronias

Origen

Synod of Antioch (325)

Urk. 18: 11–12

Synod of Bithynia (320?)

Urk. 5: 10

Synod of Palestine (321/322?)

Urk. 10: 11

Tertullian

Adv. Marc. 1.22: 166

Adv. Prax. 1–2: 38
Adv. Prax. 8: 42

Theodoret

HE 1.7.10: 12
HE 1.20.4: 14
HE 2.2: 12

Theophrastus

On Piety: 94

INDEX OF MODERN AUTHORS

INDEX OF GREEK WORDS